Writing the Global Riot

Writing the Global Riot

Literature in a Time of Crisis

Edited by
JUMANA BAYEH
HELEN GROTH
AND
JULIAN MURPHET

OXFORD
UNIVERSITY PRESS

Great Clarendon Street, Oxford, OX2 6DP,
United Kingdom

Oxford University Press is a department of the University of Oxford.
It furthers the University's objective of excellence in research, scholarship,
and education by publishing worldwide. Oxford is a registered trade mark of
Oxford University Press in the UK and in certain other countries

© Oxford University Press 2023

The moral rights of the authors have been asserted

All rights reserved. No part of this publication may be reproduced, stored in
a retrieval system, or transmitted, in any form or by any means, without the
prior permission in writing of Oxford University Press, or as expressly permitted
by law, by licence or under terms agreed with the appropriate reprographics
rights organization. Enquiries concerning reproduction outside the scope of the
above should be sent to the Rights Department, Oxford University Press, at the
address above

You must not circulate this work in any other form
and you must impose this same condition on any acquirer

Published in the United States of America by Oxford University Press
198 Madison Avenue, New York, NY 10016, United States of America

British Library Cataloguing in Publication Data

Data available

Library of Congress Control Number: 2023942877

ISBN 9780192862594

DOI: 10.1093/oso/9780192862594.001.0001

Printed and bound by
CPI Group (UK) Ltd, Croydon, CR0 4YY

Links to third party websites are provided by Oxford in good faith and
for information only. Oxford disclaims any responsibility for the materials
contained in any third party website referenced in this work.

Acknowledgements

This collection would not have been possible without the support of an Australian Research Council Discovery Grant. Over the duration of this project, which is ongoing, we have incurred many debts. A research grant from the University of New South Wales offered much needed additional support for our amazing research associate Elizabeth King, who worked tirelessly on this project for three years in the most trying of circumstances. The challenges of researching, writing, and collaborating during a global pandemic have shaped and enriched this project in unexpected ways. We were blessed with exceptional contributors and benefited from the generous insights and feedback of our anonymous readers at Oxford University Press. We are also indebted to Patricia May, who helped us in the final phases of drawing this collection together. Heartfelt thanks are also due to our respective departments and schools: the School of Arts and Media at the University of New South Wales, the Department of English, Creative Writing, and Film at the University of Adelaide, and the School of Social Sciences at Macquarie University. The isolation of the last few years has been tempered by supportive colleagues and friends; thanks to all those who have given advice, support, or offered welcome distraction. We would also like to thank our families and partners who have lived with this book along with us.

Contents

List of Tables and Figures	viii
List of Contributors	ix

Introduction. Writing and Rioting: Literature in Times of Crisis *Jumana Bayeh, Helen Groth, and Julian Murphet*	1
1. Tumultum Populi: Riots, Noise, and Speech Acts in Georgian England *Ian Haywood*	18
2. I Would They Were Barbarians: Shakespeare, Brecht, and the Global Riot *Mark Steven*	39
3. Bloody Sundays: Radical Rewriting and the Trafalgar Riot of 1887 *Helen Groth*	56
4. Rhodes Must Fall, *Ulysses*, and the Politics of Teaching Modernism *Cóilín Parsons*	71
5. Buzz, Mob, Crowd, Life: Writing the Riot in Mulk Raj Anand's *Untouchable* and Virginia Woolf's *Mrs Dalloway* *J. Daniel Elam*	88
6. Riotous Nations: Time and the Short Story of Partition *Rashmi Varma*	104
7. A Sketch of the Mob *Joseph North*	122
8. Phantom Justice and Orwellian Violence: Writing against Erasure in a Turbulent Hong Kong *Janny H. C. Leung*	137
9. The Crowd in This Moment: Troubling the Immanence of Riots in Contemporary US Literature *Julian Murphet*	153

10. 'If I write a Love poem it's against the police': The
    Abolitionist Poetics of the Riot   170
    Andrew Brooks and Astrid Lorange

11. Mobilizing the History of Protest and Dissent in Post-2011
    Moroccan Novels   187
    Karima Laachir

12. From 'Jihadi City' to 'Bride of the Revolution': The Protest
    Rhythms of Tripoli   204
    Caroline Rooney

13. Taming 'the Square': Documenting the Rioting Subject in
    Basma Abdel Aziz's *The Queue*   221
    Rita Sakr

14. Mediating the Arab Spring's Riots: Reclaiming Egypt's Lost Archive 238
    Jumana Bayeh

Selected Bibliography   254
Publisher's Acknowledgements   262
Index   263

List of Tables and Figures

Table 1. Recent titles of *Breakazine*, p. 206   146

Figure 1. Louis Philippe Boitard's *The Sailor's Revenge or the Strand in an Uproar: A Tragi Comical Farce exhibited before a numerous Audience of yr Mobility and others* (Robert Sayer, August 1749). © The Trustees of the British Museum.   23

Figure 2. [Isaac Robert and George Cruikshank], *Acting Magistrates committing themselves being their first appearance on this stage as performed at the National Theatre Covent Garden* (18 September 1809). Courtesy of the Lewis Walpole Library, Yale University.   29

Figure 3. [Thomas Rowlandson], This is the House that Jack Built (Thomas Tegg, 23 September 1809). Public domain, from The Met Open Access Initiative.   31

Figure 4. [Isaac Robert and George Cruikshank], Kings Place and Chandos Street in an Uproar (S W Fores, 20 October 1809). © Victoria and Albert Museum, London.   33

Figure 5. Mother Red Cap's Public House in Opposition to the King's Head Tavern (George Humphrey, 4 August 1821). Courtesy of the Wilhelm Busch Museum.   36

List of Contributors

Jumana Bayeh is Senior Lecturer at Macquarie University, Australia. She is the author of *The Literature of the Lebanese Diaspora: Representations of Place and Transnational Identity* (2015) and several articles on Arab diaspora fiction. She co-edited *Democracy, Diaspora, Territory* (2020), and a special issue on "Arabs in Australia" in *Mashriq & Mahjar* (2017). She is currently working on an Australia Research Council-funded project that examines the representation of the nation-state in Arab diaspora literature from writers based in Australia, North America, and the United Kingdom.

Andrew Brooks is a writer, artist, and teacher living on unceded Wangal land who lectures in Media Studies in the School of Arts and Media at UNSW. His current research proposes strategies for reading and listening to contemporary media events, systems, and infrastructures, with a particular focus on social movements in the context of circulatory capitalism, infrastructural inequality, and the politics of race. He is a founding member of the Infrastructural Inequalities research network and one half of the critical art collective Snack Syndicate. He co-edits the publishing collective Rosa Press. *Homework*, co-written with Astrid Lorange, was published in 2021. *Inferno*, a collection of poems, was published in 2021.

J. Daniel Elam is Assistant Professor in the Department of Comparative Literature at the University of Hong Kong. He is the author of *World Literature for the Wretched of the Earth* (Fordham, 2021) and the editor of *The Bloomsbury Anthology of Twentieth-Century Aesthetic and Political Thought from the Global South*.

Helen Groth is Professor of Literary Studies at the University of New South Wales, Australia. She is the author of *Victorian Photography and Literary Nostalgia* (2003) and *Moving Images: Nineteenth-Century Reading and Screen Practices* (2013), co-author of a third monograph *Dreams and Modernity: A Cultural History* (2013) and is at work on a fourth, *Riotous Lives and Nineteenth-Century Writing*. She is the co-editor of a number of collections, including the forthcoming *Edinburgh Companion of Literature and Sound Studies*.

Ian Haywood is Professor of English at the University of Roehampton, London. He was President of the British Association for Romantic Studies 2015–19, and organizes the 'Romantic Illustration Network'. He is the author of a 'trilogy' of monographs on Romanticism: *The Revolution in Popular Literature* (Cambridge UP, 2004), *Bloody Romanticism* (Palgrave, 2006), and *Romanticism and Caricature* (Cambridge UP, 2013). He has also co-edited *The Gordon Riots* (Cambridge UP, 2012), *Spain in British Romanticism* (Palgrave, 2018), and *Romanticism and Illustration* (Cambridge UP, 2019). His most recent book, *The Rise of Victorian Caricature*, was published by Palgrave in March 2020. His next two books will be *Queen Caroline and the Power of Caricature in Georgian England* (Palgrave) and *Frankenstein and Romantic Visual Culture* (Bloomsbury).

Karima Laachir is Director for the ANU Centre for Arab and Islamic Studies (The Middle East and Central Asia). Her research focuses on cultural studies in the Middle East and North Africa region or the intersection between culture and politics (cultural politics). She also works on Comparative Literature and Postcolonial Studies from the perspectives of the Global South. She was the Maghreb-lead of a large ERC-funded project "Multilingual Locals and Significant Geographies: For a New Approach to World Literature" http://mulosige.soas.ac.uk/, a project that offers a bottom-up approach to discussions on World Literature from the multilingual, localized, and comparative perspective of the Global South (2016–21).

Janny H. C. Leung is Professor of English and Dean of the Faculty of Liberal Arts at Wilfrid Laurier University. She was Professor of Linguistics and Head of School of English at the University of Hong Kong. Her research revolves around the study of meaning, especially at intersections between language and law. Her monograph *Shallow Equality and Symbolic Jurisprudence in Multilingual Legal Orders* (OUP) won the Faculty Research Output Prize in 2020. She has written about language rights, legal interpretation, unrepresented litigation, courtroom discourse, legal translation, representations of law in the media, and the regulation of speech in the digital society. She served as an elected member of the Executive Committee of the International Association of Forensic Linguists between 2017 and 2021.

Astrid Lorange is Senior Lecturer at UNSW Art & Design. She lives on unceded Wangal land. Her research focuses on the social movements and cultural practices that emerge as forms of resistance to state-managed violence. Her current project focuses on documentary practices in contemporary poetry and art. She is one-half of the critical art collective Snack Syndicate, whose book of essays *Homework* was published by Discipline in 2021. Her scholarly monograph *How Reading Is Written: A Brief Index to Gertrude Stein* was published by Wesleyan University Press in 2014 and her poetry collection *Labour and Other Poems* was published by Cordite Books in 2020. She co-edits Rosa Press.

Julian Murphet Jury Chair of English Language and Literature at the University of Adelaide. He is the author of *Modern Character, 1888–1905* (2023) and *Prison Writing in the Twentieth Century: A Literary Guide* (2024).

Joseph North is the author of *Literary Criticism: A Concise Political History* (Cambridge: Harvard UP, 2017). He is currently at work on two books: the first a history of the concept of the 'mob', and the second a history, analysis and critique of political centrism, especially as it has played out in literature over the last two centuries. He teaches literature at Yale.

Cóilín Parsons is Associate Professor of English and Director of Global Irish Studies at Georgetown University in Washington, DC. He is the author of *The Ordnance Survey and Modern Irish Literature* (Oxford, 2016), and editor or co-editor of *Relocations; Reading Culture in South Africa* (Cape Town, 2015), *Science, Technology, and Irish Modernism* (Syracuse, 2019), and *Transnationalism in Irish Literature and Culture* (Cambridge, 2024).

Caroline Rooney is co-investigator on the ESRC funded research grant 'The Crime-Terror Nexus: Investigating the Overlap between Criminal and Extremist Practices, Narratives and

Networks in Tripoli, Lebanon' and Professor Emeritus of African and Middle Eastern Studies at the University of Kent. She is the co-director of the documentary film *White Flags* (on trust-building in post-conflict Lebanon), and her most recent book is *Creative Radicalism in the Middle East: Culture and the Arab Left After the Uprisings* (Bloomsbury I.B. Tauris, 2020).

Rita Sakr is Lecturer/Assistant Professor in Postcolonial and Global Literatures at Maynooth University, Ireland. Among various other publications, she is the author of *Monumental Space in the Post-Imperial Novel: An Interdisciplinary Study* and of '*Anticipating' the 2011 Arab Uprisings: Revolutionary Literatures and Political Geographies*. Recent publications include an article on Behrouz Boochani's decolonial imaginaries of sanctuary in *Crossings: Journal of Migration & Culture*, a chapter on Atef Abu Saif's *The Drone Eats With Me: A Gaza Diary* in the Edinburgh UP volume *Literary Representations of the Palestine/Israel Conflict After the Second Intifada*, and a chapter on Arabic diasporic literary trajectories in the Cambridge UP volume, *Diaspora and Literary Studies*. She is completing a new monograph project, focusing on (im)mobilities, especially in relation to 'necropolitics' across contemporary Arab literature.

Mark Steven is the author of *Red Modernism* (Johns Hopkins) and *Splatter Capital* (Repeater), and is editor of *Understanding Marx, Understanding Modernism* (Bloomsbury). He is also Senior Lecturer in 20th and 21st Century Literature at the University of Exeter.

Rashmi Varma teaches English and Comparative Literary Studies at the University of Warwick in the UK. She is the author of *The Postcolonial City and Its Subjects* (2011) and co-editor of *Marxism and Postcolonial Theory: Critical Engagements with Benita Parry* (2018). She has also co-edited a special issue of the journal *Critical Sociology* on 'Marxism and Postcolonial Theory: What Is Left of the Debate?' She is a founding editorial collective member of the journal *Feminist Dissent* and has published numerous essays on postcolonial and feminist theory, activism, and literature in edited volumes and journals.

Introduction
Writing and Rioting
Literature in Times of Crisis

Jumana Bayeh, Helen Groth, and Julian Murphet

In the final chapters of Australian Wiradjuri writer Tara June Winch's novel, *The Yield*, traditional owners and environmental protestors combine forces to resist the mining of Massacre Plains: the fictional lands where the story unfolds. August Gondiwindi, the novel's heroine, joins the protest finally armed with the evidence of continuous connection and language needed to lodge a Native Title claim and potentially stop the mine.[1] The narrative moves hectically at this point: water hoses tear clothes from the backs of protestors chained to a fence and tear gas sears 'their eyes, noses, throats', seeping through the protective layers of goggles and bandanas. Fragments of direct speech—'To riot is the voice of the unheard', 'They can't arrest us for sitting in', 'Sacred ground girl'—mark time between moments of physical violence as August's thoughts move in and out of focus, synchronizing with the carefully orchestrated chaos of the riot:

> August had forever felt like she was a remaining thing of the past that she wanted to destroy, a face she wanted to scratch off, a body she wanted broken, her skin torn to shreds. She was feeling something close to that against the fence, hosed and chained. She was chained like the people, the Gondiwindi who came before her, but it was her choice then, she thought. It felt that everything was so close, that they could all feel the past, that it gnawed at their ankles. That it filtered into their voices as they screamed together 'Re-sist!' into the dying light. She felt whole, fighting for something, screaming in the field rather than eating it, tasting it, running away.[2]

---

[1] In Australia, Native Title is governed by the Native Title Act (1993). This Act was introduced in response to the historic Mabo decision in which the Australian High Court ruled that Australia was not Terra Nullius—a land belonging to no-one—when it was 'discovered' by white settlers. The decision recognized Aboriginal and Torres Strait Islanders as Australia's first people and acknowledged that their right and interests in the land and waters continued despite colonial settlement. Native Title requires that a case be made before a national level tribunal that establishes continuous and unbroken connection to the land claimed since colonization.

[2] Tara June Winch, *The Yield* (London: Hamish Hamilton, 2019), pp. 301–302.

A hyphen breaks the word 'Re-sist' apart, opening out a resonant space for multiple pasts to reverberate amidst the present cacophony of screaming voices. August's scream channels the silenced history of her ancestors, once chained by white settlers on Country never ceded, while her fellow protesters draw on other traditions of civil disobedience, notably Martin Luther King's much-quoted call for America to listen and make good on 'the promises of freedom and justice' that had not been met: 'To riot is the voice of the unheard.'[3]

Invoking King's famous redefinition of what it means to riot reads as an act of pre-emptive legitimation at this stage in the plot, foreshadowing the negative connotations the same word will assume in the media coverage of the protest that the narrator implies will follow. Sensitized to the resonance of the word 'riot', Winch's writing is potently comparative at this moment, inviting readers to acknowledge the overlapping histories and multiple senses that resound when this word is read. Narrative translations of the language of the Wiradjuri people progressively attune the reader to the connectivity of words in this novel, building multiple pathways through the history of the land and its connection to other places, times, and peoples. This translative world-making extends into Winch's imagining of the social space of a riot where the voices of the rioters, purposefully defining their intentions, are heard above the noisy outrage of the journalists gathered to cover the event, or the laws that entitle riot police to suppress a protest. Such imaginative expansion of the duration and social space of the riot is not new, of course, as this collection's chronological and geographical span demonstrates. Winch uses the familiar techniques of free-indirect style to access August's agonized interiority as she joins the protest, before turning the reader's attention to the direct speech that interlaces King's definition of the riot with the language of indigenous storytelling. By giving form to both the unassimilable wildness and resolute connectivity of riotous resistance in this way, Winch's writing also asserts the 'untranslatable' specificity of the struggle her novel animates.[4] And yet, King's words still resonate in unpredictable ways, inviting comparisons with the work of other writers, including the subjects of the following chapters, who have variously harnessed the formal wildness of rioting for creative and sometimes explicitly political purposes.

This collection contends that the literary archive, understood as an inherently incomplete disparate gathering of textual forms, models ways of understanding this new era of riots in which we currently live. The prevalence of rioting as a tactic for expressing collective dissent may seem to epitomize the volatility of

---

[3] Winch, p. 301. Martin Luther King, 'The Other America', delivered August 1967, Stanford; reprinted in Cornel West, ed., *The Radical King* (Boston: Beacon Press, 2016), pp. 235-244. The original context and wording of King's famous phrase is: 'I think America must see that riots do not develop out of thin air. Certain conditions continue to exist in our society which must be condemned as vigorously as we condemn riots. But in the final analysis, a riot is the language of the unheard.'

[4] This interpretation draws on Emily Apter's mobilizing of the concept of untranslatability in her critique of world literature in 'Untranslatables: A World System', *New Literary History* 39, no. 3 (Summer, 2008), pp. 581-598.

contemporary global politics, but literary writers have long registered the riot's insurrectionary appeal and risks. Literature, as Sarah Cole reminds us, with its 'restless urge to rewrite inherited stories, has always offered an exemplary forum for making violence knowable'.[5] The writers that form the focus of this collection exemplify literature's long relationship to the quasi-political form of the riot; a relationship which has been complex and varied, sometimes participatory, reactive, incendiary, anthropological, epistemological, but above all archival and aesthetic. Assuming representational responsibility for popular activities that the nation state typically perceives as ephemeral, destructive, and disconnected from any responsible political sequence (and routinely crushed into oblivion), literary writers have fashioned instead a parallel archive that has sought to capture rioting's many forms and repertoires. The spontaneous logic of riotous activity, as well as its chaotic sensory and affective manifestations, present especially demanding experiential conditions to the artist. Embracing this challenge, writers have not merely documented riots over the years, they have developed diverse ways of seeing them, ways that are more acutely attuned to the phenomenology and expressive nature of rioting than historiographical explanations, sociological classifications, or political denunciations could ever be.

Attending above all to the acoustic, expressive, and aesthetic dimension of rioting in literature, this collection traces these constants across multiple political, historical, geographical, and cultural horizons, to show what changes, and what stays the same. The chapters cohere around the following questions: how has the noise, cacophony, tumult, and discord of rioting been recorded, and with what effects on riotous self-understanding, as well as on the practice of literature? How does the spirit of 'creative destruction' invest a crowd and animate its acts within a single episode of rebellious refusal? How do cultural and demographic differences inflect this creative destruction? How have literary texts helped to configure an historical knowledge of political praxis that takes unofficial, often violent forms? To what extent does the literary tradition of rioting become self-conscious and internationalized?

One of the key contentions of this collection is that literature has done far more than merely record or register riotous practices. Rather, literature has, in variable ways, used riotous practices as raw material to stimulate and accelerate its own formal development and critical responsiveness. For some writers this has manifested in a move away from classical norms of propriety and accord and towards a more openly contingent, chaotic, and unpredictable scenography and cast of dramatis personae, while others have moved towards narrative realism or, in more recent times, digital media platforms to manifest the crises and damage that riots unleash. Keenly attuned to these and other formal variations, the chapters in this collection

[5] Sarah Cole, *At the Violet Hour: Modernism and Violence in England and Ireland* (Oxford: Oxford University Press, 2012), p. 4.

analyse literature's fraught dialogue with the histories of violence and intolerance that are bound up in rioting as an inherently volatile form of collective action.

Riots, Crowds, and Literary Form

The history of modern rioting parallels the development of the modern novel and the modern lyric. Yet there has been no sustained attempt to trace or theorize the various ways writers over time and in different contexts have shaped cultural perceptions of the riot as a distinctive form of political and social expression. Contrasting with this relative dearth of critical attention, there is a daunting body of sociological, literary, and historical analysis of crowds that typically treats the riot as a subset of the former's dominant, yet limited, 'collective repertoire of gestures', to invoke Charles Tilly's phrasing.[6] In Gustave Le Bon's *The Crowd: A Study of the Popular Mind* (1895) the European mob is located on a descending trajectory as the crowd moves through the phases of submergence, contagion, and suggestion: 'by the mere fact that he forms part of an organised crowd, a man descends several rungs in the ladder of civilisation. Isolated, he may be a cultivated individual; in a crowd, he is a barbarian—that is, a creature acting by instinct.'[7] Riots and strikes are 'immediate' unthinking responses to the remote germination of 'new ideas whose force and consequences are a cause of astonishment' in Le Bon's theory of the crowd's suggestibility.[8]

Elias Canetti reversed Le Bon's hypothesis, arguing that power was drawn to the many and various forms that the crowd assumed, rather than the crowd to the hypnotic force of charismatic leaders. While rioting is never explicitly categorized in *Crowds and Power* (1960), Canetti's first-hand experience of the explosive violence that plagued the Weimar Republic during the inflation crisis of the 1920s and erupted in Vienna during the July Revolt of 1927, where he moved in 1924 to continue his studies, proved a vital creative catalyst. Haunted by these experiences, Canetti turned first to fiction. His second novel, *Auto-da-Fé* (1935), draws on the rioting and book-burning that he had witnessed as the Palace of Justice in Vienna was overrun by protesters. Versions of this destructive iconoclasm also surface in the lyrical anecdotal movements of *Crowds and Power*. In Canetti's telling, the crowd in its more riotous incarnations is a sensitive multifaceted thing. It may take the form of a panic, a combustible eruption that refuses limits, a querulous energy that revels in the noise of destruction, to name just a few of its many

---

[6] Charles Tilly, *Popular Contention in Great Britain, 1758–1834* (Cambridge, MA: Harvard University Press, 1995), p. 41.
[7] Gustave Le Bon, *The Crowd: A Study of the Popular Mind* (Marietta, GA: Larlin Group, 1982), p. 36.
[8] Le Bon, *The Crowd*, p. 1.

incarnations, all of which are consumed from the inside out by a 'feeling of being persecuted'.[9]

Countering these more speculative, sometimes literary, accounts of the irrationality of the 'group mind', George Rudé's 'face-to-face' histories of crowds and riots, as Nicholas Rogers has argued, made it difficult to see the 'urban riot as a collective pathology, a frenzied protest of the uprooted'.[10] Rudé's archival commitment to writing a history from below aligns with E.P. Thompson's insistence on the riot's essential place in any critical analysis of the moral character of the English eighteenth-century crowd. 'It has been suggested', Thompson contended, 'that the term "riot" is a blunt tool of analysis for so many particular grievances and occasions. It is also an imprecise term for describing popular actions.'[11] Subverting typical characterizations of forms of 'direct action' as spontaneous and inchoate 'squabbles outside London bakeries' or 'affrays' in local mills, Thompson emphasized the 'discipline' and 'pattern of behaviour' that shaped these events: 'The central action in this pattern is not the sack of granaries and the pilfering of grain or flour but the action of "setting the price"'.[12] In this reading the riot's legible distinction from the organized crowd hinges on the former's unifying and conscious economic intent.

Inspired by Thompson's call for a more systematic analysis of the economic catalysts for rioting, Joshua Clover enlists Marx's labour theory of value and crisis in *Riot. Strike. Riot* to develop a theory of the riot as 'a privileged tactic' of a larger category of 'circulation struggles' that manifest in forms of the 'blockade, the occupation and, at the far horizon, the commune'.[13] According to Clover's chronology, which draws on both Tilley and Thompson, the strike surpassed the riot as the ascendant form of collective resistance in the nineteenth century, only to emerge once more in our current post-industrial era—or 'time of riots', to invoke Alain Badiou's phrase.[14] Adhering to 'the tradition of world-systems analysis', Clover elaborates a framework for understanding 'both the global breadth and *long durée* within which to think the localised event of the riot'.[15] Conceding that there are limits to this extension that justify his focus on 'early industrialising and now deindustrialising nations of the west', Clover's polemic maps a terrain where the shape of pre-industrial food riots finds an echo in the post-industrial struggles of urban Black communities against an increasingly militarized carceral state; and

---

[9] Elias Canetti, *Crowds and Power*, translated by Carol Stewart (London: Penguin, 1992), p. 24.
[10] Nicholas Rogers, *Crowds, Culture and Politics in Georgian Britain* (Oxford: Clarendon Press, 1998), p. 8.
[11] E.P. Thompson, 'The Moral Economy of the English Crowd in the Eighteenth-Century', *Past and Present*, no. 50 (February, 1971), pp. 107–108.
[12] E.P. Thompson, 'The Moral Economy of the English Crowd in the Eighteenth-Century', p. 108.
[13] Joshua Clover, *Riot. Strike. Riot: The New Era of Uprisings* (London: Verso, 2016), p. 31.
[14] Alain Badiou, *The Rebirth of History: Times of Riots and Uprisings*, translated by Gregory Elliot (New York, NY: Verso, 2012), p. 8.
[15] Clover, *Riot. Strike. Riot.*, p. 7.

the various struggles of nineteenth-century radicals and twentieth-century union organizers against a rapidly expanding capitalist market can be read along a riot–strike–riot continuum that explains the 'systematic import of the riot's return' in the current post-industrial world order.[16]

Testing the validity of Clover's heuristic approach to theorizing the global riot is not our project here: as he himself concedes, heuristics, by definition, simplify 'reality's endless complexities'.[17] It is, however, worth dwelling on one of Clover's few literary allusions, which is to Percy Bysshe Shelley's *The Mask of Anarchy: Written on the Occasion of the Massacre at Manchester*.[18] Demonstrating the poem's enduring place in 'the library of the riot', as he suggestively describes it, Clover names a series of instances where Shelley's allegorical representation of the Peterloo Massacre (legally defined as a riot) has been mobilized as a call to resist, if not necessarily to riot.[19] Clover draws attention to the enlisting of Shelley's verse by Chartists in 1842; by the leaders of the Ladies's Garment Workers Union in 1911; by student activists protesting cuts to the social wage in London in 2010; and by activists across the 2011 movement of the squares, including the Occupy movement, and the Arab Spring.[20] According to Clover, the lasting resonance of Shelley's poem for generations of activists hinges on the final stanza:

> Rise like lions after slumber
> In unvanquishable number—
> Shake your chains to earth like dew
> Which in sleep had fallen on you—
> Ye are many—they are few.[21]

While it is true that these lines have served as a 'kind of marching song for struggle after struggle' (the balladic tetrameter couplets and triplets are intentionally populist), Clover's avowedly wishful suggestion that it 'might be possible to persuade you that the sounds in the first line, *rise/lions/after*, want you to hear the word *riot*. It is hard not to' is less convincing.[22] Lost in the polemical momentum of Clover's search for literary echoes of just riots is what many have read as Shelley's aesthetic defence of non-violent resistance to the anarchic force of state

---

[16] Clover, *Riot. Strike. Riot.*, p. 39.
[17] Clover, *Riot. Strike. Riot.*, p. 8.
[18] Clover, *Riot. Strike. Riot.*, p. 70.
[19] The Riot Act was notoriously read twice inaudibly to legitimate the cavalry charge on a peaceful protesting crowd gathered in St Peter's Field on Monday, 16 August 1819 to demand parliamentary reform.
[20] Clover, *Riot. Strike. Riot.*, p. 72.
[21] Percy Bysshe Shelley, *The Mask of Anarchy. Written on the Occasion of the Massacre at Manchester*, in *Shelley's Poetry and Prose*, selected and edited by Donald H. Reiman and Sharon B. Powers (New York, NY: W.W. Norton & Company, 1977), pp. 301–310.
[22] Clover, *Riot. Strike. Riot.*, p. 72.

sponsored violence (the latter being the unjust riot).[23] The legacy of this poetic celebration of passive resistance has been traced by Timothy Morton and others in the non-violent political movements in India (notably Ghandi's recitations of the poem during his campaign for a free India), South Africa, as well as student-led protests in Tiananmen Square.[24] This is not to argue that these many contingent translations of *The Mask of Anarchy* discredit Clover's literary allusion, but rather to offer just one illustrative instance of the transmissive affordances and conative resilience of literary form in times of crisis. Resonant with multiple histories of violence, Shelley's words sound and mean differently as they are taken up by new readers and activists in diverse global settings. Implicit here is Wai Chee Dimock's argument for a theory of resonance as a means of conceptualizing why and how literary texts endure. As Dimock puts it: 'Texts are emerging phenomena, activated and to some extent constituted by the passage of time, by their continual transit through new semantic networks, modifying their tonality as they proceed.'[25]

Attuned to the semantic networks that shape the meaning of words like 'Crowd' and 'Riot' in nineteenth-century literature, John Plotz usefully elaborates the etymological and grammatical anomalies of both in an analysis that stresses their synonymity. Plotz notes that both words, along with other similar words—push, mob, press, throng, group, gang, mass—are alike in both verbal and nominative forms, but, more significantly, the '"noun/verb", or "thing/action" confusion also insinuates itself into a longstanding tradition of disputes on the ethical and legal status of behaviour in a crowd'.[26] Can one person be held responsible for the behaviour of the crowd? Where does a person's complicity in the behaviour of the crowd end? What number of people defines a crowd? Who bears the responsibility for representing the crowd? As Plotz reminds us, to one British nineteenth-century writer 'a crowd was a set of bodies collected on the street, while to another it was the dispersed citizenry of certain social classes, and to yet another it was the English nation'.[27] This parsing of the semantic unfixity of 'crowd' however, risks reducing rioting to a sub-strand of the history of the crowd. Conversely, if rioting

---

[23] This distinction between just and unjust riots draws on Jonathan Havercroft's argument for a normative theory of the riot. See Jonathan Havercroft, 'Why is There No Just Riot Theory?', *British Journal of Political Science* (2020): pp. 1–15.

[24] Timothy Morton, 'Receptions', in *The Cambridge Companion to Shelley*, edited by Timothy Morton (Cambridge: Cambridge University Press, 2006), p. 40; Meena Alexander, 'Shelley's India: Territory and Text, Some Problems of Decolonization', in *Shelley: Poet and Legislator of the World*, edited by Betty. T. Bennett and Stuart Curran (Baltimore: Johns Hopkins University Press, 1996), pp. 169–178; Madhu Benoit, 'Scatter My Words among Mankind', in *Keats-Shelley Review* 11 (1997), pp. 53–80; Andrew Franta, 'Shelley and the Poetics of Political Indirection', *Poetics Today* 22, no. 4 (2001), pp. 765–793.

[25] Wai Chee Dimock, 'A Theory of Resonance', *PMLA* 112, no. 5 (October, 1997), pp. 1060–1071, p. 1061.

[26] John Plotz, *The Crowd: British Literature and Public Politics* (Berkeley, CA: University of California Press, 2000), p. 6.

[27] Plotz, *The Crowd*, p. 7.

is treated as the primary term, as Clover contends, an alternative history comes into view: a history that focuses on riots as discrete phenomena that emerge from the place where crowds intersect with some aspect of the state and market that is 'closed' to democratic control, be it the police force, the fixed price, the powers of conscription, censorship, segregated housing policy, apartheid, or some other modality of enclosure.

Global Rioting and Literary Worldmaking

In his attempt to explain the resurgence of the riot in the wake of the Arab Spring, Alain Badiou compares the 'naïve' and 'scattered' form of riots that took place in 2011 to the 'first insurrections' of the nineteenth century, before claiming that 'we find ourselves in a *time of riots*' in which we can somehow transcend the mistakes of the past and find a different descriptive repertoire from the 'anti-popular idiom' of nineteenth-century European writers.[28] This loose genealogy presumes a global consensus on the riot that never existed, allowing 'the past' to be repurposed as a salutary warning to present rioters. Instead of an obsolete or marginal record of anti-popular sentiment, the multiple literary worlds that this collection explores makes the extensive, portable, and constantly evolving descriptive repertoire of rioting newly audible. As a tenacious manifestation of popular expression that erupts on the pages of an early modern text, yet still resonates with contemporary writing that has sought to capture the volatility of Tahrir Square, or more recently, the violence in Ferguson and Baltimore, the riot has put deep cultural roots in literary work, where it figures as a formal incentive to break from preconceived models of social cohesion and accord, and to reach beyond the knowable coordinates of social existence into the unpredictable and chaotic processes of violent contestation.

While the catalyst for Badiou's study may be the Arab Spring, his history of the riot retains a Eurocentric focus and assumes that it was only in 2011 that the Arab people massed in the streets and squares to resist the tyranny of their dictators. This assumption reflects a common misconception that is also prevalent in Middle East studies—that of the stability of the region. Veteran Middle East expert Gregory Gause III highlighted the danger of this assumption when he asked, alongside many others, 'why Middle East studies missed the Arab Spring': an oversight which he attributes to 'the myth of authoritarian stability'.[29] Gause goes some way to shedding light on what researchers in the field have overlooked, but his focus on the Arab dictators who rose to power in the mid-twentieth century

---

[28] Badiou, *The Rebirth of History*, p. 5.
[29] Gregory Gause III, 'Why Middle East Studies Missed the Arab Spring: The Myth of Authoritarian Stability', *Foreign Affairs* 90, no. 4 (2011), pp. 81–90.

replacing colonial-backed leaders, some of whom were ousted through popular revolt, neglects a longer history of riots and popular tumult. In stark contrast, as the case studies that explore Middle Eastern writers in this collection demonstrate, this sort of oversight has not been a feature of the region's literature and cultural production. Indeed, the history of mass, spontaneous violence in the region has been shaped by contemporary authors who have sought to trace a longer arc of riots and revolutions. Part of the reason for this preoccupation is that the literary and cultural fields have engaged a deeper archival suite of resources that demonstrate a substantial history of mass resistance. This wider scope does not ignore eruptions of violence because they supposedly failed to have a significant transformative impact on the region. Rather, for literary writers and researchers, documenting past uprisings and riots is an act of resistance itself, a form of decolonial praxis that challenges various Orientalist images, such as the passive, despotic worshipping Arab or the uncivilized and inherently violent Arab, instead centring instances of their popular will and agency. Jason Bahbak Mohaghegh's *The Writing of Violence in the Middle East* (2013) is an example of this mode of literary activism.[30] While his study does not exclusively focus on the representation of riots by Middle Eastern writers, its unorthodox form and written style, using fragmented prose and shifting generic registers, allows Mohaghegh to enact what he terms a textual riot. In doing so he simultaneously illustrates to readers how Middle Eastern writers have narrated their own histories of violence and reveals the deep reservoir of resistance and crowd violence that has challenged authoritarian power, be it local dictators or colonial masters.

The Orientalist trope of the violent and rioting Arab subject has also been widely challenged by writers of fiction. Mahmud Tahir Haqqi's *The Maiden of Dinshaway* (1906) is a literary representation of the 1906 Dinshaway Incident, a confrontation between Egyptians and occupying British soldiers.[31] While the imperial record recalls this incident as one where residents of Dinshaway attacked and murdered British soldiers, Haqqi's novella captures the riot that followed the biased British tribunal and brutal punishment of the Egyptians. Haqqi broke with Arabic literary convention at the time using colloquial rather than formal Arabic to render the dialogue of peasant characters, giving his story, as Zachary Lockman claims, a wide mass appeal.[32] This colloquial register brings the readership closer to the peasant classes, and represents their riotous response to the British as one of self-defence. It is also a narrative that exposed the shared interest of upper and peasant Egyptian classes, as both reacted negatively to the brutality of the British.

---

[30] Jason Bahbak Mohaghegh, *The Writing of Violence in the Middle East: Inflictions* (Bloomsbury 2013).

[31] Mahmud Tahir Haqqi, *The Maiden of Dinshaway* (1906), translated by Saad El-Gabalawy, in *Three Pioneering Egyptian Novels* (Fredericton: York Press, 1986).

[32] Zachary Lockman, 'Imagining the Working Class: Culture, Nationalism, and Class Formation in Egypt, 1899–1914', *Poetics Today* 15, no. 2 (1994): pp. 157–190.

The novella thus anticipates the nationalist unity provoked by the Dinshaway Incident, a nationalism that spread across the country and remained unabated until the 1952 revolution against the British.

This interest in popular resistance to the British is also evident in Isabella Hammad's *The Parisian* (2019), which is set almost entirely in early twentieth-century Palestine and includes a lengthy description of the Nebi Musa riots that erupted in Jerusalem in 1920. Mawsim al-Nebi Musa was a festival held in honour of the Prophet Moses in the Palestinian Muslim calendar, with celebrations, which included a procession, lasting a week. In 1920, however, the procession triggered a confrontation between Palestinians on one side and the British army and a Zionist militia on the other. The catalysts for this riot were the 1917 Balfour Declaration and the 1919 Paris Peace Conference, which Palestinians understood as evidence that European imperial powers were enabling Zionist ambitions in Palestine. Midhat Kamal, the central character in *The Parisian*, finds himself in the centre of the violent melee. Initially he expresses a sense of joy at being part of the march but soon, after losing his companions Jamel Kamal and Basil Murad, fears the danger of being subsumed by the crowd. Unable to find Basil or Jamel, Midhat concludes that 'There was nothing for it but to submit. He pressed forward with the multitude.'[33] The Nebi Musa riots have been generally understood as a spontaneous uprising, feeding the Orientalist narrative of the naturally violent and irrational Arab who cannot be trusted or allowed to congregate even to mark a religious event.[34] But what Hammad's novel shows is how various Palestinian characters recognized the encroaching threat on their land and knew they had to organize against it. On their way to the Nebi Musa procession, Basil asks Midhat 'Have you heard of Jabotinsky? ... He is a Zionist. He is starting a Zionist army. If we want to beat them we have to train ourselves.'[35] During the violence, such attempts at organizing are revealed when a 'speaker [steps up] on the balcony [to begin] his oration'. The drumbeat that set the rhythm of the crowd's chant '*Falastin arad-na!* ... Palestine is our land!' went 'quiet like a dead breeze' and behind 'the speaker a banner was unfurled with Emir Faisal's [the leader representing Arab interests] likeness'.[36] All this suggests that the riot was a loosely organized protest, not a spontaneous event or reflective of the supposed Arab will to violence. Thus, Hammad's complex narration of this riot sequence emphasizes not just Palestinian resistance to British forces and Zionist nationalists, but also the Palestinian quest for autonomy and self-determination.

---

[33] Isabella Hammad, *The Parisian* (London: Jonathan Cape, 2019), p. 293.

[34] Roberto Mazza, 'Transforming the Holy City: From Communal Clashes to Urban Violence, the Nebi Musa Riots in 1920', in *Urban Violence in the Middle East: Changing Cityscapes in the Transition from Empire to Nation State*, edited by Claudia Ghrawi, Nelida Fuccaro, Nora Lafi, and Ulrike Freitag (New York, NY: Berghahn Books, 2015), pp. 179–194.

[35] Hammad, *The Parisian*, p. 289.

[36] Hammad, *The Parisian*, p. 301.

Hammad and Haqqi's concern with British imperial violence moulds their literary output, centring the riot not as a discrete episode in history but as part of a sequence of violent events where emancipation from the oppressive forces of the state motivates crowd action. This is further evident in the chapters that focus on the Arab world in this volume, only in these cases the brutality of early twentieth-century imperialism has been replaced by corrupt local leaderships. Rita Sakr and Jumana Bayeh's chapters highlight the concern with the failed Tahrir uprising in the texts of three contemporary Egyptian authors—Omar Robert Hamilton, Yasmine El Rashidi, and Basma Abdel Aziz. While Hamilton and El Rashidi take a more realist approach and Abdel Aziz employs a surrealist register, their novels reveal literature's unique capacity to capture the fervour and chaos of those uprisings and their aftermath. This is evident in Abdel Aziz's novel, where the erasure of the documentary evidence that records the repressive practices of state authorities is supplemented by the literary text, and in Hamilton and El Rashidi's work where characters's use of sound recordings, video footage, and citizen journalism fail to fully capture the complexity of Tahrir, again stressing the potency of writing the riot in fiction. Likewise, the Moroccan and Lebanese contexts of Karima Laachir and Caroline Rooney's contributions further delve into how literature can best record and memorialize the riot. Laachir and Rooney unpack the vital role of memory in political mobilization, and the relevance of literature to what Laachir, following Toni Morrison, refers to as 're-memory'. In the case of Morocco, literary accounts of its history challenge state-imposed politics of silence and propose a suppressed counter-history; in the Lebanese context literature tracks the anarchic energy that defines Tripoli, Lebanon's second largest city, not as a reflection of what is widely perceived as its inherent disunity, but of the recent demonstration of peaceful popular unity among its denizens.

In challenging myths of Middle Eastern stability these novelists resonate with the more cultural and aesthetic emphasis in recent histories of popular resistance in the region. John Chalcraft's *Popular Politics in the Making of the Modern Middle East* (2016), for example, draws not only on conventional historical sources and evidence, but also cultural artefacts, such as literature, art, and graffiti, to understand what he refers to as the contentious politics that defined the region across the nineteenth and twentieth centuries.[37] Influenced by E.P. Thomson's focus on the economic reasons for rioting and protest, and Charles Tilly's interest in the crowd's 'conception of how its [own] aims and rights inform its action and influence its very readiness to act', as well as prompted by the 2010 self-immolation of Muhammad Bouazizi in Tunisia, Chalcraft shifts the focus from the decisions made by those in power, to the diverse array of practices—including riots,

---

[37] John Chalcraft, *Popular Politics in the Making of the Modern Middle East* (Cambridge: Cambridge University Press, 2016).

uprisings and protests—to narrate the history of the region.[38] Pnina Webner, Marin Webb, and Kathryn Spellman-Poots's edited collection *The Political Aesthetics of Global Protest* (2014) shares Chalcraft's approach to writing about protests and crowd violence.[39] While the Arab Spring is used as a catalyst for examining the performativity of protests and riots in and beyond the Arab region, comparative focus in Webner, Webb, and Spellman-Poots's volume expands to consider parallel events in India, Botswana, London, Athens, Wisconsin, and New York. What unites these sites are the rhythmic chants, songs, and slogans performed by protestors, highlighting the primary role of voice, sound, and rhythm for all riots, irrespective of geographical context.

Race, Riots, and Writing

All around the world, the modern quest for styles of life that are 'errant, fugitive, recalcitrant, anarchic, willful' has been spearheaded by Black and Brown communities in collective acts of resistance to state and corporate control over the commons; it has taken root within these communities because the 'avid longing for a world not ruled by master, man or the police' is most conspicuous in social formations characterized by racial capitalism, and it has most frequently taken the defensive/expressive form of riotous rebellion against the very structures of everyday life.[40] The compound 'defensive/expressive' seems inescapable in discussions of modern race rioting, since riot is both what is inflicted on communities of colour in a racist state and the spontaneous mode of protection from it. As Saidaya Hartman comments on the race riots of 1919 in New York City, 'What the riot made clear was that the color line was hardening and that segregation and antiblack racism were not only augmented by way of state and federal policy, but also stoked by the antipathy and the psychic investment of even the poorest whites in black subordination and servility.'[41] And the most symptomatic response to this unliveable condition is a kind of improvised wildness, a waywardness drawn to the riot as an expressive repertoire of tactics:

> Wayward: to wander, to be unmoored, adrift, rambling, roving, cruising, strolling, and seeking. To claim the right to opacity. To strike, to riot, to refuse. To love what is not loved. To be lost to the world. It is the practice of the social

---

[38] Thompson, 'The Moral Economy of the English Crowd in the Eighteenth-Century'; Charles Tilly, *From Mobilization to Revolution: CRSO Working Paper No. 156* (Michigan: University of Michigan, 1977), pp. 2–48.
[39] Pnina Webner, Marin Webb, and Kathryn Spellman-Poots (editors), *The Political Aesthetics of Global Protest: The Arab Spring and Beyond* (Edinburgh: Edinburgh University Press, 2014).
[40] Sàidiya Hartman, *Wayward Lives, Beautiful Experiments: Intimate Histories of Social Upheaval* (London: Serpent's Tail, 2019), p. 227.
[41] Hartman, *Wayward Lives*, p. 174.

otherwise, the insurgent ground that enables new possibilities and new vocabularies; it is the lived experience of enclosure and segregation, assembling and huddling together. It is the directionless search for a free territory; it is a practice of making and relation that enfolds within the policed boundaries of the dark ghetto; it is the mutual aid offered in the open-air prison.[42]

This depiction of the contemporary complexion of racial capitalism chimes with what Fred Moten and Stefano Harney gesture towards in *The Undercommons*, 'a wild place that is not simply the left over space that limns real and regulated zones of polite society; rather, it is a wild place that continuously produces its own unregulated wildness'.[43] This unregulated space and its constituent errancy defines at once the 'real' places in which riots erupt to contest police control and starvation wages, and the combative literary zone in which Black and Brown writers write back against the constricting norms of polite publishing and prizes. There is an emphasis here on improvisation, on jazz aesthetics and noisy imperfection, in the codification of this wildness in song, poem, and story. Such forms point to an 'undercommons' of tenacious resistance, to a shared, subtending field of unmapped resources for social expressivity yet to stabilize into fixed structures: rogue, external, vagabond, unruly, crazed, riotous, rapturous. It is vital that we construe the literary archive of riot not simply as representational, but at a deeper and more sustaining level, as *representative*: a pioneering act of pointing outward, into the beyond, 'out into the world, the other thing, the other world, the joyful noise of the scattered, scatted eschaton, the undercommon refusal of the academy of misery' (118).

In any event, perhaps the most enduring and emblematic form of rioting in the Americas is the race riot. Prior to its semantic redefinition after World War II, the dominant form of the race riot in the USA was violent attacks on Black, Chinese, Italian, Polish, and Jewish workers by poor working whites. It was, in that sense a kind of pogrom or population control whose specific impetus was almost always racialized labour relations and struggles over the white wage. Along with its rural form of organized lynching, race rioting in American cities gouged a grisly scar of agony in defence of the 'colour line' after the Civil War, running through urban centres and townships north and south, and leaving a broken trail of literary testaments behind it. A proper literary resistance began to coalesce only once the vanguard of a national Black press had appeared in the first decade of the twentieth century, and once W.E.B. Du Bois and Carrie Clifford had loaned their pens to the task of documenting the abominable carnage of Atlanta,

---

[42] Hartman, *Wayward Lives*, pp. 227–228.
[43] Jack Halberstam, 'The Wild Beyond', in *The Undercommons: Fugitive Planning & Black Study*, edited by Stefano Harney and Fred Moten (Wivenhoe: Minor Composition, 2013), p. 7.

1906.[44] With the conscription of hundreds of thousands of Black Americans in the First World War, spreading communist labour militancy on the shop floor, and the shock of unemployment and housing scarcity after demobilization, the situation was set for a dramatic escalation of race riots across the country. In the 'Red Summer' of 1919 the USA witnessed the most destructive urban conflict since the Civil War—many riots, all instigated by white terror mobs and perpetrated against communities of colour.[45] But rather than capitulate, Black writers took the offensive and inscribed in letters of fire their open rebellion against the unquestioned assumptions of white supremacy and open shop capitalism. The result was one of the greatest flowerings in the history of American literature— the New Negro movement and its aftermath, the so-called Harlem Renaissance, which began when the Jamaican poet Claude McKay, working as a Pullman waiter when New York and Chicago erupted, wrote his incendiary sonnet 'If We Must Die' (1919).[46] James Weldon Johnson, Carrie Clifford, Jean Toomer, Fenton Johnson, Andy Razaf—many were the Black writers who, seared by the flames of 1919, forged in the smithy of their outrage a new and unquenchable literary spirit, unassimilable to the prevailing liberal temper of American letters.

Time and again, the American race riot has served as a crucible for a Black literary renaissance. The radical Black Arts movement of the late 1960s and 1970s is unimaginable without the sequence of violent events that broke out just prior. As Juliana Spahr enumerates: 'Major uprisings and riots took place at the start of 1964 in Rochester, Philadelphia, Harlem, Chicago, Jersey City, Paterson, and Elizabeth; then, Watts in 1965; Cleveland in 1966; Newark, Detroit, and Minneapolis-St. Paul in 1967; Chicago, Baltimore, Washington DC, and Cleveland in 1968. Many sources attribute over 150 various rebellions in 1967; over 125 after the shooting of Martin Luther King Jr. in 1968.'[47] Without this riotous alembic, there is no Amiri Baraka, no mid-career Gwendolyn Brooks, no Ishmael Reed, no Watts Prophets, no Audre Lorde, no late-career James Baldwin. It is as if the American race riot conditions an urgent kind of literary productivity pitched against the state, against capital, and against complacent white denialism. It is a dynamic we witnessed again, briefly, after Los Angeles in 1992, and which has branded itself onto contemporary literary life with the sequence that runs from Ferguson, through Baltimore, Charlottesville, and Minneapolis, with all their riotous national and international

---

[44] See Dolen Perkins-Valdez, '"Atlanta's Shame": W. E. B. Du Bois and Carrie Williams Clifford Respond to the Atlanta Race Riot of 1906', *Studies in the Literary Imagination* 4, no. 2 (2007): pp. 133–151.

[45] See David Krugler, *1919, The Year of Racial Violence: How African Americans Fought Back* (Cambridge: Cambridge University Press, 2015).

[46] See Barbara Foley, *Spectres of 1919: Class and Nation in the Making of the New Negro* (Chicago, IL: University of Illinois Press, 2003), and Wayne F. Cooper, *Claude McKay, Rebel Sojourner in the Harlem Renaissance* (Baton Rouge, LA: Louisiana State University Press, 1987).

[47] Juliana Spahr, *Du Bois's Telegram: Literary Resistance and State Containment*, Kindle edition (Cambridge, MA: Harvard University Press, 2018), loc. 1830 of 4833.

rhizomes, and perhaps receives its most ghastly emanation in the assault on Capitol Hill by white rioters in early 2021. The race riot is more than an incidental feature of the literary life of the American state; it is one of the prime movers of formal and generational evolution, as, decade after decade, as century chases century, the deepest structural realities of the racial-capitalist state impress their pitiless logics on the bodies of Black men and women, and once again the business of writing is seared with the responsibility of bearing witness to the apparently inadmissible fact that *Black Lives Matter*.

In this volume, the chapters by Andrew Brooks and Astrid Lorange, and Julian Murphet, pry into these processes and contradictions to unearth a convulsive tradition of wild and wayward writing at the interface of militant self-protection and 'the joyful noise of the scattered, scatted eschaton'.[48] While their emphases differ (Brooks and Lorange are more openly affirmative, while Murphet seeks to reacquaint contemporary romanticism with the grim history of US race rioting) these chapters between them chart a vital pattern of riotous writing at the very social locations where literature seems least affordable. Proving once and for all that to write the riot means contesting the very norms of literary discourse, these chapters make a convincing case for the representative nature of riot-writing for communities of colour today, imprisoned by the structures of the racist state and yet digging tunnels into the edifice of late capitalism with a poetic and a rhetoric forged in the undercommons of a shared, fugitive life.

Riots, Literature, and the Legacies of Empire

To speak of the structures of contemporary racist states is to also acknowledge that many of 'these structures and strategies', as Olúfẹ́mi O. Táíwò reminds us, 'have their roots in the colonial era of the nineteenth and twentieth centuries, when national-level institutions functioned like franchises under the global racial empire's logo, each territorial army, colonial government, and national stock exchange linked together in a powerful cartel'.[49] The global legacy of empire links many of the case studies in this collection. Mark Steven argues that the 'collective subject of the riot' is today's answer to the barbarian—'an embodiment of the apparent savagery disavowed by capitalist civilisation'. Tracing a long and global historical arc, from the sixteenth to the mid-twentieth century, Steven reads two texts that 'conceive of riot and barbarism together as one'—William Shakespeare's *Coriolanus* and Bertolt Brecht's unfinished reimagining of that play in the

---

[48] Stefano Harney and Fred Moten, 'The General Antagonism: An Interview with Stevphen Sukaitis', *The Undercommons: Fugitive Planning and Black Study* (Wivenhoe: Minor Compositions, 2013), p. 118.

[49] Olúfẹ́mi O. Táíwò, *Elite Capture. How the Powerful Took Over Identity Politics (and Everything Else)* (London: Pluto Press, 2022), p. 4.

aftermath of World War Two. Shakespeare serves here as an index of the 'riot's globalization' and captures, according to Steven, the ambivalence of the word riot itself in the early modern period, an ambivalence that intensifies in Brecht's conjuring of the animus of Fascism in his reimagining of Caius Marcius Coriolanus's barbaric attacks on 'foreign people' under the guise of the just suppression of rebellious insurgents. Joseph North traces an equally long arc following the movement of the word mob from the seventeenth century to contemporary First Nations writing. North contends that mob, typically understood as a cognate term for riot, was developed in the seventeenth century and used disparagingly to warn against the dangers of 'the rule of the common people'. North then turns to the affirmative invocation of mob in the writing of the First Nations peoples of Australia and New Zealand, challenging us to move beyond the word's pejorative history.

Cóilín Parsons's chapter shares North and Steven's focus on legacies of violence and empire. Reading between the claims made for Joyce's *Ulysses* as an epic of decolonization and the emergence of decolonial thinking on university campuses in South Africa, Parsons questions the global and transhistorical resonance of *Ulysses*. Daniel Elam's chapter takes a more chronologically contained approach, in his consideration of how novels from the British Empire in the 1920s and 1930s cast riots and crowds as central characters. Interweaving close readings of Mulk Raj Anand's *Untouchable* (1936) and Virginia Woolf's *Mrs Dalloway* (1927), with contemporary theorizations of crowds and riots in the work of Gustave Le Bon, Gabriele Tarde, and Emile Durkheim, Elam counters recent claims that read *Untouchable* as a belated colonial response to Joyce's *Ulysses*.

While Elam's chapter rereads Woolf and Anand in conjunction with the General Strike of 1927 and the violent reverberations set off by the Rowlatt Act of 1919— which criminalized 'anarchical movements' in British India—Rashmi Varma's chapter focuses on tales of riots generated in the wake of Partition in 1947. Varma argues that the riot is the most spectacular aspect of South Asian Partition narratives. Addressing the prevailing evasion of 'the epistemological and narratological dimensions of the riot' in the scholarship on the literature of the Partition, Varma turns to the short story form as a site for representing the Partition in which the riot was a key form of violence, arguing 'that the short story is better able to narrate the episodic and spectacular nature of the riot'. Short form fiction is also one of many textual forms that are central to Janny Leung's analysis of the literary movement that emerged alongside the street protests (dubbed riots by the government) in Hong Kong between 2019 and 2021. Leung moves from syncretic heteroglossic works generated by multiple authors, to autobiographical first-hand accounts of the social movement, to Koji Akita's manga, to a burgeoning diasporic literature, culminating with novels and short stories by Hong Kong based authors, arguing that these various forms of writing serve both as a means of cultural survival and of practising freedom.

Resonating with Elam's account of the literary reverberations of the Rowlett Act, Leung's analysis of the violent redrawing of the boundaries of legal and literary geographies in contemporary Hong Kong also aligns with another entangled history of legal and literary fictions that Helen Groth and Ian Haywood elaborate. King George I's Riot Act of 1714 forcefully redrew the boundaries of the modern riot. To riot, as defined by the Riot Act, which was subsequently enacted in various forms in the British colonies, was to assemble unlawfully in numbers of more than twelve and to fail to disperse within one hour after the reading of the order. Haywood considers the paradox at the heart of the performative reading of the Riot Act in the open chapter of this collection. In his exploration of the soundscapes of the Strand Riot of 1749, the Old Price Riots of 1809, and the Queen Caroline controversy of 1820, Haywood notes not just the logistical absurdity of one magistrate's 'declaration of illegality' being heard above a riot's 'deafening clamour', but also how the very text of the Act already 'prejudges the social order it describes'. Groth's chapter also begins with a reading of the Riot Act that transformed a protest on Trafalgar Square on 13 November 1887 into a legally defined riot, authorizing the violence and bloodshed that followed. Reading the literary and visual renderings of the Trafalgar Riots by artists and writers who were present that day, Groth argues that what emerges from these works is a retrospective imagining of the riot as a complex event: a collective interpretive process that is intentionally redistributive and aesthetic.

Covering the riot across multiple contexts and periods, the case studies in this volume are an urgent reminder of the enduring legacies of empire, segregation, racial violence, and oppressive authoritarianism. More importantly, the following chapters highlight the centrality of literature in connecting seemingly disparate geographical and historical contexts, cutting across siloed national or regional literary archives to compile a more diverse and inherently comparative literary repository.

1
Tumultum Populi

Riots, Noise, and Speech Acts in Georgian England

Ian Haywood

This chapter argues that insufficient attention has been given the acoustic dimension of popular disturbances in Georgian England. The introductory section, 'Reading the Riot Act', considers the paradox at the heart of the new 1715 law. In order to quell a tumultuous commotion, the lone magistrate had to declaim in a barely credible 'loud voice'; put another way, the declaration of illegality should, by definition, be drowned out by the deafening clamour to which it responds and demarcates. Further questions then arise about the discursive and legal agency of 'reading'—both annunciating and comprehending—a piece of talismanic text which prejudges the social disorder it describes. Following this preamble, three case studies explore the soundscape of riots, in each instance drawing heavily on caricature prints, the only art form equipped to visually represent noisy spectacle. Each of these examples will also give particular attention to the visual and vocal agency of women. The first example is the so-called Strand Riot or 'Sailor's Revenge' of 1749, an intriguing confrontation between customary rights of protest and state power, and an event which produced the earliest satirical images of urban rioting. The second case study is the Old Price Riots of 1809, a prolonged outburst of popular resentment against a rise in the ticket prices at Covent Garden theatre. This episode took aural disruption to new levels as its main tactic was the interruption of theatrical performances, a transfer of traditional charivari from the streets to the symbolic heart of the Georgian cultural industry. The third and final example comes from the Queen Caroline controversy of 1820, a remarkable outpouring of popular protest which defied the Six Acts and generated an extraordinary number of caricatures. In an attempt to discredit her transformation into a populist political icon, Caroline's opponents depicted her as 'Mother Red Cap', a disloyal, flirtatious, low-life rabble rouser, but this attack can be read against the grain as a confirmation of her super-charged role as a sublime amplifier of public opinion and the 'vox populi'.

Reading the Riot Act

Though the idea of reading the Riot Act has passed into common parlance as a familiar, familial, and not-to-be-taken-too-seriously threat of dire consequences to come if misbehaviour persists, to consult the original 1715 Act today is a chilling experience.[1] To begin with, the atavistic typographical appearance and absurdly official and repetitive phraseology is ominous and foreboding, incantatory black letters for a black Act. Then there is the ghoulish purpose of the new law, the constant reminder that offenders 'shall suffer death as in the case of felony without benefit of clergy', the latter clause intentionally evoking a state of terror as it removed the defendant's right to plead for a lesser sentence. And what was the crime that merited such draconian punishment? What did it mean, in fact, to riot—or, more precisely, to riot in such a way that a lethal legal threshold was passed?

This may seem a silly question to ask, as riots were an enduring feature of European societies, and it was common sense that a riot comprised an unlawful destruction of property by large numbers of people, but reading the original document suggests the answer is less straightforward. The riot was already a capital offence, but the new law recalibrated the numbers of rioters, specifying that twelve or more people 'being unlawfully, riotously and tumultuously assembled together, to the disturbance of the public peace' constituted a mob. It is also noteworthy that the number twelve is redolent with ironic symbolism, a last supper for the doomed and deluded, and the addition of the synonymous adverbs 'unlawfully' and 'tumultuously' to 'riotously' constitutes an unholy trinity of transgression—a visible state of damnation which is as obvious as it is contradictory, already unlawful before being judged so in the courts. The Act also points to the recent Jacobite rebellion as a justification for its harshness—'of late many rebellious riots and tumults have been in diverse parts of this kingdom ... with an intent to raise divisions, and to alienate the affections of the people from his majesty'.[2] Though this appeal to a national crisis of treason and rebellion seems disproportionate when placed against the relatively modest scale of a dozen rioters venting their fury, supporters of the Act often argued that any disturbance could escalate into a political riot if left unchecked.[3] But to modern eyes and sensibilities, even this laudable aim of

---

[1] 'An Act for Preventing Tumults and Riotous Assemblies, and for the more speedy and effectual Punishing the Rioters', *Anno Regni Georgii Regis: At the Parliament Begun and Holden at Westminster, the Seventeenth Day of March, Anno Dom 1714. In the First Year of the Reign of Our Sovereign Lord George, By the Grace of God, of Great Britain, France, and Ireland, King, Defender of the Faith &c, being the First Session of this Present Parliament* (London: John Baskett, 1715).

[2] Riot Act 1714, s 1.

[3] According to a spin-off publication, the aim of the Act was 'to suppress all such traitorous rebellions' (*The History of all Mobs, Tumults and Insurrections in Great Britain, From William the Conqueror to the Present Time. to Which Is Added, The Act of Parliament and Proclamation Lately Published for Punishing Rioters* (J Moore, n.d. [1715]), Preface).

nipping sedition in the bud grates with Britain's bloody penal code, meting out the death penalty for offences against property.[4] The valuing of possessions over people was further enshrined in the Act's granting of immunity against prosecution for law officers: any rioter injured or even killed during an arrest deserved their fate as they were already, by definition, guilty.

A close textual engagement with the Riot Act illuminates some of the problems which the Georgian state apparatus faced in trying to control the customary violence which underpinned the moral economy of the English crowd.[5] Yet the real innovation of the Act was not its redefinition of scale but its methodology: the reading aloud of the Riot Act in situ and in medias res became the legal mechanism for both determining and punishing a riot. In other words, a riot became a textually performative event, a speech act, a public proclamation which took its place among the cacophony of Georgian street cries, though this new utterance was elite and potentially fatal. The stentorian oration of the magistrate was, at least in theory, the state's answer to the tumultuous racket of the mob. To adapt Percy Shelley's post-Peterloo rallying-cry in *The Mask of Anarchy*, 'they are many, you are few'. As the Act declared:

> the order and form of the proclamations that shall made by the authority of this act, shall be as hereafter followeth (that is to say) the Justice of the Peace, or other person authorized by the Act to make the said proclamation, shall, among the said rioters, or as near to them as can be safely come, with a loud voice command, or cause to be commanded silence to be while proclamation is making ...[6]

But without any means of voice amplification (and there is no evidence that megaphones or speaking trumpets were routinely used), this procedure was, to say the least, challenging. The absurdity of a single 'loud voice' commanding 'silence' from a noisy crowd, even of twelve people, does not seem to have struck the drafters of the Act. If the proclamation—actually a short text contained within the Act—was read aloud but could not be heard, 'the authority of this act' was undermined, as indeed was the case at Peterloo and the Old Price riots. Hence the most important feature of the Riot Act acknowledged the hyper-audibility of rioting without finding the credible means to suppress or surpass it. Perhaps the mere sight of the recitation, which was usually delivered from an elevated position such as a balcony or upper window by a well-dressed person, was regarded as sufficient to deter the

---

[4] On the bloody code, see Douglas Hay et al. (eds), *Albion's Fatal Tree: Crime and Society in Eighteenth-Century England* (London: Pantheon, 1976); and Vic Gatrell, *The Hanging Tree: Execution and the English People* (Oxford: Oxford University Press, 1994).
[5] E.P. Thompson, 'The Moral Economy of the English Crowd in the Eighteenth Century', *Past and Present* 50 (1971), pp. 76–136.
[6] Riot Act 1714, s 1.

rioters, but the very brief proclamation makes clear that 'all persons, being assembled' were meant to hear the command and 'immediately to disperse themselves' within one hour, 'upon the pains contained in the Act'. Once these words were uttered, a riot was officially declared and the alleged perpetrators faced the 'pains' of arrest and execution. Acoustics was a matter of life and death.

The Riot Act set the stage for a prolonged conflict between the vox populi and the 'commanding' voice of the authorities, huzzas against hussars.[7] Many objectors regarded the Act as an infringement of customary modes of protest which, as Robert Shoemaker has argued, were grounded in carnivalesque social festivities and traditional rituals of community punishment and shaming such as charivari.[8] The latter, also known as skimmington, combined physical and vocal humiliation in equal measure, and it served, along with the adoption of quasi-militaristic cries, as a model for the intimidatory or inspiring power of noisy protest.[9] At the same time, the authorities regarded deafening commotion as a stereotypical feature of a riot, regardless of the social discipline on display or the declared peaceful intentions of the 'assembled' multitudes. As R. Murray Shafer explains, a demotic din was only permissible at 'imperial' spectacles such as royal or military festivals and commemorations, while unsanctioned hubbubs were 'nuisance noise'—intrusive, unstable, volatile, inflammatory, and always potentially riotous.[10] Reformers and radicals rebutted this caricature with the utopian, enlightenment ideal of clamour as the sublime expression of collective identity, democratic agency, and irrepressible public opinion: the vox populi in action. In the loud words of the London Corresponding Society, Britain's first mass working–class political movement, 'We contend that THE VOICE OF THE PEOPLE OUGHT TO BE HEARD IN THE COUNCILS OF THE NATION.' This goal would be achieved through a principled use of freedom of speech, 'the *whole nation*, deeply impressed with a sense of its wrongs, *uniting*, as it were with one voice'.[11] The people's 'one voice' is the radical counterweight to the singular 'loud voice' of the Riot Act.

Against this acoustic background, the following case studies look at the ways in which 'nuisance' sound articulated and amplified a 'sense' of the nation's 'wrongs' in Georgian England.

---

[7] On the longer acoustic perspective, see: Peter Denney et al. (eds), *Sound, Space, and Civility in the British World, 1700–1850* (Abingdon: Routledge, 2019), especially Chapters 6–9; Ian Haywood, 'Pandemonium: Radical Soundscapes and Satirical Prints in the Romantic Period', *Republic of Letters* 5, no. 2 (2017): pp. 1–26.

[8] Robert Shoemaker, 'The London "Mob" in the Early Eighteenth Century', *Journal of British Studies* 26, vol 3 (1987): pp. 273–304.

[9] See E.P. Thompson, *Customs in Common: Studies in Traditional Popular Culture* (London: Merlin, 1991), pp. 467–531.

[10] R. Murray Shafer, *The Soundscape: Our Sonic Environment and the Tuning of the World* (London: Destiny Books, 1994), p. 76. The terms are used throughout the book.

[11] *Reformers No Rioters* (n.p. July 1794), p. 5.

The Sailors' Revenge

On the evening of 1 July 1749, a group of sailors marched up the Strand in central London and attacked a brothel. Their aim was to exact revenge on a 'house of ill-fame' in which a fellow sailor had been robbed and forcibly ejected.[12] They forced an entry, ransacked the building, and expelled scantily-clad women and many of their possessions into the street. Items of furniture were defenestrated and promptly turned into a bonfire. According to press reports, the spectacle quickly attracted 'multitudes of spectators' who 'huzza'd' the rioters.[13] Buoyed up by this popular acclaim, the sailors vandalized several more bawdy houses the next day, including one called the *Star*. By this point the authorities had called for military assistance and arrests took place, but the sailors were brimming with confidence and forced the prisons to free some of their colleagues. When the melee was over, six rioters were in custody, three went to trial, and just one, a Cornish wigmaker called Bosavern Penlez, was executed. The fact that Penlez was from a respectable background drew attention to the case and when pleas for clemency were ignored there was a considerable public outcry. This is one reason why the Strand riots are so well known. The other is that the incident generated several caricature prints, the Georgian equivalent of visual reportage.[14] The most important of these is Louis Philippe Boitard's *The Sailor's Revenge or the Strand in an Uproar: A Tragi Comical Farce exhibited before a numerous Audience of yr Mobility and others* (Figure 1).[15] The allusions to theatre in the title and subtitle emphasize the idea of a riot as a spectacular performance, a sensorium of sight and sound that is conveyed artistically through dynamic visual effects and (unique to caricature) a liberal use of speech bubbles. This image, together with the pamphlet literature surrounding the Penlez controversy, provide valuable insights into the cultural construction of rioting in mid-eighteenth-century England.

The polarized debate about Penlez's execution was rooted in differing interpretations of the legality and seriousness of the riot. There was no denying that Penlez was present at the attack on the *Star*, but to his supporters his guilt was mitigated by two factors, his casual or accidental involvement when compared to the ringleaders, none of whom were punished, and the righteousness and popularity of the sailor's cause. In Shoemaker's words, 'pulling down' a bawdy house was regarded as a 'licensed disorder', an accepted form of rough justice and social cleansing sanctioned by the 'spontaneous participation of passersby and spectators'.[16] The Sailor's

---

[12] *Gentleman's Magazine* 19 (1749): p. 329.
[13] *Gentleman's Magazine* 19 (1749): p. 329.
[14] In addition to the print discussed here, see *The Tar's Triumph, Or Bawdy House Gallery* (London: Charles Mosley, 1 July 1749). British Museum Satires, 3036.
[15] Louis Philippe Boitard, *The Sailor's Revenge or the Strand in an Uproar: A Tragi Comical Farce Exhibited before a Numerous Audience of yr Mobility and Others* (London: Robert Sayer, August 1749). British Museum Satires, 3035.
[16] Shoemaker, 'The London Mob', pp. 293, 281.

Figure 1. Louis Philippe Boitard's *The Sailor's Revenge or the Strand in an Uproar: A Tragi Comical Farce exhibited before a numerous Audience of yr Mobility & others* (Robert Sayer, August 1749)

Revenge seems to support this lenient, carnivalesque view of the affray. A female spectator in the upper right corner of the scene shouts 'a Joyfull Riddance', and the verbal contribution of both perpetrators and victims is light-hearted, consisting mainly of bawdy puns in sex-industry jargon. Like performers in a farce, each character has a funny one-liner: the lewdest quip emanates from the rowdy centre of the scene where a sailor waves his hat and shouts, 'this will teach 'em to fling seamen'. In reality, it would be almost impossible to hear this joke, but the satirical lens presents the din as a theatrical 'uproar', a noisy rapport between the riotous actors and the audience within and beyond the picture's frame. Using the hyperbolic licence of caricature, the print captures the sense of community consent for the riot, as if the whole event was a form of popular, raucous street entertainment in which no one would be hurt. In the words of a pro-Penlez publication attributed to John Cleland, local residents reacted with 'perhaps more glee and mirth, than if they had been at a droll in *Bartholomew Fair*, seeing the painted scene of the renown'd *Troy* town in flames'.[17]

The Cleland pamphlet is an extraordinary defence of what Ronald Paulson calls a 'Whig riot', an assertion of the fundamental liberties of the English people.[18] From this perspective, the sailor's 'cruzade' or 'frolic' was not really a riot at all, a claim reinforced by the fact that the 'Proclamation for dispersing was never read'.[19] Furthermore, the violence at the *Star* was not directed at the prostitutes but at the property of their pimp or 'pandar', a cowardly bully who, in Nicholas Rogers' words, got his 'comeuppance'.[20] To further bolster their heroic potential, Cleland idealizes the sailors or tars (as they were commonly known) as icons of 'antient manliness' in a period of political corruption and national decline.[21] Taking the law into their own hands was justified by their professionalism and restraint: they 'went to work as if they were breaking up a ship, and in a trice unrigg'd the house from top to bottom'. They also managed the bonfire with 'decency and order' to protect both the crowd and adjacent houses.[22] This emollient narrative is reflected in *The Sailor's Revenge*'s depiction of a voluble crowd who are clearly enjoying the fracas, including the two bonfires. The conspicuous noisiness of the scene, evident in the print's garrulous participants and theatrical allusions, is also addressed by Cleland. His first point is that brothels are commonly sites of 'brawls, quarrels,

---

[17] [John Cleland], *The Case of the Unfortunate Bosavern Penlez. By A Gentleman Not Concern'd* Second Edition (T. Clement, 1750), p. 19.

[18] Ronald Paulson, *The Art of the Riot in England and America* (Baltimore, MD: Owlworks, 2010), pp. 28–30.

[19] [John Cleland], *The Case of the Unfortunate Bosavern Penlez*, pp. 21, 16.

[20] [John Cleland], *The Case of the Unfortunate Bosavern Penlez*, p. 8; Nicholas Rogers, *Mayhem: Post-War Crime and Violence in Britain, 1748–53* (New Haven, CT and London: Yale University Press, 2012), p. 66.

[21] [John Cleland], *The Case of the Unfortunate Bosavern Penlez*, p. 46.

[22] [John Cleland], *The Case of the Unfortunate Bosavern Penlez*, p. 18.

noises and disturbances' which 'prove such nuisances to a quiet neighbourhood', so the meting out of punishment by a 'hot-headed, wild, and impetuous' mob is a kind of (rough) poetic justice, the quelling of one 'disturbance' by another.[23] But Cleland also highlights the dichotomy between the unthreatening vox populi and the lethal 'efficacy' of the state's verbal power:

> Besides, that the very sound of storming a bawdy-house carry'd nothing in it so extremely awful: and that *sound* is not of so light weight, may be collected from the efficacy of the word *riot*, towards taking away this young fellow's life, when there was so little more than the sound of it against him, if intention may be allowed to extenuate, if not annihilate, his crime.[24]

The commotion may have been 'light weight', but the invocation of the Riot Act was instrumental in 'taking away' Penlez's life, even though 'there was so little more than the sound of it against him'.

Penlez's fate was a reminder that the Riot Act was alive and kicking, even though it had been rarely used. This point was made by Henry Fielding, the novelist-magistrate who authorized Penlez's arrest and prosecution. The unpopularity of Penlez's execution prompted Fielding to publish a vindication of the judicial process, and this text neatly counterpoints Cleland's robust defence of the right to riot. Though Cleland asserted that 'the mob is generally seen on the side of liberty and property', Fielding argued that the 'light or ludicrous colours' in which the riots were painted—a likely reference to *The Sailor's Revenge*—was an irresponsible dilution of a brazen, criminal assault on private property.[25] Moreover, Fielding insisted that the Riot Act was read, and that it was a response to the danger of escalation: 'the cry against bawdy-houses might have been easily converted into an out-cry of a very different nature, and goldsmiths might have been considered as great a nuisance to the public as whores'.[26] The key slippage is from 'cry' to 'out-cry', an acoustic raising of the stakes which signals Fielding's concern that (in Rogers's words) 'social relations had reached a crisis of confidence in which plebeian rebellion and licentiousness threatened to overwhelm the system of government'.[27] Penlez's fate demonstrated the Riot Act's 'efficacy': he was executed with fourteen others on 18 October 1749 for 'being feloniously and riotously assembled,

---

[23] [John Cleland], *The Case of the Unfortunate Bosavern Penlez*, pp. 15, 45.
[24] [John Cleland], *The Case of the Unfortunate Bosavern Penlez*, p. 40.
[25] [John Cleland], *The Case of the Unfortunate Bosavern Penlez*, p. 46; Henry Fielding, *A True State of the Case of Bosavern Penlez, Who Suffered on Account of the Late Riot in the Strand* (A. Millar, 1749), p. 48.
[26] Henry Fielding, *A True State of the Case of Bosavern Penlez*, p. 49.
[27] Nicholas Rogers, *Mayhem*, p. 67.

to the Disturbance of the public Peace', a sentence read out in court, and published in the Newgate bulletin, where it could be read.[28]

But the last word on this riot should go to the women. From a twenty-first-century perspective, the idea that 'licensed disorder' was a justified way to deal with 'disorderly houses' hardly seems to be 'on the side of liberty and property', even if, as Cleland argues, the real target was the male 'caitiff' who (dis)regarded a prostitute as 'touzed, and rumpled, like a bit of dirty paper', and 'enslaved, in short, so thoroughly, that nothing, no, not her own person, is her own property, or at her disposal'.[29] Another way to read *The Sailor's Revenge* is therefore as an ironic exposé of the Hogarthian destiny of the Georgian harlot who was 'turned out' onto the street.[30] Though they have little control over their plight, at least the speech bubbles allow the women to comment on their condition and to participate in the 'tragi-comical' drama in which, as the print's subtitle announces wryly, 'the Speeches [are] adapted to the Characters'. The verbal exchanges, replete with bawdy jargon, and the lament of the young woman with the billowing dress in the right foreground that she will have to relocate to the ironically named 'Goodmans Fields', give these otherwise marginalized and silenced figures a degree of agency and audibility.

Old Price Riots

Sixty years after the Strand riot, a more prolonged commotion erupted from within the heart of the Georgian entertainment industry. In September 1809 the actor-manager John Philip Kemble announced the opening of the newly built Covent Garden theatre. The building had burnt down the previous year and Kemble had lavished an enormous amount of money on its reconstruction. In order to recoup these costs, he increased ticket prices and replaced some public galleries with private boxes reserved for the social elites (the Georgian equivalent of today's corporate seating). Kemble anticipated some public disapproval of these measures, but he could never have imagined the ferocity of the theatre-goers' response. The opening night on 18 September was intended to be a showcase of architectural and cultural splendour, but instead it became a launchpad for an unprecedentedly prolonged campaign of deafening popular protest. As the capacity audience entered the building, they were already 'hissing and exclaiming'; as they witnessed the grandeur of the theatre's interior, they were temporarily 'silenced by the beauty

---

[28] THE ORDINARY of NEWGATE'S ACCOUNT of the Behaviour, Confession, & Dying Words Of the FIFTEEN MALEFACTORS Who were executed at TYBURN On Wednesday the 18th of OCTOBER, 1749. Reproduced in *Old Bailey Online*, reference number OA17491018, https://www.oldbaileyonline.org/browse.jsp?name=OA17491018. Accessed 12 September 2022.
[29] [John Cleland], *The Case of the Unfortunate Bosavern Penlez*, p. 9; Henry Fielding, *A True State of the Case of Bosavern Penlez*, p. 50.
[30] [John Cleland], *The Case of the Unfortunate Bosavern Penlez*, p. 10.

of the spectacle', but once inside the auditorium, the full force of the vox populi asserted itself.[31] As soon as the national anthem had been sung, the heckling and barracking began. Kemble's customary opening address was completely drowned out by audience's protests (and to rub this point in, this lost text was reprinted in *The Times* the following day). That evening's entire performance of *Macbeth* and a farce called *The Quaker* were also rendered inaudible by the chorus of disapproval:

> hisses, groans, yells, screeches, barks, coughs, shouts, cries of 'Off! Lower the prices! Six shillings! Pickpockets! Imposition! Cut-purse!' &c &c served to vary, but nothing could add to, the clamour of the house.[32]

As 'the uproar still continued', three well-dressed men then 'made their *debut* on the stage'. These strangers were assumed to be magistrates, but their performance was no more commanding than Kemble's. They 'attempted to speak altogether', but 'not being able to command respect or hearing, one of them produced a paper, which was conjectured to have been the Riot Act'. Newspaper reports relished the theatrical ironies of this humiliating audition: 'The audience burst into a fresh eruption at this, and emitted, "No Magistrates, no Police in a Theatre!" The ill-advised men retired bowing.'[33] The people had triumphed and the authorities sent packing. The authority of the Riot Act, in which '*words* were *acts* of riot', was acoustically delegitimized.[34] Instead of a 'wanton or mischievous riot', it was a 'noble sight to see so much just indignation in the public mind'.[35] Despite this setback, Kemble kept the theatre open and continued with the season's schedule, even though almost every performance was ruined: 'The uproar every where prevail'd'.[36] The disruption continued for over sixty days until Kemble gave way and reinstated the 'old price' regime.

As this brief summary of events shows, the Old Price commotion was a stunning example of 'tumultum populi' in action. Compared to the Strand riots, the significant new development was the literalization of performance: the stage was no longer an analogy for spectacular protest but the actual site of the disruption. The 'clamour of the house' turned the auditorium into a symbolic battleground between the 'licensed disorder' of the people and the governmentally licensed,

---

[31] 'Covent-Garden Theatre', *The Times*, 19 September 1809, p. 3. *The Times Digital Archive*, accessed 17 September 2022.
[32] 'Covent-Garden Theatre', *The Times*, p. 3.
[33] 'Covent-Garden Theatre', *The Times*, p. 3. Compare the *Morning Chronicle*, 19 September 1809: 'And even two or three respectable Magistrates turned actors ... came forward on the stage ... as if it had been a dramatic piece got up for the occasion'. Cited in Elaine Hadley, 'The Old Price Wars: Melodramatizing the Public Sphere in Early Nineteenth-Century England', *PMLA* 107 (1992): pp. 524–537, p. 529.
[34] *The Rise, Progress and Termination of the O.P. War* (Thomas Tegg: 1810), p. 5.
[35] 'Covent-Garden Theatre', *The Times*, p. 3.
[36] *The Rise, Progress and Termination of the O.P. War*, p. 3.

monopolistic authority of the patented theatres. As critics have noted, the apparent over-reaction of the audience to quite modest price increases can be explained by a popular perception of corruption and national decline which projected wider social and political injustices onto Kemble's 'impositions': the ongoing, unpopular war against Napoleon; the Mary Clarke and Duke of York scandal; and resentments at the over-commercialization of culture which pandered to social elites, lavished salaries on foreign performers, and generally ignored home-grown talent and traditions.[37] The political opposition helped to prolong the protests as it saw an opportunity to embarrass the government, while Kemble's heavy-handed hiring of pugilist security staff only fuelled class-conscious accusations of tyrannical tactics. These are all important factors behind the duration and impact of the Old Price riots, but more attention and recognition needs to be given to the most defining feature of the protests: their sheer noisiness.

The Cruikshank brothers's caricature *Acting Magistrates committing themselves being their first appearance on this stage as performed at the National Theatre Covent Garden* (Figure 2) brilliantly captures the symbolic moment on the first night when the Riot Act was acoustically neutralized.[38] The print shows the transformation of the auditorium into a confrontation between two sets of performers, the magistrates on the stage and the hostile audience. The rough music of the latter is clearly more powerful than the outnumbered and exposed trio who appear to be singing, the only applause coming from Kemble who stands behind them in a pose that also resembles a prayer. The small sheet entitled 'Riot Act' is massively outflanked by the banners and placards which festoon the seating areas (and which constitute a more substantial 'read' than the puny piece of paper on the stage), and this discursive imbalance is accompanied by another crucial innovation, the cacophonous 'pittite' orchestra which has displaced the theatre's professional musicians. The lone remaining member of the theatre's orchestra, possibly the conductor, desperately faces off his rivals, brandishing his wand like a cudgel. The replacement of the official theatre soundtrack by its demotic travesty is the turning point in the audience-protestors's success: the chorus of 'hisses, groans, yells, screeches, barks, coughs [and] shouts' is already clamorous, but the addition

---

[37] See: Marc Baer, *Theatre and Disorder in Georgian England* (Oxford: Clarendon Press, 1992), pp. 65–84; Peter Spence, *The Birth of Romantic Radicalism: War, Popular Politics and English Radical Reformism, 1810–1815* (Aldershot: Ashgate, 1996); Gillian Russell, *The Theatres of War: Performance, Politics and Society, 1793–1815* (Clarendon Press, 1995), pp. 95–96; Jane Moody, *Illegitimate Theatre in London, 1770–1840* (Cambridge University Press, 2000), pp. 62–69; Julia Swindells, *Glorious Causes: The Grand Theatre of Political Change* (Oxford: Oxford University Press, 2001), pp. 28–29; Tony Fisher, *Theatre and Governance in Britain, 1500–1900: Democracy, Disorder and the State* (Cambridge: Cambridge University Press, 2017), pp. 204–213.

[38] [Issac Robert and George Cruikshank], *Acting Magistrates committing themselves being their first appearance on this stage as performed at the National Theatre Covent Garden* (London: 18 September 1809). British Museum Satires, 11418.

Figure 2. [Isaac Robert and George Cruikshank], *Acting Magistrates committing themselves being their first appearance on this stage as performed at the National Theatre Covent Garden* (18 September 1809).

of bugles, bells and rattles is altogether deafening. The Old Price orchestra is acoustically unassailable, drowning out its elite adversaries including the 'caterwauling' Angelica Catalani, the overpaid, Italian superstar singer. Dissonance, discord, and disharmony is the order of the day.

Other satirical prints riffed wittily and inventively on this motif. The third panel of Thomas Rowlandson's *This is the House that Jack Built* (Figure 3) shows Catalani ('the Cat engaged to squall') facing off the Old Price band.[39] Interestingly, the xenophobic reimagining of Catalani as an impostor means that the aim of the heckling is not to undermine professional talent with dissonance but to simply overwhelm her already discordant tones with a much louder, democratic cacophony. Another important detail is that there are significant numbers of women in the mob, though it is mostly the men who wield the instruments. The most salient figure is John Bull who, in the fourth and fifth panels, blows a horn like a cross between a military bugler, town crier, master of the hunt, and mythical harbinger of Fame. In the fifth panel he has been manhandled outside by one of the hired security staff but still refuses to stop bugling. In the final panel the lone figure of Kemble is no match for the boisterous buskers who are spilling onto the stage. One placard alludes wryly to the Riot Act: 'Be silent Mr Kemble's head <u>aitches</u>', a reference to the way Kemble pronounced the word 'aches', but clearly a double pun, firstly on the proverbial dropping of aitches (the distinction between posh and common speech), and secondly on his acting ability, the implication being that, like Catalani, his fame is undeserved.

Kemble's failure to successfully perform *Macbeth*—'the tragedy thus tragediz'd'—was also ripe for parody.[40] Isaac Cruikshank's print *Is this a Rattle I see Before Me?* shows Kemble staring at an uncannily suspended rattle and uttering a new version of the famous soliloquy:

> Is this a Rattle which I see before me?
> Its deaf'ning sound portends the din of war
> And warns me that my only
> Safety is in flight ... or suffer this continual Rattle in
> Mine Ears.[41]

According to Samuel Johnson's Dictionary, a rattle was 'An instrument, which agitated makes a clattering noise'.[42] The Old Price riots ensured that there

---

[39] [Thomas Rowlandson], *This is the House that Jack Built* (London: Thomas Tegg, 27 September 1809). British Museum Satires, 11414.
[40] *The Rise, Progress and Termination of the O.P. War*, p. 3.
[41] Isaac Cruikshank, *Is this a Rattle I see Before Me?* (London: S W Fores, 30 October 1809). British Museum Satires, 11422.
[42] Samuel Johnson, 'rattle, n.s.', *A Dictionary of the English Language* (1755, 1773), edited by Beth Rapp Young, Jack Lynch, William Dorner, et al. https://johnsonsdictionaryonline.com/views/search.php?term=rattle, accessed 12 September 2022.

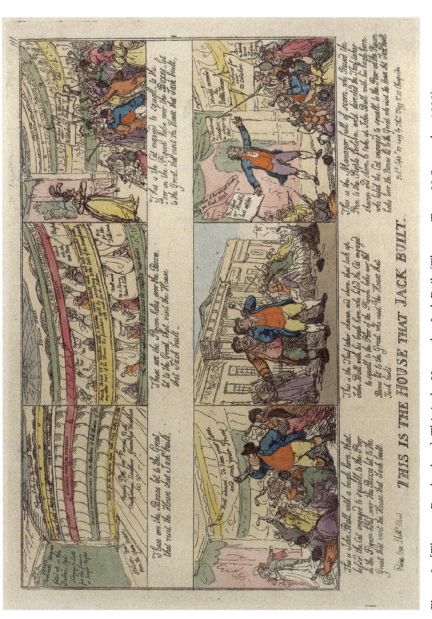

Figure 3. [Thomas Rowlandson], This is the House that Jack Built (Thomas Tegg, 23 September 1809).

was sufficient 'agitation' to keep up this 'continual Rattle' in Georgian ears. In another caricature of the same speech, Kemble declaims, 'It is the hurly-burly that informs / Thus to mine Ears / The yell throughout the House / Would raise the dead', but even this mock-gravitas is deflated by a footnote which states that 'here the clamour and cry for old price is so great that he gives himself up to despair'.[43]

The Old Price rioters appropriated the stereotypical raucousness of the mob and transformed this clamour into a highly effective weapon of protest which relocated charivari from the streets to the auditorium. This had the effect of intensifying the performative and especially the acoustic aspects of rioting. The 'tumultum populi' and its tinpot orchestra drowned out the voice of the state, whether (un)heard in the stentorian tones of the patent theatre or the inadequate readers of the Riot Act. But as in the Strand riot, it is important in conclusion to hear one other voice, that of victimized female sex-workers. Old Price propaganda condemned the new private boxes as nests of sexual depravity, little more than miniature brothels in which libertines entertained their harems in flagrant view of the audience. In the words of a satirical poem called *The O-Pœiad*, one aim of the Old Price campaign was to 'hunt the vermin' from these 'filthy holes' installed by theatre managers, the 'pimps and pandars of the British nation'. To justify this purge, the poem imagines a noisy invasion of prostitutes from 'city kennels, that with filth o'erflow'. As the women 'gain the house, and rush resistless in' they emit a 'discordant blast' and 'dreadful din!'[44] Seen and heard from this perspective, the Old Price disturbance was another 'licensed' act of vigilante violence against the Georgian sex industry. It was only in the caricatures that these women were allowed to protest their fate were given satirically mediated vocal and visual agency. In the Cruikshanks's *Kings Place and Chandos Street in an Uproar* (Figure 4), Kemble is tossed in a blanket by a group of 'bawds' from a nearby house of ill-fame whose business is suffering.[45] Behind them a procuress promotes her 'ware', two young women who are superior to 'noble whores', and the whole performance is cheered on by John Bull and the pittite orchestra. Unlike the 1749 'uproar', it is the women who are now taking their 'revenge' on the male 'pandar', duly cheered on by the male spectators. The speech bubbles make clear that the women are only acting out of self-interest, but this stereotyping does not efface the powerful impression of organized, effective, 'vociferated' protest.[46]

---

[43] [Charles Williams], *A Parody on Macbeth's Soliloquy at Covent Garden Theatre* (London: Walker, October 1809). British Museum Satires, 11423.
[44] *The O-Pœiad, A Satire. By Mad Bull* (London: 1810), pp. 8, 16, 15.
[45] [Isaac Robert and George Cruikshank], *Kings Place and Chandos Street in an Uproar* (London: S W Fores, 20 October 1809). British Museum Satires, 11421.
[46] *The Rise, Progress and Termination of the O.P. War*, p. 11.

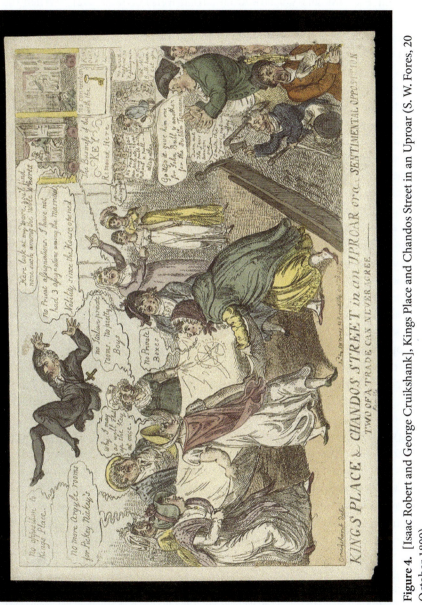

Figure 4. [Isaac Robert and George Cruikshank], Kings Place and Chandos Street in an Uproar (S. W. Fores, 20 October 1809).

Queen Caroline and Mother Red Cap

The third and concluding example of an uproarious Georgian tumult emerges from the extraordinary Queen Caroline controversy of 1820–1821.[47] When the Prince of Wales became George IV in January 1820, his estranged wife Caroline of Brunswick asserted her right to become the Queen Consort. The new king, however, was determined to deny her this prize. He had married Caroline in 1796 to clear his gambling debts, and the couple separated soon after and never reunited. Caroline lived for many years in exile and was *persona non grata* at the English court. Probes into her private life were unable to prove infidelity, so when she announced her intention to return to England, George and his Tory regime panicked. Caroline was offered a substantial sum of money to stay away, and when this was refused, the government placed her on trial for adultery. The response of the British public was overwhelmingly in support of the 'injured' queen. From the moment she set foot on English soil, public opinion went into overdrive. The media attention was unprecedented, generating millions of words of reportage as well as memorabilia, merchandise, portraits, and a bevy of caricatures. Caroline's cause mobilized and unified diverse socio-economic and political groups including women, trade unions, and the radical opposition. The government was already unpopular as the previous year had seen the Peterloo massacre and the introduction of the Six Acts restricting freedom of speech and rights of protest, so the Carolinite controversy was the first serious challenge to these repressive measures.[48] The Cato Street conspiracy of early 1820 and republican uprisings in Europe further intensified the sense of crisis, and there was widespread anticipation that Caroline's campaign could topple the government. When the trial found her guilty of adultery by a narrow margin, Lord Liverpool's ministry dropped its case. The national celebrations which followed were tantamount to an unofficial coronation, but Caroline failed to capitalize on her success and by the time of the king's coronation in July 1821 her reputation had been undermined by persistent government propaganda, including many caricatures.[49] She died in August 1821.

As this summary of the controversy indicates, the massive support for Caroline was both spectacular and extremely noisy, especially in London. Wherever the queen went, she was met with large, boisterous crowds. The presentation of Addresses—formal letters or statements of support from groups of individuals or organizations, many thousands of which were produced in this controversy,

---

[47] For a good overview of the controversy, see Jane Robins, *Rebel Queen: How the Trial of Caroline Brought England to the Brink of Revolution* (London: Simon and Schuster, 2006).

[48] See Malcolm Chase, *1820: Disorder and Stability in the United Kingdom* (Manchester: Manchester University Press, 2013), Chapter 6.

[49] The caricature offensive was spearheaded by the publisher George Humphrey. See Kristin Flieger Samuelian, *Royal Romances: Sex, Scandal and Monarchy in Print, 1780–1821* (Basingstoke: Palgrave Macmillan, 2010), Chapter 4. See also Ian Haywood, *Queen Caroline and the Power of Georgian Caricature* (Palgrave Pivot Series, 2023), Chapter 4.

including from women—became a regular ritual, with huge processions marching through central London to Brandenburgh House, Caroline's residence in Hammersmith. Once her trial began, her daily appearance at the House of Lords (where she was not allowed to speak) was met with a clamorous reception of massed ranks of supporters. One report described her rapport with the public as a 'telegraphic communication', as if she commanded and conducted the sublime acoustic power of vox populi.[50] To her enemies, however, she was guilty of whipping up hysterical and dangerous emotions which, as advocates of the Riot Act warned, could escalate into wider and potentially subversive disorder. This was not an entirely groundless fear, as radicals were using the conflict to press for sweeping democratic reforms. The authorities were also rattled by the fact that Caroline was an inspirational figurehead for women, thousands of whom were politicized for the first time.[51] Given that many caricatures showed Caroline triumphing over her political enemies in spectacular fashion, it was vital that government-backed propaganda found an effective way to recast her as a disreputable rabble-rouser.[52] This takes us to her caricature transformation into Mother Red Cap.

A hallmark of Caroline's popularity was her enthusiastic embrace of the public, so it was relatively easy for loyalists to lampoon this intimacy as socially and ethically inappropriate. In Robert Cruikshank's *A Late Arrival at Mother Wood's*, for example, a very restrained Caroline is shown on the balcony of the central London house of Alderman Matthew Wood, one of her closest companions and advisors.[53] In the street below her is a raucous gathering of men who are waving hats and cheering. Despite Caroline's reserve, her mere presence is enough to send some of these admirers into an over-excited frenzy, and several younger men are scaling the portico of the house to attempt to get closer to her. Speech bubbles reveal that their motivation is sexualized: 'I can see the whole of her', says one boy. The scene is not yet riotous, but the viewer wonders how the crowd would respond if Caroline became more animated and encouraging. George Cruikshank answered this query by turning Mother Wood into Mother Red Cap, the symbol of a very rowdy pub (Figure 5).[54] The new satirical moniker skilfully evoked an

---

[50] *The Whole Proceedings on the Trial of Her Majesty, Caroline Amelia Elizabeth, Queen of England, for 'Adulterous Intercourse' with Bartolomeo Bergami; With Notes and Comments* (London: John Fairburn, 1820), vol. 1, p. 140.

[51] Thomas Laqueur, 'The Queen Caroline Affair: Politics as Art in the Reign of George IV', *Journal of Modern History* (1982), pp. 417–466; Leonora Davidoff and Catherine Hall, *Family Fortunes: Men and Women of the English Middle Class, 1780–1850* (Chicago and London: University of Chicago Press, 1987), pp. 150–155; Anna Clarke, *Scandal: The Sexual Politics of the British Constitution* (Princeton, NJ: Princeton University Press, 2004), Chapter 8.

[52] See Ian Haywood, 'Queen Caroline in Caricature', *Romantic Illustration Network*, June 2020–September 2021, https://romanticillustrationnetwork.com/2020/06/05/queen-caroline-in-caricature-june-1820/.

[53] Robert Cruikshank, *A Late Arrival at Mother Wood's* (London: George Humphrey, 19 June 1820). British Museum Satires, 13734.

[54] George Cruikshank, *Mother Red Cap's Public House in Opposition to the King's Head Tavern* (London: George Humphrey, [4 August 1821]). Wilhelm Busch Museum.

Figure 5. Mother Red Cap's Public House in Opposition to the King's Head Tavern (George Humphrey, 4 August 1821).

actual London pub, a notorious landlady from folk tradition, and an allusion to the French revolutionary red cap, a shorthand for Jacobinism. The scene shows the disorderly Mother Red Cap facing ('in opposition to') the much more sedate, orderly, and exclusively male King's Head, the repose of loyalism. The inebriated mob that spills out of Caroline's pub is clearly out of control (two small children are fighting over booze), extremely loud (a man plays pipes and a drum, several others are yelling) and—judging by the stern look on the face of John Bull, who is positioned beneath the King's Head sign—dangerously close to vandalism. To rub this point in, the accompanying broadside text opens:

> See round old Mother Red Cap's
> The motley mobs assemble,
> And riot reigns in revelry,
> And none a wish dissemble ...
> And now the rout sends up a shout
> Which echo rattles down
> From Brandenburgh along the Thames
> And all around the town.
> 'Hail! Hail! OLD MOTHER RED CAP!
> At length return'd to town;
> Thy house shall be our tippling shop,
> Well pull the KING'S HEAD down ... '

It is quite possible that this self-condemnatory utterance of the vox populi was not meant to be taken too seriously, but the satirical reimagining of Caroline as the leader of a proto-regicidal mob clearly struck a chord with the public, as this image was reprinted several times in different formats.[55] Cruikshank's artistry no doubt contributed to the print's success: for example, viewers with a modicum of art history would have enjoyed the reworking of Hogarth's famous twinned series *Gin Lane* and *Beer Street* (1751), while more sophisticated consumers could have appreciated the playful self-referentiality of 'opposing' symbols and signs. There is also the conspicuous figure of John Bull to reckon with. He is carefully positioned between the mob and the ruling class, as if taking stock of the situation, and though his concerned look signifies disdain, it may also convey an understanding of the underlying motivations and grievances. As the crowd declaim:

> 'Red Cap shall be our CROWN AND ANCHOR
> Our SPAFIELD, PETERLOO,
> Here *Smithfield Meetings shall be held*,
> And battle Stephensloo.'

[55] 'Curator's comments', British Museum Collection website, https://www.britishmuseum.org/collection/object/P_1862-1217-407. Accessed 22 September 2022.

The satirical coinage 'Stephensloo', an allusion to St Stephens Hall, the chamber of the House of Commons, is a witty encapsulation of the stark polarization between rulers and ruled which the Caroline conflict exposed. The incongruity between this articulation of postwar radicalism and the visual depiction of wild, incoherent disorder is perhaps the key to the print's popularity, for as much as the Hogarthian rabble can be consigned to a carnivalesque past, they are nevertheless a potent factor in what William Hone called the 'irresistible force of Public Opinion', as the daily press reports of deafening massed gatherings revealed.[56] The print both registers and mediates these tensions through the reassuring presence of John Bull. But Caroline's inspirational role is also underscored, and though she is silent in this image (being literally a 'sign'), her 'telegraphic' sonic power is on display. Mother Red Cap is the satirical apotheosis of marginalized female discourse: she is the madam of yet another 'ill-famed house', but unlike her victimized predecessors in the Strand and Old Price riots, she now runs the show.[57]

The disparity between sheer 'nuisance' racket and 'irresistible' demands for social and political justice makes *Mother Red Cap's Public House* an appropriate place to pause this brief journey through the tumultuous cultural history of Georgian riots. The conservative stereotype of the baying mob, a motif that prevails into the present day, could never fully contain the radical, disruptive force of the vox populi in which 'licensed disorder' and disciplined protest co-existed. The Caroline protests blasted through the gagging clauses of the Six Acts, amplified the power of the vox populi, and impelled a new phase in the hegemonic struggle for the control of public opinion.[58]

---

[56] The phrase occurs in William Hone's printed design of *The Printer's Address to the Queen* (December 1820). See British Museum Collection website, https://www.britishmuseum.org/collection/object/P_1868-0808-13716. Accessed 22 September 2022.

[57] The Six Acts attacked women's open involvement in politics as a disreputable echo of French revolutionary women who were (allegedly) recruited from 'bagnios and public brothels'. See *Parliamentary Debates*, XLI (1819–1820), columns 390–391, columns 1665–1666. UK Parliament, Hansard, https://hansard.parliament.uk/commons/1819-11-29/debates/f2c19fae-012c-4d17-b487-9c1d5d6802af/SeditiousMeetingsPreventionBill. Accessed 22 September 2022.

[58] See Dror Wahrmann, 'Public opinion, violence, and the limits of constitutional politics', in James Vernon, ed. *Re-Reading the Constitution: New Narratives in the Political History of England's long Nineteenth Century* (Cambridge: Cambridge University Press, 1996), Chapter 4.

2
I Would They Were Barbarians

Shakespeare, Brecht, and the Global Riot

Mark Steven

If 2020 was a year of riots, it was also the year of barbarians. The collective subject of the riot, not necessarily revolutionary but nevertheless a potential agent of revolution, is today's answer to the barbarian: an embodiment of the apparent savagery disavowed by capitalist civilization. This is why, according to the militant research collective known as Endnotes, the tonality of the political present is one of insurgent barbarism. The passage 'out of our anarchic era', they say, is now to be found in what might best be described as 'non-movements', coalitions of desperate persons taking up arms and to the streets in a 'hunger for human community' denied to all of us under the depredations of capital. It is only in such a sociality, brought together and made visible as riot, that we encounter a powerful revolutionary impulse, manifest through an incoherence of political ideology as well as in the world-shattering violence of collective actions: 'in their confusion', they write, 'we can identify the eclipse of the social forms that we call capital, state and class'.[1] This affirmative use of 'barbarian' derives from Amadeo Bordiga's 1951 essay 'Avanti, Barbari!' in which the Italian communist champions barbarism as the ensign of civilizational collapse: 'we want', reads the statement of intent, 'the gates of this bourgeois world of profiteers, oppressors and butchers to be struck by a powerful barbaric wave capable of burying this world among itself'.[2] As a narrative container for ideologies of the riot, barbarism is a way for the defenders of capitalist civilization and the advocates of organizational politics to dismiss the riot as thoughtless and spasmodic violence. But it is also a crucial way to affirm the riot as an attack on capital led not by those it exploits but by those it excludes. Designating any person outside of known or knowable civilization (non-citizens in every sense), barbarism describes a principal source of social change in the present: an overgrown and racialized surplus population comprising the hundreds of millions

---

[1] Endnotes, 'Onward Barbarians', 26 May 2020, https://endnotes.org.uk/other_texts/en/end-notes-onward-barbarians. Accessed 30 May 2022.

[2] Amadeo Bordiga, 'Avanti, Barbari!' *Battaglia Comunista* 22 (November 1951), https://libriincogniti.wordpress.com/2018/02/23/on-the-thread-of-time-forward-barbarians/. Accessed 30 May 2022.

of men and women and children from all across the globe that capital has no way of or no interest in exploiting and who subsist only to be managed by police and paramilitaries into prisons, ghettos, camps, and the grave. But this kind of barbarism is no modern phenomena. Since Thucydides, 'barbarian' has designated any person who is neither Greek nor Roman, or who does not belong to Christian civilization. 'The need of protection is sure to be felt in some degree in every well-organized state', wrote Hegel: 'each citizen knows his rights and also knows that for the security of possession the social state is absolutely necessary. Barbarians have not yet attained this sense of need—the want of protection from others.'[3] And so on, from Nietzsche through Fanon, barbarian would denote those to whom humanity is denied absolutely, the very opposite of civilization and its political edifice, a people upon whose exclusion everything has come to depend. Yet while historically the barbarian might be illiterate, the proximity of riot to barbarism is as much literary as it is social. We find evidence of this in that essential foundation to so much of Western literature, the *King James Bible*. 'I shall be unto him that speaketh a Barbarian, and he that speaketh shall be a Barbarian unto me,' we read in Paul's letter to the Corinthians, a phrase that would be repeated by the translators as their statement of intent, naming that irreducible barbarism at the core of all civilizing missions.[4]

Combining these historical invocations of the barbarian, this chapter returns to a comparably influential vision of the polis and that which it excludes: the one imagined by William Shakespeare. For Shakespeare, like Endnotes and like Bordiga, barbarism serves as a form-giving metaphor that exemplarily discloses the movement and essence of not only the disorderly social mass locked outside the city gates but also—as this chapter will demonstrate—of their riots. 'I will not jump with common spirits', announces Arragon in *The Merchant of Venice*. 'And rank me with the barbarous multitudes.'[5] By looking to Shakespeare, this chapter argues that literary writing has been sensitive to a representational dialectic in which the riot is simultaneously denigrated and declaimed as the stuff of 'barbarous multitudes' and their 'common spirits'. The argument is made over a long and global historical arc, ranging from the late sixteenth century through the mid-twentieth and briefly into the twenty-first, and performs readings of two texts that conceive of riot and barbarism together as one: Shakespeare's *Coriolanus* and Bertolt Brecht's unfinished adaption of that play, worked on and abandoned in the early 1950s. If Shakespeare's play shows how the riot coincides with the emergence of the modern state, where the disavowal of its rioting masses as barbarian is used

---

[3] G. W. F. Hegel, *Lectures on the Philosophy of History*, translated by J. Sibree (London: Henry G. Bohn, 1861), p. 384.
[4] 1 Corinthians 14:11, *King James Bible* (Oxford: Oxford University Press, 1997).
[5] William Shakespeare, *The Merchant of Venice* in *Shakespeare: Complete Works*, edited by W. J. Craig (Oxford: Oxford University Press, 1966), p. 202. All further references to the works of Shakespeare refer to this edition.

to justify proto-fascistic military power, Brecht's reimagining of that play in the aftermath of World War Two presents a radical version of the riot as a force whose horizon is social revolution. It should of course go without saying here that Shakespeare is an index to the riot's globalization, the proper name bestowed upon a body of work that arrived at the advent of the modern world-system, at a time when all the populated continents were becoming interlinked by trade. 'During his lifetime', notes Anston Bosman, 'cultural exchanges multiplied not only among European nations, but between Europe and the Atlantic and, more slowly, Pacific worlds. Many of these growing interdependencies left their mark on Shakespeare's writing and theatre, from advances in stage design to an explosion of literary sources in print.'[6] More than that, however, if it is true that globalization began in the year 1571, when Spain established Manila as a port city connecting Asia and the Americas, Shakespeare came to literary maturity not only in a newly globalized world but also in a world whose primary means of connection, an emergent mercantile capitalism, would precipitate riots. And just as this arrival of the modern world-system sent English literature out along global economic currents, so too it allowed for the recombination of insurgent energies with and within those texts. As Sylvia Federici has argued, Shakespeare gave voice to 'the possibility of alliances between whites, blacks, and aboriginal peoples, and the fear of such unity in the European ruling class' imagination, at home and on the plantations', and that ideological fissiparousness, which combines collective human vitality with reactionary paranoia, is what we find in his many depictions of riot, as the formal impress of early modern history whose legacy is still with us today.[7]

Stagecraft and Statecraft

For Shakespeare, like Chaucer before him, riot was originally a term of moral indictment, synonymous with desire, wantonness, and lechery—and, while ethical instead of political, psychological instead of social, this kind of riot nevertheless describes an extraordinary challenge to individual will. In short, the riot actualizes material causes that transcend any one sovereign being. We encounter this in Sonnet XLI, which features the only riot in Shakespeare's poetic output, providing us with an expression of what Helen Vendler describes as lascivious grace, 'irresistible because beautiful in its essence', a threat to order that does not and cannot belong to any one individual.[8] If this immanent eclipse of the self-contained individual

---

[6] Anston Bosman, 'Shakespeare and Globalization'. In *The New Cambridge Companion to Shakespeare*, edited by M. De Grazia and S. Wells (Cambridge: Cambridge University Press, 2010), p. 285.
[7] Silvia Federici, *Caliban and the Witch: Women, the Body and Primitive Accumulation* (Brooklyn: Automedia, 2004). Ebook.
[8] Helen Vendler, *The Art of Shakespeare's Sonnets* (Cambridge MA: Harvard University Press, 1997), p. 213.

by interior forces is unique to Shakespeare's art—where, in Leon Trotsky's soviet construal, 'individual passion is carried to such a high degree of tension that it outgrows the individual, becomes super-personal, and is transformed into a fate of a certain kind'[9]—it persists, exteriorized onto the social, as a well-documented feature of the riot. For Alain Badiou, 'an immediate riot is always indistinct when it comes to the subjective type it summons and creates', which in turn promotes a subject that is no longer 'human' in the sense proscribed by capitalist civilization. 'Because this subjectivity is composed solely of rebellion, and dominated by negation and destruction', he reasons, 'it does not make it possible clearly to distinguish between what pertains to a partially universalizable intention and what remains confined to a rage with no purpose other than the satisfaction of being able to crystallize and find hateful objects to destroy or consume.'[10] Rather than impose this contemporary definition of riot on Shakespeare, here we can trace the ambivalence of the word itself, and the fact that, in the early modern period, there was significant passage between two dominant meanings: moral dissoluteness of the individual, on the one hand; and tumultuousness of the people, on the other.

In the tragedies especially, where passion is most likely to overwhelm and annihilate subjective reason, riot is invoked from within scenes of collapsing royalty as the life-form of destabilizing debauchery, the incursion of an all-corrupting lust. We encounter this kind of riot in *Antony and Cleopatra*, in *Hamlet*, and in *King Lear*. For Lear's daughters in particular, to speak of riot is to reckon not only with the derangement of their father's mind but also the disintegration of royal lineage, the disappearance of their inheritance, and betrayal of the military apparatus. Sensing this political meaning, invocation of the term is to place the king within a group context of what Goneril describes as knights who 'grow riotous' and again as the 'insolent retinue' with their 'not-to-be-endured riots'.[11] Likewise, in *Henry IV* and *V*, riot names an irrepressible urge to depravity and dissolution— one that threatens theatrical character and the monarchical embodiment of the state alike. Between Lear and Henry, it is as though Shakespeare had pre-empted the Coronation Riots of 1714 and King George's Riot Act of the same year, which would be read out by officers on behalf of 'Our Sovereign Lord the King' in order to either disperse or charge the 'riotous assemblies'.[12] From the standpoint of the throne, riot is nothing more than an unpredictable, all-consuming anarchy. The exemplary expression of this statist conservatism, in which the two senses of riot become directly imbricated, is to be found in Henry IV's speech to his son, Harry,

---

[9] Leon Trotsky, *Literature and Revolution*, translated by William Keach (Chicago, IL: Haymarket, 2005), p. 197.
[10] Alain Badiou, *The Rebirth of History: Times of Riots and Uprisings*, translated by Gregory Elliot (London: Verso, 2012), p. 25.
[11] Shakespeare, *King Lear*, p. 915.
[12] Adrian Randall, *Riotous Assemblies: Popular Protest in Hanoverian England* (Oxford: Oxford University Press, 2006), p. 25.

which reframes familial psychodrama as a matter of politics whereby the old king's demise ('Give that which gave thee life unto the worms') and the young prince's ascent are rendered synonymous with riots in the streets.

> Up, vanity:
> Down, royal state. All you sage counsellors, hence.
> And to the English court assemble now,
> From every region, apes of idleness.
> Now, neighbour confines, purge you of your scum.
> Have you a ruffian that will swear, drink, dance,
> Revel the night, rob, murder, and commit
> The oldest sins the newest kind of ways?
> Be happy, he will trouble you no more.
> England shall double gild his treble guilt;
> England shall give him office, honour, might;
> For the fifth Harry from curb'd license plucks
> The muzzle of restraint, and the wild dog
> Shall flesh his tooth on every innocent.
> O my poor kingdom, sick with civil blows!
> When that my care could not withhold thy riots,
> What wilt thou do when riot is thy care?
> O, thou wilt be a wilderness again.
> Peopled with wolves, thy old inhabitants![13]

The most striking aspect of this speech is the atavistic recourse to animals. The time of the riot is, in this formulation, the time of beasts: apes, wild dogs, and wolves all abound in the kingdom, in what reads here as a prefiguration of the Hobbesian state, whose spiritual as well as social commitment is to protect a citizenship from its arrant lycanthropy—a state of wild nature that could only be, in Carl Schmitt's summary, 'a domain of werewolves'.[14] The riot, announced by the outgoing monarch in chiasmic relation to its antipodean form, care, is the abdication of the state from its duty of protection, and with that comes a wild and bestial return of the repressed. For the denizens of court, the royals and the nobles, riot is a fanged beast.

But why harmonize the personal and the political in this way? In a narrative mode where psychodrama found itself intensified by the machinations of the court and where Eros served double duty as Elizabeth, the answer to this question is to be found in the proximity of prosody to power during the advent of capitalist

---

[13] Shakespeare, *Henry IV, Part II*, p. 463.
[14] Carl Schmitt, *The Nomos of the Earth in the International Law of the Jus Publicum Europaeum* (New York, NY: Telos, 2003), p. 95.

statecraft in early modern England. Robert Brenner's compact summary of the conjuncture is useful here:

> No longer needing to possess what was in effect a piece of the state, be it a lordship or an office, to maintain themselves economically, what the greater landed classes of England now merely required was a state able to protect for them their absolute private property—initially, both from marauding bands of neo-feudal magnates and from peasants seeking to conquer what they believed to be their customary rights to the land; ultimately, from landless squatters. They therefore associated themselves ever more closely during the early modern period with the monarchy in the construction of an increasingly powerful and precociously unified state that succeeded, by the early seventeenth century, in securing (at least in formal terms) a monopoly over the legitimate use of force. This monopoly of force was, from one point of view, extraordinarily effective in guaranteeing landed-class property.[15]

This interlocking of economic and biopolitical interests is the social unconscious residing not so much below but within the form of Shakespeare's writing. As Robert Matz has argued, 'many of the words that we might now understand only metaphorically—such as riches—or whose full implications we might miss—such as "friends" or "state"—when read in historical context begin to evoke a hard world of social status and courtly favour from which the writer feels outcast', in such a way that this language might contain within itself the germ of historical realism.[16] According to this logic, the riot would give shape to anything irruptive that might threaten the machinations not only of the state but also of the human subject, itself was a creation that belonged to this moment in history.

Without abandoning the residual and still dominant moral sense of the term, according to which the riot is fundamentally alien to a politics understood as procedure and bureaucracy, elsewhere in the plays it also serves as a practical means of doing politics otherwise: a premeditated assault directed at the sovereign state from those who have been marginalized and forgotten, exploited for what they have and then abandoned to rot. The exemplary mobilization of riot as political technology in this sense belongs to *Timon of Athens*. Betrayed by his friends and allies, Timon departs the city for the wilderness and makes his home in a cave where he discovers a trove of gold. Timon uses this fortune to fund an insurgent movement, paying bandits and prostitutes to assault the city and spread pestilence among its citizenry, thus combining both senses of the term, so that the bodies of riotous individuals might inflict their 'potent and infectious fevers' upon the state. Indeed, sustaining that moral sense of riot, it is specifically 'youths' in 'green virginity' and their susceptibility to 'lust and liberty' that are at issue, not yet 'the

---

[15] Robert Brenner, *Merchants and Revolution: Commercial Change, Political Conflict, and London's Overseas Traders, 1550–1653* (London: Verso, 2003), p. 652.

[16] Robert Matz, *The World of Shakespeare's Sonnets* (Jefferson: McFarland, 2008), p. 42.

whole race of mankind'. Nevertheless, Timon's declaration of vengeance comprises a scene unto itself, and stands now as one of the great explosions of rhetorical levelling in world literature. Its final words are these:

> Lust and liberty,
> Creep in the minds and marrows of our youth,
> That 'gainst the stream of virtue they may strive
> And drown themselves in riot. Itches, blains,
> Sow all th' Athenian bosoms, and their crop
> Be general leprosy! Breath infect breath,
> That their society, as their friendship, may
> Be merely poison! Nothing I'll bear from thee
> But nakedness, thou detestable town!
> Take thou that too, with multiplying bans.
> Timon will to the woods, where he shall find
> Th' unkindest beast more kinder than mankind.
> The gods confound- hear me, you good gods all-
> The Athenians both within and out that wall!
> And grant, as Timon grows, his hate may grow
> To the whole race of mankind, high and low!
> Amen.[17]

A sermon on misanthropy, it is worth noting that the philosophical cynicism Timon is said to have adopted derives in name from canine animality ('cynic' originates in the Greek word for 'dog'). But if, in what has since become one of Shakespeare's most overquoted lines, assassination would 'let slip the dogs of war', unleashing an organized force of military destruction, here the canine analogy is that much wilder: 'O thou wall / That girdles in those wolves, dive in the earth / And fence not Athens!'[18] Timon's invective, like King Henry's prophecy, abounds with snarling, creaturely life, a lycanthropy that abides within as well as from without the city walls. But more than that, and making this speech distinctive from those earlier invocations of the riot, is an emphasis on what Perry Anderson would describe as the 'subterranean archaism' of absolutism. Timon's speech is both a description of ancient Athens and, simultaneously, a description the Elizabethan state, 'an apparatus for the protection of aristocratic property and privileges, yet at the same time the means whereby this protection was promoted could simultaneously ensure the basic interests of the nascent mercantile and manufacturing classes', here conjoining the social structure of slaves and servants with what are, for Shakespeare, the modernizing forces of lust and liberty.[19] While the contradictions between feudalism and capitalism will soon position riot as the culmination

---

[17] Shakespeare, *Timon of Athens*, p. 809.
[18] Shakespeare, *Timon of Athens*, p. 809.
[19] Perry Anderson, *Lineages of the Absolutist State* (London: Verso, 1974), p. 40.

of multiple linking criminalities, that form is here, as before, presented as both a cause and consequence of social disorder, a vortex in which the citizens are admonished to 'drown themselves'.

All of which brings us to the culminating riot within Shakespeare's oeuvre, an augury of the modern world-system in the making, which establishes the dramatic shape of *Coriolanus*: the last of the tragedies and, as Frank Kermode insists, 'his most political play—not in the sense that it alludes openly to the politics of 1607–08, its probable date, but more abstractly'.[20] It is in the overlay of contemporary politics in England and Plutarch's account of Ancient Rome with a sense of literary vocation that we can witness the emergence of the social riot. In the permutations we have encountered, riot has been an expression of destabilizing, destroying lust—an all-consuming desire often made relative to licentiousness—but here riot transitions into a new frame of reference, no longer principally a moral indictment but also and primarily the concrete description of political process, taking a form that is inextricable from literal hunger. The play opens in revolt, with 'a company of mutinous citizens, with staves, clubs, and other weapons', who together and as one resolve 'rather to die than to famish'.[21] While this action takes place in Rome shortly after the expulsion of the Tarquin kings, during the Roman–Volscian wars, the food riot was very much alive in the social imaginary of Elizabethan England.

As John Bohstedt conveys in his compendious history of the early modern period, between 1550 and 1820, 'food riots were the most frequent and basic kind of collective violence', not least because, in the nascent emergence of the market economy, 'working-class households spent the lion's share of their budgets on food and most of that on bread, the fuel of work, dearth caused acute social tensions', with riots becoming 'so common as to be commonplace'.[22] Forming a battlecry with the citizens' resolution, the rioters of England risked death, fighting under a slogan that, in Bohstedt's formulation, they would 'rather be hanged than starved!'[23] This, to be sure, is the motivating tension at the core of Shakespeare's tragedy, the need to feed a growing population of men and women and children for whom no lord, employer, or state is willing to provide adequate provision. More than social diagnostic or inclement prophecy made by the ruling class, however, what makes this play unique is that its logic is spoken by the rioters:

> Care for us! True, indeed! They ne'er cared for us yet. Suffer us to famish, and their storehouses crammed with grain; make edicts for usury, to support usurers; repeal daily any wholesome act established against the rich, and provide more

---

[20] Frank Kermode, *Shakespeare's Language* (London: Penguin, 2001), p. 243.
[21] Shakespeare, *Coriolanus*, p. 701.
[22] John Bohstedt, *The Politics of Provisions: Food Riots, Moral Economy, and Market Transition in England, c. 1550–1850* (London: Routledge, 2010), p. 2.
[23] Bohstedt, *The Politics of Provisions*, p. 10.

piercing statutes daily to chain up and restrain the poor. If the wars eat us not up, they will; and there's all the love they bear us.[24]

The citizens's ire is directed at Caius Marcius Coriolanus, military veteran, nobleman, and—in the words of the citizens's ringleader, 'chief enemy to the people' and 'a very dog to the commonality'.[25] His death, they proclaim, is more than assassination; it is, for them, a necessary means of securing social provision. The nobility his embodiment sustains sustains is a superannuated social system whose chief purpose is militarism at all costs: he is representative of what Anderson has described as 'a landowning class whose profession was war: its social vocation was not an external accretion but an intrinsic function of its economic position', an expression of their species being, which 'beckoned them inexorably as a social necessity of their estate'.[26] As the old world dies and the new one struggles to be born, in the absolutist monstrosity of Coriolanus, feudal hierarchy coexists with pre-capitalist dispossession. 'Let us kill him', the citizens agree, 'and we'll have corn at our own price.'[27]

Before being spoken down to by a silver-tongued patrician, who uses the Aesopian fable of the belly and its members to rehearse an early-modern version of trickle-down economics, the citizens's leader accounts for the riot in terms that reveal its motivation and give it form and substance:

> What authority surfeits on would relieve us; if they would yield us but the superfluity, while it were wholesome, we might guess they relieved us humanely; but they think we are too dear: the leanness that afflicts us, the object of our misery, is as an inventory to particularize their abundance; our sufferance is a gain to them. Let us revenge this with our pikes ere we become rakes: for the gods know I speak this in hunger for bread, not in thirst for revenge.[28]

This reads less like an expression of slave society or feudal bondage and more like the relative 'freedom' of capitalism. Note the interlock of classes, the opposing us and them of this speech, and how 'sufferance' and 'gain' are not just coincident but mutually contingent. There is a calculus of resources at work: 'surfeits' and 'superfluity' provide the state with an accumulated surplus hoarded away from the citizens. Note, too, the choice of metaphor, 'ere we become rakes', which is an ancient proverb about becoming lean with hunger (familiar from both Chaucer and Spenser) but also an invocation of agrarian labour: the grain hoards have presumably been created by these citizens, who have to work to survive and who are

---

[24] Shakespeare, *Coriolanus*, p. 702.
[25] Shakespeare, *Coriolanus*, p. 701.
[26] Anderson, *Lineages*, p. 15.
[27] Shakespeare, *Coriolanus*, p. 701.
[28] Shakespeare, *Coriolanus*, p. 701.

now debarred from even the means to subsistence. That is why 'our sufferance is gain to them', why there is no relief offered to the people, in that scarcity of resources is a guarantee of labour and so of sustained production. And this is why the citizens riot.

Not exploitation alone but exploitation enabled by dispossession, in the form of enclosure, would provide the grounds for modern capital; the eventual accumulation of wealth is only enabled by the privatization of everything, a legal and political process that has its origins in the period during which Shakespeare was both writing his plays and hoarding grain. Jayne Elisabeth Archer, Howard Thomas, and Richard Marggraf Turley explain this in their literary history of food: 'Combining legal and illegal activities—and grain hoarding during a time of shortage was regarded with particular opprobrium—this Warwickshire man was able to retire in 1613, at the age of 49, as one of the largest property owners in his hometown, Stratford-upon-Avon. His two daughters, who inherited their father's leases, land and property, married well and lived in sizeable town houses nearby. This man was William Shakespeare.'[29] While not quite the logic of primitive accumulation, which displaces human communities from the land and into pauperism, hoarding a useful commodity is nevertheless a proto-capitalist tendency and so relative to the social admixture of privation and privatization that caused the Midland Revolt of 1607, a wave of riots that consumed much of Northamptonshire, Leicestershire, and Shakespeare's home county, Warwickshire. This uprising was, on one level, an expression of anger at genuine food shortages, but on another it was also a response to the existential threat imposed by the enclosure of common land—it was, in other words, a riot against the system itself, a mobilization against the socio-economic causes of poverty, whose spectral presence can be felt in the opening of *Coriolanus*.

Around fifty rioters were killed in battle during the Midland Revolt, or by drawing and quartering when the riot was suppressed, and we should keep in mind this bloody force of state repression when reading how Coriolanus responds to the riot. As an embodiment of the superannuated nobility but also a military man conscripted to the modern state at the historical moment of its emergence, in these words the riot meets its opposition:

> I would they were barbarians, as they are,
> Though in Rome litter'd; not Romans, as they are not,
> Though calved I' th' porch o' th' Capitol.[30]

It is as though all of Rome depends on the competing grammatical moods of the first line. Between the conditional and the indicative, barbarism is invoked to

---

[29] Jayne Elisabeth Archer, Howard Thomas, and Richard Marggraf Turley, 'Reading Shakespeare with the Grain: Sustainability and the Hunger Business', *Green Letters: Studies in Ecocriticism* 19, no. 1 (2015): p. 10.

[30] Shakespeare, *Coriolanus*, p. 719.

distance the rioters from the state, to imagine them outside the city walls and therefore as the killable mass of bare life, yet they are also contained within the state as its citizens. The state or at least the republic and its demos are thus called into being by the riot, in the appearance of that surplus humanity otherwise banished from political discourse, whom Coriolanus conjures away in a double-negative that inverts the previous line: their status as non-Romans, in the nobleman's eyes, is precisely what makes them barbarians; and yet, there they remain, in the Roman Capital, as animal life both 'litter'd' and 'calved' into being. Precisely at the moment of its denunciation, the riot secures a relationship between surplus humanity and the state, and there Coriolanus's aggression completes the circuit of early modern biopolitics. Here, finally, is the social chiasmus mapped in Shakespeare, from a play written at a moment in history when the modern state first emerged as a means to manage surplus populations and at which that surplus population responded with riot. The modern state exists, in other words, to contain the barbarians within.

Fragments in History

The genius of Bertolt Brecht's unfinished adaptation of *Coriolanus* can be located in its attempt to resolve the class contradiction of the riot as a material form of dramatic character. That is, by turning that inchoate collective subject, the barbarians and the wolves and the calved and littered social detritus, into an embodiment of historical agency capable of transformative action: namely, the actor. While Shakespeare's play had been abused as educational propaganda preaching military bravery and heroism in Hitler's Germany, it was also banned in France during the 1930s and then by the American occupying forces in Germany in the immediate aftermath of the war. During this time, questions of barbarism predominated in the German political imaginary. For the martyred socialist Rosa Luxemburg, whose advocacy of the mass strike as revolutionary strategy contained within it a denunciation of the riot as disorganized anarchy, Europe had, come 1916, reached a crossway. 'Bourgeois society stands at the crossroads', so reads Luxemburg's rewrite of Engels and Kautsky, 'either transition to Socialism or regression into Barbarism.'[31] For Walter Benjamin, barbarism would be the underside to all human endeavour: 'There is no document of civilization which is not at the same time a document of barbarism.'[32] And for Theodor Adorno, European fascism and the Holocaust were the epitome of barbarity, while the 'sole adequate praxis after Auschwitz is to put all energies toward working our way out of

---

[31] Rosa Luxemburg, 'The Junius Pamphlet' in *The Essential Rosa Luxemburg* (London: Haymarket, 2017), p. 24.
[32] Walter Benjamin, *Illuminations*, translated by Harry Zohn (New York, NY: Schocken Books, 2007), p. 256.

barbarism'.[33] Brecht would likewise make use of the term when framing the fascist antipode to socialism, but his gloss would reframe the term as much closer to its historical use, in such a way as to demystify those words of Coriolanus. 'We attacked a foreign people and treated them like rebels', we read in one of Brecht's stories about wartime atrocity. 'As you know, it's all right to treat barbarians barbarically. It's the desire to be barbaric that makes governments call their enemies barbarians.'[34] If this summarizes the ideology of conservative statehood when met with the violence of riot, showing a real sensitivity to the manipulation of political discourse around both exclusion and insurrection, Brecht's unfinished adaptation asks how to portray the riot, as a social form that is so often repudiated on both left and right as a kind of barbarism, an insurgent populism on its way to becoming fascism, as articulately opposed to the system that set it loose on the world. How, in other words, do you solve a problem like Caius Marcius?

Brecht's answer is the dialectic. 'It is only by studying the unity of opposites that a proper disposition of the opening scene of Coriolanus becomes feasible', he insists; 'and this is the foundation on which the entire play rests.'[35] This unity of opposites takes place at two levels simultaneously, which together index the riot and the state—one vertical, between Coriolanus and the citizens, and another horizontal, between the citizens themselves. Writing from within the crucible of twentieth-century political extremes, in which popular energy is just as likely co-opted by the forces of reaction as by the means to liberation, Brecht insists on reframing an apparent individualism at the core of Shakespearean tragedy, the bootstrap egotism of Coriolanus. But this is no simple matter of denying a psychology of the one in favour of the sociology of many; instead, it necessitates a rigorous historicizing of the tragic hero, so as to reinterpret their individuality not as the result of some kind of transhistorical human nature or moral autonomy but of systemic forces and social relations:

> As for enjoying the hero and the tragic element, we have to move beyond a mere sense of empathy with the hero Marcius in order to achieve a richer form of enjoyment. We must at least be able to 'experience' the tragedy not only of Coriolanus himself but also of Rome, and specifically of the plebs. There is no need to ignore the 'tragedy of pride,' or for that matter to play it down; nor, given Shakespeare's genius, would this be possible. We can accept the fact that Coriolanus finds it worthwhile to give his pride so much rein that death and collapse 'just don't count.' But ultimately society pays, Rome pays also, and it too comes close to collapsing as a result. While as for the hero, society is interested in another aspect of the question, and one that directly concerns it, to wit the hero's belief that he

---

[33] Theodor W. Adorno, *Minima Moralia. Reflections on a Damaged Life* (London: Verso, 2005), p. 268.

[34] Bertolt Brecht, 'A Question of Taste' in *The Collected Short Stories of Bertolt Brecht* (London: Bloomsbury, 2015), p. 257.

[35] Bertholt Brecht, *Berliner Ensemble Adaptations*, edited by David Barnett (London: Bloomsbury, 2014). Ebook.

is indispensable. This is a belief to which it cannot succumb without running the risk of collapse. Thereby it is brought into irreconcilable conflict with this hero, and the kind of acting must be such as not only to permit this but to compel it.[36]

Rather than 'dethrone' Coriolanus, stripping him of ego and pride and the martial valour so essential to his being, the task for modern theatre is to promote a dialectical view of the world as its basis for understanding political conflict, proposing with its staging that any individual behaviour in dialectical interaction with the social environment from which it emerges. Whereas, in Shakespeare, the relationship between the commander and his citizens is purely antagonistic, with Coriolanus wishing the expulsion of these citizens into subsistence outside of Rome, here the narrative strives to emphasize the socially mediated relationships between the rioting citizens and the beneficiaries of the state.

To account for Brecht's political theory when it comes to this adaptation is to explain why the citizens riot as opposed to undertaking any other kind of collective action. Rather than presuppose anything like class solidarity, a cultural identity that unites them into a singular collective subject or what might be called a proletariat, the realities of economic and social exclusion are a problem of method for political strategy no less than dramaturgy. Brecht had been working through this problem since the late 1920s, when he first read the works of Marx, and began to insist that proletarianization, in Michael Shane Boyle's summary, 'does not entail a worker's potential to work, but their inevitable exclusion from production', a belief that therefore 'went against the grain of the labor movements of its time, which, in affirming the wage earner as the proper political and economic subject, excluded or gravely limited the participation of women, racialized groups, and others who did not conform to the normalized identity of a worker'.[37] Reflecting on the patrician's speech, the 'phony ideology' of his trickle-down economics, Brecht insists that, if the citizens were convinced, it would only 'be a possible scene, for such things happen, but a horrifying one', in which the dispossessed accept their dispossession as necessary for some spurious collective good.[38] Immiseration, Brecht notes, is just as likely a source of disunity and oppression as it is a cause of solidarity and action. While the turning point from alienation to insurrection is the citizens's recognition that their poverty is political, a social arrangement designed for the benefit of others and at their expense, the potential for collaborative action remains as distantly elusive as the firmament, or so Brecht describes it:

> I don't think you realize how hard it is for the oppressed to become united. Their misery unites them—once they recognize who has caused it. 'Our sufferance is a gain to them.' But otherwise their misery is liable to cut them off from one

---

[36] Brecht, 'Enjoying the Hero', *Berliner Ensemble Adaptations*.
[37] Michael Shayne Boyle, 'Theatrical Proletarians', in *Understanding Marx, Understanding Modernism*, edited by Mark Steven (London: Bloomsbury, 2020), p. 152 (London: Bloomsbury, 2020), p. 152.
[38] Brecht, 'Study of the First Scene of Shakespeare's *Coriolanus*', *Berliner Ensemble Adaptations*.

another, for they are forced to snatch the wretched crumbs from each other's mouths. Think how reluctantly men decide to revolt! It's an adventure for them; new paths have to be marked out and followed; moreover the rule of the rulers is always accompanied by that of their ideas. To the masses revolt is the unnatural rather than the natural thing, and however bad the situation from which only revolt can free them they find the idea of it as exhausting as the scientist finds a new view of the universe.[39]

And yet, at the play's start—in both versions—the citizens are already armed for revolt, driven as though spontaneously but in reality by hunger into conflict with the state and its spokespersons. Their reasons for rioting are given as both ethical and social, demanding either reform or revolution, with the first option swiftly conjured away. 'The unnecessary food the good citizens stuff into their bellies could save us from starvation', announces one citizen, with a child. 'Even if they gave us their leftovers, we'd be saved. But they don't even think that much of us. Their food tastes better when they see us starving.'[40] The citizens's speaker, in a rewrite of Shakespeare's social diagnosis of poverty, counters this claim, reminding the citizens that their immiseration, their poverty, is not an ethical choice made by this or that leader but the very structure of the state. 'Leave us to starve when their storehouses are crammed full of grain', he says. 'Every day they repeal another good law against the rich and every day they grind out another cruel regulation to chain the poor.'[41]

This kind of provisional unity, mobilized through immiseration and poverty as opposed to unions or the party, is that of the non-movement: its social mass is not the organized workforce of the strike or the political vanguard of the movement proper but, instead, the inchoate mass of the riot. The citizens are acting together, but their sense of togetherness is highly contingent: 'neither we', writes Brecht, 'nor the audience must be allowed to overlook the contradictions that are bridged over, suppressed, ruled out, now that sheer hunger makes a conflict with the patricians unavoidable'.[42] If riot is the unavoidable form of that unity, for Shakespeare and Brecht alike its contradictions are resolved, even if only temporarily, by war, which historically has been both the creative destruction of surplus and an organizer of citizens on the inter-classist and counter-revolutionary basis of national feeling. 'If the wars don't eat us up, they will', announces the first citizen.[43] This grim metaphor, which turns people into food, enacts the social logic of exploitation at the level of rhetoric, but it also gestures towards an incipient militarism,

---

[39] Brecht, 'Study of the First Scene of Shakespeare's *Coriolanus*', *Berliner Ensemble Adaptations*.
[40] Brecht, 'Coriolanus: William Shakespeare Adaptation', *Berliner Ensemble Adaptations*.
[41] Brecht, 'Coriolanus: William Shakespeare Adaptation', *Berliner Ensemble Adaptations*.
[42] Brecht, 'Study of the First Scene of Shakespeare's *Coriolanus*', *Berliner Ensemble Adaptations*.
[43] Brecht, 'Coriolanus: William Shakespeare Adaptation', *Berliner Ensemble Adaptations*.

when the riot understands itself as the local counterpart to international competition, the civil war happening alongside the war between nations. 'How else', asks Brecht, 'is the director to bring out the difference between Menenius, Agrippa's phony ideological attempt to unify patricians and plebeians, and their real unification as a result of the war?'[44] If, in the sixteenth century, war allowed for the continuation of feudalistic protectionism into absolutist statecraft—what Brenner describes as the landed ruling class recognizing 'their most fundamental interests as dependent on the strengthening of a unified national state'—during the middle years of the twentieth century, and especially in the aftermath of World War Two, such conflicts had been met by revolutionary logic.[45]

'There's no need to fear or hope', Deleuze once suggested, 'but only to look for new weapons.'[46] The presentation of weaponry here is what materially preserves the difference between the riot as a revolutionary attack on the state and the clash of empires that would subsume the riot into the tyrannical logic of the state. When Coriolanus arrives at the scene of the riot, the patrician initially claims to have stopped the citizens 'with a fairy tale', before conceding, in a perfect chiasmus, that his words only achieved their desired effect when uttered in presence of the state's armed forces: 'The sword of my voice but rather the voice of your sword', is what turned the citizens away.[47] While there is a clear distinction between the patricians and the plebeians at the level of form—with the state speaking in blank verse and the dispossessed in unmeasured prose—this metaphor also underscores what Brecht describes as a 'strengthening' of the original text, in which the citizens's hesitation is not due to the speech but is, instead, responding 'to the changed situation arising from the appearance of armed men behind the speaker', which reveals at once that the ideology of pacifism despite poverty 'is based on force, on armed force, wielded by Romans'.[48] In discussing the staging, Brecht and the ensemble deliberate over how, exactly, the citizens are to be armed. 'They've got to be poorly armed,' says his collaborator and choreographer, Ruth Berghaus, 'but they mustn't be weak, or they could never win the war for Marcius and the war against him', for there is the armament of a 'sudden popular uprising', in which their class character reveals itself through props. 'So presumably their weapons are improvised ones', Brecht clarifies, 'but they can be good improvisers. It's they who make the army's weapons; who else? They can have got themselves bayonets, butchers' knives on broom-handles, converted fire-irons, etc. Their inventiveness can arouse respect,

---

[44] Brecht, 'Four Short Notes', *Berliner Ensemble Adaptations*.
[45] Brenner, *Merchants and Revolution*, p. 655.
[46] Gilles Deleuze, 'Postscript on the Societies of Control.' *October* 59 (1992), p. 4.
[47] Brecht, 'Coriolanus: William Shakespeare Adaptation', *Berliner Ensemble Adaptations*.
[48] Brecht, 'Study of the First Scene of Shakespeare's *Coriolanus*', *Berliner Ensemble Adaptations*.

and their arrival can immediately seem threatening.'[49] This presentation, according to which the citizens oscillate between necessity and conviction in combat both for and against the state, ultimately points up the indeterminate political fate of the lumpenproletariat as such: on call to the highest bidder, in ideological if not directly monetary terms, liable to revolt but also susceptible to ethno-nationalist co-option.

It is this kind of modification of the original, applied to staging and emphasis less than narrative, that brings this text closer still to the historical present. The social system that was first emerging when Shakespeare was writing and which had matured into its 'late' stage by Brecht's arrival is one whose 'general law' is the 'progressive production' of a population forced to survive on less than subsistence: 'the working population therefore both the accumulation of capital and the means by which it itself is made relatively superfluous; and it does this to an extent which is always increasing.'[50] As we enter the terminal phase of this system, a catastrophe that has pauperized two-thirds of the planet's population, it stands to reason that the representational dynamic alive in both Shakespeare and Brecht will be with us today, in a new age of riots. The 2011 film adaption of *Coriolanus* bears out the truth of this claim and once again modifies the form of the text to meet the changing shape of society, with both its riots and its state. If Shakespeare and Brecht combined anachronistic historical moments—reading early modern England and the modern world-system into Plutarch's Rome—this film is set against the backdrop of a different kind of globalized conflict: the expansion of NATO into Eastern Europe in the 1990s, or what Tariq Ali describes as the advent of 'a mobile, global police force which can hit a target state anywhere in the world to defend the interests of the United States, defined, of course, as "human rights" and the "free market"'.[51] Filmed in Belgrade, and billed as 'a place calling itself Rome', the film's setting is of high-rise tenement blocks and bombed-out ruins. It is—in Slavoj Žižek's phrase, 'a colonial city-state in crisis and decay'.[52] If this film, an English production released the same year as the riots that erupted after the police murder of Mark Duggan in Tottenham—London, does little to capture the racialized dimension of the contemporary riot, its staging should nevertheless put us in mind of the brutal enforcers of state power in the present. While the opening scene depicts the citizens's riot outside a militarily securitized grain warehouse, instead of soldiers, Coriolanus appears before the crowd flanked by riot shields, all clearly labelled POLICE. From Berlin to Belgrade, from Mexico to Minneapolis, this is the essentially contemporary feature of the riot's staging. 'The police', write Endnotes,

---

[49] Brecht, 'Study of the First Scene of Shakespeare's *Coriolanus*', *Berliner Ensemble Adaptations*.
[50] Karl Marx, *Capital: A Critique of Political Economy*, vol. 1, translated by Ben Fowkes (London: Penguin, 1992), p. 783.
[51] Tariq Ali, 'Springtime for NATO', *New Left Review* 1, no. 235 (1999): https://newleftreview.org/issues/i234/articles/tariq-ali-springtime-for-nato. Accessed 30 May 2022.
[52] Slavoj Zizek, *A Year of Dreaming Dangerously* (London: Verso, 2012), p. 119.

'are not an external force of order applied by the state to an already rioting mass, but an integral part of the riot: not only its standard component spark-plug, acting via the usual death, at police hands, of some young black man, but also the necessary ongoing partner of the rioting crowd from whom the space must be liberated if this liberation is to mean anything at all; who must be attacked as an enemy if the crowd is to be unified in anything; who must be forced to recognize the agency of a habitually subjected group.'[53] This, a further modification of Shakespeare's narrative and Brecht's staging, is what secures this early modern text as relative to the present crisis, our crisis, and to the fate of a surplus population in a dying city: 'these are the specific and local conditions for almost every major rebellion in recent history', Joshua Clover describes the policing of exclusion. 'If the state's solution to the problem of crisis and surplus is prison—carceral management—the riot is a contest entered directly against this solution—a counterproposal of unmanageability.'[54] Played with menace by Ralph Fiennes, Coriolanus berates the rioters without the presence of any patrician, removed from this production as though to signal the state's progression beyond a need for any ideology but that of force. 'Go', he berates them, 'get you home, you fragments'. With such a line—delivered in a city and to a people so wasted and ruinous we cannot help but hear T.S. Eliot—the riot reveals itself, once more, as an impossible unity of the excluded, the barbarians both within and without the city gates, as Coriolanus retreats into the wall of police, now banging truncheons on shields, now marching on the riot.

---

[53] Endnotes, 'A Rising Tide Lifts All Boats,' *Endnotes* 3 (2013): p. 98.
[54] Joshua Clover, *Riot. Strike. Riot: The New Era of Uprisings* (London: Verso, 2016), p. 163.

3
Bloody Sundays
Radical Rewriting and the Trafalgar Riot of 1887

Helen Groth

On 13 November 1887, a march to protest recent government restrictions on public meetings in London and Ireland became the first Bloody Sunday when a magistrate read the Riot Act and violence ensued.[1] Memories of this first 'Bloody Sunday' have been overshadowed by the more recent violence of 30 January 1972, when English soldiers killed thirteen unarmed Irish civilians and seriously wounded fifteen others (one fatally) in response to a protest against the structural inequalities and discrimination suffered by the Northern Irish Catholic minority in Derry. If historians scan the archive for precedents for this 'Bloody Sunday', Peterloo (the 1819 massacre of unarmed citizens gathered on St Peter's Field to demand parliamentary representation) rather than the Trafalgar Square Riot of 1887 is the more likely point of reference. To exemplify, Graham Dawson contends in his essay on the enduring reverberations of the violence of 1972: 'This event, known as "Bloody Sunday", is the most devastating instance of the British state's use of armed force against a section of its own citizens since Peterloo in 1819.'[2] This rhetorical suturing of two distinct protests reroutes historical memory through formal analogy; both led to traumatic loss of life and are the subject of many commemorative retellings, fictional and non-fictional. Both also instance the stochastic resonance of naming. Respectively dubbed 'Bloody Sunday' and 'Peterloo', these names invite re-reading beyond the immediate present of their

---

[1] The passage of Arthur Balfour's *Criminal Law and Procedure Act* (1887) defined intimidation and conspiracy and gave resident magistrates in Ireland the power to suppress organizations they deemed subversive. This Act continued the precedent of the Coercion Acts, which began with the Suppression of Disturbances Act (1833). The Coercion Acts permitted the imposition of a range of restrictions, including curfews, and detention without trial for up to three months. 'Coercion Acts', entry in S.J. Connelly (ed.), *The Oxford Companion to Irish History* (Oxford: Oxford University Press, 2007), online edition. The convergence of the passage of Balfour's Act, the Home Rule debate, and the London Chief of Police, Sir Charles Warren's public order of 8 November (1887) prohibiting all meetings in Trafalgar Square all contributed to the violence of 13 November 1887.

[2] Graham Dawson, 'Trauma, Place and the Politics of Memory: Bloody Sunday, Derry 1972–2004', *History Workshop Journal* 59 (2005): pp. 151–178; 151. In an American context, of course, the 'Bloody Sunday' that took place in Selma on 7 March 1965 when the Civil Rights protestors were attacked by Alabama state troopers on the order of the Governor overshadows all previous events that bear the same name.

Helen Groth, *Bloody Sundays*. In: *Writing the Global Riot*. Edited by: Jumana Bayeh, Helen Groth, and Julian Murphet, Oxford University Press. © Oxford University Press (2023). DOI: 10.1093/oso/9780192862594.003.0004

occurrence; readings that impute new meanings, amplify previously unheard versions of the event, and generate narrative trajectories from otherwise random acts of state violence.[3]

The consequences of naming are central to this chapter's analysis of the multiple literary engagements with the first Bloody Sunday of 1887. The violence of that day was, as many have argued, a catalysing moment for London's Socialist organizers, who keenly felt the parallels with the bloody suppression of the Paris Commune of 1871 and the more recent Chicago Haymarket Massacre in 1886 which, for William Morris and other protesters marching that day, represented a like suppression of free speech.[4] Anne Janowitz observes in her reading of William Morris's *The Pilgrims of Hope*, a long narrative poem inspired by the events of 1871 and written a year prior to the Trafalgar Riots, the Commune 'was an important screen onto which British Socialism came to project its own representation and fantasies'; it 'survived as an image of purity ... of a people's self-government which, while resembling the practices of the medieval and rural communes, was contemporary, urban, and suffused by a new sense of power amongst the labouring poor'.[5] More recently, Oscar Holland has revealed further overlapping strands of literary and political history that connect the Place Vendome to Trafalgar Square as sites of protest and resistance.[6] As Holland argues, these national monuments to imperial triumph were obvious 'symbolic targets' and focal points for internationalist and anti-colonial resistance.[7]

---

[3] This analysis is indebted to Wai Chee Dimock, 'A Theory of Resonance', *PMLA* 112. 5 (October 1997): pp. 1060–1071.

[4] While the events of the Paris Commune are more well known, the Chicago Haymarket Riot is worth glossing in this context. It took place on 4 May of the preceding year, 1886. Although the catalyst for the protest that preceded the riot was very different to the Trafalgar Riot—thousands of labour activists and anarchists rallied in Chicago's Haymarket Square against the violent police suppression of strike action that had been taken at the McCormick Reaper Works over intolerable working conditions. It was initially a peaceful protest that turned violent when an unidentified person threw a bomb that killed a policeman. Chaos ensued and ten prominent activists were arrested for the bombing. On 11 November, just two days before the Trafalgar Riot, four anarchists were hung for the bombing, although their guilt was not proven by material evidence. Herman Melville's *Billy Budd* would retrospectively allegorize the violence and inherent injustice spawned by the blind force of legal nomenclature that the Haymarket Affair raised. William Morris wrote a number of editorials in the *Commonweal* linking the American and English struggle for free speech: 'America', *Commonweal* 2 (6 November 1886): p. 254; 'Free Speech in America', *Commonweal* 3 (8 October 1887): p. 324; 'America', *Commonweal* 3 (17 November 1887): p. 374. See also Walter Crane, 'Freedom in America', *Commonweal*, 3 (15 October 1887): p. 333. Support of the link between Trafalgar and Chicago was not shared by all. Both Besant and George Bernard Shaw strenuously opposed the connection, see Shaw's 'A Refutation of Anarchy', *Our Corner* 12 (July 1888): pp. 8–20.

[5] Anne Janowitz, *Lyric and Labour in the Romantic Tradition* (Cambridge: Cambridge University Press, 1998): pp. 228–229.

[6] Kristin Ross offers an influential account of this translation of the politics of the Commune to English Socialist discourse through the interconnections between Marx, Kropotkin, Reclus, Morris, and Shaw in *Communal Luxury. The Political Imaginary of the Paris Commune* (London: Verso, 2015).

[7] Oscar Holland, 'From the Place Vendome to Trafalgar Square', *Key Words: A Journal of Cultural Materialism* 14 (2016): p. 98.

During the 1880s Trafalgar Square became a popular site for political protests and occupations, but few matched the scale and violence of 13 November 1887, as the subjects of this chapter attest. Writers and activists all, Margaret Harkness, Annie Besant, Walter Crane, and William Morris, crafted their first-hand experience of Bloody Sunday into literary and visual forms that parsed the official nomenclature of the riot as an act of wilful misreading and specious naming. Swept up in the riot itself, they were exposed to the literal risks of political action and violent suppression orchestrated by the state's nominative force. None were left in any doubt that the reading of the Riot Act was explicitly used to reverse the perceived direction of the violence and legitimate the measures taken to restore the peace.

What emerges from the work of these writers is a retrospective reimagining of the riot as a complex event, a collective interpretive process that is intentionally redistributive and aesthetic.[8] Abstracting from their immediate affective experience of the violence, each writer and or artist enlists a different genre—autobiography, the ballad, utopian, realist fiction, illustration—to reconfigure the riot's seemingly chaotic formlessness into narrative and poetic sequences that challenge the rhetoric of irrational spontaneity that characterized contemporary media accounts which sensationally named the events of that day, Bloody Sunday.[9]

Contesting Media

In the days following 13 November *The Times* narrated a version of the events that Besant, Harkness, Morris, Crane, and their fellow activists remembered very differently. With a predictable stress on law and order, the spectacle of heroically restrained force, the performative ritualized reading of the Riot Act, and a heavy reliance on martial metaphors, the first of two articles in *The Times* devoted to the riots was entitled 'The Defence of Trafalgar Square: Serious Riots in London (From our Reporter in The Square)'.[10] Taking the reader behind the lines of the police armed with 'staves', Life Guards, and Foot Guards, the reporter recasts the progressive occupation of the square by unemployed workers in the weeks leading up to 13 November, as a spontaneous form of social disruption (a mob in other words) that exposed the vulnerable citizens of London to risk, suffering, and

---

[8] Jacques Rancière, *The Politics of Literature*, trans. Julie Rose (Cambridge: Polity, 2011), p. 4.
[9] This reading of the media coverage of Bloody Sunday is indebted to E.P. Thompson's criticism of the conventional characterization of riots as spontaneous and inchoate events, as well as to Charles Tilley's extensive research which evidences the complex formations riots assume, as well as the continuous political sequences to which they belong; see E.P. Thompson's criticism of the 'spasmodic view' of popular history in 'The Moral Economy of the English Crowd in the Eighteenth Century', *Past and Present* 50 (February 1971), p. 76; Charles Tilly, *Popular Contention in Great Britain, 1758–1834* (Cambridge, MA: Harvard University Press, 1995).
[10] 'The Defence of Trafalgar Square: Serious Riots in London (From our Reporter in The Square)', *The Times* (Monday, 14 November 1887), p. 6.

uncivil displays of public emotion.[11] Voices of both protesters and law enforcers are invoked with little pretence made to unbiased reporting. Setting the scene, the minimally cited official rhetoric of the order issued by Sir Charles Warren, the Chief of Police, on 8 November prohibiting all meetings in the Square 'until further notice' is opposed to multiple instances of incendiary speech uttered by the radical organizers whose principle demands were: the release of the Cork MP William O'Brien, who had recently been imprisoned and charged for incitement for organizing a rent strike in his constituency, and the recognition of the lawful right of Londoners to protest. 'Are you prepared to submit?' cries one poster circulated in South and East London, according to the reporter, 'If not, come in tens of thousands. Preserve your dear bought liberties at all risks.'[12]

Annie Besant, a writer, Fabian socialist, and ardent supporter of Irish and Indian home rule, is singled out as one of the more intemperate delegates of the protest organizing committee. *The Times* reporter observes with some alarm Besant's rhetorical efforts to persuade her comrades to take the risk of attending to ensure 'that the numerical strength of those present in the square would by "mere pushing" effect an entrance'. This polarizing characterization establishes Besant as a seditious termagant in contrast to the more civilized discourse of resistance uttered by William Morris. Addressing the gathering of protesters on Clerkenwell-Green that afternoon, Morris is represented expressing 'sympathy' for O'Brien, and then, according to this reporter, speaking in relatively genteel terms of their 'bounden duty' to resist any constraint on 'free speech' and 'press to the square like orderly people and like good citizens'. Besant's speech, by contrast, is reported as 'vigorous' in its challenging of the legality of Sir Charles Warren's ban on public meetings in the square and advocacy of the necessity of sedition in the face of tyranny: 'She went on to say that they were told not to talk sedition, to which she replied that the other side ought not to talk tyranny. If the authorities tried tyranny they would have to try sedition.'

Besant predictably described these scenes very differently. In the days leading up to the riot, London had become in Besant's words, a 'chaos'. She writes in a Miltonic vein: 'In this weltering seething mass of living things we seek in vain for any possibly unifying faith, any centralising hope; all is formless, inchoate, not even embryonic in this whirling deep ... drifting towards Revolution, as Paris drifted, one hundred years ago.'[13] Contradicting *The Times* portrayal of an

---

[11] The protesters were described as a disorganized mob in preceding coverage of the occupation of Trafalgar Square by homeless and unemployed Londoners in the weeks leading up to the 'riot', see 'The Police and the Mob', *The Times* (Monday, 7 November 1887), p. 6.

[12] 'The Defence of Trafalgar Square: Serious Riots in London (From our Reporter in The Square)', *The Times* (Monday, 14 November 1887), p. 6.

[13] Annie Besant, 'London', *Our Corner* (January 1888), pp. 24–29. 24. *Our Corner*, was in Besant's words 'a six-penny magazine edited by Besant for six years and publishing the work of key figures such as Ernst Haeckel, George Bernard Shaw, and Constance Naden, see Annie Besant, *Autobiography* (p. 286). The Miltonic resonances here summon associations with the second book of *Paradise Lost*— of Chaos in 'his dark pavilion spread / Wide on the wasteful deep'. See John Milton, *Paradise Lost*,

outraged majority disrupted by a riotous minority, Besant's London is a fractured metropolis haunted by legacies of colonial violence perpetuated by a venal police force that 'are the slaves of wealthy vice' and the brutal 'tyrants of poverty-stricken despair'. Besant argues that Sir Charles Warren has transformed the police into an imperial 'military caste' by migrating colonial policing tactics to the streets of London, serving private interests and 'ruling by outside authority instead of serving the civic will' (24). In response, the inhabitants of London's slums defiantly claim the light and space Trafalgar Square afforded. The resulting conflict, to invoke Seth Koven, left 'an indelible imprint of the volcanic potential' of the collective resistance of East Londoners on the wealthy denizens of West London: an impact that the accounts of the riots in *The Times* strive to rhetorically contain as an aberrant situation.[14]

In a further iteration of her experience of the riot, 'The Story of Trafalgar Square', Besant expanded on the details of the activities that culminated in the riots, the intimate histories of loss, prosecution, repair, and radical organizing. Again, in contrast to the depiction in *The Times* of chaotic assemblage and spontaneity, Besant stresses continuous community and attachment. While, as she says, all 'the world knows the story of "Bloody Sunday" with its crowds of peaceful, unarmed, men approaching the Square', Besant takes it on herself to bear witness to the local affective experience of the riot—what it felt like to be on the Square on that day, the mixture of anger and expectation that defined the everyday lives of activists organizing in the months prior to the riots, and the specific damage done to bodies on the ground, whether they were hospitalized or imprisoned. These things, Besant contends, are not 'matters of history'.[15] Notably, Besant isolates the name 'Bloody Sunday' with inverted commas: it is an identification imposed from outside, and after the fact. Marks on a page, signalling an unease with the elliptical contraction and analogical suturing that such sensational naming enables; a making public of the event that excludes the personal stories of people that her story of the riot names and traces from the Square to their homes, from court to prison, and in some cases, to their graves.

Besant's multiple versions of Bloody Sunday oscillate between commemorative, polemical, and testimonial registers. Intent on creating what Jonathan Flately describes as a 'revolutionary counter-mood', Besant's prose is driven by the urgency of what needed to be done to create a 'world-altering moment' where 'new alliances, new enemies and new fields of action' could become visible to

---

in William Kerrigan, John Rumrich, and Stephen M. Fallon (eds), *The Complete Poetry and Essential Prose of John Milton* (New York, NY: Random House, 2009), lines 960–961, p. 355.

[14] Seth Koven, *Slumming. Sexual and Social Politics in Victorian London* (Princeton, NJ: Princeton University Press, 2004), p. 236.

[15] Annie Besant, 'The Story of Trafalgar Square, 1887–1888', *Our Corner* (April 1888): pp. 223–233.

her readers.[16] Besant's belief in the transformative force of writing and reading is palpable in her vivid characterization of the colonial-style policing typified by the violence of Bloody Sunday. Deliberately raising the emotional stakes to draw her readers into nothing less than a collective struggle for the soul of London against a corrupted imperial agenda, Besant's prose also manifests an implicit faith in the cognitive dimensions of affect that resonates with Flately's analysis of a like dynamic in Lenin's revolutionary manifesto *What is to be Done?* Lenin, Flately argues, 'asserts that the feeling will bring with it an irresistible desire to act as well as a knowledge of *how* to act, what to do … this knowledge arises from the feeling, without reflection or theorization, as if it were already there, a kind of 'thought unknown'.[17]

The Times portrayal of Besant whipping up an, apparently, unthinking crowd into a riot captures 'an official' investment in arguing against the possibility of a thinking riot or mob, united by a knowledge and understanding gleaned from 'being-with-others', to quote Flately.[18] In contrast, the transformative possibility of being and thinking with others drives Besant's further return to Trafalgar Square in her *Autobiography*, which locates the riot on a long trajectory of activism and collaboration that defined the 1880s: a synthesis of writing and political organizing that she shares with Margaret Harkness, William Morris, Eleanor Marx, Clementina Black, and so many others who protested that day.[19] Contrasting with the noise and violence of the police who ultimately confront them, Besant's final autobiographical account takes her readers inside the experience of walking expectantly down the narrow streets from Clerkenwell-Green to Trafalgar Square. Besant describes herself 'moving quietly and slowly' alongside her fellow protesters and then scattering with no resistance in the face of a military scale operation that beat 'law-abiding workmen, who had never dreamed of rioting' into submission.[20]

Riot, Ephemera, and Elegy

William Morris's elegiac ballad *A Death Song* memorializes Alfred Linnell, who was trampled by a mounted constable's horse while protesting on Trafalgar Square on 20 November 1887. Like so many of his fellow Londoners, Linnell, undaunted

---

[16] Jonathan Flately, 'How a Revolutionary Counter-Mood is Made', *New Literary History* 43.3 (Summer 2012): pp. 503–525; p. 504.
[17] Flately, 'How a Revolutionary Counter-Mood is Made', p. 509. Flately cites Christopher Bollas here (which I have retained because the reference provides necessary clarification of the point); Christopher Bollas, *The Shadow of the Object: Psychoanalysis of the Unthought Known* (New York, NY: Columbia University Press, 1987).
[18] Flately, 'How A Revolutionary Counter-Mood is Made', p. 509.
[19] Besant, *Autobiography*, pp. 331–332.
[20] Besant, *Autobiography*, pp. 324–325.

by the violence of 'Bloody Sunday' came to the Square the following week to continue the struggle and was fatally injured when the police charged into the crowd repeating the violence of the previous week. Linnell was one of Besant's 'law-abiding workmen, who had never dreamed of rioting', a poignance that Morris's lament for his violent death captures and Harkness's characterization of the innocent rioter Jos in her novel *Out of Work* echoes. Morris's *A Death Song* initially formed part of a penny pamphlet designed to memorialize Linnell and raise funds for his orphaned children.[21] The pamphlet included a title page featuring a memorial design by the prominent Socialist illustrator Walter Crane, as well as eyewitness accounts that highlighted Linnell's experience before, during and after the violence, a musical score composed by Malcolm Lawson to accompany Morris's song, followed by a conventional printed version of the poem. This syncretic document evokes divergent temporalities—the ephemeral topicality of the riot as an event with the associated urgencies of bearing witness and demanding justice for the victims, and an elegiac stress on collective memory, legacy, and futurity that the ballad form orchestrates. Read in sequence each iteration of the poem materializes the intrinsic portability of the poetic song, read or sung at events and meetings with ease: an iterability amplified by Crane's illustration of one of the Socialist movement's defining moments, designed to migrate across multiple formats from penny pamphlet to the pages of publications, such as William Morris's *Commonweal*.[22]

Crane's illustrative design suspends time and the riot. The constable's rearing horse and raised truncheon pause above Linnell's prone body. The lines of the constable's cloak draw focus towards Nelson's Column encircled by a banner urging the viewer not only to 'Remember Trafalgar Square' but to remember the riots differently; to bear witness to the intimate details and personal tragedy involved when the police are instructed to use violence to limit the people's right to peaceful protest. Driving this point home Crane allegorically embodies Liberty and Justice as two female figures who hover protectively over Linnell's body. One mirrors Linnell's self-defensive gesture—her hand raised to halt the impending harm—the other, arms raised, bears a banner naming the riot as a violation of both Justice and Liberty. This scene has a war-like tenor that resonates with Crane's personal memory of the organized violence of 'Bloody Sunday': 'I never saw anything more like real warfare in my life—only the attack was all on one side'.[23] Eleanor Marx (who

---

[21] William Morris, *Alfred Linnell: killed in Trafalgar Square, November 20, 1887: a death song: by Mr. W. Morris; memorial design by Mr. Walter Crane*, 1887. Gale Nineteenth Century Collections Online, link.gale.com/apps/doc/LQXMWX255001933/GDCS?u=unsw&sid=bookmark-GDCS&xid=e46626c4&pg=1.

[22] Morna O'Neill provides a more extensive analysis of the political ballad and Crane's designs in her excellent analysis of the politics and aesthetics of Walter Crane. See p. 113 in O'Neill, 'Cartoons for the Cause? Walter Crane's *The Anarchists of Chicago*', *Art History* (February 2015): pp. 106–117.

[23] Walter Crane, *An Artist's Reminiscences* (c.1907, Cambridge: Cambridge University Press, 2015), p. 249.

was wounded by a constable's truncheon), Morris, and Shaw variously echoed Crane's description of the riot as an unjust war. Morris recalled standing in the midst of the chaos: 'I will never forget how these unarmed crowds were dispersed into clouds of dust'.[24]

Following on from Crane's design, a series of accounts of the events of 20 November and the ensuing court case serve as descriptive preludes to Morris's ballad, anchoring his elegiac plaint in the present urgency of 'what is to be done'—to invoke Lenin's phrasing. The artefactual form of the pamphlet ties these urgent representations to their material contexts—on the square, the streets, halls, and domestic spaces where they were exchanged for a penny in the service of remembering what took place on Trafalgar Square over multiple bloody weekends in November 1887. Like Besant and Harkness's rewriting of Bloody Sunday, the testimonies of Linnell's fellow activists explicitly counter *The Times* coverage evoking visceral scenes of unjust violence, as well as dutifully recording the ensuing legal struggles of those arrested on the day. In the first of these Linnell's death is portrayed as an act of revenge, explicitly referencing *The Times* coverage of 21 November, where Linnell and his fellow protesters were described as a rabble hooting at the police and deserving of legally sanctioned suppression:

> There was a rush as for life, and in the rush Linnell fell. In a moment the police cavalry were upon him, and the charger of one of the constables trampled him as he lay, smashing his thigh bone beneath the horse's hoof. Then they rode on, leaving Linnell writhing on the ground.[25]

Morris's ballad resonates with these unifying calls for justice and redress. 'Communitarian' like much of his political verse of the 1880s and 1890s, the November protests assume a global significance as the poem progresses.[26] The opening stanza is a gathering rhetorical performance that sets the scene as thousands of protestors calmly march towards Trafalgar Square:

> What cometh here from west to east a-wending?
> And who are these, the marchers stern and slow?
> We bear the message that the rich are sending
> Aback to those who bade them wake and know.
> Not one, not one, nor thousands must they slay,
> But one and all if they would dusk the day.[27]

---

[24] E. P. Thompson, *William Morris: Romantic to Revolutionary* (New York, NY: PM Press, 2011), p. 490; Rachel Holmes, *Eleanor Marx* (London: Bloomsbury, 2014), p. 299.

[25] Morris, *Alfred Linnell*, p. 2.

[26] Anne Janowitz describes Morris's Romantic interventionist poetics, exemplified by *Pilgrims of Hope*, as communitarian in *Lyric and Labour*, p. 195.

[27] This version of the ballad appears in the original penny pamphlet. See Morris, *Alfred Linnell*, pp. 5–8.

These incantatory lines appear twice in the pamphlet. The first time set to Lawson's music; a residual trace of the voices raised in unison at Linnell's funeral where it was first sung.[28] The second in a poetic form that could be read aloud at the countless meetings that Morris envisaged extending far beyond the immediate moment of communal protest and grieving in a none too subtle channelling of the spirit of Shelley's stirring allegorical rendering of Peterloo in *The Mask of Anarchy*. Such 'medium-shifting', to invoke Elizabeth Helsinger's phrasing, was integral to Morris's use of verse 'to work on minds through bodies joined in song, motivating them, at marches and rallies or in the after-hours sessions with comrades that he loved, to imagine a new kind of fellowship in a socialist future'.[29] This imagined futurity depended on the amplifying resonance of the song, its inherent porosity affording a more expansive understanding of the event to emerge over time.

Morris's abiding commitment to memorializing and reanimating the spirit of the Paris Commune haunts the above rallying cry to march towards a collectively envisaged future that will not end until all are slain in the streets. The conventional rhyme scheme (ababcc), pentameter rhythm and alternating quatrain and couplet refrain—'Not one, not one, nor thousands must they slay, / But one and all if they would dusk the day'—amplifies and guides future protesting voices towards an insurgent crescendo. Not one, but many voices transform into a chorus in the final quatrains, a chorus that speculatively realizes a utopian desire to be heard by those who 'will not learn' and 'have no ears to hearken' and to be freed from the prisons of injustice and inequality. Like Besant's account of moving slowly and quietly towards the square, Morris's marchers are 'stern and slow', sibilance and meter combining to evoke measured movement and considered collective action. Countering the dissonant sounds and riotous images of spontaneous mob violence that filled the pages of *The Times* that month, literary form redistributes the sounds of the protest into organized phalanxes of marching and poetic feet united by a common purpose. Morris's relish for a mnemonic refrain ensures each stanza ends with a call to remember the collective sacrifice that Linnell's death typifies.

Three years later Morris would return to the events of Bloody Sunday in *News from Nowhere*. The seventh chapter bearing the title 'Trafalgar Square' notably transforms the once 'great space surrounded by tall ugly houses, with an ugly church at the corner' into a lush sun-drenched orchard of apricot trees featuring a 'pretty gay little structure of wood, painted and gilded, that looked like a refreshment stall'.[30] A strange sensation overcomes Morris's narrator, William Guest.

---

[28] Veronica Alfano describes this collective aspect of Morris's chants as a form of 'collaborative voicing' in 'William Morris and the Uses of Nostalgia: Memory in the Early and Late Poetry', *Victorian Studies* 60, no. 2 (Winter, 2018): pp. 243–254.

[29] Elizabeth Helsinger, 'Poem into Song', *New Literary History* 46.4 (Autumn 2015): pp. 669–690. See pp. 671, 686–687.

[30] William Morris, 'News From Nowhere', in *News From Nowhere and Other Writings*, ed. Clive Wilmer (London: Penguin 1993), p. 77.

He shuts his eyes 'and for a moment there passed before them a phantasmagoria of another day':

> the roadway thronged with a sweltering and excited crowd, dominated by omnibuses crowded with spectators. In the midst a paved be-fountained square, populated only by a few men dressed in blue, and a good many singularly ugly bronze images (one on top of a tall column). The said square guarded up to the edge of the roadway by a four-fold line of big men clad in blue, and across the southern roadway the helmets of a band of horse-soldiers, dead white in the greyness of the chilly November afternoon—[31]

The ensuing dialogue between William Guest and Dick (his guide to Nowhere) reconstructs 'Bloody Sunday' as a failed precursor to the utopian future enabled by the bloody revolution of 1952; the latter triggered by a similar struggle on Trafalgar Square that shifts in a subsequent chapter into an imaginative synthesis of the violence of Bloody Sunday and the massacre of the Communards on the Place Vendome in 1871. In this first iteration of Bloody Sunday in *News from Nowhere*, Morris shares Margaret Harkness's critical view of the futility of the suffering caused when a crowd of 'unarmed and peaceful people' were attacked by armed 'ruffians'. 'That seems too ridiculous to be true', proclaims Dick, 'but according to this version of the story, nothing much came of it, which certainly *is* too ridiculous to be true.'[32]

Shifting from a chapter identified with a place (Trafalgar Square) to a chapter that rewrites the historical record as part of a utopian manifesto ('How the Change Came'), Morris, through the memory of Old Hammond, retells the story of Bloody Sunday as a riot that shocked a culture into Nowhere—a revolutionary future divested of the rapacious pursuit of capital and empire. Read alongside the versions of Bloody Sunday discussed thus far, Morris's narrative return to Trafalgar in 1890 makes those dissenting voices newly audible through an intentionally redistributive narrative act. Fragments of direct speech from a single eyewitness metonymize the collective surge of voices that bore witness to both Bloody Sunday and the Commune in the ensuing years and decades:

> it seemed as if the end of the world had come, and to-day seemed strangely different from yesterday. No sooner were the soldiers drawn up aforesaid than, says an eyewitness, 'a glittering officer on horseback came prancing out from the ranks on the south, and read something from a paper which he held in his hand; which something, very few heard; but I was told afterwards that it was an order for us

---

[31] Morris, 'News from Nowhere', p. 77.
[32] Morris, 'News from Nowhere', p. 78.

to disperse, and a warning that he had legal right to fire on the crowd else, and that he would do so. The crowd took it as a challenge of some sort, and a hoarse threatening roar went up from them; and after that there was comparative silence for a little, till the officer had got back into the ranks. I was near the edge of the crowd, towards the soldiers,' says this eyewitness, 'and I saw three little machines being wheeled out front of the ranks, which I knew for mechanical guns. I cried out, "Throw yourselves down! They are going to fire!" But no one scarcely could throw himself down, so tight as the crowd were packed. I heard a sharp order given, and wondered where I should be the next minute; and then—It was as if the earth had opened, and hell had come up bodily amidst us.['][33]

Mimicking the transcribed orality of an eyewitness statement, this passage resonates with the 'medium-shifting' ephemeral iterations of *A Death Song* in the penny pamphlet memorializing Linnell's death. The prose of *Nowhere* orchestrates the noise and scramble of the riot, modulating the soundscape of violence so that the representative voice of a single eyewitness can be heard above and beyond the immediate chaos of the massacre—barely registering the reading of the Riot Act and testifying to the unequal contest between the crowd and their armed opponents. Thus, a literary representation of the riot again evokes divergent temporalities. Although written in the past tense, the urgency of direct speech mimics the ephemeral topicality of newspaper reportage (the reading of the Riot Act barely heard and quickly disregarded, the unequal forces of the crowd and armed soldiers), while the apocalyptic metaphors that dramatize the explosive force of bullets mowing down the crowd mythologize and elegize the dead. Although it is worth noting in this context, as Matthew Beaumont reveals in his reading of England's anti-Communist imaginary in these years, visions of hell were equally prevalent in contemporaneous reactionary representations of the Trafalgar riots as a Milton-like vision of a Satanic 'bloody saturnalia' released from the gates of hell onto the civilized middle-class denizens of London's West-End. These 'cacotopias', as Beaumont describes them (drawing on Bentham's coinage) presented a feverish anti-utopian vision of the riotous many that countered the idealized progression from riot to revolution of which Morris dreamed.[34]

Documentary Fictions

Margaret Harkness's rewriting of Bloody Sunday likewise diverges from Morris's Shelleyean vision of the riot as an 1880s Peterloo. In two very different novels—*Out of Work* (1888) and *George Eastmont, Wanderer* (1905)—Harkness portrays

---

[33] Morris, 'News from Nowhere', p. 144.
[34] Matthew Beaumont, 'Cacotopianism, the Paris Commune, and England's Anti-Communist Imaginary, 1870-1900', *ELH* 73.2 (Summer, 2006): pp. 465–487; 475. Cacotopia, according to Beaumont, was coined by Jeremy Bentham in 1818. Derived from the Greek *kakos* meaning bad, Beaumont applies the term in his reading of the 'dominant current of anti-utopianism in the late Victorian period' which depicted 'domestic class antagonism as inherently dystopian', hence 'its grisly fascination is with chthonic insurrection rather than the corrupt power structures of the putative socialist state' (p. 465).

Bloody Sunday as a grim chaotic spectacle that emerges out of the unemployment crisis that consumed London in the 1880s. In *George Eastmont, Wanderer*, the eponymous hero is briefly imprisoned for his participation in the Trafalgar Riots before continuing his activism by playing a key role in a thinly veiled fictional version of the 1889 Dockworker's strike, as Harkness did herself. In *Out of Work*, which focuses far more extensively on the riot and its aftermath, the political issues of free speech that consumed middle-class activists, such as Morris and Besant, barely register. Although Harkness knew other writers who protested that day, such as Eleanor Marx, Beatrice Webb, and Clementina Black, and was a member of the Socialist Democratic Federation at that time, the event of the riot is less a 'world-altering moment' than a symptom of a complex systemic problem.[35]

An activist, social researcher, fiction writer, and journalist, Harkness turned to the novel to build dense and complex worlds around the voices and lives that her research into the everyday lives of London's precariat dutifully captured. Expanding the narrative scope of the case study that was central to her sociological method and non-fiction writing, Harkness's characters slowly unravel in hostile environments that actively thwart their ambitions and desires. An anti-individualist ethos shapes these novels, acts of care draw characters together seemingly at random rather than by design, but these affective attachments are not sustaining, and the central protagonists soon revert to their respective downward spirals. In this fictional sequencing, rioting is an inevitability, a predictable recursive pattern that the techne of realist characterization and free-indirect narration amplify and propel.

In *Out of Work*, a magistrate reads the Riot Act and a protest transforms into a riot. Harkness's prose captures the dynamic convergence of the unemployed occupants of the square and banner-wielding protesters unified by their resistance to the state's suppressive force. Moving in and out of the mind of the novel's out of work hero Jos as he is sucked into the tumultuous surge that fills the square, the narrative voice oscillates between capturing the riot from inside the chaos and retrospective moralizing about the ultimate futility of the protest.[36] Unimpressed by the romance of revolution that energized Morris's ballad, Harkness's novel is driven by more prosaic ambitions. Only the radical structural change engineered by the writing of new labour laws, she argued, could ultimately make sense of the occupation of the square by out-of-work and homeless Londoners in the months preceding the riot.

Harkness's priority in *Out of Work* is the starving workers and the homeless, typified by the novel's central character, Jos, who after following the girl he loves to London, finds himself rejected, unemployed, and homeless. Wandering the streets of London while succumbing to the lure of gin, Jos befriends an altruistic thief and flower seller called Squirrel, as well as a Socialist dock worker, and an Anarchist poet who dismisses William Morris as 'only a Socialist'.[37] Each encounter

---

[35] Flately, 'How a Revolutionary Counter-Mood is Made', p. 504.
[36] John Law (Margaret Harkness), *Out of Work* (London: Swan Sonnenschein & Co, 1888).
[37] Law (Harkness), *Out of Work*, p. 155.

invites Harkness's readers to experience the escalating tensions that culminate in the chaos of the Trafalgar Riot, pointedly exposing the lack of constitutive activism required to build alternative forms of community and work beyond the pages of the novel:

> Then 'on there came a hungry people', north, south, east, and west of the square, with music and banners. The police grew furious. They fell upon one club after another, led by the mounted constables ... Denser and denser grew the crowd about the square. Louder and louder came the hisses. Nearer and nearer the people pressed on to the cordon of policeman that shut them off from the place which belongs to the public.
>
> The Squirrel and Jos were sucked into the mob, and could not get out again. They felt it moving like one man towards the square, and felt it surge back, hissing.[38]

Harkness's minimal prose subdues and humbles the heroic exuberance of riotous resistance that Morris, Crane, and Besant embrace. Instead, the reader is drawn into an intimate sensory experience of the riot as a collective modality—heaving, hissing, palpitating, and cleaving. Sucked into this dynamic, Jos is an ambivalent impassive participant in events over which he has no control. At the level of the plot, the riot is just one more violent force that accelerates Jos's ultimate demise, while on a political level Harkness utilizes the particularity of the riot to dramatize her frustration with the present failure of Socialist organizers to build better social forms, relations, and institutions. Harkness's literal argument for the necessity of 'a just collective amidst desperate interdependence', to quote Anna Kornbluh's eloquent formulation, may threaten the aesthetic integrity of her prose, yet it also exemplifies the lure of fiction as a politically affirmative and connective social medium.[39]

Literary character for Harkness is labile and distributive, a tool she uses to open up new ways for her readers to access a more immediate experience of the social spaces of the Square, the East End, and Docks that a failed artisan and casual labourer, like Jos, would have navigated on any given day. In *Out of Work* London feels like the chaos Besant describes in her story of the weeks leading up to Bloody Sunday, fractured, uneasy, and policed like a rebellious colony. This was neither the environment, nor the character that Friedrich Engels suggested Harkness create in a much-cited letter responding to her first slum novel, *City Girl* (1887). Recommending Balzac's passionately drawn republican heroes in *The Human Comedy* as a model for the type of character she should adhere to in

---

[38] Law (Harkness), *Out of Work*, p. 199.
[39] Anna Kornbluh, *The Order of Forms. Realism, Formalism, and Social Space* (Chicago, IL: The University of Chicago Press, 2019), p. 5.

future novels, Engels urged Harkness to write less hopeless working-class characters.[40] Instead, as Rob Breton argues, Harkness shaped her prose according to 'the affective grammar' of the working people she spent her time documenting and researching, people far removed from Engels's vision of the enduring historical agency required of a 'typical' proletariat hero.[41]

While Harkness's decision to restage Bloody Sunday as an ephemeral convergence of incommensurable intentions and forces, did resonate with Engels's criticism of the riots on the square in the year prior to 'Bloody Sunday', as 'a mass ready for any "lark" up to a wild riot', her naturalistic style did not conform to his advice.[42] Glyn Salton Cox even suggests that Harkness's selection of Zola as a model, rather than Balzac, in the first novel she wrote after receiving his letter, could be read as a 'riposte to Engels, whose letter had stressed that Zola was a poor model for a socialist novelist'.[43] When Jos is imprisoned for rioting, the narrator explicitly names Zola as a stylistic reference to intensify the grim immediacy of the cell he inhabits. This descent into naturalistic pessimism contracts Jos's past and future into a hopeless present: a literary scene that radically diverges from the temporal and spatial expansiveness of Besant's autobiographical rewriting of Bloody Sunday, Morris and Crane's elegiac insistence on the revolutionary potential of vernacular visual and literary media, as well as Engels's theory of the more affirmative form that a successful Socialist novel should take.[44] In *Out of Work* the time and space of the riot effectively compresses into a single day that is soon forgotten by those condemned to survive the present.

These various aesthetic reformations of Bloody Sunday retrospectively channel the riot's anarchic nature into literary arrangements that conjure experiences and voices that were not the subjects of history, to paraphrase Besant. In their mutual drive to make things happen Besant, Harkness, Crane, and Morris configure multiple social spaces and forms of the riot that simultaneously capture its inchoate

---

[40] Friedrich Engels, Letter to Margaret Harkness, London, April 1888, cited in Margaret Harkness, *A City Girl* (Peterborough, Ontario: Broadview Press, 2017): pp. 132–134.

[41] Rob Breton, 'The Sentimental Socialism of Margaret Harkness', *English Language Notes*, 48.1 (Spring/Summer, 2010), pp. 27–39; 29. Ruth Livesey's reading of Engels's letter to Harkness provides another salient reading of this divergence from Engels' advice in 'Soundscapes of the City in Margaret Harkness', in *A City Girl* (1887), Henry James, *The Princess Casamassima* (1885–1986), and Katherine Buildings, Whitechapel', in Flore Janssen and Lisa. C. Robertson (eds), *Margaret Harkness: Writing Social Engagement 1880–1921* (Manchester: Manchester University Press, 2019).

[42] Friedrich Engels, *The Times*, 10 February 1886, cited in Gareth Stedman-Jones, *Outcast London: A Study in the Relationship between Classes in Victorian Society* (London: Verso, 2013), p. 43.

[43] Glyn Salton Cox, 'Uncivil Society', *Key Words: A Journal of Cultural Materialism*, no. 16 (2018): pp. 23–40; 33–34.

[44] Both Lynn Hapgood and Matthew Beaumont contextualize this generic divergence from her contemporaries. Lynn Hapgood, 'Margaret Harkness, Novelist: Social Semantics and Experiments in Fiction', in Flore Janssen and Lisa. C. Robertson (eds), *Margaret Harkness: Writing Social Engagement 1880–1921* (Manchester University Press, 2019): pp. 130–146. Matthew Beaumont, '"A Little Political World of My Own": The New Woman, the New Life, and "New Amazonia"', *Victorian Literature and Culture*, 35.1 (2007): pp. 215–232.

and ephemeral sensations, as well as its connective and relational affordances. These disparate acts of rewriting unsettle any fixed meaning of the event named Bloody Sunday, intentionally challenging the interpretive authority of the law that named the convergence of a protest and occupation a riot on 13 November 1887.

4
Rhodes Must Fall, *Ulysses*, and the Politics of Teaching Modernism

Cóilín Parsons

The reception history of early-twentieth-century Irish theatre is rich with riot. Productions of the plays of John Millington Synge, Seán O'Casey, and others were occasions for scandalized, aggrieved, or opportunistic theatregoers to 'disgrace' themselves, as W.B. Yeats would have it, bringing notoriety and income to both playwrights and theatres.[1] Elsewhere in Europe, Stravinsky was setting the pace for angry audience reactions, with the May 1913 premiere of his *Rite of Spring* famously evoking a furious and violent response. Modernist performance and audience agitation go hand in hand, but Modernist novels–less of spectacle in themselves–provoke less spectacular reactions, and their controversies often played out in courts of law rather than in the street. In the audience at the Théâtre des Champs-Élysées on that night in May 1913 was James Joyce, one of the few, it was later reported, to 'remain calm and even amused'.[2] His equanimity is perhaps not surprising, given that Joyce's work would itself be the subject at the end of the decade of its own prudish obscenity trial that hung on the question of the artistic independence of modernist culture.

While the refracted presence of the obscenity trial of *Ulysses* is central to the brothel scenes of the 'Circe' episode, the riotousness of the episode is more stylistic than referential. There is, however, one set-piece scene of political protest and riot in the novel: in the 'Lestrygonians' episode, as Leopold Bloom wanders the city before heading to Davy Byrne's pub for his Gorgonzola sandwich and glass of Burgundy, he walks past Trinity College. As he passes the front gate, he remembers a protest against the Colonial Secretary, Joseph Chamberlain, that he got caught up in. Bloom's protest is one of the ubiquitous historical traces that fill the pages of the novel—there was indeed a protest that took place on that spot on

---

[1] Roy Foster, *W.B. Yeats: A Life II. The Arch Poet, 1915–1939* (Oxford: Oxford University Press, 2003), p. 305. For a comprehensive account of the riotous responses to Irish theatre in the early twentieth century see Joan Fitzpatrick Dean, *Riot and Great Anger: Stage Censorship in Twentieth Century Ireland* (Madison, WI: University of Wisconsin Press, 2004).

[2] Mary Burke, 'The Riot of Spring: Synge's "Failed Realism" and the Peasant Drama', in *The Oxford Handbook of Modern Irish Theatre*, edited by Nicholas Grene (Oxford: Oxford University Press, 2016), pp. 87–102.

18 December 1899. Chamberlain was being honoured with a degree from Trinity College, and a sizeable group of activists turned up to highlight the injustice of the award for Chamberlain while the South African War was taking place.[3] The protestors, whose sympathies lay with the Boers, were forced down Dame Street away from Trinity. When they were met on Parliament Street by mounted policemen from Dublin Castle, violence broke out; protest and riot began to shade into each other at the point at which the demonstrators encountered the law. True to Bloom's form, it is difficult to parse his allegiances at this moment in the novel, as memories of the sounds and confusion of the day come crowding back into his head:

> That horsepoliceman the day Joe Chamberlain was given his degree in Trinity he got a run for his money. My word he did! His horse's hoofs clattering after us down Abbey street. Lucky I had the presence of mind to dive into Manning's or I was souped. He did come a wallop, by George. Must have cracked his skull on the cobblestones. I oughtn't to have got myself swept along with those medicals. And the Trinity jibs in their mortarboards. Looking for trouble. Still I got to know that young Dixon who dressed that sting for me in the Mater and now he's in Holles street where Mrs Purefoy. Wheels within wheels. Police whistle in my ears still. All skedaddled. Why he fixed on me. Give me in charge. Right here it began.
> —Up the Boers!
> —Three cheers for De Wet!
> —We'll hang Joe Chamberlain on a sourapple tree.
> Silly billies: mob of young cubs yelling their guts out. Vinegar hill. The Butter exchange band. Few years' time half of them magistrates and civil servants. War comes on: into the army helterskelter: same fellows used to. Whether on the scaffold high.[4]

Was Bloom there out of solidarity with the Boers? Was he just caught up in it all? Did he think the protestors 'Silly billies' at the time or just now in hindsight? And if the real action of the day took place on Dame Street and Parliament Street, south of the river Liffey, why was Bloom ducking into a pub on Abbey Street, north of the river? Manning's pub, at 41 Upper Abbey Street, was near enough to the action to be a reasonable point of escape, but the distance from the action is also revealing. The protest had actually started on Beresford Place (not, as Bloom suggests, outside Trinity) and was broken up early on by police, with the leaders and

---

[3] A lively account of the pro-Boer activity in Dublin in the last years of the nineteenth century can be found in Donal P. McCracken, *The Irish Pro-Boers, 1877–1902* (Johannesburg and Cape Town: Perskor, 1989).

[4] James Joyce, *Ulysses*, edited by Hans Walter Gabler (New York, NY: Vintage, 1986), 8.423–440. All further citations will refer to the episode number and line numbers from the Gabler edition.

a crowd behind them moving on to the gates of Trinity. Bloom was 'swept along' with the medical students and doesn't seem to have been at the start of the protest on Beresford Place.

There is no real sense at any point here that Bloom has thought through the politics of this protest; what we are left with is rather impressions of the cacophonous and onomatopoeic soundscape (clattering, wallop, cobblestones, skedaddle, helterskelter—a jumble of consonants tumbling down on top each other). If there is one identifiable reason for Bloom to be there on the day it is his dislike for the police, but how that dislike is articulated with the anti-colonial politics driving the protest is left for us to imagine. The whole series of reminiscences had been set in train by Bloom seeing a 'squad of constables' and musing on when the best time would be to attack them (at 'pudding time', apparently, when you can give a policeman 'a punch in his dinner').[5] After the memory of the excitement of the day flashes into his mind, he turns to a quietist and gradualist position more identifiably Bloomian, dismissing the flash of youthful rebellion in the Trinity students. But the riot of that day cannot be so easily dismissed. Its shadow lives on in the streetscape of the novel, while its echoes can be heard in its soundscape. Something has ruptured and all the good-natured (though also, in this episode, hungry) musings of Bloom as he traverses the city on a sunny Thursday in June cannot dispel the fact and the memory of the rupture of that day. Public space retains a riotous memory.

This is not the only protest in *Ulysses*, which is acutely concerned with the nuances of life under colonialism at the tail end of empire—we could think of the moment when the carriage of the Lord Lieutenant glides by John Wyse Nolan in the 'Wandering Rocks' episode, and he smiles 'with unseen coldness', while the Poddle river hangs out 'in fealty a tongue of liquid sewage'.[6] But it is the only scene in which protest becomes riot, unless we count a drunken dust-up at the end of the 'Circe' episode, which has none of the planning and organization of the Pro-Boer action in 1899. 'Circe' too is shot through with Bloom's political prevarications and colonial fantasies. When confronted by British soldiers in Nighttown Bloom (or at least, the version of Bloom who appears in this episode, which is something quite different) claims, 'I'm as staunch a Britisher as you are, sir. I fought with the colours for king and country in the absentminded war under general Gough in the park and was disabled at Spion Kop and Bloemfontein, was mentioned in dispatches. I did all a white man could.'[7] The other character who is on the scene in 'Circe' is of course Stephen Dedalus, whose unwavering commitment to a politics of critique (and critique of politics), even when he feigns disengagement, contrasts with

---

[5] Joyce, *Ulysses*, 8.406, 411.
[6] Joyce, *Ulysses*, 10.1211, 10.1195.
[7] Joyce, *Ulysses*, 15.797–800.

Bloom. While Bloom may waver, Stephen's declaration of '*non serviam*' remains solid.[8]

*

In early 2012, I taught *Ulysses* for the first time. I was teaching in what was then the Department of English Language and Literature at the University of Cape Town (UCT) in South Africa, where final-year students had to take a semester-long lecture series on modernism.[9] While the attendant seminars ranged widely across anglophone modernism, including African literature, the lecture series took a narrower line on what constituted modernism. Eliot loomed large, as did Woolf, Pound, and *A Portrait of the Artist as a Young Man*. It was an unremarkable course that would be familiar to any student of modernism at the turn of the twenty-first century. In 2011 my colleagues and I decided that we would experiment with adding *Ulysses* to the syllabus, knowing that it would reach some of the 200 or so students in the class who would read it to the end, and perhaps not others. There were intellectual and ethical risks involved in choosing *Ulysses* for a lecture series and giving students just three weeks to read it. At the very least, there was the question of its notorious difficulty, which was particularly acute given the linguistic landscape of South Africa, where under ten per cent of the population at the time (though a much larger percentage of UCT students) spoke English as a home language.[10]

One of the greatest challenges in teaching *Ulysses* was to find ways to connect a forbidding ninety-year-old European text to the experience of a generation of southern Africans born mostly just before the first free elections in South Africa in 1994. The work of a generation of scholars writing mostly in the 1990s and early 2000s pointed to a possible approach: reading *Ulysses* as a rich historical document that offers an account of the structure of feeling of a day under colonial rule, written as that colonial rule came under increasing strain from protest and revolution. The contrapuntal co-emergence of the Irish state and *Ulysses* is readily documented in Enda Duffy's *Subaltern Ulysses* (1994), where Duffy writes that the novel 'is nothing less ... than *the* book of Irish postcolonial independence'.[11] The claim was explosive and somewhat overblown (like the IRA bomb with which the book opens), but Duffy's book made a strident and profoundly influential argument for *Ulysses* as a novel fundamentally oriented towards anti-colonial politics. It was not however, a 'manifesto for postcolonial freedom', Duffy argued, but 'a representation of the discourses and regimes of colonial power being

---

[8] Joyce, *Ulysses*, 15.4226, but see also James Joyce, *A Portrait of the Artist as a Young Man*, edited by Jeri Johnson (Oxford: Oxford University Press, 2001).
[9] The department now goes by the more expansive name of the Department of English Literary Studies.
[10] In the early 2010s over 60% of UCT students had English as a home language, though the percentage among those enrolled in final-year English was likely much higher. See 'A Language Plan for the University of Cape Town', http://www.mep.uct.ac.za/usr/mep/downloads/languageplan.pdf. Accessed 29 September 2022.
[11] Enda Duffy, *The Subaltern Ulysses* (Minneapolis: University of Minnesota Press, 1994), p. 3.

attacked by counterhegemonic strategies that were either modelled on the oppressor's discourses or were only beginning to be enunciated in other forms.'[12] The argument is canny, and accounts for the novel's orientation towards but inability to yet annunciate, a political horizon beyond empire. At the same time, the nuanced position has a tendency to get lost behind a thoroughgoing argument in most of the book for Joyce as an *engagé* anticolonial activist.[13]

At the same time as it negotiates the Irish revolution, the novel also traces quite carefully the South African War of 1899–1902, which features regularly and often obliquely, and not just in Bloom's memory of the protest in Dublin. There is no shortage of ways to read this as a novel with a particular, if submerged, South African obsession, written by a writer who thought twice about emigrating to South Africa.[14] Stephen's reference to Khaki hamlets, the absent-minded beggar, a rumour that Parnell had escaped to South Africa to become a Boer general, and much more, all offer a sense of the omnipresence of one anticolonial rebellion (even if a rebellion by a violent and racist settler population) in the unfolding of another.[15] And of course Joyce's work has been a lodestar of sorts for many South African writers in the last century.[16] This is a reading of *Ulysses* and South Africa that drew on postcolonial approaches to the novel in order to signal its availability to readers in contemporary southern Africa. But it is also an approach that is, as Nicholas Brown writes disapprovingly, 'more or less "vulgar" or thematic', relying on a shared colonial history (no matter how radically different) to insist on the capacity of the novel to offer insights into the African continent today. I have spent much of the time since I first taught *Ulysses* rethinking this position, and asking what the future is for this postcolonial reading of the novel. If the postcolonialism of those voices of the 1990s and 2000s has in many cases been superseded by a

---

[12] Duffy, *Subaltern Ulysses*, p. 21.
[13] Duffy was, of course, not alone in delineating the postcolonial Joyce; we can see this position also in the work of Seamus Deane, Emer Nolan, Marjorie Howes, Vincent Cheng, Declan Kiberd, Kevin Whelan, Kevin Barry, Elizabeth Butler Cullingford, and a whole generation of scholars whose Joyce scholarship reclaimed the supposedly rootless cosmopolitan for a committed politics.
[14] Tony Voss, 'Notes on Joyce and South Africa: Coincidence and Concordance', *Current Writing: Text and Reception in Southern Africa* 26, no. 1 (2014), pp. 25–26.
[15] See M. Keith Booker, *Ulysses, Capitalism, and Colonialism: Reading Joyce After the Cold War* (Westport, Connecticut: Greenwood Press, 2000); Marilyn Reizbaum, 'An Empire of Good Sports: Roger Casement, the Boer War, and James Joyce's *Ulysses*,' *Kunapipi: Journal of Postcolonial Writing* 23, no. 1 (2001), pp. 83–96; Barbara Temple-Thurston, 'The Reader as Absentminded Beggar: Recovering South Africa in *Ulysses*', *James Joyce Quarterly* 28, no. 1 (1990), pp. 247–256. See also Cóilín Parsons, 'Planetary Parallax: *Ulysses*, the Stars, and South Africa', *Modernism/modernity* 24, no. 1 (2017), pp. 67–85. The traffic is not all one way: *Ulysses* turns up in South Africa. In a very material way, the first copy of *Ulysses* to be sold in South Africa was imported in the early 1930s by a Johannesburg bookshop owner named Fanny Klennerman. Jonathan Hyslop, 'Gandhi, Mandela, and the African Modern', in *Johannesburg: The Elusive Metropolis*, edited by Achille Mbembe and Sarah Nuttall (Durham, NC: Duke University Press, 2008), p. 119.
[16] Writers like NP van wyk Louw, Lewis Nkosi, André Brink, J.M. Coetzee, Njabulo Ndebele, Zoë Wicomb, Ingrid Winterbach, Damon Galgut, Eben Venter, Niq Mhlongo, and more have enjoyed a long relationship with Joyce's work in general (*A Portrait* and *Dubliners* featuring strongly) and at times with *Ulysses* in particular. See Voss, 'Notes on Joyce and South Africa' for a more comprehensive account.

newer generation of critics and questions, and has been hollowed out from one side by World Literature and from another by Global South Studies, what future is there for the postcolonial *Ulysses*? Postcolonialism as a field has always made an explicit bargain with the politics of the present, a capricious guide, and has insisted on its own attention to history.

Brown reminds us that, in terms of *Ulysses,* 'historical content is not the same as historical movement'.[17] Just because the novel is overstuffed with details of life in the colony does not therefore mean that it can be read as a manifesto for anticolonial or decolonial aesthetics: 'Fanon the critic of the nationalist bourgeoisie is perfectly applicable, while Fanon the theorist of revolutionary violence is considerably less so'.[18] I cannot agree with Brown's assessment that *Ulysses* offers no 'hint of the political future'—or rather, I hesitate to seek in a novel set in 1904 nascent elements of a decade later, though hints and possibilities of the violence of 1916 and after are threaded through the novel, not least in the constant shades of surveillance patterning both the actions (such as they are) of the day and the forms and styles through which those actions are mediated.[19] And yet Brown's diagnosis of *Ulysses* rings true, in that it points to a surprising disidentification between the minute attention to the experience of life under colonialism in Dublin in 1904 and a later politics of anticolonialism. Any attempts to read *Ulysses* as thematically absorbed by colonialism 'tend eventually to rub up against the text's own universal ambitions'.[20] To dedicate one's work to 'finding virtually endless affinities between Joyce's work and postcolonial literature', as a strain of Joyce scholarship (including my own) has done in the last couple of decades, is to find oneself constantly stymied by a novel in which style is given more substance than history.[21] At times it feels that to ground a postcolonial poetics in *Ulysses* is about as promising a pursuit as forming a feminist politics out of a novel filled with men who treat women as little more than sexual objects. As Gayatri Chakravorty Spivak wrote archly many years ago about Julia Kristeva's relationship to Joyce's writing, 'There is something ... faintly comical about Joyce rising above sexual identities and bequeathing the proper mind-set to the women's movement'.[22] And yet it is true that *Ulysses* is '*the* book' of Irish political decolonization, and that the discourse of decolonization has been thrust back into view in the last few years, from new quarters and with new imperatives.

*

---

[17] Nicholas Brown, *Utopian Generations: The Political Horizon of Twentieth-Century Literature* (Princeton, NJ: Princeton University Press, 2005), p. 38.
[18] Brown, *Utopian Generations*, p. 38.
[19] Duffy, *Subaltern Ulysses*, p. 19. For a convincing argument about the myriad traces of the 1916 Rising in *Ulysses*, see Luke Gibbons, *James Joyce and the Irish Revolution:* The Easter Rising as Modern Event (Chicago, IL: Chicago University Press, 2022).
[20] Brown, *Utopian Generations*, p. 38.
[21] Brown, *Utopian Generations*, p. 37.
[22] Gayatri Chakravorty Spivak, 'French Feminism in an International Frame', *Yale French Studies* 62 (1981), p. 169.

Ulysses takes place on a date of great significance in South Africa: 16 June 1976 was the day that high school students in Soweto walked out of school to protest the introduction of Afrikaans as the medium of instruction. While 16 June 1904 in Dublin was a day of no particular significance, the first day of the Soweto Uprising saw the deaths of dozens of students at the hands of the police, to be followed by hundreds more in the days that followed. The day is marked now as Youth Day, a solemn reminder of the activism of children who marched into certain danger on that day. It is a traumatic anniversary (so far removed from the comic cast of the sunny day in Dublin in 1904), but the coincidence with *Ulysses* is remarked on in Zoë Wicomb's novel *David's Story* (2000), when the ghost writer character blurts out: 'Youth Day—Soweto Day, the sixteenth of June—that's also Joyce's Bloomsday... Day of the Revolution of the Word. Imagine, black children revolting against Afrikaans, the language of oppressors, on the very anniversary of the day that Leopold Bloom started with a hearty breakfast, eating with relish the inner organs of—'.[23] She is interrupted before she can go any further, though her enthusiastic linking of *Ulysses* and Youth Day is in many ways sanctioned by *Ulysses*'s principles of coincidence and metempsychosis.

Hers is also, however, a profound misreading. Yes, perhaps *Ulysses* was a revolutionary text, but its bombs and explosions were as nothing compared to the violence of anticolonial riots that took place on those days in 1976. More importantly, the ghost writer misreads Youth Day by linking it to *Ulysses*, failing to see that the former is marked by specifically racialized violence in a way that the latter is not. While the Black Consciousness movement was at the forefront of the Soweto Uprising, and race was the principal organizing feature of the apartheid state, there was no similar racial content to either colonialism or anticolonial activism in Ireland. This fact is incontrovertible, though it remains a thorny issue for Irish postcolonial studies. This is not to say that Ireland was not colonized and was not an important node in the imperial system, but that the experience of empire as racial capitalism was quite different for Ireland than for the African continent. A riot or a protest in *Ulysses* is differentially integrated into the global landscape of riot, a fact sharply outlined by Wicomb.[24]

I never taught *Ulysses* in South Africa again after that first time, for I left later that year. Indeed, after 2015, it was hard to imagine how anyone would teach it, or at least in a way that focuses on the centrality of Ireland as a postcolonial precursor. In 2015, in a protest that would not feel out of place as a minor incident in *Ulysses*, but that had major repercussions, an activist threw shit at a statue of Cecil John Rhodes on the campus at UCT. The statue was prominently displayed on the pedestrian route from many of the student residences to the academic core of the campus, and

---

[23] Zoë Wicomb, *David's Story* (New York, NY: Feminist Press, 2000), p. 35
[24] I am grateful to Joe Cleary for his enabling work on how Ireland (and Irish culture in particular) has been 'differentially integrated' into the world system. Joe Cleary, *Outrageous Fortune: Capital and Culture in Modern Ireland* (Dublin: Field Day Publications, 2007), pp. 14–46.

Rhodes was cast, as Hedley Twidle notes, in the mould of Rodin's *Thinker*.[25] This was, of course, a brutal irony, given Rhodes's predilections and shortcomings. The activist who threw the shit was Chumani Maxwele, a student of Political Science, and he had picked up the shit in Khayelitsha, a vast suburb of mostly informal housing on the outskirts of Cape Town, where city services, among them sewer services, are totally inadequate to the size of the population.[26] The parlous state of Khayelitsha and other suburbs is, perhaps, the very embodiment of the theory of the conscious development of underdevelopment.

From that one act of protest, which had crystallized actions already underway for years to transform radically the higher education complex of South Africa, grew a movement given the name Rhodes Must Fall. It grew rapidly out of the frustrations, fears, and anger of a generation born free for whom the university system in particular and the political and economic structures of South Africa in general had failed in any meaningful way to change in the aftermath of the end of apartheid. The movement's collectively authored manifesto, published just days after the initial performative act, ranged from immediate demands—remove the statue—to some that take more significant work. The removal of the statue, the manifesto's authors wrote 'will not mark the end but the beginning of the long overdue process of decolonising this university' (one of the many signs and placards to reappear often in photos of the protests was one that read, 'We're not done yet').[27] This is one of the stated long-term goals in the manifesto:

> Implement a curriculum which critically centres Africa and the subaltern. By this we mean treating African discourses as the point of departure—through addressing not only content, but languages and methodologies of education and learning—and only examining western traditions in so far as they are relevant to our own experience.[28]

There are also demands that seek more material changes to the financial structures of the university, including those that ask the university administration to 're-evaluate the standards by which research areas are decided—from areas that are lucrative and centre whiteness, to areas that are relevant to the lives of black people locally and on the continent', and on to demands for minimum wage for employees and an end to outsourcing. The Rhodes Must Fall movement grew over the next

---

[25] Hedley Twidle, 'To Spite his Face: What Happened to Cecil Rhodes's Nose?' *Harper's Magazine* (December 2021), p. 39.

[26] A reasonably comprehensive survey of student actions and university administration responses (though perhaps too sympathetic to the latter), completed very shortly after the outbreak of protests, can be found in Francis Nyamnjoh, *#RhodesMustFall: Nibbling at Resilient Colonialism in South Africa* (Bamenda, Cameroon: Langaa, 2016).

[27] 'UCT Rhodes Must Fall Statements'. *The Johannesburg Salon* 9 (2015), p. 6. https://studentsnotcustomers.files.wordpress.com/2014/11/vfinal_vol9_book.pdf, accessed 3 October 2022.

[28] 'UCT Rhodes Must Fall Statements', p. 8.

couple of years and took root in other universities, most notably at the University of the Witwatersrand (Wits) where striking students demanded the abolition of all tuition fees.[29] At Wits, the students were met with violent force by private security and the police, and it was here that protest turned to riot most spectacularly in the interface between student anger and the security apparatus of the highly securitized post-apartheid state.

Rhodes Must Fall and Fees Must Fall have changed the landscape of higher education in South Africa, and put on notice the educated classes, especially those brought up in the spirit of South African liberalism and for whom 'transformation', that watchword of the post-apartheid era, has been a useful object of worship. An early passage of the UCT Rhodes Must Fall manifesto highlights Steve Biko's coruscating criticism of white liberals: 'The (white) liberal must understand that the days of the Noble Savage are gone; that the blacks do not need a go-between in this struggle for their own emancipation.'[30] The pace and the goals of transformation have been too slow for, and inadequate to, the project of achieving racial justice in the wake of apartheid. A protest in 2015, or 2023, is always and will remain, a renewal with a difference of 1976, or whichever prior date with which it rhymes, as long as the injustice remains intact. The Rhodes Must Fall activists took pains to suture their protest to an inherited activist past and yet not have it be defined solely by the past; the memories of Rhodes Must Fall are dynamic and active. For Keith Michael Baker and Dan Edelstein, every moment of political revolution is in some sense scripted in advance in this way, with the script constituting a 'frame within which a situation is defined and a narrative projected'.[31] Far from this reading of riot and revolution refusing agency to those who renew them every time, Baker and Edelstein's formulation insists on the radical yield of understanding political action as transhistorical: 'There is ... a very significant difference between seeing a revolution as an event ... or conceiving it as a dynamic and ongoing process of contestation and conflict, or as a mode of collective action directed toward the goal of radical transformation.'[32] Collective action of this kind, they suggest, always has antecedents and descendants, participating in a long historical fight for justice.

---

[29] The actions at UCT also inspired a long-running similar set of protests and actions at Oxford, SOAS, Queen Mary, Princeton, Harvard, Ghana and elsewhere, including my own university, Georgetown. A good deal of attention has been focused on Oxford, and a book by the Oxford Rhodes Must Fall activists perpetuates that focus. Rhodes Must Fall, Oxford, *Rhodes Must Fall: The Struggle to Decolonise the Racist Heart of Empire* (London: Zed Books, 2018). For a clearer sense of the lines of influence from South to North see A. Kayum Ahmed, '#RhodesMustFall: How a Decolonial Student Movement in the Global South Inspired Epistemic Disobedience at the University of Oxford', *African Studies Review* 63, no. 2 (2020), pp. 281–303.
[30] 'UCT Rhodes Must Fall Statements', p. 8.
[31] Keith Michael Baker and Dan Edelstein, 'Introduction', in *Scripting Revolution: A Historical Approach to the Comparative Study of Revolutions*, edited by Keith Michael Baker and Dan Edelstein (Stanford, CA: Stanford University Press, 2015), p. 3. I am grateful to Darragh Gannon for bringing this work to my attention.
[32] Baker and Edelstein, *Scripting Revolution*, p. 3.

For Joshua Clover, writing of a landscape of global riot after 1968, this transhistorical thinking is a feature of riot now: 'bread riot and race riot, those paired misnomers, retain a deep unity'.[33] Behind the neat formulation is an insistence on the historical continuities of political action, the passages of resistance from the eighteenth century to today that draw long trains of both economic circumstances and signification through centuries to fill the riot action of our current moment. Clover designates our current landscape of political action 'riot prime', arguing that the shift in the nineteenth century (recognized by Charles Tilly before him) from riot to strike was succeeded not by a simple return to riot post-1968, but by the emergence of what he calls 'riot prime'. Whereas the 'proper place' of the first two are the market or the port and the factory floor, respectively, the last is located in 'square and street'.[34] We might add to that, on the campuses of universities. While Clover's argument relies on a single model of historical change that is far too closely aligned with economic conditions in the Global North ('riot prime' is keyed to 'late capitalism, financialization, post-Fordism', as if those were equally the markers of our moment globally), his identification of a global movement of disorder distinguished by a 'spectacular encounter' with the state (rather than a market trader or a factory owner) rings true. The encounter will not necessarily be, as Clover suggests it will, played out in the economic sphere, with looting and economic destruction, but the 'square and street' of 'riot prime' is filled with a deep sense of the continuities of history and the politics of signification. Bread riot and race riot are inextricable across times and spaces.

This sense of the overlapping and recurring significations of political actions over centuries sustains the layered landscape of Joyce's Dublin, with its portals and passageways from present to past and future as a form of radical re-formation of time. At the same time, the litany of Global South writers of Joycean descent (though Joyce's script is always renewed under contestation) make for a different kind of transhistorical imagination, which Michaela Bronstein has written about in her study of modernist writers from the early twentieth century whose work reappears 'out of context' later in the century, as well as other locations. Bronstein offers a theory of how novels reach into a future unknowable to them, not by avoiding history but by adapting to history:

> To read transhistorically is neither to read ahistorically nor to suggest that art is in some way 'universal.' The transhistorical, in this sense, does not merely oppose the historical; it is its own form of history ... Literature is embedded in history, but not always and only the history of its moment of production. It makes an aesthetic appeal to the future, but an appeal that has political uses.[35]

---

[33] Joshua Clover, *Riot. Strike. Riot: The New Era of Uprisings* (London: Verso, 2016), p. 28.
[34] Clover, *Riot. Strike. Riot*, p. 11.
[35] Michaela Bronstein, *Out of Context: The Uses of Modernist Fiction* (Oxford: Oxford University Press, 2018), pp. 7–8.

But by what means do we mediate the transhistory of the text, and with what tags does it emerge into the present, and indeed how is that emergence negotiated by geographical context? And how does a protest, a riot, an action, or a revolution open a rift in the transhistorical transmission of the text?

These are the questions that are raised by the work of reading *Ulysses* as a guide to the current moment of decolonization. Though we might insist on its capacity to explain and absorb the shocks of the present, to provide comfort or explanation, there must be a point at which we stop trying to accommodate *Ulysses* to the present and ask about modernism's historicity, its strangeness our moment. How do we see the origins of our present possibilities in the literature of the past without collapsing differences or romanticizing the ruptures of the present as re-emergences of a hallowed past? The genealogy of South African protest is alien to *Ulysses*, and *Ulysses* to it.

*

In the midst of the Rhodes Must Fall protests, a collective of UCT students, 'some of whom were involved and some affected by the movement', devised a play about the movement.[36] The original cast and authors of this play, *The Fall*, had just finished presenting a different play together when they turned their minds and bodies to documenting and reliving the early days of the protests. The play they had just finished was *Black Dog*, a multilingual, workshopped play by Barney Simon and his company. First performed in 1984, its subject is largely the 1976 Soweto Uprising, but *Black Dog* also reflects on the actions of 1976 through the experience of an upsurge in violence in 1984, and the play's re-presentation in 2015 creates a chain of echoes, solidarities, and transitions. *The Fall* takes part in that chain of actions and reflections, stitching together 1976, 1984, and 2015. The complex passages of retrospection and introspection are made clear in *The Fall*'s authors's note, in which they write that the play 'came as a reply to and a follow-up of *Black Dog*, but simultaneously as a retrospective gaze and reflection on the events after the #RhodesMustFall Movement started—most importantly, from the perspectives of students of colour'.[37] Debuting in October 2016, the play was performed in the Baxter Theatre, a venue with its own place in the lore of Irish modernism, since it was here that a famed multiracial *Waiting for Godot* was performed under apartheid, with Beckett's blessing.

The Fall is a moving piece of theatre, both on the page and on the stage, weaving quiet reflection and rousing call-and-response singing, a spare stage and projected images of mass protest (and violence against the protesters). Where the play sometimes tends towards rehearsal of political positions, it almost immediately undercuts those with personal accounts; ambivalence and righteousness rub up

---

[36] Ameera Conrad, Cleo Raatus, Kgomotso Khunoane, Oaribile Ditsele, Sihle Mnqwazana, Sizwesandile Mnisi, Tankiso Mamabolo, and Thando Mangcu, *The Fall* (London: Oberon Books, 2017), p. 7.
[37] Conrad et al., *The Fall*, p. 8.

against each other. It was, the authors's note, 'written solely from the students' perspectives and homes in on their individual and intersectional challenges in the movement'.[38] Its final monologue, by the character of Qhawekazi, is breathtakingly moving, a direct plea to the audience to remember that 'We used to be people. We used to dream about a future where we didn't need to protest anymore, or call ourselves brave and fearless ... I'm tired. My soul is tired.'[39]

The part of the play that is relevant, if tangentially, to *Ulysses* comes in the third of ten short scenes ('Sharing in Downtime'), in which the characters sit around while occupying the administration building on campus and talk about what brought them to this place and to this protest. Later we will see the statue come down and a march on parliament during which police blocked all the streets but one and chased the protestors down that one remaining street (they had learned their trade alongside the Dublin Metropolitan Police who rounded up the protestors in 1899). For now, though, the students construct, speech by speech, an aetiology of a movement, a protest, and a riot. They tell the story of how, as Cahya says in the first scene, 'We went from UCT students to uMkhonto weSizwe [the armed wing of the ANC] real fast':[40]

QHAWEKAZI: You know, the first time I felt othered in this university, was in first-year English class. (*To Camilla.*) Ya, you were there! The lecturer was brilliant. The only reason I knew he was brilliant, was because of how much the white kids mmm'd and aaah'd every time he spoke. He kept throwing around those big English words and the only people who could catch them were the white kids and ones who went to Model C schools.
CHWAITA: I loved him!
QHAWEKAZI: Ugh, she 'loved him'? Dude, the content ... It was ridiculous; we read these two problematic books, one after the other. Uhm ... *Passage to India* and *Heart of* ...
CAHYA: *Heart of Redness.*
CAMILLA: No, that's Zakes Mda.
CHWAITA: *Heart of Darkness*—Joseph Conrad!
QHAWEKAZI: Okay ...? Anyway now, if you've read those books you know that black people are portrayed as savages, and the lecturer just throws them at us! No discussion! He doesn't even—
CAHYA: He doesn't even make you critically analyse the Western view of the black body.
QHAWEKAZI: And then, when we finally got to do African Literature, for, like, two—just two—months out of the entire year, the white students sat at the back of the lecture hall and made fun of the African lecturer's accent.[41]

---

[38] Conrad et al., *The Fall*, p. 7.
[39] Conrad et al., *The Fall*, p. 57.
[40] Conrad et al., *The Fall*, 11.
[41] Conrad et al., *The Fall*, pp. 26–27.

Qhawekazi probably did not do her degree in English, but if she had, she would not have been swayed, I imagine, by attempts to make Joyce African. It may have struck her as a new universalism in the name of postcolonialism. There are callouts to other disciplines too—History and Film and Media Studies—but it is the English curriculum that is highlighted here, at the point at which protestors's general principles are translated into specific curricular action points. While the Rhodes Must Fall manifesto offers principles that anyone who thinks about racial justice today would struggle to disagree with, the outworking of those principles on a course-by-course, discipline-by-discipline basis is arresting. Modernism in the crosshairs. Not, of course, that the play is such a brittle application of the manifesto; it is, in fact, a very subtle meditation on the wide spectrum of grievances, solutions, fears, and hopes of committed and tentative Fallists. These critiques of European modernism are familiar, and many of us have probably levelled them ourselves, even as we appreciate Forster and Conrad's place in the development of modernist prose, and the centrality of a liberal anti-imperialism to their work. But here, on the stage, they are felt and communicated in a way that leaves no room for uncertainty—protest, riot, and the rapid dismantling of a curriculum that no amount of nuanced reframing can now salvage.

Suren Pillay, in a speech in April 2015 (given to protesting students in the occupied and renamed administration building, Azania House, where the dialogue above takes place) put to the protestors a question that has been asked before and since, but that takes on urgency in the face of an occupation: 'How do we recruit new knowledge into our universities that breaks with geographical and linguistic apartheid so that the antiquated idea of a Department of English can be a department for the comparative study of Literature? And how do we bridge the continental fault lines between Anglophone, Francophone, Lusophone, and Arabic knowledge?'[42] Pillay's question has been in the back of the minds of so many literature teachers for decades, as intellectual puzzle more than institutional imperative. But, as Cahya points out in the play, 'It's amazing, really, how everyone got lit over some pota-pota on a statue, but there was some very hard work around transformation long before he did that.'[43] Cahya's rejection of event-focused politics in favour of an understanding of the long and ramifying history of actions against colonial monuments and colonial thinking sutures the present to both past and future. We may say the same thing about curricular change: there has been hard work for decades, but it takes a riotous, performative, collective protest to open up the possibility for a new organization of knowledge, and to take steps not just to add but to cut from the curriculum. Pillay asks, 'Should we settle for a supplemental concept of history, where we now add African Studies onto the existing curriculum with the danger of once more ghettoizing it from the other mainstream

---

[42] Suren Pillay, 'Decolonizing the University', *Africa is a Country*, 6 July 2015. https://africasacountry.com/2015/06/decolonizing-the-university, accessed 3 October 2022.

[43] Conrad et al., *The Fall*, p. 16.

disciplines?' The answer is clear, and there is no assured place here for a literature of a different decolonization. Where does *Ulysses,* the postcolonial classic, fit in this new curriculum? How do we find space for it in an emerging critical conversation? Or should we?

At the very least, *Ulysses* enters its second century from a less assured position in the global classroom and with an unsure future. Readers and teachers will be challenged to say how its concerns are articulated with a new phase of decolonization, one that centres the Global South as a producer of knowledge and a generator of theories, and one in which the Irish experience of decolonization is, unlike in the early twentieth century, not a template for a global movement. The point may well be not to wield *Ulysses* as a guide to the politics of the future, but to revisit its pages through the lens of what seems to us, from this vantage point, and provisionally, a politics of the future. It is not the case that we somehow *must* continue to teach *Ulysses* everywhere literature is taught, but that if we *do* continue to teach it that it must be with an eye to the avant-garde of our own moment. There are many reasons why critics, including Brown, do still start a reading of postcolonial modernism with Joyce, and start a reading of *Ulysses* with its postcolonial potentialities.

This line of argument brings us back to the question of the transhistoricism of the novel, or its potential to 'resonate' in the present, to borrow a phrase from Wai Chee Dimock. For Dimock, literary texts have the capacity to resound and transform across time, 'moving farther and farther from their points of origin, causing unexpected vibrations in unexpected places'.[44] Rather than the enduring literary text remaining somehow a stable and timeless object that transcends history, it is marked by a 'timeful unwieldiness'.[45] Dimock's suggestion is promising, for it pointedly refuses to play the game of identifying literature that transcends time and place, choosing instead to value texts that are 'diachronic', yielding their words 'differently across time, authorizing contrary readings across the ages and encouraging a kind of semantic democracy'.[46] But as new as Dimock's reading is, it also enacts a refreshed form of canonization and insists on the possibility of the object itself remaining central, thanks to its elasticity. A novel can be transhistorical thanks to some innate features that distinguish this one from another, a suggestion that is carried forward into arguments about world literature in the last two decades that seek to define and institutionalize the translatable novel.[47] If Rhodes Must Fall and the movements to decolonize knowledge in the Global South (protests and riots over knowledge itself), teach us anything, it is to reject

---

[44] Wai Chee Dimock, 'A Theory of Resonance', *PMLA* 112, no. 5 (1997), p. 1061.
[45] Dimock, 'A Theory of Resonance', p. 1062.
[46] Dimock, 'A Theory of Resonance', p. 1067.
[47] See, for example, Rebecca Walkowitz, *Born Translated: The Contemporary Novel in an Age of World Literature* (New York, NY: Columbia University Press, 2015).

the work of finding a path for old materials to re-emerge with a new lustre, ready to tackle the present crisis. And yet embedded within *Ulysses*, entangled with those moments of riot and protest, of monuments and their downfall, is already a form of transhistorical thinking that, though it does not guarantee the novel's continued relevance across time and space, does at the very least toy with the idea of timelessness and timefulness.

*

Dublin too (the innocence of that 'too'—so easy to write and yet fraught with elisions—now fully in question) is a city of contested monuments, and of course the contestations are brought to light with glancing irony by *Ulysses*. Take, for example, Bloom's claim that we saw earlier that he 'fought with the colours for king and country in the absentminded war under general Gough in the park'. The general to whom he refers as being 'in' the Phoenix Park is not the Gough (Hubert de la Poer Gough) who commanded the troops in South Africa, but his uncle Hugh, who fought in the First Opium War, won a Victoria Cross for his defence of Lucknow during the 1857 Indian rebellion, and became Commander-in-Chief in India. A statue in his honour was erected in 1878. Monuments, colonial wars, and anticolonial rebellions shade into one another in Bloom's mind, each one signifying another across time and space in a novel that is saturated with real and imagined, remembered and forgotten riots, protests, and rebellions. Gough's supposedly glorious career began with the suppression of anticolonial revolt, and like Rhodes', his statue was the victim of many attacks in the post-independence era, including one in which his horse was beheaded.[48] This is one of many instances in *Ulysses* in which traces of the 1857 rebellion in India leave their mark on the pages, becoming yet another node in the network of riots, protests, and rebellions that spreads through the novel. Joyce sets up a complex of allusions that sketch out a world in which one time, place, character, or story is never simply itself—it is always a shadow of a coming or a past event, a far distant shore or a half-remembered place. There is a constant, unrelenting, and often corrosive transference taking place between one time and another, one place and another. Transhistoricism in this case describes not (or not primarily) the post-publication life of the century-old novel, but it is a central feature of the slippery time horizons of that unbounded day in Dublin.

At the centre of both the city and a parable told by Stephen Dedalus is Nelson's Pillar, a phallic monument to Horatio Nelson completed in 1809 in the middle of Sackville Street. A few years later, the General Post Office would open beside the

---

[48] Ronan McGreevy, 'State Papers: Repatriation of Phoenix Park Statue Equestrian Statue Not Permitted', *The Irish Times* online, 29 December 2018. https://www.irishtimes.com/culture/heritage/state-papers-repatriation-of-phoenix-park-equestrian-statue-not-permitted-1.3735857, accessed 3 October 2022.

Pillar, both monumental testaments to the power of the unevenly consolidating colonial administration in Ireland. Stephen tells a faltering and interrupted story of two 'vestal virgins' who climb the spiral staircase to the top of the tower to see the sights of Dublin. When they reach the top they become dizzy, and the city is unrecognizable to them from the lofty heights of the Pillar. They sit down to steady themselves, and eat some plums that they had bought earlier, spitting the pits on to infertile ground below. The story is all feints and parries, indecision and tentative advances, and the view from the dominating heights of the Pillar amounts to nothing but a confusing mass of spires and domes. The title of the story, Stephen tells his small audience, is 'the Parable of the Plums, or A Pisgah Sight of Palestine'.[49] Like Moses's glimpse of the Promised Land from atop Mt Pisgah before he died, it is a vision that is revealed but will never be attained.

Much of the irony of these monumental settings is invisible and unknowable to the characters who stalk the pages of the novel. It will unfold over time, between the setting in 1904 and the publication in 1922, or even later. The General Post Office will be occupied in the 1916 Rising and severely damaged by shells from a British warship a few days later. The offices of the *Freeman's Journal* newspaper, where Stephen starts to tell his parable, will be razed entirely in 1916. As Enda Duffy writes, Dublin in the 1910s was 'rising in fiction, being destroyed in fact'.[50] But the temporality of the monuments in *Ulysses* stretches farther than just the moment of political decolonization in what would become the Free State. Gough's statue is not the only one to fall after independence: in 1966, just before the fiftieth anniversary of the 1916 Rising, Nelson's Pillar was blown up in the middle of the night by members of the Irish Republican Army (IRA). Stephen's two pilgrims were afraid that it would fall, but neither they nor Joyce were yet able to articulate the manner of its demise. The act was spectacular and symbolic, but while the destruction of the Pillar wiped a symbol of colonial violence off the cityscape of Dublin, the act was curiously illegible. No one took responsibility, and the IRA denied it. It was not until 2000 that an IRA volunteer admitted to having set the charges.[51] While the monument was overdetermined in its situation in the heart of the city, the act of destruction was underdetermined, an ambiguous act of spectacular but not fully interpretable violence. By contrast, as activist and artist Thulile Gamedze writes, the slow and deliberate removal of the Rhodes statue by a crane hired by UCT was something of an anti-climax and a co-opting of the radical voices of the movement

---

[49] Joyce, *Ulysses*, 7.922-1056. On *Ulysses*'s accounts of monuments and monumental spaces see Rita Sakr, *Monumental Space in the Post-Imperial Novel: An Interdisciplinary Study* (New York, NY: Continuum, 2021), pp. 41-81. See also David Spurr, *Architecture and Modern Literature* (Ann Arbor: University of Michigan Press, 2012), pp. 187-203.

[50] Enda Duffy, 'Disappearing Dublin: *Ulysses*, Postcoloniality, and the Politics of Space', in *Semicolonial Joyce*, edited by Derek Attridge and Marjorie Howes (Cambridge: Cambridge University Press, 2000), p. 38.

[51] Donal Fallon, *The Pillar: The Life and Afterlife of the Nelson Pillar* (Dublin: New Island Books, 2014), pp. 101-103.

by the university administration. She would have preferred it to have been blown up. Or even to have had its nose taken off, as had happened to another Rhodes statue (there are so many to be toppled) just up the slopes of Table Mountain from UCT.[52]

Ulysses stages, repeatedly, the transhistoricism of the revolutionary moment, with monuments and their downfall, protests, and riots overlapping and reappearing (in a form of metempsychosis, that watchword for the whole novel) in ways that challenge the reader to stitch together the threads of causality and remembrance, of desires and justifications, that make up the riotous event. At the centre of these moments of anti-colonial action is a transhistoricism *in* the novel rather than *of* the novel. This is a key distinction, as it leads us in the direction of a more contingent articulation of *Ulysses* with new forms of decolonial action. It is not the case that *Ulysses* is prepared in advance for a future that Joyce could not have known, but that the very question of the transnational and transhistorical affiliations of decolonization is set as an enabling feature of the novel. *Ulysses*'s slippery temporalities mean that it is, as Dimock would call it, 'timeful', but not therefore necessarily resonant in all times and places. While this reading preserves the messy politics of the novel, it sutures *Ulysses* to our present by foregrounding the possibilities of transhistorical routes that could illuminate a series of jagged passages through history. The Rhodes Must Fall protests have brought into sharp focus the means by which literary history (among other disciplines and fields) is constructed in the postcolony, and have highlighted how protest and riot unsettle and recalibrate the politics of temporality, forging alliances and influences that move backwards and forwards across time and space. Protest, riot, occupation—these are modes by which we interrupt and reset literary histories as well as political histories, plotting out a new 'geopolitics of knowledge'.[53]

---

[52] Thulile Gamedze, 'Destruction Styles: Black Aesthetics of Rupture and Capture', *Radical Philosophy* 2, no. 8 (2020), p. 55. On the question of the nose, its removers, and the proliferation of Rhodes statues, see Twidle, 'To Spite His Face'.

[53] The phrase 'geopolitics of knowledge' is drawn from the work of Raewyn Connell, especially in *Southern Theory: Social Science and the Global Dynamics of Knowledge* (New York, NY: Routledge, 2020).

5
Buzz, Mob, Crowd, Life

Writing the Riot in Mulk Raj Anand's *Untouchable* and Virginia Woolf's *Mrs Dalloway*

J. Daniel Elam

Novels across the British Empire in the 1920s and 1930s relied on the riot and the crowd as key 'characters'. Mulk Raj Anand's *Untouchable* (1936) and Virginia Woolf's *Mrs Dalloway* (1927) both feature crowds as key figures in the wake of riots.[1] This chapter draws on multiple genres of writing—literary, bureaucratic, and sociological—to explore how the riot played a central role in the imperial and anti-imperial imagination and emerges as a literary figure in the two novels.

Reading Anand's *Untouchable* in conversation with Woolf's *Mrs Dalloway* recharts the geography of modernist literature by returning to the shared historical conjuncture of the interwar period as a truly global phenomenon. Both novels take place over the course of a single day and revolve loosely around a single character from whom a city and its milieu unfolds. Although Anand is rarely given credit for experimenting with linear narration, both novels feature juxtapositions between the ostensibly 'single' day and past experiences, dreams, and an omniscient narrator who both hews closely to and strays far from the protagonist. The 'single day' becomes, for both novels, a metonym for a full, if quotidian, life. There is also the fact that both novels are organized around a single task, though in horrifying contrast: Clarissa Dalloway is to pick up flowers, and Bakha is to pick up human waste.

This list of intertextual playfulness and parallels only offers us the groundwork for the conversation we might recreate between the novels. What the novels share is a global and particularly modernist discussion about modern life after World War I, especially the modern social unit of 'the crowd'. While political and social theory attempted to answer these questions, literature revelled in their provocations and used the figure of the crowd for literary experimentation. If the twentieth century was to be the 'era of the crowd', as Gustav Le Bon proclaimed in 1898, it makes sense that early twentieth-century literature reflected a global conversation

---

[1] Mulk Raj Anand, *Untouchable* (London: Penguin, 1986); Virginia Woolf, *Mrs Dalloway* (Oxford: Oxford University Press, 1998).

about this new epoch.[2] The trouble was that 'the crowd' as a nascent sociological concept, was largely undefined. Where does 'the crowd' begin and end? Do humans, upon entering into contact with it, become something less or something more than individuals? What do crowds want? While political and social theory attempted to answer these questions, literature revelled in its provocations and used the figure of the crowd for literary experimentation.

By the 1910s and 1920s, the 'crowd' was a sociological and political unit that was something *more* than a collection of individuals gathered together and also, paradoxically, something *less* than a collection of individuals gathered together. Early sociologists's metaphors are telling. Crowds were uniquely modern, born of human action. Riots were crowds of adults who *became* children, barbarians, or animals: irrational, unpredictable, motivated by unmediated sensory experience, or easily prone to sentiment. Darwin's theories (as well as less rigorous theories inspired by Darwin, including social Darwinism) made biology the most useful source of metaphors for the realm of the 'social', its intrinsic components, and its unpredictable progression.

Sociology hardly stopped at the animal world for its analyses. Crowds were also 'chemical reactions': new substances produced from discrete parts. Crowds were beaches or 'piles of autumn leaves in the wind'. Crowds were 'biological phenomena'.[3] Early sociological theory about crowds borrowed heavily from chemistry and biology for metaphors conducive to crowd analysis; twentieth-century political philosophy relied on those metaphors for figuring out how to harness this new subjectivity for political purposes. Rather than threats to individuality, crowds were a fungible substance that an individual could move in and out of.

Crowds were the most visible unit of 'society', a concept that was the basis for a nascent academic discipline: sociology. In the early twentieth century, sociologists were concerned with articulating the contours of their new field. This included thinkers like Gustav Le Bon and William James, who wrote social psychology under the influence of Henri Bergson's vitalist philosophy, and were attempting to extend psychology beyond the individual subject. This meant that early social theorists could revel in disciplinary promiscuity. In 1908 William James wrote that sociology 'made biology and psychology continuous'.[4] German sociologists like Max Weber and Ferdinand Tönnies (along with James and Durkheim) drew on philology and comparative religion to describe the foundations of 'society'.

In 1904, Gabriel Tarde and Emile Durkheim debated the conditions of disciplinary autonomy and direction for sociology. Durkheim wanted to move away from philosophy towards social facts, while Tarde insisted on the promiscuous

---

[2] Gustave Le Bon, *The Crowd: A Study of the Popular Mind* (Dover: Dover Press, 1902), p. xiii.
[3] Gabriel Tarde, *On Communication and Social Influence* (Chicago, IL: University of Chicago Press), p. 112. See also Terry N. Clark's introduction to this edition for an excellent explication of Tarde's interest in the 'biological' underpinnings of sociology.
[4] William James, *Pluralistic Universe* (Cambridge, MA: Harvard University Press, 1977).

plurality of methodological approaches for the social sciences.[5] Their shared focus, however, was crowds: crowds were the clearest empirical realization of the abstract category of 'society'. In other words, Anand and Woolf were writing when sociology was emerging as its own discipline, and was therefore a fairly heady blend of philosophy, psychology, anthropology, vitalism, and metaphysics. In response to or alongside the formation of the disciplinary social sciences, Mark Bevir notes, 'artists and moralists—including, most famously, the Bloomsbury Group—turned away from individual and social duties towards good states of mind and personal relations. So E.M. Forster and Virginia Woolf wrote in more uncertain voices about more fragmented and private worlds than had Charlotte Bronte and Charles Dickens.'[6] As most writers in this high modernist moment realized, fiction was the first realm through which new subjectivities like crowds and riots might be theorized and brought to life. Anand and Woolf understood both projects to be motivated by the emergence of new sociological subjectivities available for literary experimentation.[7]

Compared to the nineteenth century, when crowds were undefined 'mobs' to be avoided, the twentieth-century crowd was new. The institutionalization of sociology, advances in photographic technology, and the global spread of democratic politics at the *fin de siècle* brought the crowd into stark relief. In the early twentieth-century novel, crowds become characters. Unlike the nineteenth-century 'mob', both Le Bon and Tarde use 'crowd' and 'riot' somewhat interchangeably, noting the difference between them is not necessarily 'violence' per se but rather the threat of violence. In other words, the difference between the terms is one of political judgement rather than sociological description. Most often a crowd (*foule*) becomes a riot (*émeute*) when physical violence occurs. The same is true for Georges Sorel, whose mobilization of the *idea* of violence motivates revolutionary crowds, not riots. At the same time, Sorel notes, 'riot' is the name given to crowds by the police and the state.[8] This is certainly illustrated by the Rowlatt Report, where crowds and riots are fuzzily distinguished by their relationship to law and order.[9]

The literary crowd is also a response to contemporaneous political activity across the British Empire. In 1926, the Trade Union Congress called a general strike of 1.7 million British workers after a failed negotiation with the British

---

[5] Tarde, *On Communication and Social Influence*, pp. 136–138.
[6] Mark Bevir, *Modernism and the Social Sciences* (Cambridge: Cambridge University Press, 2017), p. 5.
[7] One of the conversations Anand and Woolf share is a discussion of how the General Strike and Indian Independence share common political concerns, a conversation Anand dubbed 'Tea and Empathy with Virginia Woolf' in his memoir/book *Conversations at Bloomsbury*. See Mulk Raj Anand, *Conversations at Bloomsbury* (London: Wildwood House, 1981), pp. 120–129.
[8] Georges Sorel, *Reflections on Violence* (Cambridge: Cambridge University Press, 1999). Sorel discusses throughout this text, but an exemplary iteration appears on pp. 61–62.
[9] Rowlatt et al., *Reports of the Sedition Committee, 1918*. Government of India: Indian Culture, https://indianculture.gov.in/reports-sedition-committee-1918, accessed 9 October 2022.

government over wage reductions. The strike lasted nine days, from 4 to 13 May. The strike was ultimately unsuccessful, but tensions were high in London throughout the spring. H.G. Wells's novel *Meanwhile* (1927) was one of the first novelistic accounts of the strike.[10] Woolf and Anand were both in London at the time, and Anand later recalled that the strike had a significant impact on his literary and political self-cultivation.[11] We might imagine Anand and Woolf watching on as men moved in lackadaisical formations through the city of London, stirring a collective effervescence that was likely contagious. Anand, recalling the strikes much later in his life, felt drawn to be a part of it.[12]

The crowd was also a fundamental anxiety of British Rule in India. In 1918, Sir Sidney Rowlatt, a civil servant in the British Raj, published his notes to support the Rowlatt Act of 1919, which sought to criminalize 'anarchical movements' in British India by way of a focus on mass political gatherings. At nearly 300 pages, the Rowlatt Report is a modernist work of colonial bureaucratic fiction in its own right. Although its tracking of anticolonial activism officially begins in 1906, the Report moves circuitously in time—from the seventeenth century to the future 1920s; from the minor mutinies of the late nineteenth century to the large-scale riots in 1910s Bengal. Rowlatt's Committee Report details crowds and their behaviour in Punjab, Bengal, and Maharashtra in 1917 and 1918. Lurid details about crowd behaviour fill the report, and in ways that prefigure Woolf's and Anand's depictions a few years later. The Rowlatt Report offers a vision of an urban crowd that is semi-autonomous and is therefore profoundly threatening to British rule, which had allegedly tasked itself with creating liberal individuals. As Chris Moffat and I have written, it might be best read alongside the great crime and spy novels of its age, like Joseph Conrad's *The Secret Agent* (1907) and G.K. Chesterton's *The Man Who Was Thursday* (1908).[13]

The Rowlatt Report was not an esoteric report by a handful of colonial bureaucrats: it revealed the logic of the British Raj, whose panic and insecurity about its reign in South Asia prevented it from discerning the difference between a 'riot' and a 'crowd'. This failure was the cause of violent atrocities committed by Raj police. In April of the same year that the Rowlatt Report was published, police in Amritsar opened fire on a peaceful gathering in Jallianwala Bagh, killing at least 500 people and injuring over 1200. But the Rowlatt Report also received an unexpected readership in South Asia: anticolonial activists and dissidents. Gandhi and his opponents often claimed ownership over the 'Indian masses' by proclaiming, counterintuitively, not their leadership over but their *identification*

---

[10] H. G. Wells, *Meanwhile (The Picture of a Lady)* (New York, NY: George H. Doran, 1927).
[11] See Mulk Raj Anand, *Apologies for Heroism* (Bombay: Kutub Popular, 1946); and Mulk Raj Anand, *Conversations at Bloomsbury*.
[12] See Anand, *Conversations at Bloomsbury*, pp. 120–129.
[13] Chris Moffat and J Daniel Elam, 'On the Form, Politics and Effects of Writing Revolution', *South Asia: The Journal of South Asian Studies* 39, no. 3 (2016): pp. 513–524.

with crowds. In 1929, the same year that Anand moved to his ashram, Gandhi was part of a national debate about who among the anticolonial activists was the *least* authoritative and therefore most adaptable to crowd politics.[14]

Anand would have inherited both of these riotous experiences. According to Anand, the first draft of *Untouchable* was written while he was a copyeditor at the Woolfs's Hogarth Press, and under the influence of James Joyce. Upon completion of the draft in London, Anand moved to M.K. Gandhi's Sabramati Ashram in India, where Gandhi allegedly urged him to rewrite the book entirely in a less Joycean and more Gandhian idiom. No 'Joycean' version exists, but Anand remained insistent about this anecdote. Although the book has been relegated to the rubrics of 'colonial social realism', it nevertheless retains some elements of the 'modernism' scholars tend to associate with Bloomsbury.[15]

To recall, briefly: *Untouchable* charts a day in the life of an untouchable boy, Bakha, as he sweeps human waste in a mid-sized north Indian city. The novel follows Bakha as he performs his daily tasks of cleaning latrines and waste. When he is not sweeping, Bakha tries to dress up in Western clothes ('farungi fashun'), play sports with other boys, and help others. He is beaten, hit, mocked, chastised, and chased away. Although Bakha is 'untouchable', he and the novel are infinitely sensing: Bakha smells, tastes, sees, hears, and *touches* everything around him. The mid-sized north Indian city is absorbed and processed entirely through his sensations (by way of free indirect discourse, and by way of an extra-diegetic narrator). At the end of the day, having finished his sweeping tasks, Bakha allows himself to be somewhat overcome by the surge of a crowd in its rush to see Gandhi.

Mrs Dalloway moves across a London milieu over the course of a single day, as the eponymous Clarissa Dalloway plans for a party she hosts in the evening. The novel moves almost seamlessly between an extra-diegetic narrator and the internal reflections of multiple characters, most of whom Clarissa meets while running errands. Although each character intensely reflects on their own experiences, they are each infinitely sensing: of others, of their social standing, and of their personal lives. The novel toggles between narration that might be called

---

[14] J. Daniel Elam, 'Commonplace Anticolonialism: Bhagat Singh's Jail Notebook and the Politics of Reading', *South Asia: The Journal of South Asian Studies* 39, no. 3 (2016): pp. 592–607.

[15] Jessica Berman and Ben Consibee Baer have suggested, in different ways, that *Untouchable* is the colonial response to James Joyce's *Ulysses* rather than *Mrs Dalloway*. Berman points out that the shared one-word titles beginning with 'u' cannot be an accident. Baer writes that *Untouchable* is national allegory where Bakha stands in for India, which he claims is the 'untouchable' colony of the British Empire. The alignment has its merits, but I am sceptical of these analyses. *Ulysses* is the colonial *Ulysses*: it is, after all, a book about Dublin written in self-imposed exile. Additionally, India was far from the untouchable colony of the British Empire: it was often considered its most prestigious holding. Finally, and most importantly, we might be wary of the claim that *Untouchable* is the belated response to *Ulysses*, which places the colonies always one step behind the metropole in literary merit. This 'modernism' reifies a particular time and place of literary production: namely, Europe of the 1920s, for which all other literary production is perpetually belated. See Jessica Berman, *Modernist Commitments* (New York, NY: Columbia University Press, 2011); Benjamin Conisbee Baer, 'Shit Writing: Mulk Raj Anand's *Untouchable*, the Image of Gandhi, and the All India Progressive Writers' Association', *Modernism/modernity* 16, no.3 (2009): pp. 575–595.

'stream-of consciousness' and 'shared consciousness', as time is measured by the collective experience of hearing Big Ben chime the hours of the day.

Mrs Dalloway progresses by moving, in a somewhat viscous fashion, between the semi-interior states of its characters—not unlike Gabriel Tarde's theories of 'imitation' and contagion.[16] Woolf focuses on a semi-permeable cast of characters who intersect either in the space of the narration, or by way of filmic-style cuts. No one's interiority is fully enclosed. Instead, the novel treats protagonists like members of a crowd: they are alone together and the individualism they possess is only produced in relationship with others. Further, Woolf throws each of the individual characters to the crowds of London, from the moment Clarissa leaves her house in search of flowers:

She stiffened a little on the kerb, waiting for Durtnall's van to pass....

For having lived in Westminster—how many years now? over twenty,—one feels even in the midst of the traffic, or waking at night, Clarissa was positive, a particular hush, or solemnity; an indescribable pause; a suspense (but that might be her heart, affected, they said, by influenza) before Big Ben strikes. There! Out it boomed. First a warning, musical; then the hour, irrevocable. The leaden circles dissolved in the air. Such fools we are, she thought, crossing Victoria Street. For Heaven only knows why one loves it so, how one sees it so, making it up, building it round one, tumbling it, creating it every moment afresh; but the veriest frumps, the most dejected of miseries sitting on doorsteps (drink their downfall) do the same; can't be dealt with, she felt positive, by Acts of Parliament for that very reason: they love life. In people's eyes, in the swing, tramp, and trudge; in the bellow and the uproar; the carriages, motor cars, omnibuses, vans, sandwich men shuffling and swinging; brass bands; barrel organs; in the triumph and the jingle and the strange high singing of some aeroplane overhead was what she loved; life; London; this moment of June.[17]

Stepping into the street, Clarissa enters into the lively chaos of 'the swing, tramp, and trudge; the bellow and the uproar', which Clarissa identifies as simply 'life'. Provocatively, the crowd of the city includes human and non-human elements of modernity: automobiles, technology, and the boisterous working classes are all present. 'Life', then, signals two things. First, it is Clarissa's treacly reaction to a pleasant June day—a conclusion which suggests the reader might stand at some critical distance from Clarissa. Second, it is Woolf's theoretically rich borrowing of biological metaphors to account for 'modernity'—that moment around 1910 where, as Woolf put it herself, 'human character changed'.[18]

---

[16] Gabriel Tarde, *On Communication and Social Influence: Selected Papers*, edited by Terry N. Clarke (Chicago, IL: Chicago University Press, 1969).
[17] Woolf, *Mrs Dalloway*, pp. 3–4.
[18] Virginia Woolf, *Mr. Bennett and Mrs. Brown* (London: Hogarth Press, 1924), p. 4.

Untouchable operates in a similar way, though it hews closer to Bakha. Employing similar filmic-style cuts, the novel weaves between Bakha and his sister, Sohini—as well as various upper-caste men whose waste Bakha is forced to sweep. Like Septimus, Bakha has an extended flashback in which he envisions the history of Indian civilization from the perspective of the waste he sweeps. Just before Gandhi arrives at the end of the novel, Bakha stumbles into a church, where his stream of consciousness weaves in and out of a prayer. In later notes on the novel, Anand wrote that *Untouchable* is like 'looking at outcaste consciousness from the side' as a way of seeking 'deeply human life' without celebrating individualism.[19]

The crowd scene that opens *Mrs Dalloway* closes *Untouchable*. The two crowd scenes share a use of promiscuous pronouns, which confuse the boundaries between animals, humans, objects, and environment. When Clarissa emerges from the cityscape, she is first a 'part of it'.[20] What is the antecedent of 'it' here, and what exactly is Clarissa's relationship to 'it'? On one hand, if 'it' is the collective sum of these people, 'it' is the crowd assemblage of which these pieces form the whole. Clarissa's 'being part of it' suggests that Clarissa has in fact given herself over to anonymous chaos—what Emile Durkheim called 'collective effervescence'.[21] On the other hand, the narration suggests Clarissa remains, somehow, removed from 'it'—she emerges, at the end of this sentence, as the individual host of a party. In short, Clarissa is simultaneously *a part* of this crowd and *apart* from this crowd.

The stakes of this are clearer in Clarissa's Indian counterpart, Bakha, whose untouchability should, according to caste norms, prevent him from being part of society at all. And yet, in the rush to see Gandhi, a new political formation emerges:

> Beyond the bowers, on the oval, was a tumult, and the thronging of the thousands who had come to worship. The eager babble of the crowd, the excited gestures, the flow of emotion, portended one thought and one thought alone in the singing crowd—Gandhi. There was a terror in this devotion, half-expressed, half-suppressed, of the panting swarms that pressed round. Bakha stopped short as he reached the pavilion end of the cricket ground. He leant by a tree. He wanted to be detached. It wasn't that he had lost grip of the emotion that had brought him swirling on the tide of the rushing stream of people. But he became aware of the fact of being a sweeper by the contrast which his dirty, khaki uniform presented to the white garments of most of the crowd. There was an insuperable barrier between himself and the crowd, the barrier of caste. He was part of a consciousness which he could share and yet not understand. He had been lifted from the

---

[19] Mulk Raj Anand, *Roots and Flowers* (Dhar-war: Karnatak University Press, 1972), p. 12.
[20] Woolf, *Mrs Dalloway*, p. 6.
[21] See Durkheim's analysis of this in Emile Durkheim, *Elementary Forms of Religious Life* (Oxford: Oxford University Press, 2008).

gutter, through the barriers of space, to partake of a life which was his, and yet not his. He was in the midst of a humanity which included him in its folds, and yet debarred him from entering into a sentient, living, quivering contact with it. Gandhi alone united him with them, in the mind, because Gandhi was in everybody's mind, including Bakha's. Gandhi might unite them really. Bakha waited for Gandhi.[22]

Here is the emergence of 'the crowd' as a character on its own terms. It is made up of people—Anand provides us a demographic list in one paragraph earlier—but it operates with one 'consciousness' and one 'life'. Like Woolf, Anand stresses the ways in which this 'consciousness' is semi-penetrable. The crowd is neither homogenous nor homogenizing. Bakha moves in and out of it, to be included in its folds and yet debarred from full 'sentient, living, quivering contact with it'. Like Clarissa, Bakha is both part and not part of a 'life'.

Anand's description of this crowd reflects the ambiguity between 'riot' and 'crowd' in the modernist imagination. Eagerness and devotion are tempered by the 'tumult' and 'terror' of the crowd. Bakha's partial inclusion in this fungible collectivity allows him to experience the event in two concurrent vocabularies. The first is built on a vision of tense excitement and contagion that is internal to the crowd as it waits for Gandhi. The second is culled from an external witnessing (and perhaps surveillance) that sees in this mass of people the implicit potential for violence and eruption. The second vocabulary, of 'tumult' and 'terror', mirrors the Rowlatt Report and the British Raj's defence of the 1919 Jallianwala Bagh massacre.

It is not a coincidence that Woolf and Anand both use the word 'life' in these passages in roughly the same sense. We might speculate that they shared a conversation about the life of crowds over tea at Bloomsbury, but it seems more likely that Anand and Woolf highlight a global conversation about the intersection of literary and sociological texts in the 1920s. This type of conjoined human and non-human 'life', and its attendant vitalist imagination, was not merely a new vision of characters's relationships to one another, but a vision for a new type of collective character altogether. Like their French sociological counterparts, Woolf and Anand focused their aesthetic vision on the 'crowd' as the site where human subjectivity could be reimagined. The crowd, no longer solely a threat, emerges in Anand's and Woolf's writing as a viable form of collectivity. 'Being part of it' or 'being in sentient, living, quivering contact with it' chafes against the confines of individualism in favour of a new form of social 'life'.

According to Le Bon and Gabriel Tarde, the 'life' of a crowd is due in large part to its physicality: 'the crowd has something animal about it, for is it not a collection of

[22] Anand, *Untouchable*, p. 138.

psychic connections produced essentially by physical contacts?'[23] In opposition to Durkheim's theory of the 'collective effervesce' of social cohesion—which would, in Tarde's account, produce a 'public' rather than a 'crowd'—the crowd and the riot might be better characterized by actual bodies sharing a space. In Tarde's exciting account, crowds behave the way they do because of

> the mutual contagion of sentiments among the assembled individuals. So long as no manifestation of impatience, foot stamping, catcalling, sound of canes or of feet is produced in a group ... each individual is impressed by the sight of his neighbours' resigned or cheerful attitude, and unconsciously reflects their gaiety or resignation. But if someone (when, as at the theatre, it can help reduce the delay) takes the initiative and becomes impatient, he is soon imitated by degrees, and the impatience of each individual is redoubled by that of the others.... They elbow each other aside, but at the same time they visibly wish to express only those sentiments which are in agreement with those of their neighbours, and in the conversations which sometimes occur between them they seek to please each other without distinction for rank or class.[24]

We can see here, once again, the forces of homogenization and anonymization working simultaneously with and against assertions of individuality. This is why a crowd is simultaneously more than and less than the sum of its individual parts. Sociology's identification of crowds and riots—and, moreover, its discernment of the unit called 'society'—captures the abstraction that a crowd necessarily is. As Perrin Selcer has written, 'Sociology revealed the individual's place in and contribution to society. In this sense, sociology was as much a reaction against the perceived atomising, standardising, objectifying, and dehistoricising effects of modernity as an instrument of modernity.'[25]

Selcer's insightful analysis aligns sociology's interests with modernism's catalysing anxieties. Nevertheless, the claim that modernity's effects include the feeling of 'dehistoricization' is overdetermined by the bold claims of Ezra Pound ('make it new') and Marshall Berman (following Marx, 'everything that is solid melts into air').[26] Modernist writers foregrounded the 'rupture' of a post-World War I world as much as they were committed to the continuation of Victorian genteel values. If the riot was the site of identification with others who are physically present, it was also the impetus for identification by way of history and genealogy.

---

[23] Tarde, *On Communication and Social Influence*, p. 278.
[24] Tarde, *On Communication and Social Influence*, p. 291.
[25] Perrin Selcer, 'Sociology', in *Modernism and the Social Sciences*, edited by Mark Bevir (Cambridge: Cambridge University Press, 2017), pp. 99–129, p. 101.
[26] Ezra Pound's 'make it new' comes from a collection of essays he published in 1934. See Pound, *Make it New* (London: Faber & Faber, 1934). Berman's *All That is Solid Melts into Air* remains an outstanding overview of the historical and philosophical concept of 'modernity'. See Marshall Berman, *All That is Solid Melts Into Air: The Experience of Modernity* (New York, NY: Penguin, 1981).

For Le Bon, the crowd bears a unique relationship to history even as it acts most riotously in the present:

> It is time in particular that prepares the opinions and beliefs of crowds, or at least the soil on which they will germinate. This is why certain ideas are realisable at one epoch and not at another. It is time that accumulates that immense detritus of beliefs and thoughts on which the ideas of a given period spring up. They do not grow at hazard and by chance; the roots of each of them strike down into a long past. When they blossom it is time that has prepared their blooming; and to arrive at a notion of their genesis it is always back in the past that it is necessary to search. They are the daughters of the past and the mothers of the future, but throughout the slaves of time.[27]

There is much to say about Le Bon's pointedly gendered analysis, combined with his insistence on horticultural metaphors. The crowd's invention of its past is maternal rather than paternal; it is assured of its empiricism even though its invented genesis is a speculative 'notion'. What we can discern in any event is that a crowd or a riot demands simultaneously physical presence and an imagined shared past.

This is evident in both *Mrs Dalloway* and *Untouchable*. What begins as description of a particular post-war moment—a morning in June 1923—suddenly dives into a history of England:

> For it was the middle of June. The War was over, except for someone like Mrs. Foxcroft at the Embassy last night eating her heart out because that nice boy was killed and now the old Manor House must go to a cousin; or Lady Bexborough who opened a bazaar, they said, with the telegram in her hand, John, her favourite, killed; but it was over; thank Heaven—over. It was June…. [A]nd she, too, loving it as she did with an absurd and faithful passion, being part of it, since her people were courtiers once in the time of the Georges, she, too, was going that very night to kindle and illuminate; to give her party.[28]

At least two pasts occur in this present: World War I, which lives on in the form of ongoing despair (even if Clarissa seems to find it somewhat unseemly); and the sixteenth century, which has given the evening's party a history and tradition (as well as a genealogical reason for Clarissa's 'being a part of it').

Before Bakha feels himself to be part of the crowd on its way to see Gandhi, he notes its somewhat antagonistic relationship to Indian history:

> He saw that the fort road was too long and too congested. Suddenly, like a stag at bay, he swerved round to a little marsh made by the overflow of a

[27] Le Bon, *The Crowd*, p. 48.
[28] Woolf, *Mrs. Dalloway*, p. 2.

municipal pipe in a corner of the golbagh, jumped the fence into the garden, much to the consternation of the sweet-peas and the pansies which grew on the edges, but wholly to the satisfaction of the crowd behind him, which, once it had got the lead, followed like sheep. The beautiful garden bowers planted by the ancient Hindu kings and since then neglected were thoroughly damaged as the mob followed behind Bakha. It was as if the crowd had determined to crush everything, however ancient or beautiful that lay in the way of their achievement of all that Gandhiji stood for. It was as if they knew, by an instinct surer than that of conscious knowledge, that the things of the old civilisation must be destroyed in order to make room for those of the new. It seemed, as if in trampling on the blades of green grass, they were deliberately, brutally trampling on a part of themselves, which they had begun to abhor, and from which they wanted to escape to Gandhi.[29]

The history of the crowd that sustains and connects Clarissa is mirrored by a crowd keen to 'destroy' and 'escape' its own history in favour of a Gandhian future. We might briefly note that Anand's selection of Indian history to-be-destroyed is a peculiar one: it is the ancient India promoted by his Hindutva contemporaries, most notably V.D. Savarkar. What Bahka imagines the crowd to be trampling, in other words, is 'six thousand years of racial and class superiority'.[30]

There have been two major lines of analyses of this final scene in *Untouchable*, in which M.K. Gandhi appears before a crowd to deliver a speech—a speech which Anand copies verbatim from an actual article in Gandhi's *Young India*. The first, mostly by scholars of British modernism, is to suggest that the interruption of an actual historical event—a speech by M.K. Gandhi—represents the unification of ethical and political commitments of the modernist cosmopolitan novel.[31] This uncomplicatedly assumes that 'Gandhi' was, either for Anand or at the time in general, as 'political' a figure in the South Asian context as he was in London. To be sure, there is no doubt that Gandhi was a *politician*, but his insistence on self-purification and spirituality, especially regarding caste, meant that in the 1930s 'politics' would have been an ill fit for the variety of Gandhianism that was both popular in general and with Anand specifically.

On the other hand, postcolonial studies and South Asian area studies scholars note, by way of the conspicuous absence of B.R. Ambedkar, that *Untouchable* perpetuates the notion that caste was a moral or religious problem rather than a problem of political disenfranchisement.[32] Although certainly Anand (and Forster,

---

[29] Anand, *Untouchable*, p. 137.
[30] Anand, *Untouchable*, p. 24. V.D. Savarkar's vision of Hindutva promoted an exclusively and xenophobic Hindu nation-state with its historical origins in ancient Hindu kingdoms. In his account modern India had been colonized by both Muslims (Mughals) and the British. See V.D. Savarkar, *Hindutva* (Nagpur: V. V. Kelkar, 1923).
[31] See Jessica Berman, *Modernist Commitments* (New York, NY: Columbia University Press, 2011).
[32] Gauri Viswanathan, *Outside the Fold* (Princeton, NJ: Princeton University Press, 1998), pp. 220–222.

in his preface) frame caste as an injustice, it is an injustice produced by 'six thousand years of racial and class superiority' and religious practice—and therefore impotently beyond the realm of political action.[33]

I think a third reading of *Untouchable* is possible that moves beyond the irreconcilable debates of 'politics' versus 'morality' that these analyses have tended to produce. This proposed reading also better situates Anand in a conversation about world literature more broadly. Far from being a writer of 'national allegory' as many scholars have claimed, Anand's writings participate in a global conversation about literature as the terrain to imagine new social and political collectivities that the emergent social sciences had attempted to explicate.[34] This global discussion had little regard for the distinctions between social scientific writing and literary writing—both were invested in experimentation and the imaginative heralding of new social forms.

Gauri Viswanathan has written about the final scene in *Untouchable* to critique Anand's reliance on M.K. Gandhi as the key figure of Indian unity.[35] The narrator's claim, 'Gandhi might unite them really', in her account, elides contemporaneous anti-caste movements, with which a book about an untouchable should otherwise be sympathetic. In Viswanathan's reading, there are two characters in this final scene: Bakha and Gandhi (who delivers a lecture taken verbatim from Gandhi's writings). In my reading, there are three: Bakha, Gandhi, and the crowd. At the moment of its publication, it seems likely that Anand and his interlocutors would have conceived of the crowd as a 'life' of its own and fully deserving of character status. It is Bakha, not Gandhi, who moves in and out of its 'folds', calling into question Bakha's 'untouchability'. Although *Untouchable* is certainly written under Gandhi's influence, the Gandhi that shows up at the end of the novel sits on a platform above the crowd of which Bakha is a part. In short, the Gandhi in *Untouchable* is actually unable to be 'a part' of the 'life' of the crowd. *Untouchable* manages to celebrate and critique Gandhi at once, and on Gandhi's own terms.[36]

Viswanathan is not incorrect to point out the glaring absence of Ambedkar in Anand's book. *Untouchable* remains Anand's most famous work not simply because it came packaged with a glowing preface by E.M. Forster, but also because it faced an almost immediate backlash in India, where Dalits ('untouchables') burned the book in protest. In part, this backlash was because Anand's portrayal of caste was necessarily external to the experiences of Dalits themselves. But most incriminating is that the book is surprisingly devoid of contemporaneous Dalit activism, which was experiencing a recrudescence under the leadership of Dalit

---

[33] Anand, *Untouchable*, p. 16.
[34] See Ulka Anjaria (editor), *A History of the Indian Novel in English* (Cambridge: Cambridge University Press, 2015).
[35] Viswanathan, *Outside the Fold*, pp. 220–222.
[36] For an account of these debates, especially between Gandhi, Bhagat Singh, and BR Ambedkar, see J. Daniel Elam, *World Literature for the Wretched of the Earth* (Fordham: Fordham University Press, 2020).

leader B.R. Ambedkar, whose popularity in the 1930s rivalled Gandhi's but who remains suspiciously absent in the text, as well as in Anand's subsequent novels, like *Coolie* (1936), which are also about low-caste labour.[37]

If, as according to legend, the book was indeed written under Gandhi's supervision at Sabramati Ashram, it is unsurprising that the book offers only a condescending sympathy with Dalits. More frustratingly, it is Gandhi, rather than Ambedkar, who appears at the end of the novel to encourage untouchables to morally 'purify themselves' (rather than Ambedkar's more demanding call to abolish caste altogether). Dalits have correctly criticized Gandhi for his condescending or apathetic views on caste. Anand is slightly critical of Gandhi's message, and the novel ends on a considerably more ambivalent note than a celebration of Gandhian politics. Although Ambedkar himself is notably and troublingly absent in *Untouchable*, Ambedkar's critical contributions to anti-caste sociological thought permeates Anand's prose.

It was Ambedkar, not Gandhi, who theorized the partial consciousness produced by caste hierarchy. By the 1930s, Ambedkar had received advanced degrees in law and sociology and had returned to India to be one of Gandhi's fiercest opponents. In 1932, Ambedkar and Gandhi famously disagreed about how to eradicate caste. Ambedkar's most famous work, *Annihilation of Caste*, was published the same year that Anand published *Untouchable*. Bakha's experience of the crowd, in fact, hews closer to Ambedkar's damning diagnosis of Hindu society than it does to Gandhi's vision for unity under the rubrics of *hind swaraj*. According to Ambedkar,

> Hindu Society as such does not exist. It is only a collection of castes. Each caste is conscious of its existence.... There is an utter lack among the Hindus of what the sociologists call 'consciousness of kind'. There is no Hindu consciousness of kind. In every Hindu the consciousness that exists is the consciousness of his caste. That is the reason why the Hindus cannot be said to form a society or a nation.[38]

Ambedkar borrows the phrase 'consciousness of kind' from sociologist Franklin Henry Giddings. For Giddings, 'consciousness of kind' drew on Adam Smith's concept of the 'sympathetic' 'impartial spectator' to describe how a heterogeneous social unit coheres.[39] In other words, a 'society' is formed when multiple consciousnesses experience the same thing together. Caste, in, contrast, isolates

---

[37] Mulk Raj Anand, *Coolie* (London: Hutchison, 1947).
[38] B.R. Ambedkar, *Collected Writings of B. R. Ambedkar*, vol. 71 (Bombay: Education Department, Government of Maharashtra, 1979), p. 50.
[39] See Franklin Henry Giddings, *Studies in the Theory of Human Society* (New York, NY: Macmillan, 1922).

consciousness and therefore 'prevents common activity; and by preventing common activity, it has prevented the Hindus from becoming a society with a unified life and a consciousness of its own being.'[40] By isolating consciousness *within* caste identity, Hinduism was fundamentally 'antisocial' in spirit. Hinduism prevented the formation of sympathy, and therefore society, necessary for humanist egalitarianism.[41]

This is the tension of 'life' at the core of the crowd scene at the end of *Untouchable*: Bakha moves in and out of a shared consciousness with other Indians. His attempt to share 'life' with other Indians cannot be sustained because caste 'debarrs' sympathy, connectedness, and affiliation:

> There was an insuperable barrier between himself and the crowd, the barrier of caste. He was part of a consciousness which he could share and yet not understand. He had been lifted from the gutter, through the barriers of space, to partake of a life which was his, and yet not his. He was in the midst of a humanity which included him in its folds, and yet debarred him from entering into a sentient, living, quivering contact with it.[42]

Anand's language here—the 'insuperable barrier . . . of caste'; a 'consciousness' which was only partially available across caste hierarchy; and a humanity which 'debars' Bakha from a sustained 'sentient, living, quivering contact with it'—strays away from a Gandhian idiom and closer towards Ambedkar's sociological analysis of caste. To write the riot in the context of Hinduism—and under the conjoined influence of Gandhi and Ambedkar—is to imagine an impossible unity; Anand leaves it to Bakha to experience this tension as he waits for the Mahatma.

One of his last works, *Conversations at Bloomsbury*, chronicles Anand's time in London with the modernist milieu of T.S. Eliot, E.M. Forster, Leonard Woolf, Aldous Huxley, and Ezra Pound—and, of course, Virginia Woolf. The book situates Anand as a member of the global modernist conversation at its most fervent moment rather than a bystander and mimic of its style. Each chapter recalls a

---

[40] B.R. Ambedkar, *Collected Writings of B. R. Ambedkar*, vol. 17 (Bombay: Education Department, Government of Maharashtra, 1979), p. 51.

[41] In a conversation between Ambedkar and Anand in 1950, Anand admits to having left (at least somewhat) the Gandhian fold:

ANAND: This may not be possible without upturnings like the 1789 revolution in France.
AMBEDKAR: Strange to hear this from you! I thought that by making Gandhi the liberator of Untouchables in your novel, you have been converted to non-violence.
ANAND: I could not live up to the Mahatma's ideal. We had to face Hitler and Mussolini. I went to Spain and joined the International Brigade. Though I fainted at the sight of blood in a clinic and was asked to opt out.... But one had to take sides in the second world war. A poet called the so-called war for freedom of the democracies against fascism, the fight for a 'half lie' against a 'big lie.'

See B.R. Ambedkar, *Collected Writings of B. R. Ambedkar*, vol. 17, p. 381.

[42] Anand, *Untouchable*, pp. 137–138.

vignette of Anand's time in London, very rarely interrupted by a critical assessment of his British colleagues. Snehal Shingavi and Charlotte Nunes have argued that there were 'no conversations at Bloomsbury' and argued that Anand's time in London was mostly spent as a lackey and copyeditor for Hogarth Press rather than a proper colleague of the Bloomsbury elite.[43] Although Anand recalls a lingering afternoon of tea with Woolf, there is no corresponding corroboration from her. Amardeep Singh dismisses Forster's preface of *Untouchable* as condescending and patronising. For Singh, Forster's preface is too laudatory to be sincere, and Forster's attempt to 'translate' the job of an untouchable into a British idiom was clunky at best.[44] There is no doubt the relationships between white British Bloomsbury members and Anand were unequal, as they were fundamentally built on imperial domination. But it seems far too simple to dismiss Anand's memoirs as either self-aggrandizing or aspirational. The celebrity preface was very much *en vogue*, and Forster's support of Anand continued into the 1950s as part of Forster's broader attempt to raise awareness of Commonwealth authors.[45]

In addition to his novels and editorial work for *Marg*, Anand was a prolific essayist and lecturer, as well as an art critic. The most common theme in his non-fiction writings concerns the possibilities of Indian aesthetic form and the importance of 'humanism', a term he spent much of his life defining through examples from his own work, as well as biographical sketches of Indian politicians. In an essay entitled *Prolegomena to a New Humanism*, dedicated to Forster, whose epigraph to *Howards End*—'Only connect'—serves as the essay's inspiration, Anand defines 'humanism' as a 'continuous feeling' made of 'ethical equality of all men [sic]', which is only possible through the eradication of individualism and any notion that humans possess an interiority unshaped by their interaction with others. Connection, like collective effervescence, was a form of 'togetherness, as the attempt by men to resolve, in common with other men . . . a need for brotherliness, for tenderness among men'.[46]

Anand's humanism has ties to similar writings by other contemporaneous thinkers and was similarly political in its orientation. 'Humanism', in Anand's use, referred not simply to the collectivity of urban space—which, following Ambedkar, produced a 'contagiousness' that would eventually lead to the eradication

---

[43] Snehal Shingavi and Charlotte Nunes, 'Bloomsbury Conversations that Didn't Happen: Indian Writing Between British Modernism and Anti-Colonialism', in *Futility and Anarchy? British Literature in Transition, 1920–1940*, edited by Charles Ferrall and Dougal McNeill (London: Cambridge University Press 2018), pp. 199–216.

[44] Amardeep Singh, 'The Lifting and the Lifted: Prefaces to Colonial Modernist Texts', *Wasafiri* 21, no. 1 (2006): pp. 1–9.

[45] For a discussion of Forster as well as the broader global modernist moment, see Peter Kalliney, *Commonwealth of Letters* (Oxford: Oxford University Press, 2013).

[46] Mulk Raj Anand, *Prolegomena to a New Humanism* (Bombay: Nalanda publications, 1940), p. 111.

of caste—but to solidarity among colonized people across the world. It was literature, above all else, that enabled the global contagion of humanism to take hold. With the riot as a focus of this modernist debate, we can see these concerns in stark relief, bringing us closer to the aesthetic and political vibrancy of the early twentieth century.

6
Riotous Nations

Time and the Short Story of Partition

Rashmi Varma

The Partition of the Indian sub-continent into India and Pakistan in 1947 on the eve of their independence from British colonial rule has come to be figured as the founding wound of the two nation states in the political, literary, and cultural imagination of South Asia. In the violence that preceded and accompanied the formation of borders between India and Pakistan, more than ten million people were displaced, more than a million perished, and tens of thousands of women were abducted as families, communities, and neighbourhoods were torn asunder. The announcement of the formation of Pakistan as a separate homeland for the subcontinent's Muslims triggered nationalist feelings based on religious affiliation on both sides of the border.[1] Friends turned against friends, neighbours against neighbours, and families and communities were split apart. Houses were set on fire, businesses looted and destroyed, as bodies were raped, dismembered, burnt, found dead in wells, and piled on to trains transporting millions of refugees across the divide. While for the longest time the two governments maintained studied silence about the Partition's lacerating wound, historians and writers sought to understand and explain this watershed moment that seemed beyond comprehension and indeed beyond representation.[2] The violence had torn apart any sense of universality and common humanity.

Much of the violence took place in the form of riots that broke out often randomly but persistently throughout the run-up to the Partition that came into effect on the eve of independence on 14–15 August 1947. The riots were typically carried out by marauding mobs comprising strangers but also of groups of neighbours and friends seeking to purify the nation of the 'other'. Bodily markers of identity such as the circumcised penis, the beard, the turban, the sacred thread, and the veil were transformed into signs of an otherness that needed to be exterminated even

---

[1] See Sumit Sarkar, *Modern India: 1885–1947* (Macmillan, 1983), pp. 432–438.
[2] Tarun Saint has written of how 'in the absence of widespread societal engagement that might have facilitated processes of working through memories of traumatic occurrences, literary writings at times became a mode of surrogate testimony'. See Tarun K. Saint, *Witnessing Partition: Memory, History Fiction*, 2nd edition (Abingdon: Routledge, 2017), p. 82.

as the looting and destruction of property exposed the economic inequalities that underpinned some of the violence.

Theorists of riots have typically understood them as spontaneous and lacking central command. Riots in themselves are different from pogroms that are linked to projects of genocide. However, riots as small-scale, localized acts of violence can also be understood as subsets of pogroms, or as building blocks of large-scale and more orchestrated and planned violence. In post-independence India, riots have been a recurring form of the conduct of politics, engineered by dominant communities, political parties and vested property and capital interests to exercise power over social groups, sometimes in the name of avenging a historical wrong or as a form of social and economic cleansing and profit.

In a moving remembrance of the violence during the time of the Partition, the literary critic Alok Bhalla writes:

> As with almost every one of my generation, my childhood consciousness was scarred by the cruelties I witnessed during the riots of 1947–48 and the lamentations that I heard. Indeed, there was hardly a family which survived those years without feeling perpetually threatened by the repulsive and the ruthless; there was hardly anyone who didn't hide in some dark corner for safety as mobs outside, armed with thirst spears and the names of gods, killed each other for small and pathetic gain. Now when I look back upon those years, I realise that they carried grim forewarnings about the world that I was to grow up in—a world in which thugs, chanting a few lines of tribal lore gathered from some rag and bone shop of history, and screaming religious or racial invectives, are always ready to expel, plunder, rape or exterminate with impunity.[3]

This passage is significant for the way Bhalla displaces the agency of violence on to some anonymous 'thugs', implying that the perpetrators of violence are those who are outside the norms of civility and of society itself.

At the same time, Bhalla goes on in the passages that follow to stress the importance of grasping the 'ordinariness' of the ways in which violence was inflicted. This, he argues, is 'necessary both as evidence and as boundaries against the phantasmagoric' experience that pushes against any apprehension of reality during the time of the riot.[4] The violence engendered by the riot is thus bracketed away from reality as 'phantasmagoric' even as it infiltrates everyday forms of being and belonging. Partition narratives, in this view, provide accounts of 'everyday selves of people and their acts in profane time'.[5] Here time, which is ordinary and grasped

---

[3] Alok Bhalla, 'Memory, History and Fictional Representations of the Partition', *Economic and Political Weekly* 34, no. 44 (1999): pp. 3119–3129.
[4] Bhalla, 'Memory, History and Fictional Representations of the Partition', p. 3119.
[5] Bhalla, 'Memory, History and Fictional Representations of the Partition', p. 3120.

in terms of what Walter Benjamin theorized as the empty homogeneous time of the nation, is punctured by the 'profane'.[6]

The search for causality seems futile from the outset. Bhalla reads Partition stories only to confirm that 'each of the novels and stories finds the separation and the massacres so completely without historical or social reason' that all they can do is to record that 'the place they called "home" or "basti" was reduced to rubble, and that the memories of a society with collective rites and traditions, songs and legends, names of birds and trees, were tinged forever with the acrid smell of smoke and blood'.[7] Here, the story and the riot merge as forms that defy comprehensibility as 'the emotional and ethical map of our times' is now marked with 'indelible lines of screams, ash, smoke and mockery' or 'shocked silence'. In this, the dead are merely nameless victims, too many to be counted, serving as fodder for statistical accounting and often missing even there.

In this chapter I want to focus on what was undoubtedly the most spectacular aspect of the Partition narratives from South Asia. This is the figure of the riot through which all recognizable forms of storytelling about a shared past, community, belonging, and selfhood are split apart. On the one hand, the riot has the distinctive temporality of a flicker or a flash along the continuum of history. As such, it evades narrativization and can only be represented in the aftermath via images of ruin, loss, madness, and destruction—a burnt house, an abandoned village, a dismembered body, a lost shoe, an upturned cart, a raped woman. On the other hand, the flashing images recur as shattered memories that can be sutured together and healed through narrative. If violence is conceived as a total phenomenon that leaves nothing untouched, the riot appears as a fragment. Its temporal structure intimates to us that something terrible has happened to which there is no plot, no rational chronology or sequence. Its traces in the aftermath breach the borders between times past, present, and future. The riot then is both a signifier of the founding violence of the nation that can only be remembered in fragments and of the traces that are resistant to erasure, as it is a spectre that haunts the limits of borders, of the self and community, of time and space, and of representation. Thus, if the figure of the riot evades representation, the broken histories left in its wake find form in the short story that in turn focalizes the problem of narrative.

'An Unwritten Epic' is a story that powerfully narrativizes the problematic of writing about Partition violence as a displacing force. The Urdu writer Intizar Hussain interweaves the story of the village of Qadirpur in the central province and that of a group of wrestlers who strive to protect the village from attack by the neighbouring Hindu jats, with the writer's diary entries reflecting his inability to

---

[6] Walter Benjamin, 'Theses on the Philosophy of History', in Hannah Arendt (ed.), *Illuminations*, translated by Harry Zohn (New York, NY: Schocken Books, 1968).

[7] Bhalla, 'Memory, History and Fictional Representations of the Partition', p. 3121.

write the story as a novel.[8] All he can do is to present it as 'an unwritten epic' that can ironically only be told as a short story. What at first seems to the protagonist Pichwa as a sport ('the storm of communal riots') in which he can show his skills of using the club as a weapon of defence meets with a sense of deflation as news of the formation of Pakistan comes in: 'Certainly Pichwa was glad that the battle had been won, but he was also grieved that it was not his blood that helped buy this empire' (306). As Qadirpur starts emptying out with many Muslims leaving for Pakistan, Pichwa's fate hangs in balance. But it is at this point that Hussain's diary entry appears (3 April 1950) where he talks about the ruination of his story, for at first the

> character of Pichwa could not be contained in a short story. Justice could only be done to him in a full-length novel. Moreover, I thought, no epic poem has yet been written on riots. Now, I am no poet—so let me try writing a prose epic. And then, this is not the time for writing great poetry. Now, when we have no great epic heroes, I am surely very fortunate to have a character like Pichwa fall right into my lap. But how could I have known then that after the first riot was over, another would break out and Pichwa would come to Pakistan?[9]

The short story here is distinctively understood as a story without heroes. It becomes the quintessential form for the non-heroic, for Pichwa, who had 'confronted the riot with his own body', far from staying his ground in Qadirpur, gives it up and goes to Pakistan looking for work and survival. As Hussain muses: 'Pichwa and I are both unlucky. He was not fortunate enough to become the hero of an epic, and I am fated to treat the lives of insignificant people in worthless two-penny stories.'[10] Thus, in the face of the ruination of his novel, Hussain glimpses a truth about the short story and Pichwa. He writes: 'Pichwa wasn't a great general or a splendid and glorious king; nevertheless, he had a certain dignity and greatness. And I never said my novel had to be called a *Shahnama*. An epic can also be called *Jumhurnama*.'[11] In the next diary entry on 7 April 1950, the author muses that 'real life' had 'stolen' the hero of his epic from him.[12] In Pakistan, Pichwa is begging for food and shelter and as a common person displaced by the riots, he is 'a picture of failure'.[13] The earth of Qadirpur, 'reddened' with the blood of its heroes, does not render Pichwa akin to the hero of any *Mahabharata*, that great Indian epic about war and kinship. In the end, the author decides he must give up literature itself and

---

[8] Intizar Hussain, 'An Unwritten Epic', in Mushirul Hasan (ed.), *Inventing Boundaries: Gender, Politics and the Partition of India* (Oxford: Oxford University Press, 2000), pp. 300–317.
[9] Hussain, 'An Unwritten Epic', p. 308.
[10] Hussain, 'An Unwritten Epic', p. 308.
[11] Hussain, 'An Unwritten Epic', p. 308. *Shahnama* is the term for an epic centred around a king. *Jumhurnama* would then be an epic about common people.
[12] Hussain, 'An Unwritten Epic', p. 309.
[13] Hussain, 'An Unwritten Epic', p. 311.

focus on the practicalities of survival, becoming a mill owner in the new country of Pakistan.

Interestingly, however, the scholarship on the literature of the Partition in South Asia has largely evaded the epistemological and narratological dimensions of the riot itself, even as it has focused on the large-scale catastrophic violence of the Partition and its literary registers. Notwithstanding Muhammad Umar Memon's biting dismissal of Urdu literature on the Partition as not constituting 'lasting and enduring literature'.[14] I do take up a question that he initiates about why rioting and violence came to overwhelm the representation of the totality of experience in Partition narratives. Memon offers a tentative response, one that is based on what he acknowledges as 'the near-universal impact of the rioting itself'.[15] He writes:

> There was hardly a Muslim family that had not lost one member or more in the process of migration, or had not at least been affected in some way by the incident. The rioting had totally seized the minds of people, its memory haunted them and kept them tormented, even after they had made it to the safety of the promised land. Thus the fiction that emerged during and soon after the heat and chaos of the Partition presents little more than variations on the all-pervasive theme of communal violence.[16]

But Memon finds this explanation 'neither compelling nor sufficient'.[17] In fact, he goes on to quote, approvingly, the well-known Urdu critic Muhammad Hasan Askari, who he says 'went so far as to declare—that the rioting cannot become the subject of true literature'.[18] For Memon the obsessive focus on representing the riot revealed the limits of creative imagination on the part of writers. Memon's critique, however, still leaves the riot itself untheorized, in the ways in which its structuring role within the historical unfolding of the event of the Partition remains submerged and invisible.

In attempting to fill that gap, this chapter focuses on the short story form that emerged as one of the most significant sites for representing the Partition in which the riot was a key form of violence. If the riot in South Asia is typically understood as a small-scale, localized outbreak of irrational violence and is disaggregated from the largescale violence of pogroms and genocides, the short story is often read as a fragment of the novel and has typically been considered a minor form within literary studies in general. In fact, critics like Awadalla and March-Russell argue

---

[14] Muhammad Umar Memon, 'Partition Literature: A Study of Intiẓār Ḥusain', in *Modern Asian Studies* 14, no. 3 (1980): pp. 377–410, p. 379.
[15] Menon, 'Partition Literature', p. 380.
[16] Menon, 'Partition Literature', p. 380.
[17] Menon, 'Partition Literature', p. 380.
[18] Memon provides this citation: 'As quoted in Mumtaz Shirifi, "Pakistan adab ke char sal," in her *Mi'yar* (Lahore: Naya Idarah, 1963), p. 171'. Menon, 'Partition Literature', p. 381.

that the 'emergence' of the postcolonial short story is closely linked to its form 'as an expressive medium for themes of fragmentation, displacement, diaspora and identity'.[19] They go on to read the postcolonial short story as minor literature.[20] In the ways in which events are distilled and situation is made more central than plot and character, the short story becomes the medium through which minor events and characters are given voice, assuming the status of a dissenting form. But since both the riot and the short story involve disorientation and fragmentation of time and space in how they are experienced and read, in this chapter I suggest that the short story is better able to narrate the episodic and spectacular nature of the riot, while also being committed to narrating a sliver or fragment of reality and everyday life through which the whole must be apprehended.[21] Lukacs's theorization that the short story 'sees absurdity in all its undisguised and unadorned nakedness' and thereby gives it 'the consecration of form', such that in the short story 'meaninglessness as *meaninglessness* becomes form, it becomes eternal because it is affirmed, transcended and redeemed by form' thus provides a crucial insight for analysing the work that the Partition short story does.[22] Translating the absurdity and meaninglessness of the riot into the short story thus becomes a way of representing that which seems unrepresentable.

In his essay 'The Story-Teller', Benjamin relates the short story to the demise of oral storytelling and community in the wake of bureaucratic and technological organization of society that accompanied the industrial revolution.[23] Like the novel that is intimately linked to modernity, the short story too testifies to the emergence of the bourgeois individual living through secular, industrial time. While some critics have pointed out that this template is not easily transferable to situations in the colonized and postcolonial worlds, others have sought to link the short story to traditional forms such as the folk tale or the sketch. Thus, far from extinguishing the oral tradition, it is seen as surviving in the postcolonial short story. Pointing to the salience of the short story in the Arab and third world in general, Sabry Hafez discusses the paradox that while 'the short story has been marginalized in most advanced western cultures', in the Arab world as also in 'other developing and semi-developed countries such as India, South Africa and

---

[19] Maggie Awadalla and Paul March-Russell, editors, *The Postcolonial Short Story: Contemporary Essays* (London: Palgrave, 2012), p. 3.
[20] Awadalla and March-Russell, *The Postcolonial Short Story*, p. 6.
[21] In this I lean on the work of Lukács who interpreted the short story as a 'minor epic form' in that it 'singles out a fragment from the immeasurable infinity of the events of life'. Georg Lukács, *The Theory of the Novel* (1914), Georg Lukács Archive, https://www.marxists.org/archive/lukacs/works/theory-novel/ch02.htm, accessed 10 October 2022.
[22] Lukács, *The Theory of the Novel*.
[23] Benjamin, 'The Storyteller: Reflections on the Work of Nikolai Leskov', *Illuminations*, pp. 83–110.

Yugoslavia', the short story has emerged as 'the most popular and arguably the most significant literary medium'.[24]

In what follows, I seek to both reflect further on the formal aspects of the short story form and to provide a reading of the riot as a dialectical figure embodying and condensing many of the contradictions set loose by the tumultuous events of the Partition—such as that between totality and the fragment, community and nation, silence and speech, and between the empty homogeneous time of the nation and the 'profane' time of revolutionary eruption.

Although there have been many great novels on the Partition, short stories have arguably been the distinctive form generated by that catastrophic event mainly because it is in the short stories Sa'adat Hasan Manto, Kamleshwar, Krishan Chander, Ismat Chugtai, and others that we find the sharpest, most condensed registration of the disorientation and fragmentation of the Partition.[25] Alex Padamsee goes as far as to argue that the collective violence of the Partition found in the short story 'its first fully self-reflexive form'.[26] In particular, he focuses on the Urdu short story that he argues 'more than any other literary genre in the Indian subcontinent' was 'called on to supply the missing words in the reconstruction of the effects of Partition'.[27] Saint also points to how writers of the Progressive Writers Movement such as Sajjad Zaheer, Rashid Jahan, and Ismat Chughtai 'reinvented the Urdu *afsana* or short story form in the 1930s and 1940s while negotiating the pressures of colonial modernity and processes of internal reform'.[28] Urdu was the language of mediation across religious and communal divides that evaded, as Aijaz Ahmad has argued, the very logic of borders.[29] Padamsee, also contends that because Urdu writers came from a wide cross-section of society and regions in the north,

---

[24] Sabry Hafez, *The Quest for Identities: The Development of the Modern Arabic Short Story* (London: Safi, 2008), p. 270.

[25] Many of the short stories on Partition have been translated and collected in anthologies. These include Ramesh Mathur and Mahendra Kulasrestha (eds), *Writings on India's Partition* (Calcutta: Simant Publications, 1976); Alok Bhalla (ed.), *Stories about the Partition of India*, 3 vols (Delhi: Indus, Harper Collins 1994); Saros Cowasjee and K.S. Duggal (eds), *Orphans of the Storm: Stories on the Partition of India* (New Delhi: UBS Publishers, 1995); Muhammad Umar Memon (ed.), *An Epic Unwritten: The Penguin Book of Partition Stories* (New Delhi: Penguin Books India, 1999); Tarun K. Saint and Ravikant (eds), *Translating Partition: Essays, Stories, Criticism* (New Delhi: Katha, 2001).

[26] Alex Padamsee, '"Times Are Different Now": The Ends of Partition in the Contemporary Urdu Short Story', in Paul March-Russell and Maggie Awadalla (eds), *The Postcolonial Short Story: Contemporary Essays* (London: Palgrave Macmillan, 2012), pp. 15–32, p. 16.

[27] Padamsee, '"Times Are Different Now"', p. 17. Urdu is a language written in the Arabic script but shares vocabulary and grammatical structure with Hindi. It is spoken in northern India and Pakistan. Although associated with Muslim culture, Urdu is widely spoken by Hindus and Muslims alike. Alok Rai has pointed out that the continuation of a shared language was extinguished by the Partition. See Alok Rai, *Hindi Nationalism* (Hyderabad: Orient Longman, 2001).

[28] Saint, *Witnessing Partition*, p. 171. The Progressive Writers Association that was the spirit behind the Progressive Writers movement was formed in 1935 to bring together anti-colonial, anti-fascist writers from the Left writing in English and other Indian languages.

[29] Aijaz Ahmad, *Lineages of the Present: Ideology and Politics in Contemporary South Asia* (London: Verso, 2002), p. 104.

many could be thought of as representing a microcosm of Indian society.[30] He has pointed out that 'in problematizing the form of the Partition story', writers in Urdu 'anticipated the later emergence in trauma studies on the importance of narrative and indeed its very possibility'. They did so by 'attempting to reflect, work through and understand the elusive effects of collective violence' (2012: 16).[31] The Urdu short story, then, in addition to attending to the trauma of the unspeakable and the unspoken, also did the work of linking Partition violence to the question of literary form to negate 'complicity with the violent order'.[32]

Aamir Mufti underscores Urdu's uniqueness in the valorization of 'the short story as the primary genre of narrative fiction', especially in the time around Partition but also afterwards, in a way that definitively reverses the typical 'hierarchical relationship of novel to short story'.[33] In this 'foregrounding of the short story at the cost of the novel', Mufti sees the articulation, in aesthetic terms, of the 'ambivalent relationship of Urdu literary culture to the discourse of Indian nationhood' that results in a 'formal ambiguity'.[34] In Mufti's view, in turning to 'a "minor" epic form', Urdu helps jettison the '"major" claims of nationhood as the exclusive way of being in the world'.[35] He thus links the short story to the phenomenon of 'exile' in the ways in which it ends up 'resisting precisely the resolutions the Partition attempted to implement', which contrasts with the novel as the cultural form of national belonging.[36]

But Urdu was not the only linguistic medium through which Partition violence was recorded and remembered. Critics like Alok Rai have assessed the ways in which progressive Hindi literature took up the question of Partition violence.[37] In a study of the short stories that appeared in the legendary Hindi literary magazine *Hans* (1933–1952) in the years 1947–1948, that is in the immediate context of independence and the Partition, Rai seeks to locate writers' 'contemporary consciousness' (352) and the 'literary struggle for social justice' (361) in which an abstract sense of hope generated by independence is brutally extinguished in the face of the riots that erupted.[38] While aesthetically a mixed bag, Rai contends that the stories tried to 'draw attention to, give voice to, the disadvantaged and neglected groups, the traditionally distanced and obscured millions'.[39] In fact, he

---

[30] Alex Padamsee, 'Uncertain Partitions', *Wasafiri* 23, no. 1 (2008): pp. 1–5.
[31] See also Saint, *Witnessing Partition*, p. 171.
[32] Padamsee, '"Times Are Different Now"', p. 17.
[33] Aamir R. Mufti, *Enlightenment in the Colony* (Princeton, NJ: Princeton University Press, 2007), p. 182.
[34] Mufti, *Enlightenment in the Colony*, p. 183.
[35] Mufti, *Enlightenment in the Colony*, p. 183.
[36] Mufti, *Enlightenment in the Colony*, p. 208.
[37] Alok Rai, 'The Trauma of Independence: Some Aspects of Progressive Hindi Literature 1945-7', in Mushirul Hasan (ed.), *Inventing Boundaries: Gender, Politics and the Partition of India* (New Delhi and Oxford: Oxford University Press, 2000), pp. 351–370.
[38] Rai, 'The Trauma of Independence', pp. 352, 361.
[39] Rai, 'The Trauma of Independence', p. 362.

writes that 'The orgy of communal violence unleashed by the partition' accompanied by 'the enforced regression of national politics to a brutal, primitive level' led to a loss of 'the feeling of centrality' among writers. The riots not only tore apart the fabric of community and nation and challenged available frameworks of political understanding, they manifested themselves as 'a problem of aesthetic representation'.[40] Before the 'holocaust' of the Partition, Rai argues that communalism was seen as a mystification brought about by 'malign colonial forces' as also 'a rationalization of comprehensible forms of economic conflict'.[41] But this set of 'enlightened explanations' suffered a blow 'in the face of a monstrous upsurge of mass violence', in whose wake 'one is left only with the horror—and the incomprehensibility of this horror'.[42]

However, even as the corpus of short stories on the Partition reflects attempts to foreground voices, situations and events left in the margins of national history, the limits of Urdu and Hindi progressive literature's focus on shock has led to a critical consensus that Partition stories, especially those written in the immediate aftermath of the violence, were more interested in recording the horror than in reflecting on questions of literary form.[43] In an essay from 1980, Memon criticizes the excessive focus on riots in the literature that neglected both a historico-ethical reckoning with the violence and a larger understanding of its causes and effects on individual subjects and communities.[44] In a similar vein, Alok Bhalla reads stories in Hindi, Urdu, and Punjabi by Sa'adat Hasan Manto, Kamleshwar, Krishan Chander, Khwaja Ahmad Abbas, Kartar Singh Duggal, Sant Singh Sikhon, Kulwant Singh Virk, and others as 'marked by a sense of rage and helplessness'.[45] These are, he argues, 'terrifying chronicles of the damned which locate themselves in the middle of madness and crime', documenting what seemed to be 'an endless and repeated cycle of random and capricious violence in which anyone can become a beast and everyone can be destroyed'. In this, there is a veritable refusal of any historical explanation, for to do so, the writers seem to think, may end up rationalizing the violence as 'political necessity for the suffering'.[46] The immediacy of recording the riot in the short story also creates an aesthetic disorientation. As Rai suggests, many short stories constituted a 'pornography of violence' that was nothing but a symptom of 'a breakdown of imagination'.[47] Along similar lines, Aijaz Ahmad has commented that Partition fiction seemed to be driven by the

---

[40] Rai, 'The Trauma of Independence', p. 364.
[41] Rai, 'The Trauma of Independence', p. 364.
[42] Rai, 'The Trauma of Independence', p. 365.
[43] See Tarun K. Saint and Ravikant (eds), *Translating Partition* (New Delhi: Katha, 2001). In their Introduction to the anthology of short stories, they claim that the collection brings together writings that move 'beyond simply attempting to record what was incomprehensible' (xi).
[44] Muhammad Umar Memon, 'Partition Literature: A Study of Intiẓār Ḥusain'.
[45] Bhalla, 'Memory, History and Fictional Representations of the Partition', p. 3123.
[46] Bhalla, 'Memory, History and Fictional Representations of the Partition', p. 3123.
[47] Rai, 'The Trauma of Independence, pp. 366–367. Rai specifically calls out Kamleshwar's 'Kitne Pakistan', Krishan Chander's 'Hum Vahshi Hain'/We Are Savages (1948), Agyeya's, 'Sharanarthi'/The

realization that 'as if what had disappeared needed now to be retrieved by transcription, and as if the act of writing itself may perhaps exorcise the ghostly memories of what had been seen far too vividly, suffered much too viscerally'.[48]

In a critical reappraisal of such judgements that questioned the literary merits of the Partition short story that aimed to narrativize the inchoate violence of the riot, Saint turns to the concept of 'fictive' testimony, arguing that many stories attempted to challenge 'the regime of melancholic recollection, allowing for the possibility of critical witnessing'.[49] Further broadening out the criticisms, in his review essay on Partition literature, Jason Francisco writes of the three thematic areas that emerge within it: 'rupture, protest, and repair'.[50] Amplifying this overview, Francisco writes:

> Stories of rupture involve a basic confusion, a groping for sense and sanity amid personal, social and sometimes existential loss. Stories of protest grow fundamentally from anger, and decry human savagery, the vitiation of values, the betrayal of social contract. Stories of repair, finally, remind us of the sparks of ethical conscience that dwell in the human soul, even in the most degraded of times, and of the healing power of positive memory.[51]

Through such a reading, Francisco acknowledges the co-presence of these themes in many stories and opens up space for Partition stories on riots and communal violence to be read beyond and in excess of the straitjacket of rupture around which a critical consensus has grown.

In what follows, I read a small and non-representative selection of stories from the Partition and its aftermath. The broad formal modality that connects these narratives is the way in which the figure of the riot is represented allegorically. This allows the stories to perform a double-move—to both reflect on the immediacy and spectacular nature of the riot and to connect that to states of loss of language and spatio-temporal disorientation and disjuncture. The structure of the riot is thus apprehended as a flashing image.

The loss of language adheres to what Ahmad wrote about as the 'absence of a language adequate to the scale and intensity of the horrid tale'.[52] In a similar vein, the anthropologist Veena Das has written of 'the mutilation of language' in Partition narratives as testimonies of 'an essential truth about the annihilating

---

Refuge Seeker (1948) as sacrificing aesthetic value in the drive to record the violence. In contrast, Manto is singled out as an exception in choosing to represent the violence as a 'black hole'.

[48] Ahmad, *Lineages of the Present: Ideology and Politics in Contemporary South Asia* (London: Verso, 2000), p. 125.

[49] Saint, *Witnessing Partition*, p. 200.

[50] Jason Francisco, 'In the Heat of Fratricide: The Literature of India's Partition Burning Freshly', in Mushirul Hasan (ed.), *Inventing Boundaries* (New Delhi: Oxford University Press, 2000), pp. 371–393.

[51] Francisco, 'In the Heat of Fratricide', p. 382.

[52] Ahmad, *Lineages of the Present*, p. 108.

violence and terror that people experienced during these riots, namely that as human understanding gives way, language is struck dumb.'[53] But taking a more dialectical view, I see the rupture caused by the flashing image and immediate sensation of the riot as also productive of protest and repair. In this I draw once again on the work of Benjamin to theorize the riot in terms of the flashing image that disturbs and interrupts the empty homogeneous time of the nation. His work on historical memory as 'an image which flashes up' helps in articulating the narrative structure of the riot with that of the short story. In his 'Theses on the Philosophy of History', Benjamin writes that:

> The past can be seized only as an image which flashes up at the instant when it can be recognized and is never seen again.... To articulate the past historically does not mean to recognize it 'the way it really was'. It means to seize hold of a memory as it flashes up at a moment of danger....[54]

Benjamin differentiates between empty homogeneous time as the time of clocks, calendars, of routinized modernization, a time that could be filled up with events and schedules and in contrast, messianic time that is revolutionary and experienced in immediate and sometimes violent ways. It consists of events strung together that explode routine and continuum. Andrew Yang points out that:

> Within fiction, homogeneous, empty time occurs within the simultaneous unfolding of multiple plotlines involving varieties of characters and locales. These plotlines coalesce into an imagined community, organized by the quantified, measured passage of time. Messianic time, meanwhile, focuses far more on exposition-climax-denouement cycles of action, centered upon transformations in thoughts, societies, power structures, and the like.[55]

In many ways, this apprehension of time can also be mapped on to the different generic registers of Partition, such that it is the short story whose structure can be read in the dialectical mode of historical materialism in which the flashing image of the riot ruptures the empty homogeneous time of the nation and its founding mythologies.

Sa'adat Hasan Manto's short story 'Open It!' ('Khol Do'), written immediately after Partition, in Manto's signature acerbic style, where a situation in which several passengers on a train have been killed or injured is described in a matter-of-fact tone: 'Quite a few passengers were killed along the way, several received

---

[53] Veena Das, 'The Anthropology of Pain', in *Critical Events: An Anthropological Perspective on Contemporary India* (New Delhi: Oxford University Press, 1995), pp. 175–196, p. 184.
[54] Benjamin, 'Theses on the Philosophy of History', pp. 253–264.
[55] https://lareviewofbooks.org/article/empire-nation-and-time/

injuries, and some just wandered off to God knows where.'[56] The story is set within the space of a refugee camp, a product of the riotous violence that fragments apprehensions of both time and space, of self, community and nation, as the displaced and the destitute find temporary shelter from the riots. 'Open It!' narrates the story of Sirajudin who wakes up from numbness caused by grief at losing his wife and 'snaps back into consciousness' as 'a series of images flitted across his mind—images of plunder, fire, stampede, the train station, gunshots, night, and Sakina'.[57] Sakina is his beautiful teenage daughter from whom he has become separated during the mayhem of the riots. But Sirajudin is exhausted and his ability to recall how exactly he lost contact with Sakina is thwarted by the memory of his 'wife's mutilated body, her guts spilling out'.[58] After six desperate days of futile searching, he comes across a group of young male relief-workers involved with rescue missions to bring back abducted and raped women and children. When they offer to assist him in his search, Sirajudin describes her beauty to them, including the distinguishing black mole on her fair cheek. The omniscient narrative voice reveals to us readers that the men do find her, but they first rape her and then abandon her by the train tracks. When Sakina's mutilated body is brought to a doctor's tent in the camp, Sirajudin identifies her after seeing the mole on her cheek. The last lines offer a chilling denouement:

> The doctor glanced at the body lying on the stretcher. He felt the pulse and, pointing at the window, told Sirajuddin, 'Open it!'
> Sakina's body stirred ever so faintly on the stretcher. With lifeless hands she slowly undid the knot of her waistband and lowered her shalwar.
> 'She's alive! My daughter is alive!' Old Sirajuddin screamed with un-bounded joy. The doctor broke into a cold sweat.[59]

The story's dark irony rests on what Benjamin has theorized as the becoming normal of the state of exception. Here the ordinary becomes the repository of unspeakable horror because all recognizable norms of community have been upturned with callous disregard—the volunteers who were meant to protect are the rapists, and the ordinary words 'open it' come to condense, in a flash, the horrific terror of the rape such that the reference to the opening of the window by the doctor is interpreted by the traumatized Sakina as an instruction to open her trousers to be violated again. The violation itself is no longer an exception.

Critics have read this story as offering no redemption as the narrative jettisons the possibility of shared language and community, indeed of humanity itself.

---

[56] Sa'dat Hasan Manto, 'Open It!', translated by Muhammad Umar Memon, *Annual of Urdu Studies* 27 (2012): pp. 74–76, p. 74. The original Urdu story' Khōl Dō' is taken from the Manto's collection *Mantō Kahāniyāñ* (Lahore: Sang-e- Meel Publications, 1995), pp. 11-14.
[57] Manto, 'Open It!', p. 74.
[58] Manto, 'Open It!', p. 74.
[59] Manto, 'Open It!', p. 76.

Bhalla reads the story as evoking 'a nightmarish quality' in which all 'moral and ethical signposts' have disappeared, as have 'the certitudes of historical or sociological explanation'.[60] Against such a reading, I want to suggest that Sirajuddin's 'unbounded joy' that his daughter is alive points to an opening into hope. In reality, of course, women raped in riots were often killed by their fathers and brothers or ended up killing themselves for bringing dishonour to the family.[61] As Das writes: 'the political history of creation of independent India and Pakistan corresponds with another history—that of the secretly carried memory of terror upon the "secret" organs of women'.[62] But traumatic as it is, in my reading the story leaves Sakina's future open-ended in the fact that her father is not only relieved but joyous to see her alive, albeit unaware of the violations she has had to endure. Within patriarchal discourse, raped women are equivalent to dead women. 'Open It!' takes a sliver of hope to crack open the darkness that envelops places and bodies torn apart by violence, both literally and metaphorically.

Manto's story 'Siyah Hashye' or 'Black Margins' develops the idea of the margins of history that disturb the very constructs of narrative itself.[63] Here the author jettisons a novel-in-the-making for the more open-ended and malleable form of the short story. The story represents not only what critics tend to see as a ruination of language by violence, but constitutes a break in the certitudes of narrative. Seemingly everyday situations are imbued with a sense of menace and with the potential to annihilate reality itself as the riot moves from one time-space conjunction to another, creating a veritable tableau of destruction. The entire text is made of a series of fragments of scenes from riots, with each section woven around a situation that first lights up and then extinguishes as a flash. The short stories within the short story are written in stripped down sentences that are evacuated of all sentimentality. Manto wrote of his acceptance of the 'nightmarish reality' of 'the consequences of the revolution' set off by Partition 'without self-pity or despair'. Of 'Black Margins' he went on to say:

> I tried to retrieve from this man-made sea of blood, pearls of a rare hue, by writing about the single-minded dedication with which men had killed men, about the remorse felt by some of them, about the tears shed by murderers who could not understand why they still had some human feelings left.[64]

In the story, each fragment is a whole unto itself, while also being part of the whole of the short story. From 'Sweet Moment' that comprises one sentence that is a

---

[60] Bhalla, 'Memory, History and Fictional Representations of the Partition', p. 3123.
[61] See Ritu Menon and Kamla Bhasin, *Borders and Boundaries: Women in India's Partition* (New Brunswick, NJ: Rutgers University Press, 1998).
[62] Das, 'The Anthropology of Pain', p. 185.
[63] Sa'adat Hasan Manto, 'Black Margins', in Mushirul Hasan (ed.), *Inventing Boundaries* (New Delhi: Oxford University Press, 2000), pp. 287–299.
[64] Manto, 'Black Margins', p. 268.

fragment of a news report from Associated Press that says 'It is learnt that sweets were distributed at several places in Amritsar, Gwalior and Bombay to rejoice the death of Mahatma Gandhi' to fragments about the bloodshed over religion that is intertwined with struggles ('looting and plundering') over food and wages in 'Wages of Labour' and 'Sharing the Loot'. Many stories narrate the grisly performance of violence over objects such as a thermos flask that becomes a 'trophy' in 'Legitimate Use' or the stolen bag of sugar that sweetens the well in 'Miracles'.[65] In 'An Enterprise', 'Fire gutted the entire mohalla' and only 'the hoarding on the shop that escaped the flames read: "A complete range of building and construction materials sold here"', existing words and signs are shown to be disconnected from their original contexts.[66] There is also humour in 'Mourning the Dead' when a man who was part of a mob that was desecrating the statue of the Hindu philanthropist Sir Ganga Ram is injured and is sent to Ganga Ram Hospital. The fragments are narrated in a deadpan style, withholding moral judgement and thereby evoking the banal brutality of the violence. In 'Jelly' an ice-cream seller is stabbed to death. As his blood mixes with the melting ice from the van, a child sees the 'coagulated blood on the road' and exclaims to his mother 'Look mummy, jelly'.[67] In fragments such as 'Sorry', the dark humour intensifies the register of casual barbarism: 'The knife slid down his groin. His pyjama cord was cut into two. "Chi, chi, chi, chi, I've made a mishtake," the assassin said with a sense of remorse'.[68] In this upside-down world, murderers also have regrets. In 'Double Cross', a man complains to his friend for selling him petrol at black-market prices, because of which 'not a single shop could be set on fire'.[69] Each fragment coheres around an image that flashes and cuts through the possibility of narrating the riot in anything but the space of the short story.

If Manto's splintered and broken texts allegorize the riot as breaking down the linear narrative of the nation and its history, the film *Garm Hawa* (*Scorching Wind*) based on an unpublished short story by Ismat Chughtai deploys the idea of broken history as only available through flashes of cinematic memory. First released in 1973, the film directed by M.S. Sathyu was part of the new wave of Indian cinema. Made on a shoe-string budget, the film was shot in a silent mode with background sounds and dialogues dubbed in post-production. Interestingly this lends a palimpsestic quality to the film as image and sound are literally and figuratively layered on one another.

The film's narrative unfolds not only in the aftermath of Partition, but crucially in the moment after Gandhi's assassination by a Hindu fanatic. When riots broke out across the subcontinent after the announcement of formal Partition in 1946,

---

[65] Manto, 'Black Margins', p. 268.
[66] Manto, 'Black Margins', p. 294.
[67] Manto, 'Black Margins', p. 297.
[68] Manto, 'Black Margins', p. 296.
[69] Manto, 'Black Margins', p. 298.

Gandhi famously undertook a visit to Noakhali, a district in the east Indian state of Bengal where Hindus were being killed and displaced by powerful Muslim forces. Images of a bare-foot Gandhi walking for hundreds of miles to survey the destruction caused by the riots have become iconic in the photographic memory of the nation. During his stay in the riot-torn district, Gandhi set up his base in a half-burnt house in the village of Srirampur. His plea for non-violence and religious tolerance, however, came to be seen as his political weakness. He was perceived by many Hindus as acquiescing to the minority within the nation, as well as by Muslim leaders who saw his presence as exacerbating the bitterness between Hindus and Muslims. Just a few months after formal Partition, on 30 January 1948, a Hindu fanatic named Nathuram Godse sprayed bullets into Gandhi as he emerged from a prayer meeting in Delhi. Manash Firaq Bhattacharjee has commented that 'Gandhi's non-violent project could not overcome the violent contradictions of the nation, as it came into being in light of one of the worst genocides in modern history.'[70] In historical hindsight one could argue that the bullet that killed Gandhi shot through postcolonial Indian history, changing its course forever. The flash of that moment recurs like the return of the repressed as riots and communal violence have intensified under the current Hindu supremacist regime under the leadership of Prime Minister Narendra Modi.

Garm Hawa can be seen as a requiem for the secular ideals that Gandhi represented, and that Indian Muslims who stayed back, like the film's protagonist Salim Mirza, had reposed their faith in. The film evokes the fading secular culture of pre-Partition India by means of music—the *qawwali* (a form of Sufi music representing the non-doctrinaire elements of Islam), as well as undulating images of historic Mughal-era monuments reflecting India's syncretic history. The film uses cinematic montage such that news reels of riots before and after Partition, Gandhi's murder, and inflammatory political speeches are set to Sufi songs about the oneness of god. The music intensifies the sensory load of images of monuments such as the Taj Mahal, evoking the pathos of the romance between the lovers Amina and Shamshad in the film and foreshadowing the impossibility of love across borders and boundaries. Bhaskar Sarkar in his book on Partition and Indian cinema points to the deployment of 'the overwrought *mise-en-scène*, the musical interludes, and modes of editing and sound-image' used in films that 'consolidate (combining, in archaic terms, content and form)—at a *performative* level—a potent and singularly Indian idiolect for cinematic mourning.'[71] These scenes create impressions that are transient, fragile, and fragmentary, against the backdrop of the permanence of history and the certitudes of linear secular narrative that is violently interrupted by the violence of the riots. Thus, although the main thrust of the film centres around

---

[70] Manash Firaq Bhattacharjee, 'Gandhi and the Trial of Noakhali', *The Wire*, 1 October 2016, https://thewire.in/history/gandhi-and-the-trial-of-noakhali, accessed 10 October 2022.

[71] Bhaskar Sarkar, *Mourning the Nation: Indian Cinema in the Wake of Partition* (Durham, NC: Duke University Press, 2009), p. 9.

the Partition violence and the fate of one family within a disintegrating nation, its images reinforce the ongoing trauma of loss—of property, community, family, and the self. As the days and months unfold, members of Salim Mirza's family leave home in India to relocate to Pakistan where they would no longer be in the minority.

The crux of the trauma in the film coheres around the fate of Sakina, Salim's beloved daughter, who is betrayed by her lover with whom she was engaged to marry. When she learns that he has been betrothed to someone in Pakistan, Sakina shuts herself in her room and slits her wrists with a blade. The blood that seeps out of her body in many ways evokes the images of the streams of blood on the riot-torn streets. Dishonoured by her abandonment by her lover, she chooses death as a fate that many of the raped and abducted women chose during the Partition riots.[72]

At its end the film, however, offers a different kind of sociality that becomes the opposite pole of the riot. Despite financial ruination when Salim's shoe factory is shut down because no one will give Muslims loans any more, and despite his son Sikander's struggles finding a job as a young Muslim man, Salim states 'we cannot live in isolation'. In this the film focalizes the question of the place of the minority in a secular, democratic society and reprises questions of political engagement. Despite all the obstacles, Sikander chooses at the end to stay back and join the march of young men protesting unemployment and economic immiseration in the newly independent nation of India that must now grapple with questions of the material wellbeing of its citizens.

There are of course many films that have sought to represent the riot through the cinematic image outside the allegorical mode. In particular, the emergence of protest documentaries by independent filmmakers such as Nakul Singh Sawhney's *Muzaffarpur Baaqi Hai* (2015) made in the aftermath of the Muzaffarnagar riots in the state of Uttar Pradesh in 2013, Rakesh Sharma's *Final Solution* on the Gujarat riots of 2002 in which over 2,000 Muslims were killed, and *In the Name of the Father* (1993) by Anand Patwardhan on the rise of the Hindu right and its use of the riot as an instrument of supremacy has been a noteworthy phenomenon as the Indian state's commitment to secularism has waned.[73] On the other hand, mainstream Bombay cinema has attempted to tackle the representation of riots in both melodramatic and sentimental registers, from early renderings of loss in films such as *Dharmputra* (1961) and *Dhool ka Phool* (1959) to films from the 1990s onwards that were made against the backdrop of post-Partition riots such

---

[72] See Urvashi Butalia, 'Community, State and Gender: Some Reflections on the Partition of India', in Mushirul Hasan (ed.), *Inventing Boundaries* (New Delhi: Oxford University Press, 2000), pp. 178–207.

[73] Nandini Ramnath, 'Documentary Muzaffarnagar Baaqi Hai Revisits the Riots that Tore Apart Western UP in 2013', *Scroll.in*, 19 February 2015. https://scroll.in/article/707824/documentary-muzaffarnagar-baaqi-hai-revisits-the-riots-that-tore-apart-western-up-in-2013, accessed 11 October 2022.

as *Bombay* (1995), *Fiza* (2000), *Mr and Mrs Iyer* (2002), *Black Friday* (2007), and *Firaaq* (2008). Across all the different registers of representation, from the realist to the neo-realist, from melodrama to romance, the riot appears as an imagistic flash that enables a turning point in the narrative, one that can only be recalled through broken memories set to film and the short story form.

I want to conclude with a brief discussion of Hansda Sowvendra Shekhar's story 'They Eat Meat'.[74] In it, a young Adivasi couple have recently moved to Baroda, one of Gujarat's main cities. Used to eating meat and eggs as an integral part of their diet like a majority of Indians and particularly those from tribal communities, they find themselves marooned in a state where majoritarianism is on the rise and where vegetarianism has been turned into a sign of belonging to the majority Hindu community.[75] The story is set on the eve of the pogrom against Muslims in 2002 and narrates how meat-eating in the intensely polarized politics of Gujarat then and India today has become a sign of otherness and foreignness. The consumption of meat is seen as a threat to the idea of a pure Hindu India that is of course willing to murder meat eaters since eating meat has been increasingly attached as a practice to being Muslim.[76] The family pines for egg, chicken, and meat and the traditional Santhal curries, but has to forego those pleasures in their new location. Their struggle to obtain meat is juxtaposed ironically with the impending violence in the form of riots as they are forced to hide in their home against marauding mobs looking to kill Muslims and all 'others'. Ultimately, the mob does arrive at the home of the only Muslim family in their neighbourhood of Subhanpura and begins to set it on fire and shouts obscenities at the women of the family. Except, of course, Shekhar offers a real twist to the story of women during riots. Here, first the women of the household and then the women of the neighbourhood start hurling their thick, heavy-bottomed steel vessels at the rioters:

> As the flames in the Mohammeds' living room spread, the forty-fifty men in the mob faced a shower of iron, steel, aluminium, tin and wooden implements. The women of Subhanpura Colony had turned out into force. Some pelted the rioters with their kadahis and katoris, others drew degchis and frying pans. Some threw old, heavy irons. Some threw sticks and brooms. Those who had nothing heavy to throw, pelted vegetables, packets of juice and butter, and bottles of oil and ketchup.[77]

---

[74] Hansda Sowvendra Shekhar, 'They Eat Meat' in *The Adivasi Will Not Dance* (New Delhi: Speaking Tiger, 2017).

[75] See Teresa Tudu, '"They Eat Meat": A Study of Tribal Culture in Non-tribal Vicinity', *Research Journal of English Language and Literature* 7, no. 3 (2019): pp. 144–147.

[76] Supriya Nair, 'The Meaning of India's "Beef Lynchings"', *The Atlantic*, 24 July 2017. https://www.theatlantic.com/international/archive/2017/07/india-modi-beef-lynching-muslim-partition/533739/, accessed 11 October 2022.

[77] Shekhar, *The Adivasi Will Not Dance*, p. 24.

In actuality, women bore the brunt of the 2002 Gujarat riots. Many were raped, including pregnant women who also had foetuses extracted from their wombs, or simply burnt alive.[78] Several thousands were left widowed and destitute. But Shekhar allows his story to imagine a different outcome for women, one in which they exercise their gendered power to overcome the rioters.

Sarkar writes that 'An elastic conceptualization of Partition, extending backward and forward in time, highlights the way in which seemingly disparate historical moments congeal in the popular imagination around the fulcrum of 1947.'[79] The riots then 'become elements of one single experiential chain that many place under the sign of "Partition" in the ways in which its legacy reverberates throughout contemporary South Asia.' As the images flash and cut through official versions of history, they also put pressure on narrative itself. Short stories on the riot provide formal space through which the dialectic unleashed by the violence is represented. It is where the empty homogeneous time of the nation confronts the eruption of the time of the riot.

---

[78] Harsh Mander, 'One Thing Was Distinctly Rotten about 2002 Gujarat Riots: Use of Rape as a Form of Terror', *The Print*, 24 April 2019, https://theprint.in/pageturner/excerpt/one-thing-was-distinctly-rotten-about-2002-gujarat-riots-use-of-rape-as-a-form-of-terror/225511/, accessed 10 October 2022.

[79] Sarkar, *Mourning the Nation*, p. 15.

7

A Sketch of the Mob

Joseph North

There are some words which we avoid using on principle, or use only when they have been so thoroughly reclaimed that they bear a meaning opposed to their usual one. The most obvious examples are racial slurs, religious slurs, slurs against women, and terms that denigrate people on the basis of sexuality or gender presentation. Debate about slurs of this kind often collapses into the unpromising idiom of polemics against so-called 'cancel culture' or 'political correctness', which makes it easy to forget that the call to consider what is at stake in our use of language is a very old one, predating current culture wars. In particular, these kinds of questions are a long-standing concern of the discipline of literary studies, one of the founding commitments of which is the insight that the character of our language strongly conditions the character of our collective experience, so that the speakability of a thing does much to determine whether or not that thing can even be imagined, perceived, or thought within the culture at large. When reflecting on this I often think of Raymond Williams's *Keywords* (1976), which revived something like traditional philology, but from a materialist standpoint: a book in which the history of each keyword was revealed as the history of an ongoing material struggle, carried out by large collective forces, over what was to be speakable and therefore imaginable, perceivable, thinkable within the culture at large. The book did not pretend to be a neutral or objective record of that history. Rather, word by word Williams demonstrated that the very building-blocks of our language had been baked in the kiln by oppressive forces, rendering it difficult for us to build our own capacities for experience, except on oppressive terms. Reading the book made it seem necessary to break the hold of oppressive forces on our language, thereby remaking it into a tool with which to experience the world more fully, freely, and equally, on our own terms. So that was quite an inspiring vision of what might be possible as an intellectual and political project—even more inspiring, perhaps, since at first glance the project might appear to be merely a dry old philological exercise in tracing the etymology of words.[1]

---

[1] Sincere thanks to Feisal Mohammed, Catherine Nicholson, Joe Cleary, Tim Kreiner, Michael Denning, and Joseph Hone for offering their thoughts on this piece at various points. I am deeply grateful to Gary Foley for believing in the larger project, and to Victoria Haskins, Ray Kelley, and everyone else at the University of Newcastle's Purai Global Indigenous History Center for supporting it. The piece was written partly in New Haven, CT, on land taken from the Quinnipiac people, and partly in Newcastle,

I will not attempt to reach anything like those heights in this chapter. But recently I have been tracing the history of a few words that I take to be keywords of political centrism: 'extremism', 'totalitarianism', 'populism', and—this chapter's word—'mob'. All these are words which centrisms past and present have used to designate their enemies, thereby defining themselves. For better or worse, I have found myself arriving at the view that we urgently need to unlearn them either by rendering them unsayable in polite conversation, or by reframing them so that they designate something quite opposed to their usual meaning.

What does 'mob' mean? It is a word closely connected to riots: indeed, today the primary definition one is usually offered is something like 'a crowd bent on violence', and that meaning has not changed much since it first appeared in the late seventeenth century. That meaning is always said to have developed out of the Latin phrase *mobile vulgus*, the 'fickle crowd', though as we will see, this is not really the whole story. 'Mob' is evidently a term of class contempt, and so it is tempting to understand it simply as another entry in the long series of terms that have been used by the upper classes to express contempt for the lower ones, such as 'plebs', 'riff-raff', or 'rabble'. But we need to be more specific here, because the new term 'mob' was drawing a different emphasis than those older terms. The most telling contrast is with 'rabble', since (as early observers themselves noted) it was specifically on the semantic territory occupied by 'rabble' that the new word 'mob' was beginning to muscle in.[2] What is the difference between the two terms? A 'rabble' is the common people imagined as various, heterogeneous, pulling in multiple directions, whereas a 'mob' is something quite different or even opposed: the common people imagined as united by a common purpose, that common purpose being irrational violence. Observing this allows one to see that the word 'mob' is not merely another way of expressing contempt for the common people, but a way of reimagining the relationship between the common people and the social order: the 'mob' is the 'rabble' reimagined as threatening in its unity and sense of purpose.

Why in the late seventeenth century did it suddenly become important to have a word with which to express this range of meaning? We begin to approach an answer when we recall that the seventeenth century was the period of the greatest constitutional crises in English history, with the Civil War, the Restoration, and then the so-called Glorious Revolution. For our purposes, the point of real significance is that this was the period when the embryo of popular sovereignty first became a live political concern in England: the only time England has

---

NSW, on land taken from the Awabakal people. Both peoples continue their struggles for justice and self-determination today.

[2] Roger North, writing in 1740, tells us that it was in the 1680s that 'the rabble first changed their title, and were called *the mob*'. Roger North, *Examen: or An Enquiry into the Credit and Veracity of an Intended Complete History* (London, 1740), 574, cited in Shoemaker, *The London Mob* (London and New York: Continuum, 2004), xii.

managed to become a Republic, and then only for eleven years.³ The term 'mob' in our sense arose in the generation after the Republic, in a period of reaction against it, when the culture was still trembling with the aftershocks of that seismic upheaval, and from the outset the word was quite clearly part of a broader movement to demonize the common people when those people sought to take power into their own hands.⁴ Bearing all this in mind, my proposal is that the word was developed in the late seventeenth century as a weapon against the new discourse of popular sovereignty, and that since then, one of the chief effects of the discourse of the 'mob' has been to conflate the rule of the common people—in effect, democracy—with the prospect of 'mob rule'.

This is the key point of the chapter: from its inception, the word 'mob' has been used not merely to indicate 'a violent crowd', nor even to demonize the common people as violent, but to demonize the common people as violent specifically in their new capacity as potential bearers of state power. We worry about 'mobs' not just when groups become violent in the street, but when groups not sanctioned by the state begin exercising state-like functions. Noticing this helps us to see why the discourse of the 'mob' tars popular action by conflating it with irrational violence, specifically, rather than by conflating it with some other repellent thing such as greed, perfidy, or incompetence. Many of the most influential theorists of the state—notably Weber and Bourdieu—have seen the state as coextensive with the claim to hold a monopoly on real and symbolic violence within a particular territory: which is to say, those aligned with the state understand the state as violence made rational, violence finally subjected to the rule of reason.⁵ It is against this background that it makes sense to feel that a non-state, a parody of a state, or an anti-state must be, specifically and first of all, a condition of irrational violence.

The older term 'rabble' may have proved insufficient in the late seventeenth century because it did not articulate this. The rabble is contemptible, but not because of its organized capacity for irrational violence: it is contemptible because it is disorderly, heterogeneous, confused, mutable. In that sense it is really the rabble rather than the mob which most resembles the *mobile vulgus*, or fickle crowd. But in the seventeenth century, when the common people began to appear rather forcefully in their new capacity as potential bearers of state power, a new word was evidently needed. Reimagining the rabble as a 'mob' perfectly encapsulates

---

³ Recent attempts to uncover germinal forms of popular sovereignty in earlier periods only confirm the importance of seventeenth-century England. See Richard Bourke and Quentin Skinner (eds), *Popular Sovereignty in Historical Perspective* (Cambridge: Cambridge University Press, 2016).

⁴ Of course, not all the Republicans were enthusiastic about popular sovereignty: on the contrary, the dominant figures, certainly including Cromwell, sought to overthrow the monarchy while guarding vigorously against the threat of democracy. See Phillip Baker (ed.), *The Levellers: The Putney Debates* (London: Verso, 2007).

⁵ The locus classicus here is Weber, *Politik als Beruf* (1919), available in English as 'Politics as a Vocation', in Tony Waters and Dagmar Waters (ed. and transl.), *Weber's Rationalism and Modern Society* (New York, NY: Palgrave Macmillan, 2015). Bourdieu adds the clause regarding *symbolic* violence in *On the State: Lectures at the Collège de France, 1989–1992* (Cambridge: Polity, 2014).

the new elite sense of the lower orders as threatening specifically in their capacity for unity and common purpose, a capacity that the word renders horrifying by conflating it with irrational violence: the precise opposite of responsibly exercised state power. A mob is a rabble with a claim to sovereignty, but a claim that can only ever end in blood and madness; a mob is a rabble with purpose and unity, but a purpose that can only ever be the destruction of the state and the erection of a non-state, an anarchy or tyranny of unchecked violence.

If this seems to strike a Hobbesian note, then you are hearing the right tune. I mentioned Weber and Bourdieu as examples of thinkers who have seen the state as defined by its monopoly on the power of the sword, but in the mid-to-late seventeenth century the name most strongly associated with that particular emphasis was Hobbes, who indeed has a strong claim to be its effective originator, at least in elite philosophical discourse in English.[6] The word 'mob' in our sense dates from the late 1680s; as it happened, Hobbes died in 1679 and narrowly missed out on the chance to hear it used. Nevertheless, I think he would have liked it. The word seems almost made for—or if you like, made by—Hobbes's purposes. It beautifully encapsulates his conviction that the state is violence subjected to reason, whereas a life outside the state is a life of unchecked, irrational violence, and I think we can see in it also something of his horror at the prospect of a 'popular' sovereignty (most immediately that represented by groups like the Levellers), and his concomitant rejection of the very category of 'the people' prior to their incorporation into the state. Indeed, I propose that the word 'mob' arrives as a kind of codification of a Hobbesian view at the level of popular language: that Hobbes spends his life hammering out, at the level of elite intellectual discourse, the very emphases that the word 'mob' will later fold into the language at large. The new word 'mob' names, as an uncanny horror, the specific prospect that Hobbes tried to render unthinkable: the prospect of a common people either sovereign over, or else living without, a state. It is then almost too convenient to recall that the earliest records of this usage in print (one of which we shall examine in a moment) date from 1688, precisely the year when the English state was effectively re-founded upon Hobbesian lines.[7]

A Mob of Three Parts

I will glance again at Hobbes, but first will expand our frame by observing that the 'mob' discourse as a whole in fact demonizes a more extensive list of political agents than I have noted so far. I have been arguing that the word 'mob' was developed, not simply to demonize crowds, nor to demonize the common people

---

[6] In Hobbes, the *locus classicus* for this claim is *Leviathan* (1651), but the claim itself is usually said to go back to Jean Bodin's *Les Six livres de la République* (1576).
[7] Thanks to Joseph Hone for this observation.

in general, but to demonize the common people specifically in their new capacity as potential bearers of state power. Yet when one studies the ways in which the term has been used, one begins to realize that from the very start, the discourse of the 'mob' repeatedly has sought to demonize popular sovereignty by conflating it with the horrible prospect of two other, seemingly quite different forms of sovereignty: the sovereignty of women, and the sovereignty of Indigenous peoples. In this sense our imagined 'mob' has always been a mob of three parts. This is an important point, not least because it is a way of tying together struggles around class, struggles around gender, and struggles around colonialism.

A Mob of the People

Let me first sum up what I see as the central emphasis of this discourse: elite horror at the prospect of a popular sovereignty gone wild. One way to grasp this is to ask: what does this discourse posit as the opposite of a 'mob'? When serious thinkers start worrying about the threat of the 'mob', they often move to contrast it not with, say, the monarch, or the aristocracy, or the bourgeoisie, or even the 'plebs' or 'rabble'—all plausible opposites, on one axis or another—but specifically with 'the people', either in something like a Hobbesian sense ('the people' as a body that springs into being the moment we contract our liberty away in exchange for the protection of the sovereign) or, more often, in a Whiggish or, later, liberal sense ('the people' as the proper subject of politics, but a somewhat notional subject that can never acquire a legitimate body and will outside a properly constituted parliament). One sees this move being made again and again over the centuries, wherever the threat of the so-called 'mob' arises. To point very rapidly to three examples: in the early eighteenth century Defoe makes it in his *Hymn to the Mob*; in the early nineteenth century Hazlitt mourns the fact that so many of his contemporaries were making it while trying desperately to distance themselves from their earlier positions of sympathy towards the French Revolution (with bitter irony, he observes that '"No connection with the mob", was labelled on the back of every friend of the People'); and in the mid-twentieth century, Arendt makes the same move again, even elaborating the slur term 'mob' into a philosophical concept and placing the distinction between 'the mob' and 'the people' at the heart of her theory of antisemitism, imperialism, and totalitarianism.[8] One could go on. My point is that the serial repetition of this move to pose 'the mob' as the opposite of 'the people' would seem to confirm once again that our imagined 'mob' is much more than simply a violent crowd: rather, it embodies the threat of popular sovereignty escaping elite control; the threat of state power falling into the wrong hands.

[8] Daniel Defoe, *A Hymn to the Mob* (London: S. Popping et al., 1715). William Hazlitt, 'Essay XIII: On the Jealousy and Spleen of Party', in *The Plain Speaker* (London: Henry Colburn, 1826) 2: 409–447. Hannah Arendt, *The Origins of Totalitarianism* (Milton Keynes: Penguin Classics, 2017), especially 'IV: The People and the Mob', pp. 138–152.

Observing this also perhaps suggests something of the historical and intellectual significance of the term. By any measure, 'the people' is one of the central concepts of political modernity. Beginning in embryo with, let us say, Machiavelli in the late fifteenth century, and then passing through a long and bloody labour across the centuries that follow, we eventually see the birth and widespread acceptance of the idea that it is from 'the people' that all political legitimacy must ultimately flow—at least in principle. But who counts as 'the people', and how do we understand their relationship to other 'peoples'? Does 'the people' ever really exist as such, except via its representatives? Who best represents 'the people': the monarch, the parliament, or the crowd in the street? And so on. Virtually all serious political thinkers accept that questions of this broad kind have been central to modern political thought. But if you ask: 'what is the opposite of the people—that other against which it defines itself?' then you will find it much harder to get a quick answer, even among serious political thinkers. One answer is 'the mob'. Viewed in this light, the concept of begins to take on a rather grander aspect as the long shadow of one of the central concepts of political modernity. If that is the case, we should not be surprised to find the term lurking in the background of many important scenes, whenever 'the people' or 'popular sovereignty' take centre stage.

A Mob of Women

As I began by noting, the word 'mob' is usually said to have developed out of the Latin phrase *mobile vulgus*, or fickle crowd, and people usually date this transformation to the 1680s. This is not wrong. But what people often fail to note is that in fact the word 'mob' already existed in English prior to 1688, though with a different range of meaning. From about 1650 one could find the word 'mob' used, not for a crowd bent on violence, but for a sex worker, and thus also, by the usual chain of extension, for a promiscuous woman, a lower-class woman, or indeed any women at all when one wanted to damn her. It strikes me that this prior life of the term as a gendered slur must have conditioned the development of *mobile vulgus* into 'mob' in our own 'unauthorized exercise of state-like power' sense of the term.

Let me point to a concrete case that suggests the truth of this. One of the earliest recorded uses of the term 'mob' in the modern sense occurs in a Restoration comedy by Thomas Shadwell called *The Squire of Alsatia* (1688)—a play best remembered today for having introduced the popular character of the shrewish Mrs Termagant (so it is a play rich in slurs against women, among other things). Our word arrives when a gentleman is encouraging a crowd in the street to beat up a sex worker. He cries: 'Here honest mob, course this whore to some purpose, a whore, a whore, a whore.' This is intended as witty wordplay: the 'mob' in the sense of crowd is being called upon to discipline the 'mob' in the sense of prostitute. Here we see how tightly the two meanings of the word are bound together, with the earlier meaning sitting right alongside the later one, the two being played off against one another.⁹ I take it Defoe is relying on the same punning sense of the term when he writes, a generation later:

> Dear MOB, To place thee now in perfect View,
> We must be to thy Failings true
> Not daub thee like a painted Whore;
> But view thee all behind, and all before[10]

That is to say, we must not simply praise the mob—one can acknowledge the sex-worker's charms, as Defoe does in the first part of his *Hymn to the Mob,* but one must not lose one's head, lest one fall for the sex worker's tricks. No, Defoe warns us, we must strip the mob and view her before and behind, to know what we are really getting.[11] And what are we getting? For Defoe, what we are really getting is a terrifying parody of 'the people'. Defoe's central rhetorical move in *A Hymn to the Mob* is to praise 'the mob' by attributing to it all the political virtues that Whig political thought normally ascribes to 'the people': the mob is the wellspring of all political legitimacy, the power of kings and princes rests on it, and so on. This unexpected praise of the mob is intended to be outrageous and entertaining. But the poem ends by returning to the expected Whig emphasis, warning us that the people should only ever try to wield their power via their proper legal representative, parliament, for whenever they presume to go beyond this, the people become a 'mob' indeed. It is at this point that the spectre of the riot becomes so important to the poem—Defoe's evocative term for it is 'Street-madness'. Yet here as elsewhere the discourse of the mob turns out to be founded on a fear, not merely of crowds rioting in the street, but of state power being seized by the wrong people: 'Contagious Madness seizes every Head, / And *all Men* follow, just as *all Men* lead. / Let not Men wonder at their *Fate*, / When *MOB* grows mad *beware the State*.'[12]

In any case it seems worth knowing that the term 'mob' was a gendered slur even before it was a class one, and that in a sense the demonization of popular sovereignty, when it arrived, went hand in hand with the demonization of female autonomy, and especially female sexual autonomy. In fact this conjunction recurs later on in the history, too: as we shall see in the next section, even when the word 'mob' has lost the range of meaning that allows it to refer specifically to women of certain kinds, we nevertheless continue to see condemnation of 'mobs', in the sense of crowds, associated with the condemnation not just of the common folk's claim to sovereignty, but of female claims to sovereignty in particular.

---

[9] I am grateful to Robert Shoemaker for pointing me towards this passage in the opening pages of his excellent book *The London Mob: Violence and Disorder in Eighteenth Century England* (London and New York, NY: Continuum, 2004).
[10] Defoe, *A Hymn to the Mob*, p. 27.
[11] Defoe, *A Hymn to the Mob*, p. 14. Emphasis in original.
[12] Defoe, *A Hymn to the Mob*, p. 14. Emphasis in original.

A Mob of 'Savages'

To see this condemnation of female sovereignty in action, and to bring us to the question of Indigeneity, let us take a single example from Edmund Burke, a century later. Obviously the late eighteenth century is a key moment for anxieties about popular sovereignty, and one might expect Burke to be one of the key users of our word, given that his *Reflections on the Revolution in France* (1790) has proved such an enduring touchstone for anti-radical and anti-popular sentiment over the last two centuries—and yes, he does make use of it in the ordinary damning sense of a crowd bent on mindless destruction.[13] But more interestingly, in *Reflections* Burke also moves to call out the word 'mob' for special attention. Boasting of the staunchness of the English resistance to radicalism, he recalls the last major instance of street protest in England, the 'Gordon Riots' of June 1780. Burke notes that Gordon 'raised a mob' and then adds in parentheses '(excuse the term, it is still in use here)'.[14]

This strikes me as a lovely aside: Burke is saying, in effect, 'You French have given up the term "mob"; your revolutionary sensibility no longer recognizes the category. You see a scene such as the King of France being paraded through the street in chains, and your sensibility is in such disarray that you misrecognize it as liberty and the sovereignty of the people. Whereas we, across the channel, still know a "mob" when we see one, and it repels us.' Burke certainly appreciates that there is something at stake, for any political sensibility, in the question of whether or not to recognize the category of the mob.

Burke makes this explicit when he describes the parading of the ex-monarch through the streets. He paints this scene in gothic terms as a kind of horror show, a spectacle celebrating irrational violence. Strikingly, he achieves this by figuring the 'mob' of the Parisian people at their moment of assuming sovereignty both as a 'mob' of 'ferocious' women and as a 'mob' of murderous, dancing 'savages':

> It was (unless we have been strangely deceived) a spectacle more resembling a procession of American savages, entering into Onondaga, after some of their murders called victories, and leading into hovels hung round with scalps, their captives, overpowered with the scoffs and buffets of women as ferocious as themselves, much more than it resembled the triumphal pomp of a civilized martial nation....[15]

This is not a throwaway comparison: Burke reiterates it a few moments later when he tells us that the assembled crowds of Paris surrounded the procession of royal

---

[13] Edmund Burke, *Reflections on the Revolution in France* (London: Penguin, 2004), pp. 279–280, pp. 348, 366.
[14] Burke, *Reflections*, p. 179.
[15] Burke, *Reflections*, p. 159.

prisoners with 'horrid yells, and shrilling screams, and frantic dances, and infamous contumelies; and all the unutterable abominations of the furies of hell, in the abused shape of the vilest of women'.[16] In both these cases we see Burke transforming the ordinary people of Paris, at the very moment they assume sovereignty, into a fantasy of Indigenous violence (the 'horrid yells', 'shrilling screams', and 'frantic dances' all quite clearly evoke the image of tribal 'savages'), and in both passages the image of the unchained beast of popular sovereignty, in all its primal savagery, leads directly to the image of women who do not respect the boundaries of nature: 'women as ferocious as themselves'; 'all the unutterable abominations of the furies of hell, in the abused shape of the vilest of women'. It seems Burke feels that it is only in this triple equation between popular sovereignty, Indigenous sovereignty, and female sovereignty that the real 'mob' quality of the revolution can be seen for what it is.

Now, this Indigenous aspect of the question might seem surprising. Why, when the word 'mob' is used to damn common people attempting to take or dismantle state power, do we so often find ourselves in a scene, not simply of violent crowds and unruly women, but of sovereign Indigenous peoples, disfigured as wild savages? It is not enough merely to observe that this is 'racist', 'colonialist', or 'culturally chauvinist'—though obviously it is all those things—since there are many other racist, colonialist, and culturally chauvinist figures Burke could have used to damn the common people of France. Why this one? To entertain one counterfactual, why not, for example, fall back here on the whole discourse of Orientalism and compare the Parisian people toppling their king to tyrannical 'Eastern potentates', or similar? After all, Burke is arguing that, since anarchy is here, tyranny is just around the corner. Why compare the newly sovereign people of Paris to Indigenous peoples, specifically?

The answer is that sovereign Indigenous peoples, recast as 'savages', seem to raise the spectre of a life without the state in a way that Orientalist figures such as the 'Oriental despot' do not. Burke wants to teach us that a state ruled by the people is not a state but an anti-state, a non-state, a state of irrational violence, and it is the figure of the stateless 'savage' that allows him to express this. Again then, Burke's move to compare the revolutionaries to Indigenous women is neither weightless nor accidental: one only has to recall Rousseau to remind oneself that the struggle for popular sovereignty within Europe had been crucially inspired by the encounter with the Indigenous peoples of the so-called 'New World'. Repeatedly the accounts of progressive Enlightenment thinkers talk up the relative virtues of Indigenous ways of life: their relative freedom from hierarchies of class and caste, and also, in many cases, their relative equality of gender, with Indigenous woman becoming a figure of powerful, disturbing, unruled or unruly womanhood. Now,

[16] Burke, *Reflections*, p. 165.

obviously these were not the only things said of Indigenous peoples, and in particular, those who resisted calls for 'democracy' were liable to agree that it did seem 'Indian', in the sense of being mere savagery—indeed, it is this anti-Enlightenment spirit which the word 'mob' so often invokes. The sentiment here that might seem distinctively Burkean, but which really resides in the much older discourse of the mob, is that if ordinary people take over the power of the state, or if women take over the power of the state, and especially if *poor* women take over the power of the state, then you have really just lost the state: the state then is nothing, and you are back in an imagined state of nature, a Hobbesian war of all against all, where life is nasty, brutish, and short.

I would like to summarize this by reflecting on a single image: the frontispiece of Hobbes's *De Cive*.[17] In a brilliant reading of this frontispiece, Quentin Skinner notes that like many humanist frontispieces, the frontispiece to *De Cive* dramatizes two sides of an argument, and offers us a choice between them.[18] Do we choose Imperium, represented on the lower left as a white woman clad in classical garments, or do we choose Libertas, represented on the lower right as an aged Indigenous woman in a grass skirt, armed for war? Hobbes wants to convince us that the choice is clear: liberty might sound good, but really it means life outside the state, and that is mere savagery. Thus in the woods behind Libertas, Indigenous people hunt one another, the state of nature being a war of all against all, whereas in the fields behind Imperium, workers gather the harvest: these are fields of plenty, in which we reap the benefits of living under a powerful state. As Skinner points out, the scene behind Libertas is based on an image of Algonquian hunters in which the implied moral was precisely the opposite: in the original image, the people are hunting deer, not other people—which is to say, it too was an image of plenty. But Hobbes turns that on its head. He is deeply afraid of the new stirrings of popular sovereignty, and he wants to insist that liberty is barbarism: that a state in the hands of its people is a state destroyed, an anti-state, a war of all against all.

That is Skinner's reading of the image, and it seems a very perceptive one. I would simply like to add that though Hobbes designed this frontispiece four decades before the word 'mob' acquired its modern sense, we are nevertheless already seeing here precisely the triple equation that the word will come to codify: a horror at the prospect of popular sovereignty, which is understood as the collapse of the state—a horror which is then refigured as the repellent double spectacle of 'unruly' women, immodest, unreasonable, out of control, and as the violence of a tribe of warlike and unrulable 'savages'. In this respect we can observe

---

[17] Thanks to Joseph Hone for pointing out this frontispiece.
[18] Quentin Skinner, 'Hobbes and the Humanist Frontispiece', in *From Humanism to Hobbes: Studies in Rhetoric and Politics* (Cambridge: Cambridge University Press, 2018), 222–315.

that Hobbes responded to the prospect of popular sovereignty in England in the 1640s in precisely the manner in which Burke responded to the prospect of popular sovereignty in France in the 1790s.

Thus, this odd three-part compound was able to maintain a striking semantic stability over 150 years. That may seem a long time, but the stability of the 'mob' discourse—and with it, the stability of the structure of social power which lies at its root, namely the state—is in fact even more striking than this, for the three-part 'mob' is still with us today. Two brief examples will indicate this. When the US 'Capitol Riots' of January 2021 came to be symbolized by a man in pseudo-Native-American cosplay, many observers read this simply as a sign of the unhinged wackiness of the US far right. It would have been better if we had been able to see the quoting itself, together with observers's fascination with it, as a continuation of the discourse of the mob as it runs in a fairly straight line from Hobbes, through Burke, to today: a discourse that the protesters were in many cases self-consciously courting (some carried pitchforks), and that outraged observers duly deployed (*New York Times*: 'the mob descended on the Capitol'. *Washington Post*: 'Americans morphed into a mob').[19] A second example: in the 2010s, the #metoo movement was regularly demonized as a brand of 'mob justice' or 'witch hunt': which is to say, demonized as an illicit attempt to abrogate to ordinary women a power of judgement which ought to belong to the state. It ought not to surprise us when we find that this demonization often involved comparing the women involved to 'tribal' 'savages'—an invocation, in effect, of Hobbes. Take for instance the Prime Minister of Australia's declaration, while defending his Attorney-General from rape allegations, that 'There is not the mob process. There is not the tribe-has-spoken process. That's not how we run the rule of law in Australia.'[20] Here we see all three elements of the discourse: the 'mob' seeking sovereignty, the 'tribe' standing in judgement, and women seeking justice, all conceived of as threats to 'the rule of law', a phrase which functions in part as a synecdoche for the liberal state. In response to sentiments of this kind, the very least one can observe is that the slur term 'mob' has evidently maintained its ability coordinate a very particular set of oppressive power relations over a very long stretch of time.

[19] The Editorial Board, 'Opinion: Jan. 6 Was Worse Than We Knew', *New York Times*, 4 October 2021. https://www.nytimes.com/2021/10/02/opinion/jan-6-trump-eastman-election.html, accessed 3 October 2022. Rachel Weiner, Spencer S. Hsu, Tom Jackman, and Sahana Jayaraman, 'Desperate, Angry, Destructive: How Americans Morphed into a Mob', *Washington Post*, 9 November 2021. https://www.washingtonpost.com/dc-md-va/2021/11/09/rioters-charges-arrests-jan-6-insurrection/, accessed 3 October 2022. Fredrick Kunkle, 'Trump Supporter in Horns and Fur Is Charged in Capitol Riot', *Washington Post*, 9 January 2021. https://www.washingtonpost.com/local/jacob-chansely-horn-qanon-capitol-riot/2021/01/09/5d3c2c96-52b9-11eb-bda4-615aaefd0555_story.html, accessed 3 October 2022.

[20] Paul Karp and Daniel Hurst, 'Scott Morrison Rejects Calls for Independent Inquiry into Rape Allegation against Christian Porter', *The Guardian*, 3 March 2021.

The Southern Exception

Sketching the history of a keyword only takes us so far: once we have determined that we are dealing with a complex slur, we want to know what to do about it. Should we continue to use the term, knowing that it was developed in seventeenth-century England as a weapon against demands for sovereignty from below, and that it remains a weapon used for that purpose today? Neither criticism nor scholarship are neutral, and it seems to me that those of us who believe in the desirability of something like democracy ought to understand 'mob', for the most part, as a hostile foreign body that has made its home in our language, rendering it very difficult for us to imagine a state ruled differently, and still more difficult to imagine the value of lives lived outside the state.

Is there an alternative? What would it mean to reject or remake the whole discourse of the 'mob'? Would doing so help us to cultivate a genuinely democratic imagination, better prepared to embrace the prospect of a state ruled by its people, and perhaps even the much more radical prospect of a sovereign society living without the state? As it happens, history has already produced something like an answer to these questions. For the last three centuries 'mob' has been used in a strongly negative sense virtually everywhere English has been spoken. The unique exceptions are Australia and New Zealand, where a different range of meanings has developed, many of them very positive indeed. In working-class Australia, for example, to speak of 'our mob' is to speak in highly affectionate terms of a loose, inclusive social grouping comprising one's family, friends, and assorted plus-ones. This should not surprise us, for the Australian prison colony was founded in a situation almost calculated to catalyse all three elements of the 'mob' discourse. It was a society of convicts—precisely the 'mob' in the ordinary late eighteenth-century sense, the criminalized poor of England and Ireland, with a handful of Irish rebels thrown into the mix—leavened by a small group of rare and therefore troublingly empowered convict women, all occupying land inhabited by the world's oldest continuous Indigenous cultures. One result of this particular mixture was a thorough reframing of the term among all the groups just mentioned. But it was specifically among the Indigenous peoples of the continent that these new, local, positive meanings of 'mob' were to become most closely and warmly held. Indeed, it is not too much to say that today there is no single word more central to Aboriginal and Torres Strait Islander self-identification: to be 'mob' is to be Indigenous in the proudest sense.

I do not have time here to trace the history of this reversal, which was effected by all three overlapping constituencies, often in violent conflict with one another, at other times working in common. But I would like to close with a brief reflection on the significance of contemporary Indigenous uses of the term, with the aim of gesturing towards one way in which remaking the dominant anti-mob discourse might help us to reimagine our relationships both to popular sovereignty and to the state. Anyone at all familiar with Indigenous life in Australia will already appreciate something of the term's importance in that context, but for the benefit of those who are not, it may help to observe simply that the term is central enough to appear regularly in titles, whether of monographs by prominent writers (e.g. Ruby Langford Ginibi's *All My Mob*, Mudrooroo's *Us Mob*); of edited collections (*Our Mob Served: Aboriginal and Torres Strait Islander Histories of War and Defending Australia, Our Mob, God's Story: Aboriginal & Torres Strait Islander Artists Share Their Faith*); of popular bands ('The Wilcannia Mob', 'Us Mob'), of state initiatives (the NSW Aboriginal Affairs agency's 'Finding Your Mob' service, the Adelaide Festival's Centre' annual 'Our Mob' exhibition), even of Australia's first Indigenous children's TV series ('Us Mob').[21] But it is not just a matter of titles: the term plays an important role in daily life. So much so, in fact, that at least one scholar—Patrick Mullins—has suggested that for many Indigenous people today 'mob' serves the function of what anthropologist Sherry Ortner has called a cultural 'root metaphor':

> a symbol with great conceptual elaborating power ... [that] formulates the unity of cultural orientation underlying many aspects of experience.... [It is a symbol that] operates to sort out experience, to place it in cultural categories, and to help us think about how it all hangs together.[22]

Mullins notes that in many Indigenous Australian contexts, the word 'mob' articulates one of the central axes of cultural life, and connotes 'connectedness, equality and togetherness', with a special emphasis on the mutual obligation to share.[23] On this basis, he goes on to argue that this English word has now come to organize a range of social values which are continuous with pre-colonial Indigenous life. Now, claims of that order make some academics wince, and it is easy to see why: any attempt to draw a straight line between pre-colonial and contemporary Indigenous life risks effacing many complexities, among them the impact of colonization itself. But in another sense Mullins is merely restating something which is taken as common sense in many Indigenous circles today: that some of the strongest, most valued aspects of Indigenous social life—notably, the presence of strong bonds of mutual care, and the presumption that goods will not be hoarded by individuals,

---

[21] Ruby Langford Ginibi, *All My Mob* (St Lucia: University of Queensland Press, 2007); Mudrooroo, *Us Mob* (Sydney: Angus & Roberston, 1995); Allison Cadzow and Mary Anne Jebb, *Our Mob Served: Aboriginal and Torres Strait Islander Histories of War and Defending Australia* (Canberra: Aboriginal Studies Press, 2019); Louise Sherman and Christobel Mattingley (editors) *Our Mob, God's Story: Aboriginal & Torres Strait Islander, Artists Share Their Faith* (Sydney: Bible Society Australia, 2017). *Us Mob*, television series, directed by David Vadiveloo (Australian Broadcasting Corporation, 2005).

[22] Sherry Ortner, cited in Patrick Mullins, 'Mobs and Bosses: Structures of Aboriginal Sociality', *Australian Aboriginal Studies* 1 (2007), p. 1, p. 33.

[23] Mullins, 'Mobs and Bosses: Structures of Aboriginal Sociality', p. 33.

but shared—are in important respects inheritances from the pre-colonial social order.[24]

To indicate how much may be at stake in this inversion of the discourse of the 'mob', I will close by glancing at just one contemporary Indigenous thinker who understands the term as expressing a range of values continuous with pre-colonial Indigenous societies: the prominent Bundjalung/Australian novelist and essayist Melissa Lucashenko. Perhaps Lucashenko's most powerful meditation on the nature of what she terms the 'classical Aboriginal world' is her 2015 *Meanjin* essay 'The First Australian Democracy'.[25] There she argues that discussions about the origins of democracy ought to begin by acknowledging that democracy was invented, not in the fifth century BCE in classical Athens, but tens of millennia before on the continent that eventually came to be known as Australia. After all, she observes, by any reasonable measure the ordinary people of classical Aboriginal societies were much closer to the relevant levers of power than were the ordinary people of the patriarchal slave-state of classical Athens, a highly stratified society in which the functional *demos* consisted of a very small proportion of the population indeed. She acknowledges that classical Aboriginal societies appear to have had patriarchal and gerontocratic elements; nevertheless she observes that at least as much can be said of all the peoples usually celebrated in histories of democracy, from the ancient Athenians through to the proud inventors of parliamentary democracy who, prisoners in tow, arrived to begin their genocide in 1788.

There is certainly room to debate which English-language political term offers the best analogue for classical Aboriginal societies: Lucashenko uses the term 'democracy', but there are certainly other terms that spring to mind. One of them is 'communism': even the much-maligned 'primitive communism' of Marx and Engels (though the adjective spectacularly fails to capture the sophistication of the classical social order). Another option, perhaps more idiosyncratic: by all accounts classical Aboriginal societies were strongly bound by inherited custom, while also being highly resistant to resource hoarding, stratification, and state formation, and thus it sometimes seems to me helpful to think of them as comparable to something like a Burkean anarchism, as oxymoronic as that may sound in European terms (especially given Burke's veneration of the state). But let us stick with 'democracy' for now. For present purposes, Lucashenko's more important observation is that the basic egalitarianism of classical Aboriginal culture—its positive resistance to stratification—had a real effect on the subjective character of social life. Lucashenko quotes the anthropologist Fred Myers, writing of the Pintupi people of the central desert in the 1970s: 'Except for very close kin, no individual simply on the basis of being an elder can tell one what to do.... There are none who *in themselves* possess authority or the right to create that which others must follow.'

---

[24] Mullins, 'Mobs and Bosses: Structures of Aboriginal Sociality', p. 33.
[25] Melissa Lucashenko, 'The First Australian Democracy' *Meanjin* 74, no. 3 (2015).

She notes that one finds the same emphasis being drawn by observers right across the continent, throughout the whole history of the colony: thus for example in 1888 we find John Bulmer, mission manager in Victoria, bemoaning the fact that 'it is difficult to get into a blackfellow's head that one man is higher than another.' For Lucashenko, an egalitarian subjectivity of this kind is the sign and product of a genuinely democratic culture. At the level of subjectivity, this is what democracy looks like—at least in part.

All of this puts us in a better position to understand the distinctive—and historically novel—range of meaning now carried by the word 'mob' in much Indigenous discourse. Lucashenko cannot be accused of idealizing contemporary Aboriginal life: her novels, set in and around the present, do not shy away from alcoholism, domestic abuse, and casual violence. This ought to make us listen more carefully when she uses the term to speak of the most positive elements of actually existing Aboriginal sociality. Thus in a recent essay about Blak life under COVID, Lucashenko tells us that that one of the central reasons Blak communities were able to band together and protect their most vulnerable during the crisis was their continued commitment to the 'mob solidarity born out of classical Aboriginal culture'.[26] Far from being an anti-democratic slur, hostile to popular sovereignty, women, and Indigenous peoples, the word here warmly valorizes precisely those aspects of collective life which persist in being democratic, in the face of the most violent pressures to be otherwise. This strikes me as a precise reversal of anything Hobbes might have wished for.

To conclude, the English word 'mob' was forged three and a half centuries ago as a weapon against the new discourse of popular sovereignty, and it continues to serve in that capacity today. Yet on the Southern continent, working in the face of continuous violence and dispossession, the collective cultural intelligence of Indigenous peoples has reforged that weapon into a tool for expressing the human warmth characteristic of a much older democratic—or, if you prefer, communistic or anarchistic—culture, living beyond the state. The idiom thus produced offers us a glimpse of what it might mean to unlearn the dominant discourse of the 'mob', the better to imagine what subjective and collective life might feel like under conditions of actual democracy, were we to have it. If that is 'mob rule', then surely we could use a lot more of it.

---

[26] Melissa Lukashenko, 'It's No Accident that Blak Australia Has Survived the Pandemic So Well. Survival Is What We Do', *The Guardian Australia*, 22 July 2020. https://www.theguardian.com/australia-news/2020/jul/23/its-no-accident-that-blak-australia-has-survived-the-pandemic-so-well-survival-is-what-we-do, accessed 3 October 2020.

8
Phantom Justice and Orwellian Violence

Writing against Erasure in a Turbulent Hong Kong

Janny H. C. Leung

In 2019, street protests in Hong Kong drew global attention. The protests receded in 2020 when the coronavirus pandemic hit, and government crackdown intensified. Less in the spotlight is a literary movement that started at the same time as the street protests, but is still ongoing as to this date. This chapter depicts this movement, focusing on an eventful two-year period between 2019 and 2021.

In the first section, I provide the legal and sociopolitical context to the social movement, with special regard to the loss of freedom of speech and the threat to civil society. The second section reviews cultural and literary imaginaries in contemporary Hong Kong, surveying imaginations about the city before and after the handover.[1] The third section provides a non-exhaustive analysis of literary publications that appeared in Hong Kong since 2019, proposing an interpretation of their significance, with an eye on mid-2020—the passing of the National Security Law (NSL)—as a demarcation line. The analysis draws attention to the evolving legal consciousness expressed in these works.[2] I argue that these works serve as a testimony, as a way of redefining community, as cultural preservation, and as a method of practising freedom. These constitute literary defences against erasure, as I conclude in the final section. While adjusting to the new legal reality, writers have used living in truth as a way of coping with loss and countering Orwellian doublespeak.

'Securing' Hong Kong: Legal Violence and Political Resistance

As China increased its imperatives for regulating national security in Hong Kong, the rule of law has been eroding in Hong Kong.[3] Ironically, such erosion is largely achieved through the imposition of law itself, as Hong Kong laws become

---

[1] On 1 July 1997, the British transferred sovereignty over Hong Kong to China.
[2] Understood here as the ways in which ordinary people understand and make sense of law. See Patricia Ewick and Susan S. Silbey, 'Conformity, Contestation, and Resistance: An Account of Legal Consciousness', *New England Law Review* 26 (1992): pp. 731–749.
[3] Cora Chan and Fiona de Londras, 'Introduction: China's National Security in Hong Kong. A Challenge for Constitutionalism, Autonomy and the Rule of Law', in *China's National Security: Endangering*

nationalized. Major protests in post-handover Hong Kong were largely a response to the threat of legal violence, such as a proposed national security law which drew half a million people to the streets in 2003; or an expression of frustration with unfulfilled legal promises—for example, opposition to an electoral reform proposal that would significantly curtail the promise of universal suffrage guaranteed in the Basic Law led to the Umbrella Movement in 2014. Since Hong Kong's common law operates under China's authoritarian system, the divergent meanings of 'national security' and 'the rule of law' in the two jurisdictions translate into legal and political doublespeak that permeates the new normal in Hong Kong.

The 2019–2020 protests were triggered by a proposed extradition bill that would allow fugitives to be extradited to Taiwan and mainland China without sufficient human rights safeguards.[4] Opposition to the bill needs to be understood in the context of a dramatic incident that took place in 2015–2016: five booksellers, all connected with a dissident bookstore in Hong Kong, disappeared one after another in Hong Kong and Thailand, with there being no immigration record of them exiting the territory. They then reappeared in mainland China, confessing to various crimes on national television.[5] The fear was that the freedoms guaranteed by One Country, Two Systems would quickly erode under the extradition bill.[6]

More than 10,000 people were arrested during the protests, and close to 3000 have charged so far (as of 2022). Over 800 were charged for rioting, a public order crime enacted during the colonial era that carries a maximum prison term of ten years. While the protests successfully forced the Hong Kong government to formally withdraw the extradition bill, protesters did not know at the time that a different draconian law would replace it. The Chinese government imposed the NSL on Hong Kong on 30 June 2020, the enactment of which bypassed the Hong Kong legislature altogether. The NSL criminalizes secession, subversion, terrorism, and collusion with foreign organizations, all of which can be committed by speech alone. All NSL offences carry a maximum penalty of life imprisonment. The NSL stamped out months of unrest, which at its peak saw a quarter of the 7.5 million population marching together; it also dismantled civil society. The democratic culture was butchered by the arrest of forty-seven opposition figures, under the NSL offence of 'conspiracy to commit subversion', for organizing and participating in a primary election. Others were disqualified from their elected seats, and many went into exile. At the time of writing, over 240 people have been arrested under NSL

Hong Kong's Rule of Law?, edited by Cora Chan and Fiona de Londras (Oxford and New York, NY: Hart Publishing, 2020), pp. 1–15.

[4] The Fugitive Offenders and Mutual Legal Assistance in Criminal Matters Legislation (Amendment) Bill 2019, CB(3)510/18-19, 29 March 2019. See Cora Chan, 'Demise of "One Country, Two Systems"? Reflections on the Hong Kong Rendition Saga', *Hong Kong Law Journal 447*, University of Hong Kong Faculty of Law Research Paper No 2019/098 (2019), https://ssrn.com/abstract=3453136.

[5] Janny Leung, 'Publicity Stunts, Power Play, and Information Warfare in Mediatised Public Confessions', *Law and Humanities 11*, no. 1 (2017): pp. 82–101

[6] One Country, Two Systems is a constitutional principle whereby under China's rule, Hong Kong would enjoy a high degree of autonomy and retain its own systems and ways of life. The Basic Law, Hong Kong's constitutional document, gives effect to this principle.

offences, including the owner of a major opposition newspaper in Hong Kong,[7] members of a student group that ran a welfare programme for prisoners,[8] and a barrister who leads a democratic group that organized an annual commemorative Tiananmen Square vigil.[9] Dozens of civil society organizations have disbanded. Books written by dissidents have been pulled from public libraries.[10] Publishers, bookstores, and book fairs have been exercising self-censorship.[11] Media outlets have been closed or restructured, and their online archives deleted. Since texts are continually speaking—in that they may be circulated and read long after the authors have stopped writing—they could be seen to endanger national security even if they were published before the law came into place. The NSL does not only threaten speech freedoms in the present and in the future, but also wipes out evidence of freedoms enjoyed in the past by requiring active erasure.

As if the NSL were not sweeping enough, the government has been pushing other legislation that further restricts speech and cultural expression. These measures include a 'fake news' law that could be used against expressions that contradict official accounts,[12] amendment to copyright laws that could restrict derivative works such as parody and satire,[13] and amendments to the Film Censorship Ordinance that would ban films that are 'contrary to the interests of national security'.[14] Since 2019, political expression in Hong Kong has thus gone from robust to frail, with the introduction of the NSL being the watershed moment in the middle. It is against this background that the flurry of literary activities seen in the same period will be analysed.

---

[7] The newspaper ceased operations in June 2021. Johnny Patterson, 'Denial of Bail to Jimmy Lai Marks a "Legal Watershed" as Court of Final Appeal Confirms It Cannot Consider Constitutional Challenges to the NSL', *Hong Kong Watch*, 9 February 2021, https://www.hongkongwatch.org/all-posts/2021/2/9/denial-of-bail-to-jimmy-lai-marks-a-legal-watershed-as-court-of-final-appeal-confirms-it-cannot-consider-constitutional-challenges-to-the-nsl.

[8] Reuters, 'Hong Kong Police Arrest Three Members of Student Prisoner-Support Group', *Reuters*, 20 September 2021, https://www.reuters.com/world/china/hong-kong-police-arrest-three-members-student-prisoner-support-group-2021-09-20/.

[9] Eric Cheung and Jessie Yeung, 'National Security Police Arrest Organizers of Hong Kong's Tiananmen Vigil', *CNN*, 8 September 2021, https://www.cnn.com/2021/09/07/asia/hong-kong-alliance-arrest-nsl-intl-hnk/index.html.

[10] Laura Westbrook, 'Hong Kong Libraries Pull Democracy Activists' Books for National Security Review', *South China Morning Post*, 4 July 2020, https://www.scmp.com/news/hong-kong/politics/article/3091842/national-security-law-hong-libraries-pull-books-some.

[11] Associated Press, 'Self-Censorship Hits Hong Kong Book Fair in Wake of National Security Law', *The Guardian*, 15 July 2021, http://www.theguardian.com/books/2021/jul/15/self-censorship-hits-hong-kong-book-fair-in-wake-of-national-security-law; Nicolle Liu and Alice Woodhouse, 'Hong Kong's Publishers Self-Censor in Wake of National Security Law', *Financial Times*, 19 July 2020, https://www.ft.com/content/f1352a8a-3931-4160-99f2-af7bbe5b67db.

[12] Simon Shen, 'How China's Worldview Took Over Hong Kong', *The Diplomat*, 1 September 2021, https://thediplomat.com/2021/09/how-chinas-worldview-took-over-hong-kong/.

[13] Candice Chau, 'Hong Kong Gov't Mulls Copyright Law Amendments after Plans Shelved in 2011 and 2016 amid Protests', *Hong Kong Free Press HKFP*, 25 November 2021, https://hongkongfp.com/2021/11/25/hong-kong-govt-mulls-copyright-law-amendments-after-plans-shelved-in-2011-and-2016-amid-protests/.

[14] Jessie Pang, 'Hong Kong Proposes Film Censorship Law to "Safeguard National Security"', *Reuters*, 24 August 2021, https://www.reuters.com/world/china/hong-kong-proposes-film-censorship-law-safeguard-national-security-2021-08-24/.

Cultural and Literary Imaginaries in Contemporary Hong Kong

As Michael Berry points out, pain and trauma are a prominent theme in modern Chinese literature as writers represent and interpret the atrocities of the twentieth century.[15] Situated at the geographical and political margins, Hong Kong experienced these atrocities indirectly, but the events haunt Hong Kongers's imagination of their future. With the Tiananmen massacre occurring just five years after the signing of the Sino-British Joint Declaration, anxiety about the future of Hong Kong spawned a wave of emigration in the 1980s and 1990s. Artistic expressions in this pre-handover period portray what Berry describes as anticipatory trauma, which draws as much from 'fear for the future' as 'memories of the past'.[16] Famous local writers such as Xi Xi, Wong Bik Wan, Liu Yichang, and Dung Kai Cheung all published stories that envisioned a tragic future for Hong Kong. These stories are filled with violent disruptions. In a story called '1997', for example, Liu writes about a man who is preparing to emigrate but is run over by a car before he can leave Hong Kong. In a similar vein, violence, displacement, and uncertainty were central themes in Hong Kong cinema (in films such as *The Wicked City* by Tsui Hark and Fruit Chan's handover trilogy) during the same period.

Another influential account of pre-handover Hong Kong culture is offered by Ackbar Abbas. Abbas describes Hong Kong as a fragile city with not much of a pre-colonial past, always threatened with erasure as it was caught between two colonialities: Hong Kong culture is built upon the imminence of disappearance.[17] For example, Leung Ping-Kwan's poem 'At the North Point Car Ferry', which imagines a Hong Kong that was razed to the ground, though cars and people are still waiting to cross a flyover, simultaneously portrays catastrophic disappearance and a strange sense of normality. The last stanza is reproduced here:

> We came through cold daylight to get here, following a trail of broken glass. The last roadsigns pointed to rusty drums, everything smelling of smoke and burned rubber, though we couldn't see fire anywhere. In the narrow shelter of the flyover, cars and their people waited a turn to go over.[18]

The years that followed 1997 turned out to be anticlimactic. The imagined trauma did not materialize in the first two decades after the handover. No tanks rolled into the city. Protests were frequent, but violent suppression was rare. However,

---

[15] Michael Berry, *A History of Pain: Trauma in Modern Chinese Literature and Film* (New York, NY: Columbia University Press, 2008).
[16] Anticipatory trauma is 'a complex whereby angst and trepidation about the future are projected into catastrophic visions of what is to come, reinforced by historical or psychological scars from past traumas'. Berry, *A History of Pain*, p. 367.
[17] Abbas Ackbar, *Hong Kong: Culture and the Politics of Disappearance* (Hong Kong: Hong Kong University Press, 1997): pp. 1–15.
[18] Leung Ping-Kwan, *City at the End of Time: Poems by Leung Ping-Kwan*, translation by Gordon T.Osing and Leung Ping-Kwan, ed. Esther M. K. Cheung (New York, NY: Hong Kong University Press 2013), p. 48.

anxieties about the ongoing integration with China and concerns about eroding freedoms intensified over time. A longitudinal survey of ethnic identity shows that since the late 2000s, a local Hong Kong identity surged against a diminishing sense of national identity.[19] Indeed, it was very much a clash between a surging Hong Kong identity and a Chinese national identity that precipitated the massive social movement in 2019.

The decline of creative industries in Hong Kong since the 1990s is a manifestation of Hong Kong's identity crisis. A regional and global leader since the 1970s, Hong Kong films made HKD1.5 billion in box office revenue in 1992, but only HKD300 million in 2006.[20] The market share of Hong Kong film productions has been taken over by foreign language films and mainland-Hong Kong co-productions. Similarly, Cantopop has suffered in popularity since the 1990s. Chu blames these declines on the misguided emphasis on nationalization and internationalization at the cost of localization.[21] Hong Kong was 'lost in translation' when it tried to become another Chinese city and another global city. In the same vein, identity confusion, and bicultural uneasiness are recurring themes in post-handover Hong Kong literature. Lee identifies these themes at play in works such as *The Death of Lo Kei* (2018) by Wong Bik Wan and *Postcolonial Affairs of Food and the Heart* (2009) by Leung Ping-Kwan.[22]

Despite being an idealization,[23] the rule of law, or 法治 (*faat3 zi6*) in Chinese, has been regarded as a core value of post-handover Hong Kong identity, a notion in which Hong Kongers take pride to differentiate Hong Kong from the rest of China.[24] With the dramatic changes in the Hong Kong sociopolitical landscape since 2019, the same Chinese term, 法治, is now frequently used by the government to refer to rule *by* law—providing a prime example of legal doublespeak that thinly masks Hong Kong's rapid descent from a semi-democratic and relatively free society to an authoritarian order. Since the new legal reality overlays and overpowers the old without officially replacing it, the rule of law is like a phantom limb that one can feel until one tries to reach for it, only to realize that it has been amputated. As I will argue below, the resulting sense of shock and loss is a prevailing theme in Hong Kong literature today.

---

[19] H. Christoph Steinhardt, Linda Chelan Li, and Yihong Jiang, 'The Identity Shift in Hong Kong since 1997: Measurement and Explanation', *Journal of Contemporary China* 27, no. 110 (March 2018): pp. 261–276, https://doi.org/10.1080/10670564.2018.1389030.

[20] Yiu-Wai Chu, *Lost in Transition: Hong Kong Culture in the Age of China* (Albany, NY: SUNY Press, 2013), p. 92.

[21] Chu, *Lost in Transition*, p. 92.

[22] Tong King Lee, 'Hong Kong Literature: Colonialism, Cosmopolitanism, Consumption', *Journal of Modern Literature* 44, no. 2 (2021): p. 62, https://doi.org/10.2979/jmodelite.44.2.06.

[23] See Ng and Wong (2017) for a historical review of the limited rule of law during British Hong Kong. Michael H. K. Ng and John Wong, eds., *Civil Unrest and Governance in Hong Kong: Law and Order from Historical and Cultural Perspectives*, 1st ed. (London: Routledge, 2017), https://doi.org/10.4324/9781315537252.

[24] See for example a declaration of Hong Kong's core values in 2004 by civil societies in Hong Kong. Ambrose Leung, 'Push to Defend City's Core Values', *South China Morning Post*, 7 June 2004, https://www.scmp.com/article/458500/push-defend-citys-core-values.

Writing Hong Kong, 2019–2021

My review of these literary publications does not aim to be exhaustive, not least because of the challenge of surveying the plethora of publications released under the threat of the NSL.[25] I include works of diverse genres, and of varying literary quality, written in both Chinese and English. With the aim of gauging Hong Kongers's lived experience of law through the lens of literature, I examine these works with an eye to their explicit and implicit expressions of legal consciousness, and their response to Orwellian violence that struck the city with the enactment of the NSL in mid-2020.

Writing as Testimony

When the protests broke out in June 2019, an explosion of publications documented the event. There was an acute awareness that this was a historical moment, as record numbers of people took to the street. Countless volumes of photographic collections and textual chronicles were published to record history and preserve 'the truth', as protestors and the government presented contrasting accounts of what was unfolding. The protestors saw themselves as fighters of democracy and freedom, who demonstrated unity and bravery in the face of unprecedented oppression. The government, however, portrayed them as violent rioters brainwashed by foreign powers, who disrupted the social order and threatened public safety. Faceless protestors in the leaderless movement were routinely dehumanized in pro-establishment discourse: they have been described as zombies, cockroaches, and the like.

Publications like *Freedom in June* (September 2019; Chinese) remind readers of the flesh and blood behind the masks and underneath the black bloc.[26] Written by twenty-two Hong Kongers connected through the Internet, including a journalist, social worker, teacher, designer, student, cosplayer, computer engineer, writer, public servant, front line protester, banker, and historian, the book presents a chronological illustration of how the protests escalated. Even though these texts may seem to present only one side of the story, they are always heteroglossic. As Bakhtin observes, centripetal forces (official discourses) and centrifugal forces (unofficial discourses) are interdependent.[27] For example, the

---

[25] Many of these publications were printed by small independent publishers and are not carried in major bookstores (almost all of which are now owned by pro-establishment companies); some were printed in Taiwan only. Some were printed in limited quantities and sold in fundraising drives.

[26] Twenty-Two Hongkongers, *Freedom in June* 自由六月 (Taiwan: Independent and Unique, 2019).
Black bloc refers to a tactic used by protestors to conceal their identity by wearing black clothing including face coverings.

[27] Mikhail M. Bakhtin, 'Discourse in the Novel'. In *The Dialogic Imagination: Four Essays*, edited by Michael Holquist, translated by Caryl Emerson and Michael Holquist (Austin, TX and London: University of Texas Press, 1981), pp. 259–422.

texts implicitly invite the readers to decide whether the people who were involved in the movement were protestors or rioters. Similarly, *Disappearing Lennon Walls* (2019, Chinese) contains a textual and visual chronicle of the social movement between June and October 2019.[28] Inspired by the John Lennon Wall in Prague, Lennon Walls—message boards made up of post-it notes filled with handwritten words of encouragement—have been a common occurrence in protests in Hong Kong since the Umbrella Movement in 2014. Echoing Abbas's characterization of Hong Kong culture, the blurb of the book starts with an anticipation of disappearance: 'When this book is published, most Lennon Walls in Hong Kong may have been removed.' The anonymous author would be proven right—in the months to come, the walls would be torn down, rebuilt, only to be torn down again.

Some works are autobiographical, first-hand accounts of the social movement. These accounts reflect the strong sense of injustice that caused the protests to escalate in a response to police brutality. One of the first widely known victims of such police brutality was a former liberal studies teacher, Raymond Yeung Tsz-chun, who lost most of his vision in one eye after he was hit by a police projectile. His book *A Journey through the Brick Wall* (2020, Chinese) tells the story of his eight-year journey as a socially conscious teacher, from an unlikely beginning (he was a student who did not do very well in school) to an abrupt end in 2019.[29] Although only the last chapter describes his experience in the social movement, the rest of the book brings to life the portrait of a protestor in a faceless crowd. Another autobiographical book, *Dark Night in Yuen Long* (2020, Chinese), was written by a former journalist who was beaten up by thugs attacking commuters and protesters in the Yuen Long subway station on 21 July 2019.[30] That the police did not respond to the incident for hours was a turning point in the social movement, prompting some protesters to accept the use of force as a strategy for radicalizing the movement. The book not only contains the journalist's first-hand account of the incident, but also interviews with more than forty eyewitnesses. These autobiographies re-humanize participants in the protests, complicating the official rhetoric by revealing them to be real people from all walks of life.

Some autobiographical accounts provide testimonies of the emotional and social aftermath of the protests. *After Shock: Essays From Hong Kong* is a collection of English prose pieces written by eleven journalists, which does not focus on objective reportage but invites contributing authors to look inwards to reflect on how the social movement has shaped or shocked them as individuals.[31] Holmes

---

[28] Guardian of Hong Kong, *Disappearing Lennon Walls* 消失了的連儂牆 (Hong Kong: Isaiah, 2019).
[29] Raymond Yeung Tsz-Chun, *A Journey Through the Brick Wall* 逆權教師 (Hong Kong: Times C.C., 2020).
[30] Ryan Chun-kong Lau, *Dark Night in Yuen Long: My Memory and Everyone's* 元朗黑夜: 我的記憶和眾人的記憶 (Hong Kong: Lauyeah Production Ltd, 2020).
[31] Holmes Chan, 'The Adversary', in Holmes Chan (ed.), *After Shock: Essays from Hong Kong* (Hong Kong: Small Tune Press, 2020), pp. 45–54.

Chan, both a contributor and editor of the book, probes into the expressive and symbolic functions of violence, both on the part of the protestors and the police. Chan expresses deep anger about the way officials engage in doublespeak to disguise the truth about state violence—for instance, using phrases like 'use of force' in place of 'violence'. Concerned about an official rewriting of history, he reflects, 'the strength of the reality you propose does not depend on its resemblance to the world; it is measured only against the strength of the alternate reality coming from your opponent'.[32] Competing narratives in public discourse are testimonies to a trial by the public; by publishing testimonies that will allow history to judge, writers are concurrently expressing a lack of faith in the truth-seeking function of current legal institutions.

Testimonial accounts have also been published by journalists. A notable book is *Voices Out of the Darkness—Stories from the 2019 Hong Kong Protests* by Tam Wai-wan Vivian (2020, Chinese), which offers observant feature stories of ordinary people she encountered during the social movement.[33] *Our Last Evolution* (2020, Chinese) is another, which is authored by nineteen journalists who fled to Taiwan.[34] The book consists of interviews with participants who played different roles in the social movement, including those who are now in exile and some who have charges pending. Many interviewees are concerned about safeguarding the truth. For example, an interviewee who witnessed the Yuen Long attacks expresses her concern that the Independent Police Complaints Council distorted the event as 'fighting between two groups'.[35]

Preserving the truth entails not only representing an observable reality, but also articulating people's motivations and psychology amidst counter-narratives. Fictional works often engage in this kind of truth-telling. *MANGA HONG KONG DEMO GEKIDOU! 200 NICHI* (June 2020), by Koji Akita, is a manga that narrates the experience of a politically ignorant Japanese young man living in Hong Kong who gradually learns about the struggles of Hong Kongers and participates in the protest.[36] Although fictionalized, the manga documents critical events during the first 200 days of the movement, and attempts to explain controversial behaviour by protesters (such as occupying the airport and damaging property owned by Chinese businesses) to outsiders. It is interspersed with 'columns' of contextual notes that provide the reader with a full picture of events that were happening in the background of the story. First published in Japan in 2019 before being translated into traditional Chinese in 2020, the manga seems determined to educate readers about what happened in Hong Kong.

---

[32] *After Shock* p. 50.
[33] Vivian Wai-wan Tam, *Voices Out of the Darkness—Stories from the 2019 Hong Kong Protests* 天愈黑, 星愈亮: 反修例運動的人和事 (Hong Kong: Breakthrough Ltd, 2020).
[34] People under the Umbrellas, *Our Last Evolution* 我們的最後進化 (Taiwan: Alone Publishing, 2020).
[35] People under the Umbrellas, *Our Last Evolution*, p. 97.
[36] Koji Akita, TOA, *Manga Hongkong Demo Gekido! 200 Days* (Hong Kong: Humming Publishing Ltd, 2020).

After the passing of the NSL, the publication of testimonial accounts of the movement seemed to have slowed down as the crackdown continues. However, even though the NSL intends to reach individuals in any jurisdiction, these accounts continue to be published by the expanding Hong Kong diaspora. Apart from *Our Last Evolution*, another example of this burgeoning diasporic literature is *Hong Kong without Us: A People's Poetry* (2021), published by a Hong Kong poet in Berkeley, California, which began as poems on postcards distributed to draw international attention to Hong Kong's plight.[37] The English collection contained poems submitted to the Project, as well as political messages posted on the streets, on news websites, and social media platforms, that were translated and recreated as English poems. Some striking examples are wills young protesters wrote for their family, anticipating their deaths and expressing as their last wish that their willingness to sacrifice themselves for Hong Kong would be understood. Written in the shadow of NSL, the author refuses to tiptoe around questions of freedom of expression and begins the postscript with the provocative sentence, 'This is a criminal book.'

Writing as Redefining Community

What people read can serve as a barometer of the present social climate. At the Eslite bookstore in Hong Kong, some of the recent best-selling non-fiction works include *On Tyranny* by Timothy Snyder, practical advice offered by the Yale historian on what citizens can do in the age of rising authoritarian populism, and *The Power of the Powerless*, a political essay written by Czech dissident and president Václav Havel.[38] Dystopian novels such as George Orwell's *1984* and *Animal Farm* and Aldous Huxley's *Brave New World* feature prominently among best-selling fiction. The same novels were also among the most borrowed adult English fiction from Hong Kong Public Libraries in 2020.[39] Hong Kong people seem eager to gain perspectives on Big Brother and doublespeak as they navigate their new political reality.

Literature provides a pathway to collective catharsis and a means of finding strength when the reader realizes that they are not alone. In the first few months of the social movement participants found a sense of community through their collective resistance, reflected in various texts published in Hong Kong at this time. In

---

[37] Bauhinia Project (eds), *Hong Kong Without Us: A People's Poetry* (Athens, GA: University of Georgia Press, 2021).
[38] See https://meet.eslite.com/hk/tc/product/202108170001 and https://meet.eslite.com/hk/tc/product/202109020005 for recent top sellers.
[39] Hong Kong Free Press, 'Orwell Novels Leap in Popularity on "Top 100 Most Borrowed Books" in Hong Kong', *Hong Kong Free Press HKFP*, 20 April 2021, Orwell novels leap in popularity on 'Top 100 Most Borrowed Books' in Hong Kong—Hong Kong Free Press HKFP. See also Hong Kong Public Libraries, 'Top 100 Most Borrowed Books', *Hong Kong Public Libraries*, Adult Lending Fiction 2020—Collections.

a collection of literary prose, *Darkness under the Sun* (June 2020; Chinese),[40] Hon Lai-Chu writes: 'In the past, people always said, this is a rootless city. This summer, the city finally took root, one that was woven together from many wounds, and that had become our collective identity.'[41] The Hong Kong she was writing about was at a transitional stage. This is how she describes it: 'The old world has disappeared. The new world has yet to arrive. It is as though people are trapped in a long dark tunnel, uncertain of what is ahead.'[42] In her subsequent book, *Half Eclipse*, published more than a year later (July 2021; Chinese), she describes the current state of living as the bardo—which is a Buddhist intermediate state of existence between death and rebirth.[43] Even though there is hope of light at the end of the tunnel or of being reborn, the shared anxieties and loss of the past in the current state bind Hong Kongers together. If earlier literature in post-handover Hong Kong often expressed a confused sense of identity, this confusion has since been replaced by clarity. What emerges is a collective identity based less on historical roots and more on shared experience.

We can observe a similar transition in *Breakazine*, a quarterly magazine with a strong focus on social issues, just by glancing at the titles of its recent issues (see Table 8.1):

Table 8.1 Recent titles of *Breakazine*, p. 206

Issue	Publication Date	Title
059	September 2019	*Hong Kong in Tears*
060	January 2020	*Unquenchable Courage*
061	May 2020	*Live Like It's Doomsday*
062	July 2020	*Dangerous Read*
063	December 2020	*Silence*
064	April 2021	*The Way We Cook*
065	July 2021	*Leaving or Staying*

When the NSL was enacted, the magazine turned from telling stories of injustice, shock, bravery and sacrifice to exploring how to find strength when everything seems to have been shattered, including through cooking and self-care. If we think of writing as a way of defining a sense of possible community, we might observe that since 2019, literary works in Hong Kong have gradually shifted from

---

[40] Lai Chu Hon 韓麗珠, *Darkness under The Sun* 黑日 (Taiwan: Acro Polis, 2020).

[41] My Translation. The Chinese original:「以往, 人們總是說, 這是個無根的城市。這個夏天, 城市終於長出了根, 由眾多傷口盤結而成的根部, 成了我們共同的身分。」

[42] My Translation. The Chinese original:「舊的世界已經消失了, 新的世界還沒有來, 人們恍如卡在一道長長的闇黑的隧道中, 無法肯定前方還有甚麼...」

[43] Lai Chu Hon 韓麗珠, *Half Eclipse* 半蝕 (Taiwan: Acro Polis, 2021).

defining a community based on resistance, to redefining it in terms of persistence: a community with the courage to keep its spirit free.[44]

This redefined community shares wisdom about how to live under an authoritarian regime. Such wisdom may be found not only by inspecting the present, but also by revisiting the past. *Stories that Belong to Hong Kongers* (June 2021; Chinese) is a collection of short stories, written from the first-person perspective of real and fictional historical figures who recount their struggles in earlier days in Hong Kong.[45] They include a soldier from the Rajput Regiment of the Indian Army helping the British to defend Hong Kong during the Japanese invasion, who was captured and tortured by the Japanese army; he chooses death over betrayal.[46] The protagonist of another short story, entitled 'Sau Zuk, Don't Turn Back When You Leave', is a Chinese white dolphin that lives in Hong Kong waters.[47] Before the reader finds out that the story is about a dolphin, the opening paragraph contains an ambiguous portrayal that invokes the protests and their social consequences in Hong Kong: 'A few years ago, many *sau zuk* have been chased, cornered, and attacked, causing countless injuries and deaths. Surviving *sau zuk* are all talking about migrating, wanting to leave this sad place. Before every *sau zuk* leaves, I say goodbye to them.' The protagonist goes on to lament that the survival of these dolphins has been threatened by a government that places economic interests above all else. As Hong Kong sees an exodus of its population, the forced disappearance of dolphins captures the feelings of anger, abandonment, and loss that penetrate society. This collection of historical fiction thus reinvigorates social bonding, not only through its depiction of the collective struggles of the past, but also by evoking the emotions of the present.

Writing as Cultural Survival

Recent years have seen a flurry of publications on Hong Kong culture, examining topics that range from architecture to street food. One example documents old shops and sunset industries in Hong Kong, setting out to explore 'the aesthetics of disappearance' in the city and to use beauty to invite collective remembrance.[48] Another is a quarterly magazine called *Being HK*, which explores local landscapes,

---

[44] Ackbar, *Hong Kong*, p. 116.
[45] Bluegodzi 藍橘子, *Stories That Belong to Hong Kongers* 屬於香港人 (Hong Kong: Welcome Back Ltd, 2021).
[46] 'Not Yet Over', in Bluegodzi, *Stories that Belong to Hong Kongers*, pp. 44–50.
[47] *Sau zuk* is a Cantonese word that literally means 'hand and feet', used to refer to people so closely connected that they feel as though they are one. The phrase was used frequently during the recent social movement to refer to like-minded people. Hilary Leung, 'Hong Kong's Protestors Have Their Own Special Slang. Here's a Glossary of Some Common Terms', *Time*, 6 September 2019, https://time.com/5668286/hong-kong-protests-slang-language-cantonese-glossary/.
[48] Lam Hiuman, *Hong Kong Reminiscence: Document of Hong Kong's Old Stories* 香港遺美 (Hong Kong: Extraordinary Publishing, 2021).

businesses, artworks, history, and popular culture.[49] Although these publications may not be overtly political, their celebration of cultural heritage can be read as a way of protecting local identity and maintaining symbolic borders, especially as cultural survival is under threat.

An important dimension of the attempt to defend local culture is linguistic: a Cantonese literary movement has been quietly in the making. Although Cantonese literature has a long history, formal writing in contemporary Hong Kong, including official documents and 'serious' literary writing, is dominated by standard Chinese (which is based on Mandarin).[50] Written Cantonese is commonly seen in informal writing such as advertisements, subtitles, comic books, magazines, or personal communications. As local Hong Kong identity surged against a diminishing sense of national identity, there has been a movement to reinstate Cantonese as a literary language.[51] One notable effort is the launch of a Cantonese literary magazine called *Resonate* (迴響), the first issue of which was published in June 2020—the same month as the passing of the NSL. The monthly magazine features fiction and prose, and also educates its readers about how Cantonese words are written. The promotion of written Cantonese may be seen as part of a larger vernacular language movement that attempts to diminish the disconnect between the way we speak and the way we write, considering the grammatical and lexical differences between spoken Cantonese and standard Chinese. Relatedly, a series of books entitled *Hong Kongers' Speech*[52] now offer calligraphy practice with written Cantonese characters, which subverts the association between calligraphy and classical Chinese characters.[53]

The dystopian novels mentioned earlier have been popular in Hong Kong both in their English original and in their Chinese translation. Although Chinese translations of many of these classic works have been around for a long time, it is notable that many new translations appeared following the 2019 protests. For example, a translation of *Animal Farm* into standard Chinese by Shiu Ming Joseph Lau was published by The Chinese University of Hong Kong Press in 2020. More interestingly, two Cantonese translations were published in 2021.[54] The Times C.C. version, published bilingually in Cantonese and English, contains the following

---

[49] Being HK 就係香港, published by Being Media Limited.

[50] Chung Ming Wong, '粵語文學資料初探 (1900–1970) Introduction to Cantonese Dialect Literature (1900–1970)', *Journal of Modern Literature in Chinese* 現代中文文學學報 vol. 8-9, no. 2–1 (2008): pp. 112–122; Donald Bruce Snow, 'Written Cantonese and the Culture of Hong Kong: The Growth of a Dialect Literature' (Ph.D. dissertation, Indiana University, 1991), https://www.proquest.com/docview/303947953/abstract/A708344EF42C4719PQ/1.

[51] Steinhardt, H. Christoph, Li, Linda Chelan, and Jiang, Yihong, 'The Identity Shift in Hong Kong since 1997', *Journal of Contemporary China* vol. 27, no. 110 (2018): pp. 261–276.

[52] The *Hong Kongers' Speech* series is published by Enlighten & Fish.

[53] Cantonese has inherited many classical Chinese characters but it has also developed its own regional vocabulary, which adopts some written characters that are not found in standard Chinese and thus may not be intelligible to readers of standard Chinese.

[54] George Orwell, *Animal Farm*, translated by Thomas Tsoi (Hong Kong: Bleu Publications, 2021); George Orwell, *Animal Farm*, translated by Times C.C. (Hong Kong: Hillway, 2021).

paratext on its cover that helps frame the interpretation of the book: 'A fable told 70 years ago now staged in Hong Kong. Use (your) familiar language to re-read a classic; use a classic to re-read (your) unfamiliar home' (original in Cantonese; my translation). The Times C.C. translation not only uses Cantonese, but also occasionally engages in translanguaging between English and Cantonese (such as '連續幾個鐘不停loop', as a translation of 'keep it up for hours on end') to reflect the speaking habit of Hong Kongers.[55] Cultural expressions are one of the few remaining means of asserting a Hong Kong identity as nationalization continues.

Writing as Practising Freedom

Another notable shift in the literature published following the events of 2019, which reflects the shadow cast by the NSL, is to use writing as a way of testing, pushing, and exercising freedom of speech. To think of these authors as being brave to write *in spite of* fear and oppression is a mistake; they write *because of*, or *in response to*, fear and oppression. This echoes Foucault's idea that freedom is practice: even though in a state of domination, such practice may be extremely confined.[56] While the boundaries of new laws in Hong Kong are still being tested, writing is a way of practising freedoms that exist in the closing gap between the overlapping old and new legal realities.

Some authors counter the pressure of self-censorship by exposing the elephant in the room; that is by openly acknowledging that they are self-censoring. The comic book *If I Could Keep Drawing* (2020; Chinese) does so playfully.[57] The book features a cover image with a man writing on a chalkboard. His mouth is covered by a hand with a red-sleeved arm, the owner of which is not visible to the reader. The artist, vawongsir, lost his teaching job for the political comics he drew. A sense of humour, often dark, permeates the book. One of the comic strips depicts Jesus and his disciples being subjected to temperature checks and having to sit at different tables at the Last Supper, poking fun at the gathering restriction in Hong Kong during the Covid-19 pandemic. Another is entitled 'Do not call yourself a Hong Konger unless you have tried…'. The comic strip contains drawings of many famous Hong Kong snacks including egg waffles, custard tarts, pineapple buns, fish balls, and tofu pudding. A canister of tear gas appears among the food items, its presence an uncanny indicator of what one also needs to 'try' in order to call themselves a Hong Konger today. Notably, multiple comic strips contain pixelated

---

[55] Orwell, *Animal Farm* (Hong Kong: Hillway 2021), pp. 60–61.
[56] Michel Foucault, 'The Ethic of Care for the Self as a Practice of Freedom: An Interview with Michel Foucault on January 20, 1984', *Philosophy & Social Criticism* 12, no. 2-3 (July 1987): pp. 112–131, https://doi.org/10.1177/019145378701200202.
[57] vawongsir, *If I Could Keep Drawing 假如讓我畫下去* (Hong Kong: Hillway Press, 2020). Consistent with its informal style, the comic uses written Cantonese.

drawings, with a note next to the pixelation that reads '*After self-censorship. (I) don't want to be arrested!' This, along with another comic strip of a monopoly board where landing on any property leads one to jail, conveys fear of the wide latitude of the law and a lack of confidence in the legal protection of one's rights and freedom. By openly acknowledging his vulnerability and problematizing his freedom, the author persists in exercising his freedom of expression while resisting ideological assimilation. In other words, he refuses to be silent while being silenced.

Just like political suppression after the 1989 Tiananmen massacre led to a wave of allegorical literature that contains veiled depictions of violence, speech censorship in Hong Kong today has also pushed authors towards allegory, decontextualization, and abstraction.[58] By moving away from the context of contemporary Hong Kong politics, authors find the space to practice their freedom of thought. One example is the comic book *Kafka* (2021; Chinese) by veteran Hong Kong comic artist Li Chi Tat.[59] The book features absurdist short stories that take place in an unidentified setting, with architecture and a landscape that bear more resemblance to Europe than Hong Kong. All the stories revolve around characters finding themselves in precarious situations, with divergent responses. In the story *Wolves*, a wolf threatens to eat a groom-to-be, who readily concedes to feeding it, only to find the insatiable beast demanding more and more. In *Vulture*, a vulture attacks a man's feet; when a passer-by asks him why he tolerates it, he says he feels defenceless and has chosen to sacrifice them. The vulture goes on to kill him by piercing his neck. The last story in the book, entitled *War*, describes a group of masked military men invading a village and killing its people. To their shock, the men come across an old man in ragged clothes and with wings on his back. They ask why he does not fly away. The man replies, defiantly: 'Huh, why would we leave our city? Leave our home? Abandon the dead and our belief?' The fictional world in these stories is ruled by military men or by beasts, with no sign of the rule of law. Most of the stories do not have a clear ending. Despite the sense of impending doom that penetrates the stories, the narrative focus is on choices that characters still get to make in defending their freedom and survival.

In a similar vein, the graphic novel *After Havoc* tells the story of young people struggling to survive in a post-apocalyptic Hong Kong that was hit by a tsunami, where bandits imprison and extract forced labour from them and where older generation are complacent and disinterested in changing the future.[60] As the story progresses, readers are exposed to page after page of familiar Hong Kong scenery now in ruins, with people cut off from the outside world and from one another. The young protagonist relentlessly searches for a path forward despite obstacles;

---

[58] Berry, *A History of Pain*, p. 11
[59] Li Chi Tat, *Kafka* (Hong Kong: Today Publications, 2021).
[60] Pen So, *After Havoc* 災難之後 (Hong Kong: Today Publications, 2021).

he eventually dies from disease, leaving behind handwritten letters that tell his story. Even though his body succumbs, his spirit lives.

Living in Truth: Coping with Phantom Justice and Countering Orwellian Violence

From testimonial writing that serves a truth-preserving function, literature that attempts to redefine community as civil society dissolves, literature that contributes to cultural survival, to literature that practises eroding freedoms, writing Hong Kong since 2019 has been a race against erasure. Disappearance is agentless and gradual; erasure is active and rapid. Compared to the fight against legal violence that triggered the street protests, erasure is a different type of injustice that happens on the battlefields of public discourse, educational textbooks, and cultural expression. It is therefore through speech that erasure may be resisted. Compared to the digitally coordinated street protests, which are fluid and transient, literature has the potential to travel through space and time.

There is a corresponding change of mood in the literature published in Hong Kong since 2019, with the NSL, passed in mid-2020, as a dividing line. The earlier works motivate the reader, praising the courage of the protesters and illustrating the injustices they face. In later publications, while the rage remains, the writing itself requires courage. The injustice this writing seeks to counter has shifted from legal and police violence to the threatened erasure of collective memory.

At the height of the protests in 2019, despite rage and anger about the impending legal violence, Hong Kongers retained enough faith in the legal and political system that they reflexively sought to use it for protection: protesters demanded the withdrawal of the extradition bill, an independent inquiry into alleged police brutality, a halt to the characterization of protests as 'riots', amnesty to arrested protesters, and universal suffrage. All demands fell within the familiar pathways for redressing injustice that Hong Kong people knew. New laws have hollowed out the formerly acceptable way of doing things in Hong Kong: speaking up against injustice has become a dangerous endeavour, and people's faith in legal recourse has evaporated. The Basic Law guarantees freedom of speech, but people exercising this right are now being arrested because the NSL trumps other laws. At the same time, colonial laws such as sedition, which have not been used for a long time, are now being invoked to handle dissent.[61] Before the handover, Abbas notes the fragilities of a Hong Kong caught between two forms of colonialism.[62] In Hong Kong today, although the British have long since departed, the old colonial legal regime and new authoritarian legal regime form two walls that are closing

---

[61] *HKSAR v. Tam Tak Chi [2020]* DCCC927, 928, 930/2020.
[62] Abbas, *Hong Kong*, pp.1–15.

in. Between 2019 and 2021, Hong Kongers's legal consciousness quickly evolved. Hong Kong writing has registered a shift from seeing law as a protector of rights to seeing it as a tool of oppression. The popular vision of law as a pathway to social justice has disappeared.

Law is a boundary-making practice that creates lived experience.[63] As new boundaries are drawn, we reconfigure our mental maps and encounter cognitive dissonance in the form of the lingering presence of old boundaries that are still very much alive in our memories. This is not unlike losing a limb, but feeling that it is still attached. Recent literary works in Hong Kong capture the sense of disorientation and loss that results from this mental remapping. The trauma of the amputation has not been processed, and the rule of law—still actively present in public discourse with its reinvented meaning—is now a phantom limb that reminds Hong Kong of its vanishing past.

The best way of countering Orwellian violence is by living in truth, as Václav Havel suggests.[64] This is what Hong Kong writers have been doing: holding on to their identity, telling their story, practising the freedoms that they still have. Boundaries are not only geographical and institutional, but also symbolic and social; to that extent, states do not have a monopoly in boundary-making.[65] Writing can be used to renegotiate social boundaries, to find safe spaces for community, to reimagine a Hong Kong identity that crosses geographical boundaries as the diaspora grows. In turbulent times like this, social bonding can provide the security that people need for survival.[66] The more unstoppable the blurring of the actual geo-political boundaries appears to be, the more Hong Kongers feel the need to reassert symbolic and cultural boundaries.[67] This need to reassert cultural boundaries will only continue as the disappearance of a Hong Kong culture and identity remains a lurking threat, as the national security police begin to turn their attention to cultural expression.[68]

---

[63] Joel S. Migdal, 'Mental Maps and Virtual Checkpoints', in *Boundaries and Belonging: States and Societies in the Struggle to Shape Identities and Local Practices*, ed. Joel S. Migdal (Cambridge: Cambridge University Press, 2004), pp. 3–26.
[64] Václav Havel, *The Power of the Powerless* (Vintage Classics, 2018).
[65] Migdal, 'Mental Maps and Virtual Checkpoints'.
[66] Migdal, 'Mental Maps and Virtual Checkpoints', p. 14.
[67] Carol A. G. Jones, *Lost in China?: Law, Culture and Identity in Post-1997 Hong Kong* (Cambridge: Cambridge University Press, 2015).
[68] Candice Chau, 'Hong Kong National Security Police Explain Why Children's Picture Books about Sheep Are Seditious', *Hong Kong Free Press*, 22 July 2021, https://hongkongfp.com/2021/07/22/hong-kong-national-security-police-explain-why-childrens-picture-books-about-sheep-are-seditious/.

9
The Crowd in This Moment

Troubling the Immanence of Riots in Contemporary US Literature

Julian Murphet

At a certain point in his sprawling utopian novel, *The Ministry of the Future* (2020), Kim Stanley Robinson's narrator pauses to asseverate the virtues of

> Solidarity—there's no feeling like it. [...] You have to be part of a wave in history. You can't get it just by wanting it, you can't call for it and make it come. You can't choose it—it chooses you! It arrives like a wave picking you up! It's a feeling—how can I say it? It's as if everyone in your city becomes a family member, known to you as such even when you have never seen their face before and never will again. Mass action, yes, but the mass is suddenly family, they are all on the same side, doing something important.[1]

There is a tonality, a pitch, and an ethic in this encomium that catches on to a wider revaluation of riotous assemblies in contemporary US writing, springing from a shared sense of paroxysmal frustration with the usual representative processes before the staggering implications of climate change, a planetary super-oligarchy, and the rising global tide of 'surplus populations'.[2] Mass action is the only imaginable force capable of breaking through our political impasse, to be sure, but *how* imagined? This is not the organized, disciplined style of action associated with the traditional strike or peaceful protest march. Rather, 'like a wave picking you up', this solidarity is organic, spontaneous, and perfectly adventitious. 'You can't choose it—it chooses you!'

Is it a riot? There are good reasons for thinking so. Riots in the Indian subcontinent are instrumental to reconfiguring the geopolitical space of the novel, the *gilets jaunes* are an indispensable reference-point, a riot in Switzerland establishes the civil legitimacy of climate refugees, and a narratorial voice insists, 'You know the world is spinning toward catastrophe. You know it's time to act. [...] So now things have broken. We broke them; we broke them on purpose! Riot, occupation,

---

[1] Kim Stanley Robinson, *The Ministry of the Future* (London: Orbit, 2020), 515.
[2] For more on surplus populations, see Ruth Wilson Gilmore, *Golden Gulag: Prisons, Surplus, Crisis, and Opposition in Globalizing California* (Berkeley: University of California Press, 2007), 70–78.

non-compliance, general strike: breakdown.'[3] The head of the novel's titular UN institution responsible for managing the climate catastrophe, Mary Murphy, is clear that change cannot come from above; so, how? 'Occupying the offices of every politician who got elected by taking carbon money and then always voted for the one percent? Riot strike riot?'[4] The same phrase ends up as a cryptic note left on her office desk: 'Two days after a note had appeared on her desk that said only *riot strike riot*, she read that Berlin, London, New York, Tokyo, Beijing, and Moscow had experienced simultaneously, in the very same hour no matter the local time of day, teacher and transport worker strikes.'[5] Strikes persist, then, but only as vanishing mediators between the identical prior and subsequent term: *riot*. The riot is the wave of which the strike is a crest. In Robinson's books there is no more utopian figure than the wave being surfed by a seeker of truth: 'the wave picks her up and as she floats up the face she is also sliding down the face, at about the same rate of speed, so that she is both hanging there and flying along: that moment is astonishing', astonishing above all in its rapturous immanence.[6]

There is more than a passing similarity between the depiction of riotous mass action in Robinson's book and the intensely poetic figurations of 'spontaneous' praxis in Rosa Luxemburg's writings on the mass strike:

> It flows now like a broad billow over the whole kingdom, and now divides into a gigantic network of narrow streams; now it bubbles forth from under the ground like a fresh spring and now is completely lost under the earth. Political and economic strikes, mass strikes and partial strikes, demonstrative strikes and fighting strikes, general strikes of individual branches of industry and general strikes in individual towns, peaceful wage struggles and street massacres, barricade fighting—all these run through one another, run side by side, cross one another, flow in and over one another— it is a ceaselessly moving, changing sea of phenomena.[7]

Here again, strikes are moments within the organic rise and fall of social immanence under capital, cresting white-water intensities of a more general oceanic turbulence; indeed, so over-extended is the term 'strike' here that it essentially resolves into that 'changing sea' of undulating wave forms where the great proletarian masses swell across the militarized face of capital. Riot, strike, riot: the wave propels and makes possible the punctual confrontations of concerted strike action.

[3] Robinson, *The Ministry of the Future*, pp. 141, 245, 151, 412.
[4] Robinson, *The Ministry of the Future*, p. 252.
[5] Robinson, *The Ministry of the Future*, p. 248.
[6] Kim Stanley Robinson, *Aurora* (London: Orbit, 2015), 456.
[7] Rosa Luxemburg, 'The Mass Strike', *Rosa Luxemburg Reader*, ed. Peter Hudis and Kevin B. Anderson (New York, NY: Monthly Review Press, 2004), 191.

The Ministry of the Future is the second of Robinson's novels to thank Joshua Clover for his assistance with the political theory of the texts, and Clover's book *Riot. Strike. Riot* (2016) is a touchstone for many of the recent literary evocations of rioting that place it squarely on an affirmative footing.[8] What attractions does the book hold for a literary transvaluation of this mostly scorned social phenomenon? First, it offers a dynamic historical theory of the modes of collective praxis in the West, pivoting on the alternation between riot and strike action over the long arc of capitalist modernity—a theory that does not disparage the relatively 'unorganized' forms of rioting but refers them to class struggles over circulation rather than production, prices rather than wages. Second, and relatedly, the book insists that the 'meaning of the riot has changed dramatically' in our current epoch of shattered labour movements, declining rates of profit, and militarized logistics—that is to say, it offers a progressive conception of why the traditional strike may have taken a back seat to riotous behaviour in capital's 'catastrophic autumn'.[9] Third, and perhaps most importantly, the tone of the book is one of unequivocal assurance in its own propositions: its declamatory brio, the insouciance with which its modelling piggybacks on Marx's M-C-M formula, the rhetorical ring and aplomb of every sentence, all testify to the author's parallel persona as a poet-activist.[10] It is a poet's book of historical theory, battle-hardened and vocally chiselled, offered as a kind of intelligent person's user's guide for street action—and, by default, for writers striving to configure the present in a non-defeatist mode.

The justifications for rioting in Clover's book never appear apologetic, only common sense for communities in peril: a 'counterproposal of unmanageability' to the state's carceral regime.[11] Firmly located in the contradictions of the present, his account of the current phase of 'riot prime', 'borne by the troika of Toyotaization, information technology, and finance', takes root in America's systemic crisis of accumulation and the surging tides of racialized 'surplus population' generated by it.[12] 'Riot prime', or the mode of rioting specific to the present-day taking wing of capital investment, is the political reflex of racialized surplus populations—a so-called 'surplus rebellion'—in a wider horizon of struggles over circulation and the vanishing wage.[13] The time of riots is a time of radical uncertainty over larger historical ends: the ends of sustainability, of ecology, of habitability, of sociality, and of capital itself, all held in contested suspension over a growing conviction that something must give, or everything will. Clover's model offers writers an advantageous leverage on the bewildering culture-flux of the present, laser-printing

---

[8] Joshua Clover, *Riot. Strike. Riot: The New Era of Uprisings* (London: Verso, 2016).
[9] Clover, *Riot. Strike. Riot.*, p. 7.
[10] M-C-M refers to the ability of money (M) to be mediated by commodities (C) in order to become yet more money (M). See Marx, *Capital, Vol. 1*, trans Ben Fowkes (London: Penguin, 1990), pp. 247–257.
[11] Clover, *Riot. Strike. Riot.*, p. 163.
[12] Clover, *Riot. Strike. Riot.*, p. 23.
[13] Clover, *Riot. Strike. Riot.*, p. 27.

underlying tectonics and offering a coherent map of contemporary riotous phenomena that depicts them as waves immanent to a global situation. It offers the contemporary riot its proper conditions of representability.

There is, however, an overlooked element in the specifically American aspect of this larger narrative, and this is the fact that, for over a hundred years prior to WWII, the dominant form of the riot in America was violent attacks on Black (and Chinese, and Italian, and Polish, and Jewish) workers by poor working whites: the race riot as such, about which Clover says little, but of which Black literature in the USA has left a record of extraordinary documentation, outrage, and execration. The 'classic' American race riot functioned, not as a price-setting exercise, but as a reactionary type of strike action over wages: striking not against employers's profits but against the perceived wage-depressing consequences of admitting racialized minorities into the industrial workplace.[14] For over a century, assaults against communities of colour functioned economically and socially as strikes for *the wages of whiteness*.[15] Race riots, along with lynching, do not easily fit the model of 'the riot' offered by Clover's book, since they had less to do with circulation than with a caste system embedded within the free market of labour.[16] If it is true that, in his words, 'Riot goes looking for surplus populations, and these are its basis for expansion', it is not always with the political valence he gives this ringing phrase.[17] This matters because, especially in the literary record, memory is longer than theory, and semantic transformations like the one the phrase 'race riot' has undergone (from a pogrom to the apparently 'self-destructive' violence of minorities against their own urban environments and on to direct assaults against police stations and personnel) tend not to be resolved so easily into neat historical periodizations.

One way of putting the problem is to frame it in terms of immanence. If 'the capitalist system itself is no longer able to find an immanent level of self-regulated stability',[18] and, in Clover's terms, rioting has become immanent to contemporary capitalism ('The riot ... bears its police within itself ... the integration of the state's police function with *riot prime*', etc., 171), then it is also experienced as an

---

[14] See Allison Davis, 'Caste, Economy, and Violence', *American Journal of Sociology* 51, no. 1 (1945): pp. 7–15.

[15] '[T]he white group of laborers, while they received a low wage, were compensated in part by a sort of public and psychological wage. They were given public deference and tides of courtesy because they were white. [...] [T]he Negro was subject to public insult; was afraid of mobs; was liable to the jibes of children and the unreasoning fears of white women; and was compelled almost continuously to submit to various badges of inferiority. The result of this was that the wages of both classes could be kept low, the whites fearing to be supplanted by Negro labor, the Negroes always being threatened by the substitution of white labor.' W. E. B. Du Bois, *Black Reconstruction: An Essay Toward a History of the Part which Black Folk Played in the Attempt to Reconstruct Democracy in America, 1860–1880* (New York, NY: Harcourt Brace, 1935), 700–701. See also David Roediger, *The Wages of Whiteness* (New York, NY: Verso, 1991).

[16] See the discussion in Salvatore J. Restifo, Iora Phillips, and Vincent J. Roscigno, 'Racial/Ethnic Hierarchy and Urban Labor Market Inequality', *City & Community* 18:2 (June 2019): pp. 662–688.

[17] Clover, *Riot. Strike. Riot*, p. 154.

[18] Slavoj Zizek, *The Year of Dreaming Dangerously* (London: Verso, 2012), 12–13.

immanent capacity of the immiserated surplus populations who struggle with and against their exilic relation to a living wage. As with Luxemburg's 'general strike', the riot flows and bubbles, billows and crashes in 'a ceaselessly moving, changing sea of phenomena', which violently relates the broken halves of the social totality. On the other hand, American race rioting has an even longer history as a kind of transcendental interference with the innermost tendencies of the market to equalize the value of labour-power per se. That is, the riot has more frequently been deployed to pre-empt a genuinely free market in labour-power, to segregate and hierarchize the market's inbuilt tendencies towards immanence or what Marx calls 'one homogeneous mass of human labour-power'[19]—forcing Black workers, for instance,[20] into low-skilled sectors of the economy (or out of it altogether) and ring-fencing others for white labour.[21] These critical differences are related, to be sure, in the contemporary scene where the transcendental interference is no longer required: racialized surplus populations having been banished from the formal economy altogether, we can describe the immanence of riots in America today as a reflex of the final victory of a transcendental war of white terror against communities of colour—a pyrrhic victory that has engulfed organized labour's last remaining strongholds of white privilege in a maelstrom of proletarianization. Winner loses. But I want to argue that, in the American scene, this longer history of race rioting haunts the immanence of contemporary figurations of 'surplus rebellion', an uncanny sliver of transcendental terror lodged in the body of mass action, insisting on the defensive logic of the counter-strike implicit in the logic of 'riot prime'.

When Clover writes that 'the term "race riot" has an inverted sense: not that of race as cause of riot, but of riot as part of the ongoing process of racialization. It is not that race makes riots but that riots make race', I am suggesting that he says more than he means.[22] What Black American literary history teaches us is that riots make race in an intensely dialectical fashion in the US: in the first case, riots have specifically produced and maintained racialized communities of colour to keep their labour out of the market in labour-power, violently to patrol discriminations internal to that market and to coerce compliance with a de facto caste structure. Riots have thus directly yielded surplus populations. In the second place, more recently, riots return as the '*modality through which surplus is lived*'—'surplus life *is* riot,' as Clover puts it.[23] A once transcendental interference with the laws of the market, producing American racial capitalism, is henceforth rendered immanent;

---

[19] Marx, *Capital, Vol. 1*, trans. Ben Fowkes (London: Penguin, 1990), 129.
[20] But also Jewish, Polish, Italian, Chinese, Irish.... Class society is never simply a '1 + 1' equation; it invariably draws on an algebraic signifier, an '*a*'—'1 + 1 + *a*'—such that the two dominant classes have their struggles mediated by an intruder, an alien, an Other.
[21] See the discussion in Philip S. Foner *Organized Labor and the Black Worker: 1619–1981* (Chicago, IL: Haymarket, 2017).
[22] Clover, *Riot. Strike. Riot.*, p. 168.
[23] Clover, *Riot. Strike. Riot.*, p. 170.

the apparatus of white terror can now shift away from clandestine organizations and private militias to the state itself, as surplus expresses itself in a form that justifies permanent militarization. 'Within the social reorganization of the Long Crisis, the public of surplus is treated as riot at all times—incipient, in progress, in exhaustion—not out of error but out of recognition.'[24] Again, transcendence gives way to immanence; but the historical 'inversion' of the sense of race riot is preserved in the political DNA of its structure.

What I am arguing here is this: an older form of race rioting persists beneath the skin of the new 'era of riots' that has organized itself around flashpoints of racist violence in the US today. To attend to the long literary record of Black writing about the American race riot is to complicate any prematurely celebratory assessment of 'the riot' as such today, and to reinstate a deeper, more troubling history of systemic antiblack violence near the very heart of the meaning of American rioting. Only with this more ambivalent, dialectical understanding can we begin to orient ourselves responsibly towards the ongoing crisis of capitalist accumulation and its disproportionate effects of violent immiseration and disenfranchisement on communities of colour. That 'race makes riots' in the USA will always mean that white mob violence created race in the first place, long ago during the inaugural 'invention of the white race', and ever afterward in the reactive and proactive mass efforts to undo that formative national trauma.

A Longer History of Race Riots

Consider the logic of representation of the Wellington riot in Charles Chesnutt's *Marrow of Tradition* (1901): 'At three o'clock sharp the streets were filled, as if by magic, with armed white men.... If [a Black man] resisted any demand of those who halted him—But the records of the day are historical; they may be found in the newspapers of the following date, but they are more firmly engraved upon the hearts and memories of the people of Wellington. For many months there were negro families in the town whose children screamed with fear and ran to their mothers for protection at the mere sight of a white man.'[25] Chesnutt's use of the narrative lacuna and his appeal to the historical record is also a triggering of what he calls a 'slumbering race consciousness which years of culture had not obliterated' and which intuitively supplies the missing pieces of a race riot's modus operandi.[26] The race riot is imprinted in the historical consciousness of every descendant of a slave in America; it is the privileged modality of what Theodore Allen called 'the

---

[24] Clover, *Riot. Strike. Riot.*, p. 170
[25] Charles Waddell Chesnutt, *The Marrow of Tradition*, Ch. 32, in *Stories, Novels, and Essays* (New York, NY: Library of America), p. 678.
[26] Chesnutt, *The Marrow of Tradition*, p. 195.

invention of the white race'—which requires constant reinvention through violent assaults on Black bodies.[27] 'He knew the history of his country [...] and he was fully persuaded that to race prejudice, once roused, any horror was possible.'[28] In an essay entitled 'The Disenfranchisement of the Negro' (1903), Chesnutt wrote: 'day after day the catalogue of lynchings and anti-Negro riots upon every imaginable pretext, grows longer and more appalling. The country stands face to face with the revival of slavery.'[29] At the turn of the twentieth century, there was no mistake in Black minds that race riots were the primary instruments of such a revival: the violent restoration of a two-tier economy in labour and a social apartheid more generally.

Black poet Carrie Clifford transposed into verse some of the atrocious violence of what took place in Atlanta, 1906:

> Three awful nights she reveled in a carnival of crime,
>   Three days or e'er the tension was relieved;
> When her thirst for blood was sated, the whole nation stood aghast.
>   Her cry of 'Rape', no more the world deceived!
>
> Lamentations, bitter sobs, heart-wrung groans the soft winds bore
>   Thro' the streets where lay the victims of her rage;
> Helpless age and guiltless youth, innocence and trusting truth—
>   It had taken all, her fury to assuage.
>
> Dread Atlanta nevermore can the crimson stain erase,
>   Nor the foul blot wipe from off fair history's scroll;
> This fell deed shall e'er arise, ghost-like from the mists of time
>   To confront and terrify her guilty soul![30]

By 1919, one of the worst years on record for terroristic race rioting in the nation's history, anti-Black violence had reached such a peak that a coordinated national propaganda campaign had to be administered in tandem, associating Black organizations with Soviet communism and radical union militancy, thus implicitly justifying the mob violence as a patriotic defence initiative.[31] But as Barbara Foley points out, 'Whether riots were precipitated by economic pressures or simply by

---

[27] See Theodore W. Allen, *The Invention of the White Race, Vol. 2: The Origin of Racial Oppression in Anglo-America* (London: Verso, 2012).
[28] Chesnutt, *The Marrow of Tradition*, p. 196.
[29] Charles Chesnutt, 'The Disenfranchisement of the Negro', in *Stories, Novels, and Essays*, p. 878.
[30] Carrie Clifford, 'Atlanta's Shame', *Voice of the Negro* (November, 1906): 492. See the discussion in Dolen Perkins-Valdez, '"Atlanta's Shame": W. E. B. Du Bois and Carrie Williams Clifford Respond to the Atlanta Race Riot of 1906', *Studies in the Literary Imagination* 40.2, (Fall 2007), pp. 133–151, p. 174.
[31] See the discussions in Theodore Kornweibel, *'Seeing Red': Federal Campaigns against Black Militancy, 1919-1925* (Bloomington & Indianapolis, IN: Indiana University Press, 1998), and David F. Krugler, *1919, The Year of Racial Violence* (Cambridge: Cambridge University Press, 2015).

the refusal of returning black soldiers to abide by what Richard Wright was to call the "ethics of living Jim Crow", African Americans demonstrated an increasing unwillingness to respond passively to abuse and violence.'[32] 1919 marks the decisive turning point in the history of the American race riot when Black communities coordinated (using the organs of a new national Black press), armed themselves, and let it be known that 'fighting back' was their explicit intent if attacked. The phrase comes, of course, from Claude McKay's great sonnet of that year, appearing in *The Liberator* in July, the deadliest month:

> Like men we'll face the murderous, cowardly pack,
> Pressed to the wall, dying, but—fighting back![33]

In another poem, 'To the White Fiends', he wrote:

> THINK you I am not fiend and savage too?
> Think you I could not arm me with a gun
> And shoot down ten of you for every one
> Of my black brothers murdered, burnt by you?[34]

As Carita Owens Collins wrote in a similar vein of the political morality of 1919,

> Demand, come not mock suppliant!
> Demand, and if not given—take!
> Take what is rightfully yours;
> An eye for an eye;
> A soul for a soul;
> Strike, black man, strike!
> This shall not be![35]

The rioters themselves appeared in the verse of this year as so many 'mad and hungry dogs'. James Weldon Johnson's 'Brothers—American Drama' takes a lynching as a synecdoche of the wider terror; in it the white mob speaks in character:

> Now bring the fuel! Pile it round him! Wait!
> Pile not so fast or high! or we shall lose

---

[32] Barbara Foley, *Spectres of 1919: Class and Nation in the Making of the New Negro*, Kindle ed. (Chicago & Urbana: University of Illinois Press, 2008), loc. 359 of 7398.

[33] Claude McKay, 'If We Must Die', *Liberator* 2 (July 1919): p. 21.

[34] McKay, 'To the White Fiends', in *Complete Poems*, ed. William J. Maxwell (Urbana: University of Illinois Press, 2008), 132.

[35] Carita Owens Collins, 'This Must Not Be!' (1919), in Sterling Spero and Abram Harris, editors, *The Black Worker: The Negro and the Labor Movement* (New York, NY: Columbia University Press, 1931), 387.

> The agony and terror in his face.
> And now the torch! Good fuel that! the flames
> Already leap head-high. Ha! hear that shriek!
> And there's another! wilder than the first.[36]

In Chicago, Carl Sandburg, back from the USSR and having completed an exhaustive journalistic exposé of the roots of anti-Black sentiment in the city just before the riots broke out on 27 July, characterized the rioters in stark terms in his poem 'Hoodlums'.

> This is the hate my father gave me, this was in my mother's milk, this is you and me and all of us in a world of hoodlums —maybe so.
> Let us go on, brother hoodlums, let us kill and kill, it has always been so, it will always be so, there is nothing more to it.
> Let us go on sister hoodlums, kill, kill, and kill, the torsos of the world's mothers are tireless and the loins of the world's fathers are strong—so go on—kill, kill, kill.
> Lay them deep in the dirt, the stiffs we fixed, the cadavers bumped off, lay them deep and let the night winds of winter blizzards howl their burial service.[37]

Why all this hatred? One answer seemed obvious. Carrie Clifford again put to rhyme her conclusions on the East St. Louis race riots of 1917:

> ...the hellish East St. Louis 'show',
> Orgy—riot—mob—what you will,
> Where men and e'en women struggled to kill
> Poor black workers, who'd fled in distress from the South
> To find themselves murdered and mobbed in the North.[38]

This is all to underscore the incontestable fact that, for Black writers in the USA, a riot had for many long decades been not a struggle 'to set the price of market goods ... featuring the interruption of commercial circulation', but a violent assault on their right to participate as equals in the political economy of American capitalism or in the polity of Republican democracy.[39] An American race riot functioned as

---

[36] James Weldon Johnson, *The Crisis*, New Orleans Number (February 1916): p. 200.
[37] Carl Sandburg, 'Hoodlums' [Chicago, July 29, 1919], in *Collected Poems* (New York, NY: Harcourt, Brace & Co., 1950), p. 201.
[38] Clifford, 'Silent Protest Parade', in Maureen Honey, ed., *Shadowed Dreams: Women's Poetry of the Harlem Renaissance* (New Brunswick, NJ: Rutgers University Press, 2006), p. 29.
[39] Clover, *Riot. Strike. Riot.*, p. 16.

a reactionary struggle to set the price of Black labour-power at zero, often breaking out at factory gates as Black strike-breakers from the South were bused in by employers to interfere with more affirmative strike actions, and generally working in tandem with white union strikers to segregate the labour force and fix white wages as high as possible. Clover's simple distinction between riot and strike, and his stagist model of their dialectical leapfrogging, overlooks one of the most tenacious realities of American political and economic life, its defining characteristic as racial capitalism: the race riot *was* a strike action. And by the end of 1919, the will to defiance among Black communities was so strong, and the rhetoric of resistance so broadly disseminated, that this form of rioting was henceforth ceded to the state: after 1919, the race riot as a punctual event of wage-setting violence undertaken by white vigilantes was transformed into that more generalized, structural violence called *policing*.

"'How did all this get started?'" asks the eponymous narrator of Ralph Ellison's *Invisible Man* (1952) about the Harlem riot that serves as a climax to this urgent allegorical text. "'Damn if I know, man'", replies his new friend, Scofield. "'A cop shot a woman or something.'"[40] By this point the narrator himself has been wounded by police gunfire and seen another man killed by it. It is generally a cop shooting someone, as the primordial logic of the American race riot is carried over to the arms of 'law enforcement' patrolling communities of colour. By the middle of the twentieth century, the riot is indeed becoming immanent, as increasingly there is no question of inside and outside, ghetto and invader, just a permanent situation:

> The police, in this sense, are not an external force of order applied by the state to an already rioting mass, but an integral part of the riot: not only its standard component spark-plug, acting via the usual death, at police hands, of some young black man, but also the necessary ongoing partner of the rioting crowd [...] who must be attacked as an enemy if the crowd is to be unified in anything.[41]

In Ellison's riot, the prose touches on this immanence. The narrator comes across some Black men pushing a purloined safe down the street, shadowed by 'figures crouching in doorways and along the curb'; '[I was] aware to my left of the men still speeding the rumbling safe along the walk as back up the street, behind me, two policemen, almost invisible in black shirts, thrust flaming pistols before them'.[42] There is no interval here, no before and after; the grammar establishes the immediate adjacency and coevality of these two aspects of the immanent riot. 'The crowd

---

[40] Ralph Ellison, *Invisible Man* (London: Penguin, 2014), 540. In fact, the Harlem race riot of 1943, on which this climactic episode is based, was ignited when a white police officer shot a Black soldier after he attempted to intervene in the police officer's arrest of a Black woman for disturbing the peace.
[41] 'A Rising Tide Lifts All Boats,' *Endnotes* 3 (2013), p. 98.
[42] Ellison, *Invisible Man*, p. 535.

was working in and out of the stores like ants around spilled sugar. From time to time there came the crash of glass, shots; fire trucks in distant streets.'[43] Violators cannot be told from enforcers, or crime from prevention. Here is a circulation struggle indeed, with looters presumptively setting the price of all consumer goods at zero, superintended by fatal police fire. They expropriate gallons of kerosene and carry it to their neighbourhood:

> All the windows seemed empty. They'd blacked it out themselves.
> I saw now only by flash or flame.
> 'Where will you live?' I said, looking up, up.
> 'You call *this* living?' Scofield said. 'it's the only way to get rid of it, man....'[44]

Ellison's novel indelibly fixes a modern conception of the riot, a post-1919 conception, in which the 'white terror mob' has been absorbed into two now immanent functions of contemporary street violence: the police, and the Black community with nothing further to lose, prepared to burn its own habitations because in them *life does not live*.[45] But the most peculiar and telling touch of this epic depiction of a Harlem race riot is its deployment of a third figure who is reducible to neither aspect of riotous immanence. This is Ras the Destroyer: an incendiary 'alien' from the West Indies, a kind of excessive caricature of Garvey's Black nationalism, to whom the Brotherhood (Ellison's deplorable image of the CPUSA) has ceded authority in the Harlem ghetto to incite fire and bloodshed. Exceeding his satiric function, Ras, mounted on a black steed, hurling spears, 'a fur cap upon his head, his arm bearing a shield, a cape made of the skin of some wild animal', has become that nightmare element of which Conrad's Stein had spoken in *Lord Jim* (1900): 'to the destructive element submit yourself'.[46] Epitomizing terror, violence, destruction, irrationality, primitivism, wanton and all-consuming hatred, Ras is in effect the politically unconscious residue of over a hundred years of American race riots—a grotesque figure of what the Black community suffers, physically and affectively, every time a riot breaks out; a potent imaginary sliver of the damage done to them by generations of murdering white mobs. Even where one can understand and unconditionally endorse the necessity of rioting after another cop murders another Black boy or girl, Ras recalls the deeper elemental wellsprings of American race riots in the kind of terror and detestation that predates riotous immanence: a vestige of the transcendental dread that produces whiteness and blackness both.

---

[43] Ellison, *Invisible Man*, p. 538.
[44] Ellison, *Invisible Man*, p. 545.
[45] The formulation is Ferdinand Kürnberger's. See Theodor Adorno, *Minima Moralia: Reflections from Damaged Life*. Trans. E. F. N. Jephcott (London: Verso, 2005), p. 19.
[46] Ellison, *Invisible Man*, p. 556. Joseph Conrad, *Lord Jim: A Tale* (New York, NY: Everyman, 1992), p. 193.

Limits to Contemporary Immanence

It is just this residual dimension of horror and stalking fear that is missing from the riot that 'arrives like a wave picking you up' in contemporary American riot literature. Clover's own poetic work has been known to endorse the riot as the primary authenticating onto-political condition of 'the poem' as such: 'The poem must be on the side of riots looting barricades occupations manifestos communes slogans fire and enemies.'[47] In the straightforward binary his poems construct between 'calm' and 'riot', Clover situates a stark choice for the poem and for 'you', the reader who shows any sign of resiling from the ardent Benjaminian maxim: 'That things are "status quo" *is* the catastrophe. It is not an ever-present possibility but what in each case is given. Thus Strindberg: "hell is not something that awaits us, but this life here and now"'.[48] To choose calm is to choose the reproduction of the infernal existent: the 'reverie of law' that holds up captive and makes us enemies to our own best interests.

> If what you want is calm
> to be restored you are still the enemy
> you have not thought thru clearly
> what that means
> if what you want is a national
> moment of silence the indictment
> of a single police officer
> or two or three you are still
> the enemy you have chosen the reverie
> of law for you and your friends if you want
> another review panel a Justice Dept
> study a return to democracy rather than
> for riot and looting to leap beyond
> itself from county to county
> rift to rift until it becomes general
> you have not understood
> what a revolution is it's just this
> it's coming out again night after night more of us
> than there are of them it's saying no
> to every deal remember nothing

---

[47] Clover, *Red Epic* (Oakland: Commune Editions, 2018), 12. Clover is, clearly, echoing and channelling Diane di Prima's 'Revolutionary Letter #19'.
[48] Walter Benjamin, *The Arcades Project*, trans. Howard Eiland and Kevin McLaughlin (Cambridge, MA: Harvard University Press, 1999), 473.

>belongs to you because
>nothing belongs to anyone[49]

Turbulent immanence is the condition in which we come to terms with the inexistence of any remaining 'outside', any alternative to the all-or-nothing of a transformative process that is always beginning here and now, never 'to come'. If the riot is immanent to capital, and the only chance we have is to annihilate it from within, there is no option but to follow the consequences through to the end. To ride the wave, become the riot, 'night after night', in its incremental swell and crash against the bastions of order; to reach the point where 'riot and looting [...] leap beyond' themselves into social revolution.

It is a captivating, even intoxicating vision of riotous immanence, from which has been banished any lingering transcendental trace of terror, dread, horror, or fear. The sophisticated argumentative logic of *Riot. Strike. Riot.* secedes to the Brechtian *plumpes denken* of Di Prima's sing-song syllogistic construction, 'if/then', 'if/then'. Binary logic forces negative affect out of the frame. In the work of Clover's comrade Wendy Trevino, 'riot' is as endemic as ballgames and ethnic restaurants, a horizon of being:

>We watched the game
>On a flat-screen tv set up outside a bookstore
>In Downtown Oakland. Right next to a vegetarian
>Chinese restaurant that had been shot up
>During a vigil the week before. Josh wanted
>Cleveland to win. Mostly for Tamir Rice.
>Mostly hoping Black people in Cleveland would
>Finally get their riot. I want that, too.[50]

The optative mood takes root in the agons of immanence. The place for the subjunctive is in the indexical confusion between before and after, here and there, that any condition of immanence engenders in its occupants. To 'want' is to ride the wave of temporal flexion sustaining the present.

>I'm writing from the future, where all over
>The United States Black people are blocking highways
>& carrying guns to protests where the cops can see them.
>This is the week cell phone videos of 2 Black men
>Being murdered by cops go viral on consecutive days.

---

[49] Clover, *Red Epic*, p. 18.
[50] Wendy Trevino, 'Summer 2016', in *Cruel Fiction* (Oakland: Commune Editions, 2018), 25.

> Before Micah X. Johnson kills 5 cops in Dallas
> During a Black Lives Matter march.[51]

Something always 'feels different' here, because 'the same' is contoured by a conflict raised to the status of an ontological dominant. Poems themselves can become

> like highways full of people
> There's no way around & barricades & teenagers setting
> Cop cars on fire. It's inevitable. Maybe we'll see each other.[52]

The riot as a kind of proto-commune on steroids, perpetuating itself, finding the means to reproduce itself, at least in the imaginary: this is what a certain strain of contemporary US literature is conjuring from the present emergency, in an attempted adequation of Clover's definition: the 'commune [...] has a continuity with the riot' and 'is a tactic that is also a form of life'.[53] In so doing, I am arguing, these poets significantly bypass the fact that when 'Black people are blocking highways' and 'get[ting] their riot', there is rather more at stake than the flickering forth of the commune in a rowdy street party. There is, at the very least, the sacred memory of the thousands upon thousands lynched, burned alive, maimed, tortured, dispossessed, unhoused, and banished by the white race riot in its ascendant phase. This is a potent dimension of the contemporary race riot that cannot be gainsaid or leveraged unproblematically for anti-systemic uprisings—animated by terror and awe, not tending towards the commune, not instigating revolution, but commemorating and honouring the numberless dead.

Doubtless the best and most significant of the contemporary works to dwell in riotous immanence is Juliana Spahr's dextrous long poem, 'It's All Good, It's All Fucked'. Spahr is exhilarating in her breathless evocations of what it is to be caught up in the riot, up to the eyes and ears in its plural movement, crowd and police like gazelles and lionesses in some prototypical scene of the Serengeti:

> And I am so caught in the moment,
> I can't leave. I can't stop the hard beat chanting of off the pigs with.
> Then more police come around the corner, some of them rushing in
> to grab us, part of the crowd screaming, part of it trying to pull back
> those who are getting snatched, part of it running like gazelles towards
> me, and I run ahead of them, with them and away from them to get

---

[51] Travino, 'Summer 2016', p. 26.
[52] Travino, 'Summer 2016', p. 27.
[53] Clover, *Riot. Strike. Riot.*, pp. 190, 191.

out of their way. Then suddenly police running towards me and us and then I am running with in between the police....[54]

The aesthetic here is that of a motile molecularity within the surging molar forms of riotous immanence; the rapid alternations between 'I' and 'us' and 'them' suggestive of nothing less than a protean subjectivity, a mass affect and millipedal movement that expands the subject into a self-aware multitude. The relationship of rioting to aesthetics and the history of forms is an active concern of the poem. Spahr writes 'All the art that has had a crowd scene in it in which the crowd has been loved, I have loved.'[55] Yet the poem knows the danger of this kind of sentimental simplification, even as it doubles down and commits itself to it unhesitatingly:

> The crowd in this moment. Complicated, but still joyous,
> transitory, momentary, experiencing this one moment of freedom
> before what we know is to come because we know history and we know
> the crowd will not win. Just one day I noticed this, and I should say
> that I was able to notice this because I had sing-chanted with, from
> then on, a different sort of art. All art either with the crowd or with the
> police. All art coming down to that simple divide.[56]

Here the full risk of the new theory of immanence is on display; as if a 'simple divide' could ever do proper justice to the immense complication not just of political and economic schismatics, but of the methods and techniques of art itself, along with its ambiguous loyalties and undecidable intensities. The commitment is to the 'moment' itself, an immersive head-in-the-sand affirmation of what it feels like to have staked everything, or almost everything, on the timeless, eternal freedom immanent in the struggle itself, despite knowing what we always and already know. If the divide is between an art of the *polis* and an art of the police, as Rancière puts it, then this poem proclaims that it will have been worth it, after all, to have taken the losing side time and time again.[57]

Perhaps the most successful innovation of this text is its faux-naïve recourse to the perennial rhetorical figure of personification, specifically the concentration of riot itself into the beloved person of 'Non-Revolution'. On the one hand, such reductionism clearly courts the dangers of reification and simplification that dog critical studies of rioting; but on the other, handled as playfully and skilfully as Spahr does here, the device activates affective and passional attachments between

---

[54] Spahr, 'It's All Good, It's All Fucked', in *That Winter the Wolf Came* (Commune Editions: Oakland, 2015), 65–80, p. 68.
[55] Spahr, 'It's All Good, It's All Fucked', p. 68.
[56] Spahr, 'It's All Good, It's All Fucked', pp. 68–69.
[57] Jacques Rancière, *Disagreement: Politics and Philosophy*, trans. Julie Rose (Minneapolis: University of Minnesota Press, 1999), 21–42.

individual and crowd that sociology can never grasp.[58] Nomination clearly matters here, and the name for this figure of riot clarifies in advance a certain epistemological resignation that, however exhilarating the contact with this charismatic lover, they are not yet *the thing*, not *It*; they are, in fact, very specifically cast as a *Non-It*, a failure to coincide with the true historical object of desire. There appears in due course an 'historian of revolution who disdained Non-Revolution', cynically 'mocking my attraction to Non-Revolution', while undermining his Old Left sagacity by 'pressing his leg against mine'—in a flash of #MeToo exasperation.[59] Non-Revolution, bearing what they negate in their very name, dwells in 'the possibility of revolution all the fucking time' (as Clover says, riot is *continuous* with revolution), but this possibility remains only virtual, notional, aspirational, destined for ontic 'dissolution'.[60] After all, as the voice proclaims again, 'we knew history. We knew we would not be together long'.[61] To love Non-Revolution, then, is (like most relationships, as the persona muses repeatedly) to love transience, exuberance, and loss. To be in the riot, with the riot, is not to be in or with Revolution, and so it is to feel what it is like repeatedly to lose, without being permanently defeated. And that itself can be a good thing, because Revolution is decidedly not a carnival; it is hard and the costs of defeat in it are so much graver.

> I knew going into it that it never lasts with
> Non-Revolution. I never thought it would. I just knew I wanted it in
> whatever moment I could get it. If it did not end, if it became Revolution,
> I knew that would be hard. That was an entirely different lover,
> one I was not sure I was ready for and yet longed for so much that they
> often showed up in my dreams and led me by a hand into an incredible
> sadness and a high so intense that the personal sadness would
> become incidental to the possibility. I mean I will take that hand and
> be lead [sic] to whatever room when it comes because oh my god, the body
> of Revolution is something magnificent. But I also know that at that
> moment I will know the meaning of it's all fucked so hard.[62]

The problem is, then, the very association of riot with carnival as such. To cast riot as a kind of warm up for deferred revolution, a sexy street party without enduring consequences, an easy lay with fickle loyalties and promiscuous habits, is again to dissociate riot from the American story rehearsed in this essay, to suspend it

---

[58] See the discussion in Paul Bagguley and Yasmin Hussein, *Riotous Citizens: Ethnic Conflict in Multicultural Britain* (Abingdon: Routledge, 2016), esp. p. 13; and in Jumana Bayeh's chapter in this volume.
[59] Spahr, 'It's All Good, It's All Fucked', p. 69.
[60] Spahr, 'It's All Good, It's All Fucked', p. 66, p. 71.
[61] Spahr, 'It's All Good, It's All Fucked', p. 70.
[62] Spahr, 'It's All Good, It's All Fucked', p. 71.

outside of real history in an ideal ontological state. As Spahr writes after another dissipated riot,

> We fought because we became through fight. And because we don't agree and because we cared with an intensity. I am unsure of my metaphors. Were we wolves? Were we even we? Were we lovers or were we just a brief hook-up? Was Non-Revolution the hard dancing one sometimes does to feel less middle aged? Does it even matter?[63]

My claim is that it does; that racialized riots in America can only be construed as a 'kind of dancing', a 'wave', a 'proto-commune', or a 'brief hook-up', by those (largely white) writers whose ancestors, whose grandmothers and great uncles and great-grandfathers, were not hounded and murdered by white patriotic mobs, and whose sons and lovers are not today being murdered by the police who took their place. In the USA, a racialized riot is both more, and less, than a stepping-stone to a revolution, when it is also and even primarily a theatre of historical claims and turbulent griefs that stretch right back to the founding of the Republic itself. I have no argument with the claim that riots are becoming immanent to late capitalism as it desperately fends off the declining rate of profit and invests in the supply chain; nor that there is a chance for riotous phenomena to become-communal. Rather, my case is simply that writing as if the racialized riot is *already* and *only* a space of immanent political transformation and wave-surfing affective rapture is a gross underestimation of its residual quotient of horror, grief, dread, and trauma.

---

[63] Spahr, 'It's All Good, It's All Fucked', p. 72.

10

'If I write a Love poem it's against the police'

The Abolitionist Poetics of the Riot

Andrew Brooks and Astrid Lorange

Introduction

To begin, a proposition: *poetry is produced by struggle and not the other way around.* How are we to make sense of the content and context of contemporary struggle by reading a poetics of social formations that take place on the street and against state violence? How can we read the poems that emerge from collective struggle as a way to study struggle itself, to attend to the particular forms that struggle takes, and to the social (trans)formations that struggle generates? Or, to borrow Joshua Clover's question: 'What does a poetics of surplus populations look like?'[1] In this chapter, we focus on the riot as a frontline of collective resistance to the violence of contemporary capitalism and its entanglement with the state, and the riot poem as that which emerges from and documents such resistance. We argue that there is no poetry that is external to the material conditions that shape its production: the poetry that arises from struggle is shaped by the socio-political intensities of the moment that produces it. The present moment is defined by the expansion of surplus populations who have been excluded from, or made adjacent to, the discipline of the wage relation as capitalism enters an increasingly circulatory phase in which the decline in global productivity rates leads to an inevitable crisis of overaccumulation.[2] Without the discipline of the market, the state steps in to manage (largely racialized) surplus populations through the intensification of policing and the expansion of the carceral system. With the workplace no longer the central site of organized resistance, surplus populations take to the street to riot against the forms of misery that emerge from the inter-relation between the state and capital. The riot is an irruption that announces and enacts, even if only temporarily, the possibility of an otherwise to these miseries—of a meaning not yet articulated.

---

[1] Joshua Clover and Chris Nealon, 'The Other Minimal Demand', in *Communism and Poetry: Writing Against Capital*, edited by Ruth Jennison and Julian Murphet (London: Palgrave MacMillan, 2019), p. 34.

[2] For more on the production of contemporary surplus populations, see Endnotes, *Endnotes 2: Misery and the Value Form* (London and Oakland: Endnotes, 2010).

To read the poetics of riots and surplus populations, then, is to anticipate these meanings not yet articulated. The poem, which, as Clover has written, can attune to movements in and relations of time and space, offers an aesthetic form capable of apprehending possibility and transformation.[3] Sean Bonney writes that militant poetics involves what Rimbaud called 'the long systematic derangement of the senses'.[4] For Bonney 'social being determines content, content deranges form'. Bonney figures this derangement as crucial to the process whereby the '"I" of a poem becomes an "other" as in the transformation of the individual into the collective when it all kicks off'.[5] For Bonney, the poem is a vehicle for capturing the intensity of emerging collectivity and solidarity, for tracing the movement of the lyric 'I' to the 'we' who inhabit it in the shared act of reading. 'Seeing as language is probably the chief of the social senses, we have to derange that', he writes.[6] And so, when we memorize the songs of struggle, we are not simply learning what we are against—the police, for example—but rather we are attuning ourselves to the experience of transformation and the possibility of collective struggle.

This chapter reads riot poems from the late 1960s to the present, corresponding to the period that Clover, repurposing Robert Brenner's 'long downturn' schematic, calls 'the long crisis'.[7] The global oil crisis of 1973 marks the beginning of this period of extended downturn and rolling crises with global productivity entering a state of decline that continues into our present. We perform a materialist reading of this historical period (including the 1960s as a transitional period between post-war growth and the economic crisis of '73), asking how the poem can allow us to sense the shape of history, and crucially, to consider how and where radical movements might move next. Reading work by Miguel James, Wendy Trevino, Gwendolyn Brooks, and David Henderson, we argue that these poems instruct readers to engage with the specific, contingent conditions in which struggle happens and becomes learned, shared, contested, won, and lost; in short, the poetics of abolition.

The Riot Poem and Its Abolitionist Poetics

My entire Oeuvre is against the police
If I write a Love poem it's against the police

---

[3] Kristina Marie Darling, '"An Archive of Confessions": A Conversation with Joshua Clover, curated by Kristina Marie Darling', *Tupelo Quarterly* (June 2017), https://www.tupeloquarterly.com/editors-feature/an-archive-of-confessions-a-conversation-with-joshua-clover-curated-by-kristina-marie-darling/.
[4] Sean Bonney, 'Letter on Poetics: Saturday, June 25, 2011', *All This Burning Earth: Selected Writings of Sean Bonney* (Ill Will Editions, 2016), p. 15.
[5] Sean Bonney, 'Letter on Poetics', p. 15.
[6] Sean Bonney, 'Letter on Poetics', p. 15.
[7] Joshua Clover, *Riot. Strike. Riot: The New Era of Uprisings* (New York, NY: Verso, 2016), p. 130.

> And if I sing the nakedness of bodies I sing against the police
> And if I make this Earth a metaphor I make a metaphor against the police.[8]

So read the opening lines of Miguel James's poem, 'Against the Police'. The poem finds itself in a lineage of anti-police poems, a form continuous with riot poems in an epoch where riots increasingly respond to instances of racialized state violence and that includes works by Amiri Baraka, N.W.A, Lil Boosie, and RMR.[9] But what does it mean for a poem to be against the police? For James, it is not the case that this or that poem takes an anti-police position or outlines an anti-police politics. To begin, as the opening line states, the poet's 'entire Oeuvre' is against the police—every song, metaphor, figure of speech; every word, stanza, line; all prose—it is *all* against the police. 'Including', he concludes, 'this poem'. There is no way to read this poem, the poem directly tells its readers, against the force of James's political commitment; the poem's didacticism forecloses the possibility that the poem be subsumed into a liberal interpretation. In other words, the interpretation of the poem is brought into the poem itself via a rhetorical claim in which 'this' poem gives an unambiguous account of itself. In James's poem, the abolitionist politics is not to be found *in* the poem, but in the conditions of the poem's very existence. Poems, we might imagine by extension, emerge as part of James's commitment against the police and towards abolition, a commitment that comes to shape the poet's life-world outside the act of writing a poem or the poem as a particular kind of text. We might read in this particular poem an echo of Sean Bonney's 'nursery rhyme', which opens with: 'for "I love you say fuck the police"' and begins its last section with 'all other words are buried there/all other words are spoken there'.[10] For Bonney, as for James, an abolitionist poetics suggests a world of infinite translation. Any speech act can be reframed as *fuck the police*, just as any poem that speaks of the beloved is a poem that speaks against the police, since abolitionist love is love that stands against the police. In both James's and Bonney's poems, poetry is taken as one site in which the relation between political struggle and the speech that comes to be animated by it can be apprehended. James's short poem includes itself as an example of its larger claim: Bonney's 'nursery rhyme' invokes poetry's pedagogic and mnemonic functions: we learn the language of struggle by memorizing its songs.

---

[8] Miguel James, 'Against the Police' (translated by Guillermo Parra), *Typo Magazine*, Issue 18: Portable Country: Venezuelan Poetry: 1921–2001, http://www.typomag.com/issue18/james.html.

[9] See: Amiri Baraka 'Black People' in *The LeRoi James/Amiri Baraka Reader*, edited by William J. Harris (New York, NY: Thunder's Mouth Press, 1991), p. 224; N.W.A, 'Fuck Tha Police', *Straight Outta Compton* (Ruthless/Priority, 1988); Lil' Boosie, 'Fuck the Police', *Superbad: The Return of Mr. Wipe Me Down*, (Bad Azz, 2009); and RMR, 'Rascal', *Drug Dealing Is a Lost Art* (Universal Music Publishing Group, 2020).

[10] Sean Bonney, 'ACAB—A Nursery Rhyme', *Abandoned Buildings*, December 2014, http://abandonedbuildings.blogspot.com/2014/12/acab-nursery-rhyme.html.

'Look at it this way', Wendy Trevino addresses her reader in the opening words of 'When You Hear People Say "Burn Down The American Plantation"': '"sometimes you have to burn things down / To rebuild"'.[11] The quote is unattributed, perhaps because it belongs to no one. Which is to say, it belongs to everyone. The poem continues, pointing as if gesturing towards empty space:

> This is where the QuikTrip that belonged to the man
> Who called the cops on Mike Brown used to be. The precinct
> That deployed the cops who murdered George Floyd used
> To be here. & over here there used to be a Target. & over here
> There used to be a CVS.[12]

An entire precinct, a corner shop, a megastore. They are united by their absence, each has been burned down in a riot. But to say that Trevino's poem points as if to empty space, or that these sites are united by their absence, is not quite right. There is *something there* that can be pointed to, a presence that is more than a trace (of ash or metal) and more than a memory. These sites represent the real, material context in which riots took place, sites in which absent buildings mark the presence of a struggle for survival. Such ruins contain what Avery Gordon refers to as 'haunting', the absent presence of repressed social violence that continues to structure the present.[13] The poem's structure depends on the deictics 'here' and 'there' which work to orient a reader to particular places (a shop in St Louis, Missouri) and general structures (the ubiquitous CVS, enormous and illuminated on any given street corner across the US). By the end of the poem, the list of counter-memorial sites contains just the deictic itself—the final two (and a half) lines read:

> ... & when
> The marches turned into riots the cop cars were parked here
> Here, here, here, here, here, here, here, here, here, here, here[14]

The list describes a collective past. These marches became riots; this is where the cars became fire. But the list also describes a future. The immanent potential of the riot is to be found in people gathering together, claiming the streets against state power and state property. Trevino's poem asserts the destruction of the cop car as an incontrovertible expression of resistance and refusal contra the narration

---

[11] Wendy Trevino, 'When You Hear People Say "Burn Down The American Plantation"', *Destituencies*, Issue Zero (November 2020), https://destituencies.com/2020/when-you-hear-people-say-burn-down-the-american-plantation/, lines 1–2.
[12] Wendy Trevino, 'When You Hear People Say "Burn Down The American Plantation"', lines 2–6.
[13] Avery Gordon, *Ghostly Matters: Haunting and the Sociological Imagination* (Minneapolis: University of Minnesota Press, 2008).
[14] Wendy Trevino, 'When You Hear People Say "Burn Down The American Plantation"', lines 13–15.

of riots in the liberal media as opportunistic and irrational violence. The insistence that we remember the burning cop car or razed building as material facts is a reminder that the cop car may burn again, the building may fall again: more than this, the car *will burn again* and the building *will fall again*. The poem memorializes the riots it chronicles while also leaping towards a future, revolutionary horizon. For Trevino, the immanent potential of a cop car, wherever one may see it, is that it contains within it the conditions for, perhaps even promise of, fire.

Trevino's poem insists on the revolutionary nature of the abolitionist riots of 2020 which erupted in the wake of the killing of George Floyd by Minneapolis police officer Derek Chauvin and spread through the entire country over that long, hot summer. In the time that has elapsed since the riots, politicians and officials have attempted to re-narrativize the events in ways that diminish the popular fury and revolutionary intent. In a related and, by now, familiar manoeuvre, rioters were dismissed as opportunistic criminals and/or disorganized mobs lacking coherent demands. This concerted attempt to sever revolution from riot, or what Joy James refers to as 'airbrushing', is not limited to liberal media and permeates spaces of activism and academia as well.[15] The slippage from calls to abolish the police to calls to defund the police is an example of this, subsuming the revolutionary demand within a logic of reform that ultimately leaves the state and market intact. 'Alliances between abolitionists and revolutionaries', James tells us, 'are destabilised by the airbrushing of revolutionary struggles.'[16]

Trevino's poem refuses this airbrushing of struggle, imploring us to look again—'Here, here, here, here, here, here, here, here, here, here'—at the spaces where cop cars once stood. The final lines are a directive to pay attention to what the destruction of state property implies. The cop car is an extension of the cop, a figure that Guy Debord famously described as 'the active servant of the commodity, the man in complete submission to the commodity, whose job it is to ensure that a given product of human labour remains a commodity, with the magical property of having to be paid for'.[17] The destruction of the cop car symbolically and actually aims at the destruction of the commodity, a gesture that seeks the destruction of value itself. In Trevino's poem, the events of 2020 are placed in a longer durée with the invocation of a series of sites of ruin linking the murder of Floyd ('The precinct / That deployed the cops who murdered George Floyd used / To be here') to the murder of Michael Brown ('This is where the QuikTrip that belonged to the man / Who called the cops on Mike Brown used to be') to the murder of Latasha Harlins ('That used to be the deli where Latasha / Harlins was murdered by Soon Ja

---

[15] Joy James, 'Airbrushing Revolution for the Sake of Abolition', *Black Perspectives*, July 2020, https://www.aaihs.org/airbrushing-revolution-for-the-sake-of-abolition/

[16] Joy James, 'Airbrushing Revolution for the Sake of Abolition', section 4.

[17] Guy Debord, 'The Decline and Fall of the Spectacle-Commodity Economy', trans. Donald Nicholson Smith, *Internationale Situationniste 10* (March 1966), archived on *Situationist International Online*, https://www.cddc.vt.edu/sionline/si/decline.html

Du') to the murder of Rayshard Brooks ('The Wendy's where Rayshard / Brooks was murdered by cops used to be here').[18] Each instance of anti-Black violence that is named in the poem is connected to a riot: Minneapolis in 2020, Ferguson in 2014, Los Angeles in 1992, Atlanta in 2020.

The poem gestures to a periodization that Joshua Clover refers to as 'the new era of riots' which he traces back to the deindustrialization that began in late 1960s.[19] 'This used / To be the center of the world's automotive industry', writes Trevino, acknowledging that this extended period is marked by recurring crises of overaccumulation that inevitably leads to labour rationalization and racialized surplus populations. But this is not the only temporality at play in the poem, with Trevino invoking an even longer history: 'A building where slave traders sold slaves during the Civil War / Once stood here'. The shorter and longer histories of the violence and immiseration of racial capitalism unfold within the sixteen lines of the poem—the slave trading of the Civil War era is linked to the deindustrialization (and corresponding expansion of the prison industrial complex) that began in the 1960s, which in turn is joined to the repeated murders of Black people at the hands of police in the present. The time of slavery, as Saidiya Hartman tells it, is yet to pass.[20] Against the tendency to either dismiss the riot as disorganized violence or airbrush its revolutionary intent, Trevino casts the immanence of the riot as a paradigmatic response to accumulated historical conditions. The instruction to look *here*, at the ruins, is a call to pay attention to the material conditions of struggle and the historical conditions that they arise from, as well as the promise that is given in these acts of property destruction. The promise, no less, of a new world.

Dancing in the Streets

In his 1970 poem 'Keep on Pushing', David Henderson writes of the Harlem Riots in 1964.[21] Over six summer nights in July of that year, rioters assembled in the wake of the murder of fifteen-year-old James Powell by the NYPD. The poem, named for the hit song of that summer by Curtis Mayfield and The Impressions, opens with Lenox Avenue—'a big street' that 'must be so to contain the / unemployed / vigiling Negro males, / and police barricades'.[22] The capaciousness of the street, with its wide footpaths, is evoked by Henderson for its ambivalence. The street can hold an enormous assembly, just as it can accommodate a surge of police to enclose it. Or, inversely: if a single call can summon 'five hundred cops in five

---

[18] Wendy Trevino, 'When You Hear People Say "Burn Down The American Plantation"', lines 3–5, 2–3, 9–10, 11–12.
[19] Clover, *Riot. Strike. Riot.*
[20] Saidiya Hartman, 'The Time of Slavery', *South Atlantic Quarterly*, vol. 101, no. 4 (2002): 757–777.
[21] David Henderson, 'Keep on Pushing', *De mayor of Harlem: the poetry of David Henderson* (New York, NY: E.P. Dutton, 1970), pp. 31–36.
[22] David Henderson, 'Keep on Pushing', p. 31.

minutes', then 'a shot a cry a rumor' can summon an equal number of rioters.[23] In other words, and as Henderson points out, the riot represents an original struggle of and for the street, which is to say, of and for the city. But it is not a struggle over territory, nor is it a struggle over contested property. It is a struggle for and against territory, for and against property, for and against the racial capitalist order and its immiseration of the social. In Henderson's complex song of the big, busy street, we might hear an echo of Gwendolyn Brooks, who opens her poem 'Riot' with a scene of white terror in the face of Black rage:

> John Cabot, out of Wilma, once a Wycliffe,
> all whitebluerose below his golden hair,
> wrapped richly in right linen and right wool,
> almost forgot his Jaguar and Lake Bluff;
> almost forgot Grandtully (which is The
>   Best Thing That Ever Happened To Scotch);
>   almost
> forgot the sculpture at the Richard Gray
> and Distelheim; the kidney pie at Maxim's,
> the Grenadine de Boeuf at Maison Henri.
>
> Because the Negroes were coming down the
>   street.[24]

'They were black and loud', she writes. 'And not detainable. And not discreet.'[25] With an echo of both Brooks and Henderson, Fred Moten, speaking with Robin D.G. Kelley in 2016, reflects on the terms of violence that underwrite the ongoing war of state-managed anti-Blackness: '[W]e need to understand what it actually is that the state is defending itself from.... What the drone Darren Wilson [the police officer who murdered Michael Brown in 2014] shot into that day was insurgent black life walking down the street.'[26] Henderson and Brooks know this to be true, which is why their poems open with the threat posed, not (just) of the riot itself against which the police will close their ranks, but with what the riot represents—collective life that reaches for an otherwise.

Henderson's poem is structured by variations on the refrain '*Keep on pushing*', which repeats throughout the poem as a counterpoint to the violence of policing—a reminder of the sociality of the riot that exists in excess of the reaches of the state. The phrase can be read as a directive to the rioters to persist despite the 'tear gas bombs / guns / ammunition' that can be summoned by the police commissioner.[27] And yet the refrain is also the invocation of a certain rhythm and a

---

[23] David Henderson, 'Keep on Pushing', p. 31.
[24] Gwendolyn Brooks, *Riot* (Detroit, MI: Broadside Press, 1969), p. 9.
[25] Brooks, *Riot*, p. 9
[26] Fred Moten and Robin D.G. Kelley, 'Do Black Lives Matter? Robin D.G. Kelley and Fred Moten in Conversation', *Melville House*, July 2016, https://www.mhpbooks.com/132892-2/
[27] David Henderson, 'Keep on Pushing', p. 31.

certain groove—we can almost hear the falsetto gospel harmonies and the heavy, low brass riff of The Impressions's song. The new era of riots led by racialized surplus populations responding to anti-Black violence—which includes the murder of James Powell in 1964 that is the subject of Henderson's poem, through to the killing of George Floyd that sparked the mass riots of 2020—are animated by fugitivity, which Moten figures as 'a desire for and spirit of escape and transgression of the proper and the proposed'.[28] Nathaniel Mackey tells us that fugitivity, a generative excess that evades constraint, 'asserts itself on an aesthetic level, at the level of poetics'.[29] That which animates the riot also animates the poem and the song. Or to return to Bonney's formulation: 'social being determines content, content deranges form'. In Henderson's poem, the musical refrain not only implores the rioter or the reader to keep on pushing, but gestures to the insurgent sociality of Black life itself—the rioters appear 'from idle and strategic street corners / bars stoops hallways windows'.[30] These are spaces in which people come together around music in collective forms of sociality. The gaps on the page between the different locations suggests a space of possibility, a space in which the logics of enclosure are refused and resisted, marked instead by a radical openness and affectability. The movement from the bar or the stoop or the hallway or the window to the street is continuous, as is Mayfield's rhythm with the rhythm of the riot. The second movement of Brooks's 'Riot', titled 'The Third Sermon of the Warpland', draws out the relation between the sociality of the riot, the sensuality of song, and the violence of looting:

> A clean riot is not one in which little rioters
> long-stomped, long-straddled, BEANLESS
> but knowing no Why
> go steal in hell
> a radio, sit to hear James Brown
> and Mingus, Young-Holt, Coleman, John,
>   on V.O.N.
> and sun themselves in Sin.
>
> However, what
> is going on
> is going on.[31]

For Brooks, the rioters are not defined by the forms of subjugation imposed by the capital relation and white supremacy. Rather, the riot produces a moment in which Black social life declares itself through the pleasures of Black performance, even if

---

[28] Fred Moten, *Stolen Life* (Durham, NC: Duke University Press, 2018), p. 131.
[29] Nathaniel Mackey, 'Cante Moro', *Sound States: Innovative Poetic and Acoustical Technologies*, ed. Adelaide Morris (Chapel Hill: University of North Carolina Press, 1997), p. 200.
[30] David Henderson, 'Keep on Pushing', p. 31.
[31] Brooks, *Riot*, p. 14.

the sociality that coalesces around the looted radio remains illegible to white society. The musicality of the riot is also present in Amiri Baraka's 'Black People!', a riot poem written in 1966, which equates dancing and rioting through the invocation of looted radios turned all the way up.[32]

In Baraka's poem the rhythm of looting leads directly to dancing, the 'magic actions' that produce radios for the people are inextricably tied to the collective rituals that insist on the possibility of sociality not structured by individuation. Magic actions are in excess of the logic of the commodity and its value, just as the music of the Black Radical Tradition moves as a generative excess that insists on collective and improvised practices. For Baraka, the act of looting is a dance that inaugurates a different order of possession, a collective ritual that declares that the value-form is breakable. The poem becomes directive here: the language shifts to imperatives addressed to the one who riots as well as to a reader who is compelled to register the poetics of the riot. The 'magic words' that become 'magic actions' here have a dual function: they capture the revolutionary speech of the streets in which the conditions make magic possible; rendered in the poem, they cannot work their magic except by showing where and how magic has occurred and will occur again. That the riot is cast in choreographic and sonic terms reminds us not only of the aesthetic dimension of the riot but also of the affectivity of sound and movement. The noise that comes down the street and the magic dance that moves down the avenues, impress upon those that come into contact with them. 'Because everything vibrates', writes Ashon T. Crawley, 'nothing escapes participating in choreographic encounters with the rest of the living world. It's a reality of thermodynamics, of kinesthesia.'[33] Baraka's, Henderson's, and Brooks's poems all suggest that the particular vibrations of Black-led riots are irreducibly shaped by the rhythms of Black social life and the aesthetic forms that emerge from them.

For Henderson, the rhythms of Black music can not only be located in the act of rioting but are positioned in explicit opposition to the condemnation of violence and the repeated calls for a return to order that define the representation of riots in the media. In the final section of the poem, Henderson documents the whiteness of the media, including the radio station WWRL which supposedly caters to the Black community. The poem contains transcribed snippets from a radio broadcast that condemns the violence of the riot with Henderson adding bracketed asides that counters such liberal speech by suggesting that law and order, freedom and

---

[32] Baraka, 'Black People', p. 224.
[33] Ashon T. Crawley, 'Stayed Freedom Hallelujah', *Los Angeles Review of Books*, May 2015, https://www.lareviewofbooks.org/article/stayed-freedom-hallelujah/

dignity are concepts circumscribed by whiteness and tied to the preservation of the property that the rioters are out there destroying.[34] The poem returns the reader to music at the conclusion of the spoken transmission, bringing us back to the generative actions taking place in the streets:

> The Rhythm n Blues returns
> a flaming bottle bursts on Seventh Avenue
> and shimmies the fire across the white divider line[35]

For Henderson, the relation between song and struggle is inextricable; they arise from a shared history and context. To think through the continuity between Black-led riots and Black aesthetics is to consider the familiar chant of 'WHOSE STREETS? OUR STREETS!' alongside Moten and Harney, who write: 'It's not about taking the streets; it's about how, and about what, we take to the streets.'[36] Put another way, the task of the poem is to remind us that what is at stake is a conception of social life beyond the individuating logics of racial capitalism. The italicized refrains function as a call sung to those assembled in the streets: *Keep on pushing*.

The use of the refrain in Henderson's poem is one way that musicality of the Black Radical Tradition influences the formal aspects of the poem. The repetition of '*keep on pushing*' becomes a call that seems to invite a collective response, invoking the classic formats of work songs and blues music. In these improvised musical forms, which document the shared experiences of dispossession and resistance, the response is already known to the chorus being called upon to respond. The same is true in Henderson's poem which uses as its hook the enduring sentiment of pushing ahead in order to forge a new future. The call and response that the poem employs then follows an inversion that Harney and Moten describe: 'the response is already there before the call goes out', that is, 'one who is said to have given the call is really an effect of a response that had anticipated him'.[37] The poem understands Black social life as always already musical. In collaging different registers together—lyric address, overheard speech, snippets of media, and popular music—Henderson gives this musicality a contemporary poetic form. The riot is not a singular phenomenon but a multiplicity of action that unites people in antagonism, rearranges time and space, and heightens the contradictions of public/private, individual/collective that inhere in the street. And, as Henderson emphasizes, the riot tunes itself to

---

[34] David Henderson, 'Keep on Pushing', p. 35.
[35] David Henderson, 'Keep on Pushing', p. 35.
[36] Fred Moten, and Stefano Harney, *All Incomplete* (Colchester: Minor Compositions, 2020), p. 48.
[37] Fred Moten, and Stefano Harney, *The Undercommons: Fugitive Planning & Black Study* (Colchester: Minor Compositions, 2013), pp. 134, 132.

the key of the latest pop song, or rather, makes a song popular in a spontaneous street party.

In the fourth section of the poem, Henderson traces the complex relations between cop, commodity, and rioter:

> I see the plump pale butchers pose with their signs:
>   'Hog maws 4 pounds for 1 dollar'
>   'Pigs ears 7 pounds for 1 dollar'
>   'Neck bones   chitterlings   6 pounds for 1'
>   Nightclubs,   liquor stores   bars 3, 4, 5 to one block
>   3 & 4 shots for one dollar
> I see police eight to one
>   in its entirety Harlem's 2nd Law of Thermodynamics
>   Helmet
>   nightsticks bullets to barehead
>   black reinforced shoes to sneaker[38]

In this section of the poem, the price of the commodity is first set by the white butcher who sells meat on the streets of Harlem. We might read the meat for sale—pig stomach, pig ears, pig guts—as both the shopping list for a cook-up as well as a more symbolic relationship between white property (whiteness *as* property, as Cheryl Harris famously puts it) and the police.[39] The butcher is not incidental to the riot that transforms the Harlem street: the butcher is the business owner whose presence on the street requires the promise of the police's protection. And in turn, the butcher sells pig meat, a perverse representation of the police themselves. Here in the poem and through Henderson's canny construction, the police become the commodities for sale, become the stomachs, ears, and guts of the law. The poem inverts the formula that sees whiteness as property in order to turn cops into pig meat. This inversion hints at the revaluation achieved by the riot—as Clover instructs us, the riot as a particular intervention seeks to re-set the price of the commodity to *zero*.[40] In a riot, a pig's ear might be seized from the shop window, just as the assembly might out-number the police in the struggle for the street. The section continues with a sequence of ratios: there are three, four, and five bars to the block; three or four shots to the dollar in each bar; eight police for every rioter; a helmet, club, and bullet for every bare head; a boot for every sneaker. But in a flash, the poem hints, the eight to one can flip, and the calculus of the riot can be irreversibly transformed. We can read this section, again, for its resonance with Brooks. In the opening of 'Riot', Brooks introduces the white man whose terror portends the coming of the assembly. His terror, she describes,

---

[38] David Henderson, 'Keep on Pushing', p. 33.
[39] Cheryl I. Harris, 'Whiteness as Property', *Harvard Law Review*, vol. 106, no. 8 (1993): 1701–1791.
[40] Clover, *Riot. Strike. Riot.*, p. 29.

causes him to 'almost' forget the 'kidney pie at Maxim's, / the Grenadine de Boeuf at Maison Henri'.[41] His whiteness is linked to and by meat dishes and their signal institutions. Brooks continues to describe the coming assembly and the white man, John Cabot's fear:

> 'Don't let It touch me! the blackness! Lord!' he
>   whispered
> to any handy angel in the sky.
> But, in a thrilling announcement, on It drove
> and breathed on him: and touched him. In that
>   breath
> the fume of pig foot, chitterling and cheap chili,
> malign, mocked John.[42]

For Brooks, too, the riot turns on the sheer scale of the crowd. Cheap chili can feed the whole assembly (Diane di Prima would echo this idea in 'Revolutionary Letter #3 when she implored her reader to 'store food—dry stuff like rice and beans stores best / goes farthest').[43]

In Henderson's poem, cops are counted and sized up against protestors; ratios are calculated, presented as odds:

> I see police eight to a corner
> crude mathematics
> eight to one
> eight for one.[44]

This seemingly simple accounting of the presence of police gestures to the history of what Katherine McKittrick calls the 'mathematics' of Black life. As she explains, the archives that document the passage of enslaved people across the Middle Passage and into plantations in the New World operate as a ledger of violence, dehumanization, and death.[45] The reduction of people to numbers, items in account books, quantities, and values, works to enumerate Black death, transforming anti-Black violence into either a mundane occurrence (a mere data point) or a spectacle for voyeuristic consumption (an enormous and gruesome dataset). For McKittrick, 'historic blackness' is linked to this archival enumeration: 'the list, the breathless numbers, the absolutely economic, the mathematics of the unliving'.[46]

---

[41] Brooks, *Riot*, pp. 9–10.
[42] Brooks, *Riot*, pp. 9–10.
[43] Diane di Prima, *Revolutionary Letters* (San Francisco: Last Gasp of San Francisco, 2005), p. 9.
[44] David Henderson, 'Keep on Pushing', pp. 31–32.
[45] Katherine McKittrick, 'Mathematics Black Life', *The Black Scholar*, vol. 44, no. 2 (Summer 2014): 16–28.
[46] Katherine McKittrick, 'Mathematics Black Life', p. 16.

One way to understand the new era of riots is as a response to a plantation logic that renders Black life disposable and fungible, a refusal of the 'crude mathematics' in which yet another Black life is added to the breathless numbers.

For Henderson, the ratio of 'eight to one' or 'eight for one' speaks to the foundational anti-Black violence of the state and the market. The police are rendered as an occupying force, militarized 'squadrons' that patrol in groups of six or eight or twelve, as he puts it in the poem.[47] The threat to Black life is, in part, accounted for according to its size, when Henderson writes that 'The Police Commissioner can / muster five hundred cops in five minutes' he is showing both the enormity of the deployment of force against the state's own subjects and the scale and speed of resourcing. But McKittrick's reflection on the mathematics of Black life is a call to develop a different order of accounting that moves beyond what Saidiya Hartman famously termed 'the scene of subjection'.[48] 'What happens to our understanding of black humanity when our analytical frames do not emerge from a broad swathe of numbing racial violence but, instead, from multiple and untracked enunciations of black life?' McKittrick asks.[49] This question is an invitation to attend to the generativity and fugitivity of Blackness itself. The riot, we contend, is a particular form of struggle that irrupts not only as a response to premature Black death but also as a defence of Black social life. Here we might return to Moten's reading of the killings of Michael Brown and Eric Garner, which he tells us constitute an attack on the generativity of Blackness which implies something in excess of the equation of value, because it is both anti- and ante- the regulative order that brings it into being. He writes:

> I don't think he [Darren Wilson] meant to violate the individual personhood of Michael Brown, he was shooting at mobile Black sociality walking down the street in a way that he understood implicitly constituted a threat to the order that he represents and that he is sworn to protect. [...] And part of the reason that it constitutes such a profound threat is its openness, its unfixity, the fact that anybody can claim it and that it can claim anybody.[50]

The riot then can be understood as a struggle for a different order of value, a struggle to assert the 'multiple and untracked enunciations of black life'. The riot

---

[47] David Henderson, 'Keep on Pushing', p. 32.

[48] For Hartman, 'the scene of subjection' describes not only the spectacular forms that racial subjugation can take but importantly those quotidian forms of violence that can play out through concepts like humanity, enjoyment, protection, rights, and consent. Hartman develops this term in her articulation of the continuation of racial subjection in the aftermath of the formal abolition of slavery. Saidiya Hartman, *Scenes of Subjection: Terror, Slavery, and Self-Making in Nineteenth-Century America* (Oxford: Oxford University Press, 1997).

[49] Katherine McKittrick, *Dear Science and Other Stories* (Durham, NC: Duke University Press, 2021), p. 109.

[50] Fred Moten and Robin D. G. Kelley, 'Do Black Lives Matter? Robin D. G. Kelley and Fred Moten in Conversation', *Melville House*, July 2016, https://www.mhpbooks.com/132892-2/

poem is that which allows us to read the poetics of the riot in order to register this enunciation of a different order of value. If the riot is an assertion of survival that responds to state violence, a negation of the present enacted through the symbolic and actual destruction of the circulation of goods that the social reproduction of capital relies upon, then the riot poem transforms this negation into prophecy. As a mode of inquiry, the riot poem attends to the material dynamics of history that produce the present moment in order to reveal a possible movement towards the future.

In the fifth section of 'Keep on Pushing', Henderson cites the breakout hit of the summer of 1964: Martha and the Vandella's party track, 'Dancing in the Streets'. In the song, a promise hangs somewhere between the present and future tense. 'They'll be dancing (dancing in the street)' they sing, followed by, 'They're dancing in the street / Dancing in the street'.[51] When summer comes, the song promises, they'll be dancing in the street. But summer is already here—and so they are already dancing. The song lists cities across the US—New York, Baltimore, Philadelphia, New Orleans, and of course, Detroit, the band's hometown. For those who listened to the call to dance—the call to witness those already dancing—the promise of summer contained within it something bigger. For those on the street, the song was a call to revolution; for those who feared Black revolution, the song was a danger. As it became the anthem of more and more riots—as rioters understood the riot as a 'party for self defense'—radio stations began to remove the song from playlists.[52] (Decades later, in the wake of 9/11, the broadcast media company Clear Channel released a list of 150 songs to avoid playing for fear of inciting insurrection. 'Dancing in the Street' was included.[53]) Asika Touré, writing on 'Rhythm & Blues as a Weapon' in 1965 (in an essay titled, not incidentally, 'Keep on Pushing'), figures 'Dancing in the Street' as a 'Riot-song' that foreshadows revolution:

WE ARE COMING UP! WE ARE COMING UP! And it's reflected in the Riot-song that symbolized Harlem, Philly, Brooklyn, Rochester, Patterson, Elizabeth; this song, of course, 'Dancing in the Streets'—making Martha and the Vandellas legendary. Then FLASH! it surges up again: 'We Gonna' Make It' (to the tune of Medgar Evers gunned down in Mississippi: POW! POW! POW! POW! POW!) 'Keep on Trying' (to the tune of James Powell gunned down in Harlem: POW! POW! POW! POW!) 'Nowhere to Run, Nowhere to Hide', 'Change is Gonna'

---

[51] Martha and the Vandellas, 'Dancing in the Street' (Gordy, 1964).
[52] Fred Moten, 'Necessity, Immensity, and Crisis (Many Edges/Seeing Things)', Floor Journal, vol. 1, October 2011, http://floorjournal.com/2011/10/30/necessity-immensity-and-crisis-many-edgesseeing-things/
[53] Rollo Romig, '"Dancing in the Street": Detroit's Radical Anthem', The New Yorker, July 2013, https://www.newyorker.com/books/page-turner/dancing-in-the-street-detroits-radical-anthem

Come' (to the tune of Brother Malcolm shot down in the Audobon: POW! POW! POW! POW! POW! POW! POW!)[54]

For Touré, these songs are the soundtrack to the riot as well as that to which the riot responds; the soundtrack that underwrites the total climate, to use Christina Sharpe's formulation, of anti-Blackness, as well as the soundtrack that scores Black resistance.[55] In her history of Motown, called, of course, *Dancing in the Street*, Suzanne E. Smith opens the book with a description of an interrupted performance of the number one hit during a Detroit broadcast in the summer of 1967.[56] As Martha and the Vandellas began to sing, they were ushered off the stage. A riot had broken out on the streets of Detroit. The band packed up and left town—they went to New Jersey, South Carolina, but unrest followed them. The correlation between the song and the riots became a hot topic. Asked by the British press if she was a 'militant', Martha Reeves replied 'My Lord, it was a *party* song'.[57] Henderson and Touré, of course, agree: what is clear to them, and perhaps to Reeves too, is that a party can also be a riot, and when it is, it transforms dancing in the street into a matter of life against death.

Conclusion

'The poetics of the open field, especially when performed in the narrow cell', writes Moten, 'was always tied to the sociopoetics of riot, of generative differentiation as a kind of self-care, of expropriative disruption as a kind of self-defense, of seeing things as a performed social theory of mind'.[58] Moten's statement offers something of an answer to the questions we began with: What does it mean for a poem to be *against* the police? What does it mean for a poem to be *of* the riot or *for* abolition? For a poem to be against the police or for abolition it must be animated by a poetics that is linked to a social field. Poetics, which always exceeds the singular poem and the categories that delimit our reading of poems, is simultaneously social and aesthetic, a movement of generative differentiation. The continuum between dancing

---

[54] Asika Touré (writing as Rolland Snellings), 'Keep on Pushin': Rhythm & Blues as a Weapon', republished under the name 'We Are on the Move and the Music Is Moving with Us', in *Black Nationalism in America*, eds. John H. Bracey Jr, and August Meierand Elliot Rudwick (Indianapolis, IN: The Bobbs-Merrill Company, 1970), pp. 449–450.

[55] Christina Sharpe, 'The Weather', *The New Inquiry*, January 2017, https://thenewinquiry.com/the-weather/

[56] Suzanne E. Smith, *Dancing in the Street: Motown and the Cultural Politics of Detroit* (Cambridge, MA: Harvard University Press, 1999).

[57] Suzanne E. Smith, *Dancing in the Street*, p. 2.

[58] Fred Moten, 'Necessity, Immensity, and Crisis (many edges/seeing things)', *Floor Journal*, vol. 1, October 2011, http://floorjournal.com/2011/10/30/necessity-immensity-and-crisis-many-edgesseeing-things/

and rioting in the street reveals this unbreakable relation between the social and the aesthetic, the expropriative disruption that runs through both activities, the insistence that Black sociality is always a matter of life against death. The riot poem emerges from contact with the generative sociopoetics of the riot itself, which cannot but shape both the form and content of the poem. Such poems can be understood as examples of what Jasper Bernes, Joshua Clover, and Juliana Spahr describe as 'post-production poetics', which they tell us 'means something like a form of timeliness. The shape of being historical'.[59] The capacity for the poem to escape narrativization and representation leaves it open to capturing a sense of the historical in motion—it is both of the present and reaching beyond it. This too is the gift of struggle which insists on the attainability of a horizon beyond the given. The poem that is *against* the police or *of* the riot has no set form but rather captures the dynamism of this motion, which is a movement of radicalization. To return to Bonney yet again: 'social being determines content, content deranges form'.[60]

The poem that is shaped by struggle does not take a certain form, rather its formalism is its relation to the conditions of struggle which necessarily *deform* the shape of the poem in the relentless search to capture something of this double movement both to name the death inflicted by the capital relation *and* to sing the existence of otherwise possibilities. As distinct from the riot itself, the riot poem tries to capture the conditions that produced the riot as well as the intensities that comprise rioting in order to produce a document for future readers to study struggle. A riot poem makes a certain demand on its reader to consider the conditions of its making—that is, to consider the particular resistance it documents—and it also instructs a reader to be attentive to meaning as it comes to be articulated in new and unexpected ways. For these reasons, and as we have argued above, the riot poem is both a kind of counter-memorialization and a kind of prophecy: the riot poem can give shape to shared feelings and attachments that arise in times of social flux and antagonism. To read a riot poem is to be reminded of the power and capacity of what is shared. The poetic, writes Bonney in 'Letter Against the Firmament', is a fault-line:

> The moment of interruption, a 'counter rhythmic interruption', like a cardiac splinter of a tectonic shake. Again, a cracked metaphor, an abstraction or a counter-earth. Actually it's an entire cluster of metaphors, and each one of those metaphors twist in any number of directions, so that 'counter rhythmic interruption' refers, at the same time, to a band of masked-up rioters ripping up Oxford

---

[59] Joshua Clover, Juliana Spahr, and Jasper Bernes, 'Elegy, or the poetics of surplus', *Jacket2*, February 2014, https://jacket2.org/commentary/elegy-or-poetics-surplus

[60] Sean Bonney, 'Letter on Poetics', p. 15.

St., and to the sudden interruption inflicted by a cop's baton, a police cell and the malevolent syntax of a judge's sentence. We live in these cracks, these fault lines.[61]

The value of the riot poem is in its capacity to allow us to attune to the poetics of surplus populations—the timeliness and movement they imply. The militant poems we read here offer, in the words of Bonney, 'A map, a counter-map, actually, a chart of the spatio-temporal rhythm of the riot-form, its prosody and signal-frequency. A map that could show the paths *not* taken. And where to find them, those paths, those antidotes, those counter-plagues.'[62] We read riot poems and the poetics of the riot precisely in order to find those paths not taken, and to find a way to take them.

---

[61] Sean Bonney, *Letters Against the Firmament* (London: Enitharmon Press, 2015), p. 116.
[62] Sean Bonney, *Letters Against the Firmament*, p. 117.

11
Mobilizing the History of Protest and Dissent in Post-2011 Moroccan Novels

Karima Laachir

In the preface of his seminal book *Arabic Thought in the Liberal Age 1798–1939*, Albert Hourani notes the need to study how literature was used to disseminate Arab intellectual thought to broader audiences.[1] The turn to writing literary texts, including novels, by Arab intellectuals was a response to an oppressive environment. The increasing tyranny of the postcolonial state from the late 1960s created an atmosphere in which intellectuals were unable to openly express their disillusionment. Novels offered the opportunity to turn scathing attention on the state via criticism of societal norms and values. This is not merely a historical phenomenon but can be seen in the recent Arab uprisings, where culture and literature played a key role in anticipating and consolidating these events. It is certainly true that the uprisings were primarily the result of mass dissatisfaction with the authoritarian states in the Arabic-speaking world, which have entrenched social and economic inequalities and oppression. However, we also need to take into consideration the decades of civil society activism from the cultural and artistic spheres—expressed through cinematic productions, literature, popular music, arts, cartoons, and graffiti—which paved the way for the recent revolutionary fervour in the Arabic-speaking region. James Scott expresses a similar idea when he claims that behind every revolutionary movement, there is always 'a long prehistory, one comprising songs, popular poetry, jokes, street wisdom and political satire'.[2] Through their diverse works contesting hegemonic narratives of sociopolitical and economic issues, writers and artists have been at the forefront of social and political movements for change. Morocco is no exception. Cultural production in the country has been at the forefront of popular struggles for freedom against colonialism, political and social repression, and corruption.

A large number of influential Moroccan intellectuals and writers have leftist leanings. Some of them have been affiliated with leftist political parties and have been subject to imprisonment, torture, and harassment by the state; others have

---

[1] Albert Hourani *Arabic Thought in the Liberal Age 1798–1939* (Cambridge: Cambridge University Press, 1983), viii.
[2] James Scott, *Domination and the Arts of Resistance* (New Haven, CT: Yale University Press, 1990), p. 212.

never been part of the formal political system but strongly orient themselves to equality, justice, and freedom. Novels written in Arabic and French have offered a rich cultural memory of social and political mobilization; these poetics encourage rebellion against dogmatic social and political structures in the way they reinvent and reuse past struggles and uprisings, which they see as embedded in the social and political imaginary of the country. Individually and collectively, these works keep alive a memory of protest and riots that have been suppressed in official history and memory.

Memory Mobilization in Literature

This chapter examines the present engagement of Moroccan writers of literary fiction with Morocco's postcolonial projects of equality, justice, and freedom, paying attention to the way in which memory is generated and sustained through literature. In this respect, I take up the call placed by Jan Rupp to pay greater scholarly attention to 'the specific role as well as the distinctive functions of literature in memory culture'.[3] In fact, the cultural turn in the humanities was accompanied by growing interest in the idea of 'cultural memory'.[4]

In recent years, there has been an increasing effort to draw overt links between memory and political mobilization. Ann Rigney points to a bifurcation of scholarly interest between memory *of* activism (that is to say, 'how earlier struggles for a better world are culturally recollected') and memory *in* activism ('how the cultural memory of earlier struggles informs new movements in the present').[5] A handful of scholars have narrowed their focus to the intersections of literature, memory, and political mobilization. Pınar Yelsalı Parmarksız, for instance, exposes the tangled relationship between these strands in the context of the 2013 Gezi Park uprisings in Turkey.[6] Susanne Rinner undertakes a similar process in studying the German student movement, while Sarah Beth Hunt does much the same for Dalits in north India.[7] While these earlier studies have started to shift the conversation from memory of activism to memory in activism, there is clearly more work to be done to

---

[3] Jann Rupp, 'Book Review: Sarah Henstra, The Counter-Memorial Impulse in Twentieth Century English Fiction.' *Memory Studies* 4, no. 3 (2011): pp. 349–351, p. 350.

[4] See Aleida Assmann, *Cultural Memory and Western Civilization: Functions, Media, Archives* (New York, NY: Cambridge University Press, 2011); Ron Eyerman 'The Past in the Present: Culture and the Transmission of Memory', *Acta Sociologica* 47, no. 2 (2004): pp. 159–169; Felicitas Machilchrist and Rosalie Metro, editors, *Trickbox of Memory: Essays on Power and Disorderly Pasts* (Brooklyn: Punctum Books, 2020); Max Silverman, *Palimpsest Memory: The Holocaust and Colonialism in French and Francophone Fiction and Film* (New York, NY: Berghahn Book, 2013).

[5] Ann Rigney, 'Mediations of Outrage: How Violence against Protestors is Remembered', *Social Research* 87, no. 3 (2020): pp. 707–733, p. 708.

[6] Pınar Melis Yelsalı Parmaksız, 'Cultural Memory of Social Protest: Mnemonic Literature about Gezi Park Protests', *Memory Studies* 14, no. 2 (2021): pp. 288–302.

[7] Susanne Rinner, *The German Student Movement and the Literary Imagination: Transnational Memories of Protest and Dissent* (New York, NY: Berghahn Books, 2012); Sarah Beth Hunt, *Hindi Dalit Literature and the Politics of Representation* (London: Taylor & Francis Group, 2014).

understand how literature sustains cultural memory in order to inform present and future politics.

Cultural memory, it is fair to say, has taken on a kind of catch-all quality in the scholarly effort to understand the diverse and complex ways in which societies remember their distinctive pasts using a vast array of media.[8] Cultural memory refers to the way in which social groups construct a shared past via text, institutions, and practices, which in turn contribute to the shaping of communities.[9] It has been broadly established in memory studies that literature plays a particularly important role in cultural memory-work.[10] Fiction is, of course, inherently unreliable as a repository of historical truth. Indeed, fiction's stock-in-trade is the illusory and the elusive. However, it is this very quality of literature that conversely (and perversely) allows it to act as a repository and vehicle of culture and collective memory. While history 'is seen to deal in truths, remains controversial and, ironically, untrustworthy', fiction acts as an articulation of identity.[11] Literature can, as Jacques Derrida puts it, 'say everything'; and a kind of licence is given to the writer of fiction 'to say everything he [or she] wants to or everything he [or she] can, while remaining shielded, safe from all censorship'.[12] In the largely authoritarian political system functioning in contemporary Morocco, history is notoriously subject to censorship and to acts of suppression and omission. In such a context, fiction has the capacity to whisper historical truths, if not to speak them out loud.

In the case of Morocco, the Years of Lead (1961–1999) had an undeniably stultifying cultural effect, which inhibited the development, and continuing trajectory of an indigenous literature.[13] This was a period marked by repression, brutal violence, arbitrary arrests, and disappearances. The Rif Revolt (1958/59), the repression of Marxist-Leninist activists (1972–1990), the disappearance of soldiers and civilians to secret prisons (1973–1991), the mistreatment of Islamist prisoners, and the bloody crackdown on social movements from the 1960s to the early 1990s were notorious examples of state-sponsored violence under King Hassan II. Despite officially mandated efforts to come to terms with the country's recent history—not least through the establishment of The Equity and Reconciliation Commission (ERC) in 2004—there remain significant gaps and omissions in the way the past is memorialized in the present.

---

[8] Astrid Erll and Ann Rigney, 'Literature and the Production of Cultural Memory: Introduction', *European Journal of English Studies* 10, no. 2 (2006): pp. 111–115.

[9] Jennifer Terry, '"When the sea of living memory has receded": Cultural Memory and Literary Narratives of the Middle Passage', *Memory Studies* 6, no. 4 (2013): pp. 474–488.

[10] Herbert Grabes (ed.), *Literature, Literary History, and Cultural Memory* (Tübingen: Gunter Narr Verlag, 2005).

[11] Elisabeth Yarbakhsh, *Iranian Hospitality, Afghan Marginality: Spaces of Refuge and Belonging in the City of Shiraz* (Lanham: Lexington Books, 2021).

[12] Jacques Derrida and Derek Attridge, *Acts of Literature* (New York, NY: Routledge, 1992), pp. 37–39.

[13] Abdelfettah Fakihani, *Le couloir: bribes de vérité sur les années de plomb* (Casablanca, Morocco: Tarik Éditions, 2005).

In this context, literary accounts of Morocco's recent history challenge a state-imposed politics of silence and oblivion and offer a counterpoint to the official narrative of democratic transition. As Rigney puts it, 'stories stick'.[14] That is to say, narrative fiction makes events memorable 'by figuring the past in a structured way that engages the sympathies of the reader'.[15] Literature 'creates its own memory worlds with specifically literary techniques'.[16] But such memory worlds are not static: the 'act of memorization is always generative of an event'.[17] Cultural memory 'is the product of fragmentary personal and collective experiences articulated through technologies and media that shape even as they transmit memory. Acts of memory are thus acts of performance, representation, and interpretation.'[18]

In her 1987 novel, *Beloved*, Toni Morrison coins the term *rememory* to capture the non-linearity of time and the way in which past and present collapse into one another.[19] An event, while possessing a precise chronology, may not be time-bound because of the metaphorical law of accretion where it 'takes on significances outside … [its] time-frame'.[20] Importantly, literature can rememory history.[21] Amir Eshel notes the way in which literature about the past gains a prospective aspect or futurity.[22] This notion of futurity becomes important when we consider that Moroccan literature has not merely produced a record of the past but has, vitally, kept alive and present the politics of dissent and protest. A common thread in the works of writers such as Mohamed Achaari and Abdelkarim Jouaiti is a commitment to justice and social equality, indicative of a new way of performing politics in a neoliberal social and governmental milieu. On the one hand, we might consider these novels as a form of resistance against the logics of neoliberalism but, on the other, we can recognize the ways in which they are very much embedded within the contemporary neoliberal order. At the turn of the millennium, Morocco embraced neoliberal economic policies. This was ostensibly part of a shift to democracy that is yet to be fully realized. By offering paths of resistance and agency to their characters, novelists reveal how modes of opposition to neoliberal economic policies can be negotiated and contested. The novels demand the reader

---

[14] Ann Rigney, 'The Dynamics of Remembrance: Texts between Monumentality and Morphing', in *Cultural Memory Studies: An International and Interdisciplinary Handbook*, edited by Astrid Erll and Ansgar Nünning (Berlin: Walter de Gruyter, 2008), p. 347.

[15] Rigney, 'The Dynamics of Remembrance', p. 348.

[16] Birgit Neumann, 'The Literary Representation of Memory', in *Cultural Memory Studies: An International and Interdisciplinary Handbook*, edited by Astrid Erll and Ansgar Nünning (Berlin: Walter de Gruyter 2008), p. 334.

[17] Sudesh Mishra, 'Acts of Rememory in Oceania', *Symploke* 26, no. 1–2 (2018): pp. 19–32, p. 20.

[18] Marianne Hirsch and Valerie Smith, 'Feminism and Cultural Memory: An Introduction', *Signs* 28, no. 1 (2002): pp. 1–19, p. 5.

[19] Toni Morrison, *Beloved* (New York, NY: Alfred A Knopf, 1987).

[20] Shahid Amin, *Event, Metaphor, Memory: Chauri Chaura 1922–1992* (Delhi: Oxford University Press, 1996), p. 3.

[21] Marta-Laura Cenedese, '(Instrumental) Narratives of Postcolonial Rememory: Intersectionality and Multidirectional Memory', *Storyworlds* 10, no. 1 (2018): pp. 95–116.

[22] Amir Eshel, *Futurity: Contemporary Literature and the Quest for the Past* (Chicago, IL: Chicago University Press, 2013).

reflect on Morocco's political past, but also consider what sort of present is now available and what possible futures might be embraced.

Aleksandr Skidan argues that poetics and politics are 'two dimensions of the very same thing' as they are both the 'articulation (the poiesis) of the "external" and "internal", the sensorial and the rationally intelligible, the singular and the universal'.[23] The novels under examination here can be read as simultaneously poetic and political reflections on Moroccan history. However, in thinking about political poetics we need to move beyond merely emphasizing the way in which politics (and political history) is made accessible to a readership through the application of poetic or literary techniques. Rather, we need to consider how politics might itself function as a form of poetics in the present.

Literary and cultural production has always engaged with pressing social and political issues, offering alternative visions and 'imaginings' to the social and political spheres in Morocco. A number of Moroccan critics make this very point. These include Ahmed Al-Yaburi, who argues that Moroccan literature has always been engaged with its social and historical contexts through the use of shifting innovative aesthetics to reflect the shifting dynamics of Moroccan society.[24] Abdelkebir Khatibi pushes for the plurality of Moroccan culture and its multilingual diversity and argues for the 'power of the word' or what he calls 'poetic force' that can oppose the 'word of power' or hegemonic structures of power.[25] Khatibi considers the genre of the novel as 'the testimony of a time'.[26] Along these lines, the Moroccan novelist Mohamed Achaari considers 'creativity as a political choice' or a political intervention that can help correct the derailed democratic project in Morocco.[27] He states that Morocco's rich multilingual cultural field and the free movement between various languages allow for diversifying modes of expression and creativity. This, in turn, opens up 'spaces of freedom' by which 'an effective weapon is forged against restrictions on language and thought'.[28]

The Turn to History and Memory of Oppression and Protest after the 2011 Arab Uprisings

The traumatic events of Morocco's Years of Lead, during which thousands of people were arrested, tortured, and imprisoned because of their political views,

---

[23] Aleksandr Skidan, 'Political/Poetic', *Russian Studies in Literature* 54, no. 1–3 (2018): pp. 84–94, p. 90.
[24] Ahmed Al-Yarubi, *Al Kitāba al riwā'iya fī al Maghreb* (Casablanca: Sharikat al Nashr wa al tawzī', 2006).
[25] Abdelkebir Khatibi, *Le Maghreb Pluriel* (Paris: Denoel, 1983), p. 61.
[26] Abdelkebir Khatibi, *Le Roman maghrébin* (Paris: Maspéro, 1968), p. 28.
[27] Mohamed Achaari, 'Creativity as a Political Choice', *Journal of North African Studies* 21, no. 1 (2016): pp. 12–21.
[28] Achaari, 'Creativity as a Political Choice', p. 15.

inspired an outburst of literary production. Since the death of King Hassan II in 1999, there have been increasing literary references to the trauma of these years.[29] These 'personal and creative productions about the prison experience provide alternative voices and versions of events that, both in their subject matter and narrative styles, seek to subvert traditional modes of discourse in favour of the telling of a story (or stories) that is nuanced, complex, and alive.'[30] They seek recognition of the violence and suffering that went unrecognized for decades. As Alexander Elinson puts it: 'Moroccan prison writings published during or after the "Lead Years" face and oftentimes oppose an official, "authoritative discourse" of violence and control.'[31] The outburst of Francophone and Arabophone narratives on the Years of Lead touches upon the physical and symbolic violence of prison experiences, solitary confinement, and torture, including the experience of the notorious secret prison in *Tazmamart*, where political prisoners were confined in the 1970s and 1980s.[32]

Prison literature is not uniquely found in Morocco; it is common in other Arabic literary traditions because of the tyranny of most of the political regimes in Arab countries and their brutal suppression of dissent and opposition. Sabry Hafiz argues that 'Arabic literature is perhaps one of very few literary traditions that have a distinct literary genre known as the "prison novel". This is not only because a great majority of writers have themselves lived the experience of arrest, imprisonment, and even torture, but also because the history of the contemporary Arab intellectual is one of constant struggle with the authorities.'[33]

Did literary writers acquire more freedom of expression in the immediate aftermath of the Arab Uprisings in 2011? One cannot claim a fundamental change in

---

[29] There have been some literary publications on prison experiences in the form of semi-autobiographical accounts from the 1960s to the 1990s, but an increasing number of publications appeared after the death of Hassan II. El Yazami et al. state that in the period between 2000 and 2004, as many as 41 works dealing with this topic were published. See Abdellali El-Yazami, Ali Kabous, and Jaafar Akil, *D'ombre et de lumière: Bibliographie des violations graves des droits de l'homme au Maroc* (Rabat: Centre de Documentation d'Information et de Formation en Droits de l'Homme, 2004), p. 22.

[30] Alexander Elinson, 'Opening the Circle: Storyteller and Audience in Moroccan Prison Literature', *Middle Eastern Literatures* 12, no. 3 (2009): pp. 289–303, p. 290.

[31] Elinson, 'Opening the Circle', p. 290.

[32] Narratives include, among many others, Abd Al-Qadir Al-Shawi's *Al-Sāhatu Al-Shārīfiya* (2000, *The Square of Honour*); Khadija Marwazi's *Sīratu Al-Rāmad* (2000, *Biography of Ash*); and Said Haji's *Dhākiratu al-finīq: Sīratun dhātiyatun li wajhin min sanawāt al-rāsās* (2006, *Memory of the Phoenix: An Autobiography from the Years of the Lead*); Muhammad Al-Rays' Mudhākirāt's *Muhammad al-Rāys: min al-skhirāt ilā Tazmamart: tadkhirat dhahāb wa'iyab ilā al-jaīim* (2002, *Memoirs of Mohammad al-Rays, from Skhirat to Tazmamart: A Round Trip Ticket to Hell*); and Ahmad Marzouqi's *Tazmamart: Cellule 10* (2000, Tzamamart: Cell 10).

[33] Sabry Hafiz, 'Torture, Imprisonment and Political Assassination in the Arabic Novel', *Al Jadid Magazine* 8, no. 38 (2002), https://www.aljadid.com/content/torture-imprisonment-and-political-assassination-arab-novel, accessed 9 October 2022. Hafiz explains that the genre dates back to the anti-colonial times when various narratives emerged in the 1950s and 1960s about the violence of colonial powers in various Arab countries such as Algeria, Egypt, and Syria. For a discussion of torture and imprisonment in Moroccan poetry, see Muhammad Huwwar, *Al-Qabd 'alā l-jamr: tajribat al-sijn fi l-sh'r al-m 'āsir* (Beirut: al Mu'assasa al- 'Arabiyya li l-Dirāsāt wa l-Nashr, 2004).

the way literary texts reflect on social and political reality, as they have always offered a space of opposition and dissent. However, in novels emerging after the 2011 Arab Uprisings, particularly those written in Arabic, we see a critical and aesthetic agenda that crosses certain lines such as the question of the Western Sahara war and the amnesia regarding its victims.[34] Such texts also dwell on the re-imagining of local (peripheral) histories of elite Makhzenian families and their abuse of power or misuse of rule from pre-colonial to postcolonial Morocco, exploring how this abuse is perceived by the masses and how this micro-power replicates the macro-power of the rulers or the monarchy.[35] There is also a strong critique of the neo-liberal economy, state capitalism, and the monopoly of wealth in the hands of the very few. There is a focus on the corrosive effects of these forces on society, and a deep anxiety expressed by both Francophone and Arabophone writers on the question of the rise of Salafism, strict conservative Islam and the perceived restriction on social rights and freedoms.

A small number of literary texts in Arabic and French, which came out immediately after the 2011 uprisings, directly refer to protests in Morocco and the 20 February movement. They include Abdelellah Belkziz's novel *Al Haraka* (*The Movement*, 2012), Driss Ksikes's play, *N'enterrez pas trop vite Big Brother* (*Don't Bury Big Brother Too Soon*, 2014), and Sonia Terrab's *La révolution n'a pas eu lieu* (*The Revolution Did Not Take Place*, 2014).[36] Belkziz, a well-known and prolific thinker with leftist leanings, fictionalizes the events leading to the demise of the 20 February movement; he reflects on how a movement comprised of various factions disintegrated and lost its coherence and focus because of various disagreements over how to respond to state initiatives for reform and how to treat political friends and allies. Ksikes, who is also a well-known leftist secular intellectual, uses

---

[34] Morocco has been perceived as one of the Arab countries that has been the least affected by the popular pro-democracy uprisings that have swept Arab countries in North Africa and the Middle East in 2011. Demonstrations were not as large as in neighbouring Tunisia, Egypt, and Libya. The Moroccan Makhzen (security apparatus and ruling political and economic elites) swiftly reacted to contain the demonstrations using the carrot and stick approach, and the monarch quickly announced constitutional reforms. The emergence of the 20 February pro-democracy movement, led by a politically independent youth contingent, has shown the aspirations of Moroccan people for real political and social reforms. It follows other revolts in the past that marked Moroccan modern history such as the Rif Revolts of 1958/59, the 1965 Casablanca popular protests led by students, and the 1981 public protests and strikes among others. A wave of protests took place in the North of Morocco and in the Rif region in 2016–17 and were triggered by the death of a fishmonger, Mouhcine Fikri, who was crushed by security forces after jumping in the back of a garbage truck attempting to save his allegedly illegal fish merchandise from being taken by the police. The protests were met with repression and there were violent clashes between the security forces and the protests in various cities. Many protesters, including the leader of the movement, Nasser Zefzafi, were arrested and imprisoned.

[35] The term Makhzen was used in the twelfth century to refer to the warehouses where taxes were kept (whether they were in currency or in kind); today it has come to signify the royal court, the ruling elite (particularly security forces, veteran politicians, and economic elites).

[36] Abdelellah Belkziz, *Al Haraka* (*The Movement*) (Casablanca: al-Maaref Forum, 2012); Driss Ksikes, *N'enterrez pas trop vite Big Brother* (*Don't Bury Big Brother Too Soon*) (Paris: Riveneuve, 2014); Sonia Terrab, *La révolution n'a pas eu lieu* (*The Revolution Did Not Take Place*) (Casablanca: Editions La Croisée de Chemins, 2014).

his play (which was performed in Morocco and France) to refer symbolically to the burying of the 20 February movement. The play dwells on the discussion between former residents of Building 48 which was burnt down twenty years ago in mysterious circumstances. The building was a place of libertarian living, an ideal free society where religious and personal freedoms were respected. The cause of the fire—variously thought to be a hostile policeman or else Islamists who disapproved of the building's inhabitants—is not settled. The residents's debate what to do with the legacy of the building, whether to turn it into a museum preserving the past or to look to the future with hope. Terrab's novella criticizes the entrenched privileges of the upper classes in Morocco who were lukewarm about their support of the movement. It dwells on the life of a group of upper-class Moroccans completely disconnected from the country as they move in the bubble of money, privilege, and drugs.

If these literary works dwell on the immediate aftermath of the demise of the pro-democracy movement, novels that have appeared later are more outspoken and radical about the swift return of the status quo in Morocco. These include Abderahim Jouaiti's *Al Maghariba* (*The Moroccans*, 2016).[37] The novel dwells on the relationship between a soldier, who was badly disabled in the Western Sahara war and was forgotten by the state and society, and his brother, who gradually lost his eyesight in a society that does not deal well with disabilities. The novel traces the history of local landlords, Pashas and *Qaids* in the region of Beni Melal and their abuse of power in a historical genealogy of flashbacks between precolonial, colonial, and postcolonial Morocco, as a way to reflect on the micro-histories of local Makhzenian violence and how it reflects the central and absolute power of the monarchy. The history of violence is symbolized by the finding of a mass grave of hundreds of skulls without bodies by a group of builders; a mass grave that has been presented as a historical cemetery by the authorities to brush aside any public doubts as to why there are only heads without bodies.[38] To silence the growing restlessness of the masses towards the discovery of the mass grave, the authorities send a committee made up of a visually impaired archaeological expert and his assistant to verify the skulls and write a report about their history.[39]

It turns out that the expert suffers from regular emotional crises (described in the novel as similar to epileptic fits), during which he remembers and re-lives his father's arrest and torture at the hands of the security forces following the terrible events of 3 March 1973.[40] In a chapter titled 'The Rope', the expert goes through one of these fits in the presence of his assistant, the soldier and his brother. He retells the story of his father, a university professor, who was suspected of being

---

[37] Abderahim Jouaiti, *Al Maghariba* (*The Moroccans*) (Casablanca: Al Markaz Athaqafi Alarabi, 2016).
[38] Jouaiti, *The Moroccans*, pp. 137–152.
[39] Jouaiti, *The Moroccans*, pp. 147–149.
[40] Jouaiti, *The Moroccans*, p. 189, pp. 189–196.

part of the secret revolutionary wing of the leftist party USFP (Socialist Union of Popular Forces) when it led a military revolt against King Hassan II on 3 March 1973. This came after the failure of two coup d'états against the King in 1971 and 1972. The secret radical leftist cell waged a failed military attack in the town of Khenifra, leading to an aggressive security response resulting in the imprisonment, torture, disappearance, and killing of many people suspected of being part of the plot. The novel commemorates this forgotten history in the Moroccan imaginary by tracing the violence and trauma it left on the collective psyche. The expert goes into an emotional crisis as he remembers his father's torture in the family house in front of his children and wife. His father was eventually killed by five men in the secret security services in his own home. To cover for his murder, the five men convinced the young boy (the expert) to help them use a rope to hang the father so that they could give the impression that the murdered man committed suicide. The expert explains that when the police investigated the case, and despite being told by the two young children what really happened, they concluded their report by stating that the father killed himself because of marital conflict. The expert relives the guilt of a child being embroiled in his own father's murder and cover-up, but he also criticizes neighbours for knowing the truth and not having the courage to speak out in the face of fear and repression.[41]

Reflecting on the trauma of the expert, the soldier's brother extends that trauma generationally when he tells us, 'I have been thinking that the real skulls are what the expert carries inside him, and what each one of us carries, spacious and dark cemeteries with rotten gravestones: the guilt complex, resentment, mourning, fears and bitter memories.'[42] The soldier then also condemns the Moroccan people for their lack of courage and their complicit silence in the face of the crimes committed during the Years of Lead. He condemns them for accepting the state's 'reconciliation' with the new era of King Mohamed VI, which only paid lip service to the violence of the Years of Lead without really confronting the past.[43]

In drafting the report on the hundreds of skulls found in the mass grave, the expert and his assistant, with the help of the soldier, look for possible explanations in Morocco's earlier history, focusing on particular episodes when the kings and sultans sent their armies to discipline uprisings amongst tribes and regions.[44] Reflecting on this history of violence in the country, the soldier suggests that

---

[41] Jouaiti, *The Moroccans*, p. 195.
[42] Jouaiti, *The Moroccans*, p. 295.
[43] Jouaiti, *The Moroccans*, pp. 195–196. This refers to the ascension of King Mohamed VI to power in 1999 and the attempt to turn a new page in Moroccan history with the idea of national reconciliation and the establishment of The Truth and Reconciliation Commission in 2004. Although this royal initiative is rather unique in the Arab world, as it investigated state-perpetuated human rights abuses, it can also be seen as part of a set of carefully state-staged reforms to break with the state repression of the past in a way that allows public criticism of past abuses without any radical change or any safeguarding of the citizens from future abuses.
[44] Jouaiti, *The Moroccans*, pp. 291–298.

the mass grave could even be more recent—that it might be related to the dark decades of the Years of Lead, particularly the 1960s and 1970s in the region of Beni Melal, where an office of secret security forces operated and was well known for its brutal crackdowns and murders.[45] This suggestion brings back the expert's trauma and the murder of his father, who was one of the victims of the Years of Lead.[46]

Jouaiti's novel is a work of archaeology that 'digs up' the fragmented and silenced history of state violence in Morocco. As the soldier puts it 'writing is the only act of resistance left in a country whose birds stopped singing and flowers started refusing to bloom in the morning and trees stopped growing'.[47] The soldier allegorically indicates the deterioration of oppositional culture and civil society activism with the advance, in the words of the soldier, of the 'new elites' whose interest is focused on accumulating vast wealth and power at the expense of the suffering of ordinary people.[48] The move between individual and collective trauma, and the reinforcing of the intertwining of the personal and collective trauma across generations in the novel, commemorates the silenced histories of physical and psychological violence inflicted upon generations of Moroccans.

The reflection on the Western Sahara question and the intimate life of the palace or *Dar al Mulk* under Hassan II began with the work of Youssef Fadel with his Arabic novel *Qetun Abyadun Jameel Yamshi Ma'e* (*Beautiful White Cat Walks with Me*, 2011).[49] This novel describes the life of a Saharan conscript during the armed conflict with the Polisario Front from 1975 to 1991. The novel describes the corruption of the army's senior generals and the forgetfulness assigned to the soldiers who died in the war. It is the story of an estranged father and son. The father works as the court jester of Hassan II and the son, an artist who writes political sketches criticising the abuse of power, is forcibly conscripted in the Saharan conflict, where he witnesses the brutality of a war that the soldiers could not understand. In turn, Mahi Benabine's *Le fou de roi* (*The Court Jester*, 2017) traces the 'true' story of his father who was Hassan II's court jester.[50] Like Fadel's text, it is the story of a father and a son, the son in this case is a militant who was accused of taking part in a failed coup against Hassan II and ended up spending eighteen years in Tazamamart prison. The father in Benabine's story had cut all ties with his family. In both novels, Hassan II is an elusive figure: powerful, calculating, and always ahead of the game. The texts offer comic glimpses of the King's cronies and the extent to which they are willing to be humiliated by the monarch to keep their position in power.

---

[45] Jouaiti, *The Moroccans*, p. 298.
[46] Jouaiti, *The Moroccans*, p. 298.
[47] Jouaiti, *The Moroccans*, p. 145.
[48] Jouaiti, *The Moroccans*, p. 145.
[49] Youssef Fadel, *Qetun Abyadun Jameel Yamshi Ma'e* (*Beautiful White Cat Walks With Me*) (Beirut: Dar Al Adaab, 2011).
[50] Mahi Benabine *Le fou de roi* (*The Court Jester*) (Paris: Stock, 2017).

We read about powerful army generals and ministers (like the well-known brutal interior minister Driss Basri), and the rituals of submission and humiliation that they experience and in turn practise on the masses and those below them. Fadel and Benabine's novels are both acts of memory of the Western Sahara war and the forgotten history of the soldiers who perished in that war and whose stories remain largely untold and unknown.

A novel that highlights the silenced history of dissent is Mohamed Achaari's *Al 'Ayn Al-Kadima* (*The Old Spring*, 2019), which follows the itinerary of Masoud, a quietist leftist in his sixties who reflects on his 'losses' in life after his retirement, the death of his French wife and the migration of his adult children to California.[51] Masoud met his French wife in Paris and was inspired by the May 1968 protests in France, which called for workers's rights and greater freedoms. His older child Mona was born in early June 1981, during a day of rioting in Casablanca that cost the lives of many people. The 1981 bread riots in Casablanca took place at the height of King Hassan II's rule and were driven by price increases in basic food supplies. The young people from the slums of Casablanca who led these riots were brutally suppressed, with over 500 people estimated to have been killed. The novel commemorates the event through the story of Mona's birth and the anxiety of her French mother, who suspected that there was a birth swap between Mona and another male child, Osama, whose father was killed in the riots.[52] The adult Mona, who lives in California, thinks her mother never recovered from the violence with which the protests of June 1981 were met in Casablanca. She reads her mother's anxiety about the possibility of a baby swap as a protest against 'the indifference and forgetting that followed that horror'.[53] Mona returns to Casablanca to investigate her mother's story and whether there was a swap at her birth; her investigation takes her back to the memory of early June 1981 and the riots. In the slums of Casablanca where Tashafin, who is helping Mona to find the lost child who was presumed to be swapped with Mona at her birth, claims that 'revolution will come sooner or later from these slums'.[54] However, when she asks him about past riots in Casablanca, he claims that 'the matter ends faster than with which it starts and we are only left with fear' referring to the security apparatuses's oppressive reactions to these riots.[55] The memory of the 1981 riots dominates the novel and links individual trauma to the collective larger one, highlighting the continuity of struggle.

---

[51] Mohamed Achaari, *Al 'Ayn Al-Kadima* (*The Old Spring*) (Casablanca: Al Markaz Athaqafi Alarabi, 2019).
[52] Aachari, *The Old Spring*, p. 165.
[53] Achaari, *The Old Spring*, p. 160.
[54] Achaari, *The Old Spring*, p. 185.
[55] Achaari, *The Old Spring*, p. 186.

Dar Al Mulk (House of Dominion or Royal House and Entourage)

The fascination with the power dynamics in *Dar al Mulk* is replicated throughout society, from high-ranking officers of the Makhzen to those lowest. Novels like Jouaiti's *Al Maghariba* (*The Moroccans*) can be read together with Abdellah Hammoudi's study *Master and Disciple: The Cultural Foundations of Moroccan Authoritarianism*. Hammoudi argues, not uncontroversially, that the cultural foundation of political power in Morocco is based on the Sufi master–disciple relationship, which is marked by both submission and coercion, and which links political power to rituals of servitude and rites of passage.[56] In fact, Jouaiti's complex novel devotes three chapters, named 'Moroccan Hallucinations', to real extracts from famous Moroccan Sufi masters detailing the suffering of their followers, their humiliation and their total submission in order to join the Sufi brotherhood.[57]

A significant part of Jouaiti's novel is devoted to recreating the memories of tribal rebellions against unjust local authority and the authority of the sultans from pre-modern to recent history in Morocco. These rebellions were suppressed using brute force, which sometimes led to the massacre of whole tribes.[58] To justify their killing, they were accused of blasphemy; in the words of the soldier: 'religion had killed many of our ancestors more than upheavals, famines and epidemics. Whenever they [the tribes] rejected injustices and subjugation, they were accused of blasphemy.'[59] A largely unknown revolt that is commemorated in the novel is the revolt of 1960 in Beni Melal in north-central Morocco when a local leader, Bashir Athami, captured a military barrack and declared the formation of a republic.[60] For few days the rebels formed a popular republic in the socialist revolutionary tradition and were joined by some peasants in the area hoping that the revolt will spread to other areas in the region, but they were quickly crushed by the Moroccan army.[61] The novel links this history of rebellion with the present—indicating, as the soldier's brother claims, that the Makhzen has mastered the art of co-opting movements of opposition, particularly with the coming of corrupt party leaders who made the masses lose hope in politics and change.[62] The interweaving of the past and the present widens the scope of the novel's historical reference and shows that the roots of the current crisis go back deep in history.

---

[56] Abdallah Hammoudi, *Master and Disciple: The Cultural Foundations of Moroccan Authoritarianism* (Chicago, IL: Chicago University Press, 1997).
[57] Jouaiti, *The Moroccans*, pp. 241–255, 372–382.
[58] Jouaiti, *The Moroccans*, pp. 295–296.
[59] Jouaiti, *The Moroccans*, p. 296.
[60] Jouaiti, *The Moroccans*, p. 185.
[61] Jouaiti, *The Moroccans*, pp. 185–186.
[62] Jouaiti, *The Moroccans*, p. 303.

While the discourse of Jouaiti's novel recognizes the 'structuring structures' of power it laments the submission of the masses.[63] This is explained in the novel by referring to the educational system that has encouraged the masses to memorize knowledge at the expense of creativity and innovation. It also puts the blame on the choice of the Maliki School of jurisprudence that prefers safety and security to rebelling against corrupt rulers. In sum, Moroccans are a people who have been terrorized through the ages and therefore carry within them a fear of power that is difficult to break:

> Because Morocco was far away, in the abyss of empires, where the grip of the state, religion and history is diminished, it was always a common property for pretenders, dreamers of power, and big liars. A people [Moroccans] without imagination, they never dreamt of another society except through false forecasters and miserable pretenders to messianism. Wherever you turn your face, you see a nation that had distributed all its pain on tombs and singled out each one of them for healing a disease and then took a seat at the edge of history waiting for miracles.[64]

Jouaiti's novel, despite its harsh criticism of Moroccans, can be read as an act of memory of the history of dissent and rebellion in the country against unjust rulers and corruption in an attempt to mobilize that history to rebel against the present situation.

The reflection on *Dar al Mulk*, particularly under Hassan II takes another turn with Achaari's novel *Thalatha Layalin* (*Three Nights*, 2017) where he digs up the forgotten story of Hassan II's harem.[65] It brings back to memory a taboo subject about how many Moroccan women from all over the country were taken by force and kept for the pleasure of the king, and possibly married (as daughters of the Makhzen) to army Generals and other key officials. After the dismantling of the harem in 1999 by the current king, the narrator in Achaari's novel reflects:

> In a short period of time, many things happened and the most important one is the 'freeing of the women of the Harem' after centuries of close links between the harem and the practice of governance. Some newspapers spoke about the uprising of the women in the Palace of Fes ... and then spoke about the 'yashirat', or those who were saved by the royal Palace from the clutches of orphanage and need, but no one spoke about the 'protected' [mahdiyāt] ones, and it was said that the management of the royal palaces would send some high instructions on how to get rid of 'this burden'. After a few days, the subject was over and nobody spoke

---

[63] Pierre Bourdieu, *The Logic of Practice* (Stanford, CA: Stanford University Press, 1990), p. 53.
[64] Jouaiti, *The Moroccans*, p. 122.
[65] Mohamed Achaari, *Thalatha Layalin (Three Nights)* (Casablanca: Al Markaz Athaqafi Alarabi, 2017).

anymore about it, no news media enlisted itself to drumming and tooting about the greatest transformation in Moroccan State; nobody met any woman of flesh and blood who was there [confined in the Royal palaces] and she was no longer there.[66]

Achaari's novel starts with the abuse of women, their abduction and confinement in powerful houses of the *Qaids* and Pashas dating back to pre-colonial Morocco, when women were forcefully taken from their families sometimes as children or were given as gifts from tribes to pacify the sultan and his allies. The first part of the novel dwells on the story of the harem of the well-known Lord of the Atlas, the Pasha Glawi, who had more than a hundred women in his harem for his own pleasure. It then moves to the story of the harem in the royal palace of Rabat of Hassan II, focusing on the story of Rhimou, a young girl who was taken from her parents in a village near Marrakesh just because the monarch was attracted to her beauty. In the novel, her parents were murdered in mysterious circumstances when they insisted on seeing her again. She spends more than thirty years in the palace, but she is called only twice to the King's private quarter. The novel partly recounts her and other women's untold and silenced histories of oppression and confinement.

A younger generation of Arabophone writers trace the changes in the Moroccan political landscape since the 1970s to the present moment. This includes the work of the journalist and poet Yassin Adnan, whose debut novel *Hot Maroc* (2016, translated to English in 2021), focuses in particular on the death of politics and the way powerful oppositional parties, particularly those on the Left, were co-opted in the 1990s.[67] *Hot Maroc* is an urban comic novel set in Marrakesh which follows a group of middle- and working-class young people trying to make sense of their life in a city that has experienced unbridled urban development that has not benefited the majority and has been environmentally disastrous. It takes place mainly on the internet or through it, via the news site called 'Hot Maroc', where commentators and bloggers can take part in political and social discussions. The novel criticizes the decay of the culture of debate on the internet, suggesting that cyberspace has become a tool for the Makhzen or the security apparatus to direct and control political and social discussions in a way that preserves its interests and, at the same time, projects an image of the country 'debating freely'. The protagonist (an antihero) of the novel, Rahhal, is a very intelligent but shy and cowardly young man, who can only criticize society and politics via the anonymity of the internet. Rahhal is recruited by the Makhzen for that purpose. Adnan's novel also reflects on

---

[66] Achaari, *Three Nights*, p. 147.
[67] Yassin Adnan, *Hot Maroc*, translated by Alexander E. Elinson (Syracuse, NY: Syracuse University Press, 2021).

the dire living conditions of African immigrants stuck in Morocco, illegal prostitution, the corruption of the political system and the rise of a form of fundamentalist Islam.

The novel traces the memory of protest and demonstration by the National Union of Students in 1990s Morocco; a protest movement that started in the 1960s and was important in Moroccan political life.[68] *Hot Maroc* offers a rich memory of the experiences and struggles of the writer's generation of students in Moroccan universities in the 1980s and early 1990s, when competing Islamist political ideologues attempted to dominate the National Union of Students and impose their own agenda, which the novel represents as regressive and conservative. These student protests were met with oppression from the authorities using brute force, intimidation, and infiltration tactics.[69] Chapter 19 dwells on one of these many examples of organized students's protests. In this instance, the protestors were calling for better medical care for students on campus and university accommodation, and they were harshly beaten and arrested by the security forces.[70]

The strong student movement of protest that spans decades starting from the 1970s is commemorated in *Hot Maroc*. The novel focuses particularly on the era of the 1980s when Morocco was confronted with the new market economy and the IMF structural adjustment programs that further impoverished the poor and enriched the elites. Adnan's novel documents the students's recurring protests on various political and social issues, and charts how the security forces that invaded university campuses suppressed them.[71] This rich memory of protest in the novel is juxtaposed with a new era in Morocco post-2000 with the coming of King Mohamed VI. This new era saw the proliferation of Makhzenian political parties, the co-optation of oppositional political parties and the death of meaningful politics.[72] The novel shows how younger generations are disillusioned with change and the corrupt politics. They feel suffocated with the lack of opportunities, the restrictions on social mobility and the conservative social norms and values. They see migration to the rich North as the only way out, as this passage demonstrates:

Qamar Eddine wanted to flee the country by any means necessary ... his boring life at home exhausted him, as did the college, which he infrequently attended, and even the cursed cybercafé to which he seemed addicted.... The discussions of his history teachers at high school exhausted him—they came in mass to the

---

[68] The National Union of Students was established in 1956 and was closely associated in the 1960s and 1970s with the leftist party National Union of Popular Forces and other progressive parties. Its leaders were regularly arrested and imprisoned during that period for their political activities and for organizing mass protests.
[69] Yacine Adnan *Hot Maroc* pp. 453–454.
[70] Adnan, *Hot Maroc,* pp. 108–112.
[71] Adnan, *Hot Maroc,* pp. 113–117.
[72] Adnan, *Hot Maroc,* pp. 455–460.

cybercafé.... They said life under Hassan II had been worse, and the situation in the country had improved a lot with the advent of the young king, that there were margins of freedom, a new vitality, and signs of change. Qamar Eddine wasn't interested in the stories of his father's colleagues. He could see no change at all. Besides, who said he wanted to know what life had been like under Hassan II? He had been small then. Now he felt grown up and did not want to go backwards. He didn't have time to waste on such a talk. He wanted another kind of life. The life he saw in films and television. Life as lived by God's chosen people in the North. Qamar Eddine wanted to run away from here.[73]

Adnan's novel is a reminder of the rich protest and dissent culture in Morocco led by the Student Union, which was part of the struggle for democratization in the country in the 1960s up until the early 1990s when it became marred by ideological divisions. The disillusionment with the corrupt contemporary political culture may be seen as an attempt to revive that memory of dissent led by Moroccan youth. It is also a reminder that the 20 February movement in 2011 was led by young people—whose aspirations for change were again quashed with the swift response of the state and the co-optation of the movement, such that it did not challenge existing elite structures of power and dominance.

Conclusion

Moroccan novelists in the post-2011 era are maintaining an older tradition of memory-work, whereby the novel plays a key role in keeping alive the memory of protest. I have shown that this is not merely about looking *back* to the past—as important a process as that is in a context where history itself has been suppressed—but involves work of rememory, in which past, present, and future are intimately entangled. Fiction acts to shape our engagement with the past but perhaps even more importantly provides new insights to the present and an understanding of possible futures. In the sample of novels explored in this chapter, the memory of histories of riots and protest related to rural rebellions, urban riots, and students's protests reflects on various types of violence inflicted upon Moroccans including the most recent physical and psychological violence during the Years of Lead. They also suggest that the roots of the current crisis, particularly the co-optation of the once aspiring oppositional political parties, go back deep in history. The emphasis in the novels on the interplay between past and present histories of dissent (and their suppression) is also a reminder of the continuity of revolutionary movements of change. As politics continues to

---

[73] Adnan, *Hot Maroc*, p. 205.

be a battle between social and political movements with deeply divergent views on Morocco's history, its current state, and its future trajectory, novelists are significantly contributing to and shaping the multiple narratives that comprise the nation.

12
From 'Jihadi City' to 'Bride of the Revolution'
The Protest Rhythms of Tripoli

Caroline Rooney

When the Lebanese uprisings of October 2019 began, it came as a surprise that the city of Tripoli played a leading role. This was because Tripoli had long been stereotyped as Lebanon's 'jihadi city', seen as both deeply conservative and fanatically extremist, while also known to be a hotbed of crime gangs. This reputation sat in contradistinction to the image of Beirut, widely regarded as the progressive and avant-garde capital of the country. In this chapter, the insurrectionary rise of Tripoli will first be explored through an analysis of the dejected status of Tripoli prior to the uprisings. The chapter will draw on the work of Raphaël Lefèvre to throw light on the city's culture of crime gangs, and will also offer a reading of Jabbour Douaihy's novel *The American Quarter* (2014), set in one of the city's poorest neighbourhoods, Bab al-Tebanneh.[1] While *The American Quarter* shows how one of its characters is recruited into the jihadi cause, it also contains subtle traces of alternative ways forward that may be linked to new arts and popular culture movements that started to emerge in Tripoli shortly before the uprisings. The chapter will then go on to discuss how popular culture played a significant role in the 2019 uprisings in ways that serve not only to contest the centralization of power, but to challenge official national discourses concerning Tripoli.

The uprising in Tripoli defied expectations because, in a manner akin to other uprisings of the Arab Spring, it sought to express peaceful popular unity and was characterized by creativity and festive good will, in contradiction to the violent and chaotic disturbances associated with previous riotous protests in the city. That said, Tripoli's creative mode of popular mobilization shares similar motivational causes with those earlier riots, such as socio-economic deprivation, experiences of humiliation and degradation, and loss of trust in state actors and the possibility of state justice. These common catalysts mean there is always a chance that

---

[1] Jabbour Douaihy, *The American Quarter*, translated by Paula Haydar (Northampton, Massachusetts: Interlink Books, 2014).

riots could lead to revolutionary solidarity, and peaceful protest could turn into riotous mayhem. This persistent dissonance is an implicit yet resonant concern of Douaihy's novel *The American Quarter*. Douaihy's writing registers this ambient threat of riotous outbreaks that may overlap, depending on contexts, with other forms of transgression, ranging from rebellious civil disobedience to criminal activity to acts of terror. Accordingly, *The American Quarter* presents readers with numerous manifestations of violence that are not just random and discrete, even when they are introduced as such. Rather, we come to understand these violent episodes as interlinked aspects of Tripoli's layered history as will be discussed in the following section.

In *The American Quarter* we are introduced to the anarchic energies of Tripoli through the eyes of an effete upper-class character called Abdelkarim, precisely because he feels isolated from the popular dynamism of the poorer quarters. The first instance we have of this is when, as a boy, Abdelkarim is driven in the family Jaguar by a chauffeur through a deprived neighbourhood during a religious holiday. The streets are lined with happy strolling pedestrians. Suddenly, the car is surrounded by a rowdy mob of youngsters who start pounding the car with their fists, then dancing around it and rocking it. The chauffeur honks at the boys and tries to shake them off by veering down a side street. At this point, the youngsters turn angrily violent and hurl a rock through the car window, sending shards of glass onto Abdelkarim. While it might seem that this riotous incident is motivated by class resentment, this reading is too quick a conclusion to reach in terms of the observant detailed way in which the incident is narrated. When Abdelkarim first encounters the holiday merry youth on the street, he finds their exuberance compelling, and he smiles and waves to them. It is this that excites them to make contact in return through pounding and rocking the car. That is, Abdelkarim and the street kids initially share a desire to bridge the social barrier between them and make contact in a carnivalesque mood. It is only when the chauffeur starts to panic, protective of the posh car and his employer's child, that the mood turns vicious: the street children feel turned against, rejected, and put down. What causes the upsurge of violence is thus the thwarting of the carnivalesque, revolutionary desire to overturn class divisions through mutual forms of hailing or welcoming. In this scene, the street youth are implicitly interpellated by the behaviour of the chauffeur into the identity of mere hooligans, and what is noteworthy about this is the youth respond by acting in accordance with this interpellation. Positioned as hooligans, they then act as hooligans.

Neighbourhoods of Negligence and Popular Contention

Raphaël Lefèvre's *Jihad and the City* offers an in-depth study of Islamic militancy in 1980s Tripoli. Lefèvre concentrates on the formation of a group called Tawhid

(*Harakat al-Tawhid al Islami*, or Islamic Unification Movement) that emerged in 1982 to establish what it termed an 'Islamic Emirate'.[2] He writes:

> Far from homogeneously made up of hardened ideologues only, its members were committed to Islamism to various degrees and many had instrumentalized it; using ideology alternatively to channel tales of Tripolitan identity, protest against their conditions, prevail in preexisting neighborhood rivalries and social conflicts or get access to criminal networks and activities. In the shadow of Allah Square, Tawhid and the 1980s 'Islamic Emirate' of Tripoli, then, lay ideology but also local solidarities, identities, grievances and myriad older antagonisms.[3]

Tawhid is thus shaped by the conditions of its local formation, both historically and spatially, even as it can also be seen to be influenced by and caught up in wider geopolitical events such as the Palestinian struggle, the Iranian revolution, and the persistent interventions of Syria in Lebanon.

The marginalization of Tripoli within Lebanon began with the dismantling of the Ottoman Empire in 1920. Greater Syria was succeeded by the newly formed states of Lebanon, Palestine, Jordan, and Syria, and the historic regional centre of Tripoli was demoted in relation to Beirut. Initially maintaining an identification with the Syrian hinterland, Tripolitan residents came to develop strong support for Pan-Arab nationalism. While 'contentious Tripolitans', as Lefèvre refers to them, contested successive Lebanese governments, they also engaged in activism against local notables and embraced radical left-wing protest movements.[4]

What is striking about this is that the milieu out of which Islamist groups emerged had initially strong Marxist affiliations, together with a popular solidarity movement that supported the Palestinian liberation struggle. As the Syrian regime sought to undermine the PLO, this alienated the Palestinian-leftist alliance in Tripoli since the Syrian regime aimed not only to control the Palestinian struggle but also Lebanese militants. However, the growing cultural momentum of faith-based groups in Tripoli came to prove more effective in channelling local grievances in a context of neighbourhood loyalties and rivalries: in particular, those of the predominantly Sunni neighbourhood of Bab al-Tebanneh, and the bordering, predominantly Alawi neighbourhood of Jabal Mohsen. Both neighbourhoods struggled with severe socio-economic deprivation and neglect and had developed illicit economies with competing criminal gangs. The violent local gang rivalries across the two neighbourhoods were further enflamed by the Syrian backing of and influence on the Alawi youth in Jabal Mohsen, this being at odds with the rebel tradition of Bab al-Tebanneh that was often opposed to the control of

---

[2] Raphaël Lefèvre, *Jihad in the City: Militant Islam and Contentious Politics in Tripoli* (Oxford: Oxford University Press, 2021), p. 2.
[3] Raphaël Lefèvre, *Jihad in the City*, p. 3.
[4] Raphaël Lefèvre, *Jihad in the City*, p. 57.

the Syrian regime. What issued from this, particularly in the 1980s, although it extended beyond this period, was a lengthy period of 'slum warfare'[5] between the two sides in a battle for both resources and local status and power.

Tripolitan movements were also much influenced by popular leaders who emerged as the strongmen of their neighbourhoods. This phenomenon can be understood in terms of the dynamics of social banditry. The charismatic strongman or *qabaday* figures served as 'champions of mobilization', as Lefèvre explains, while being entrusted with the needs and interests of the neighbourhoods they served with the loyal support of their residents.[6] In Bab El-Tabbeneh, a prominent *qabaday* in the 1970s was Ali Akkawi, a local Che Guevarra figure leading a Marxist resistance movement that fermented local uprisings and violent public interventions. When Ali Akkawi died in 1974, he was succeeded by his brother Khalil Akkawi, who, on becoming the leader of Tawhid, took the movement in an Islamist direction in order to extend and re-orientate its appeal. This decision was influenced by the Iranian revolution: while Shia in its constituency, Iran presented the opportunity of bringing revolution and religion together in a form of Red Islam. Tawhid was eventually defeated in 1986, partly due to internal factionalism, but more significantly due to the violent repression of Bab al-Tebanneh on the part of the Syrian regime. The neighbourhood battle between Bab al-Tabanneh and Jabal Mohsen nonetheless persisted as a local conflict that continued to intersect with the regional and transnational conflicts, most recently fuelled by the Syrian civil war and global war on terror.

It is this history that closely informs Jabbour Douaihy's novel *The American Quarter*, which takes place in Tripoli. While the novel is set at the time of the American invasion of Iraq, it contains many flashbacks to earlier moments in the lives of its main characters, so that it is possible to understand how their present lives are informed by an ongoing, specifically Tripolitan, history. Indeed, Tripoli has been regarded by some critics as the ultimate character of the novel.[7]

Reconfigurations of Radicalism in *The American Quarter*

The American Quarter is a novel that revolves around the radicalization of a young Tripolitan man in the context of both the history of his neighbourhood and the so-called war on terror. *The American Quarter* is a name given to the impoverished suburb of Bab al-Tebanneh, 'so named for its association with the now abandoned American Evangelical School, in whose crumbling buildings a branch

---

[5] Raphaël Lefèvre, *Jihad in the City*, p. 115.
[6] Raphaël Lefèvre, *Jihad in the City*, p. 96.
[7] See, for example, Hebdo Readings, August 2019, https://hebdoreadings.com/the-american-quarter-by-jabbour-douaihy/.

of the dreaded Syrian Intelligence agency had been quartered for many years'.[8] The novel begins by following Intisar Muhsin on her way to work. She travels from Bab al-Tebanneh through the banking district to an affluent quarter of the town, where she is employed as the maid of Abdelkarim Azzam. Intisar is particularly preoccupied by the disappearance of her son Ismail. He has not been seen for two weeks, and religious messages keep being left on the cell phone that Ismail has given to her. She goes about a routine day's work for Abdelkarim, who cultivates his quirky obsessions of listening to operatic arias at full blast and tending to his bonsai plants. When Intisar returns home, it is to find a festive gathering at her house, glued to the television news as Ismail's fate is reported. The novel then leaves this present moment to excavate its characters's past. That is, as noted, the novel is mostly a flashback retracing a complex of local stories without which the present moment cannot be understood.

We are given insight into Abdelkarim's childhood as a 'highly envied and protected child'.[9] While he leads a pampered, isolated life, he yearns to connect with the street life of the city, as revealed in the incident analysed at the outset of this chapter. We are told that 'at a very young age, Abdelkarim started to develop the feeling that the world was somewhere he was *not*'.[10] As he grows up, he takes refuge in literature, and he is eventually persuaded into an arranged marriage that is a failure. As gang violence starts to escalate against the rich neighbourhoods of the city, Abdelkarim is sent to study in Paris. There he falls in love with a beautiful Eastern European ballerina, with whom he embarks on a passionate affair. However, when she falls pregnant, she returns to her native Belgrade, abandoning Abdelkarim without trace. Abdelkarim packs up the ballet costumes of his lover, together with her collection of bonsai plants, and returns to Tripoli. Once home, he consoles himself by getting drunk most nights, displaying the ballerina's clothes with fetishistic attachment, and blaring out recordings of European operas.

Juxtaposed with Abdelkarim's story are the stories of Ismail and Ismail's father, Bilal. Bilal is someone who has never had fixed employment in his life, and who relies on his wife to support him while offering no support in return. He lives an aimless life, letting the days drag by 'with his grey face and half-shaved beard'.[11] The only thing that gives any meaning to his life is the memory of a brief period of his youth when he was involved in local politics. Bilal finds that a rebel Islamic group seeking to boost its numbers is willing to take him in. We learn that Bilal is enamoured by the reputations of local rebel heroes: 'Everyday he heard talk of someone named Abu Khalid who'd blown up a tank at the entrance to the neighbourhood, near the traffic circle'.[12] This would seem to be a reference to *qabaday*

---

[8] Jabbour Douaihy, *The American Quarter*, pp. 1–2.
[9] Jabbour Douaihy, *The American Quarter*, p. 33.
[10] Jabbour Douaihy, *The American Quarter*, p. 39.
[11] Jabbour Douaihy, *The American Quarter*, p. 62.
[12] Jabbour Douaihy, *The American Quarter*, p. 52.

figures such as the renowned Khalid Akkawi of Tawhid. However, Bilal is a supporter of Sheikh Imad, a moderate cleric who campaigns against the militancy of the local Islamist groups while upholding Islamic pride. Bilal's one act of bravery entails firing a weapon at a railroad car when Sheikh Imad is assassinated. Bilal's pro-PLO group is then targeted in vengeance by a barely identified group. While all his comrades are killed in the attack, Bilal is spared, leading people to suspect him of being a traitor even though he has no idea why he was kept alive. Bilal, then ostracized, fades into marginalized obscurity.

Ismail, Bilal's and Intisar's son, initially lives with his maternal grandmother. This affords him a comfortable and protected early existence, but when his grandmother dies, the money for his schooling dries up and he is forced back into the cramped and shabby home environment of his parents. He joins the 'Sons of the American Quarter' gang, and soon becomes involved in neighbourhood mischief, riotous mayhem, and petty crime. He is then given a job by the local baker, who is a fervent Islamist. The baker persuades Ismail to adopt a new stance of piety and responsibility. Despising his father, Ismail stands up to him, most notably when his father attempts to assault his mother. The incident leads to Bilal confessing to Ismail his one militant act. This confession satisfies Ismail, 'knowing that his father was not a coward, was not totally useless.'[13]

It turns out that Yasin (the baker), while a socialist in his youth, embraces religion when he is imprisoned and tortured for an act of insurgency, the torture leading to his loss of faith in humanity. Influenced by Yasin, Ismail joins the Islamic Guidance Association and is crushed by the broken lives he encounters: people desperate for financial assistance, ranging from needing schoolbooks for their children to vital medical assistance. Douaihy writes that

> Their poverty and ailments were an extension of his [Ismail's] life and theirs. But when they started coming [to Ismail] as destitute beggars, he couldn't take it anymore. He would return home at the end of the day a broken man. He grew more religious and prayed intently.[14]

The American Quarter thus offers a nuanced and intimate understanding of the various ways in which people get drawn into both unruly gang culture and radicalized militant politics. The experiences of socio-economic deprivation and social humiliation emerge as a key consideration, while local networks of loyalty and support are also important. As Lefèvre's research suggests, it is not so much that doctrinal adherence to Islamic ideology drives radicalization, but that Islam, in its different vernacular forms, becomes one among many possibilities that answer to desperate circumstances. In a moment of contextualization, the narrator observes:

---

[13] Jabbour Douaihy, *The American Quarter*, p. 82.
[14] Jabbour Douaihy, *The American Quarter*, pp. 122–123.

At one time, this same city had fought off the French Mandate, and it stood in solidarity with every Arab cause: for the Algerian revolution, against the Baghdad Pact. Everyone, without exception, went out into the streets the day Nasser resigned, and in 1988 it was one of the city's men who led the Arab Salvation Army for the liberation of Palestine. But nowadays, the city couldn't be bothered. During the elections, the rich went around buying votes—rich people with fortunes amassed by questionable means.[15]

While Tripoli has a notable history of popular left wing resistance movements, the novel indicates how the defeat of Nasser constituted a crushing blow. At the same time, the novel demonstrates how disillusionment with political forms of resistance was exacerbated by widespread political corruption and factionalism. This, in part, explains the turn to religious movements as a search for ethical reorientations, that Douaihy registers in the intertwined stories of Yassin and Ismail. That said, the novel also delicately signals that militant forms of Islam may constitute a wrong turning. This, at any rate, is the view of the wise sheikhs in the novel. Apart from Sheikh Imad, already mentioned, there is Sheikh Abellatif, whom we learn is loved by the people and sought out by them. While he gives them his time, he 'grieve[s] for the Arabs and Arabism' and mocks '"the era of midgets"' represented by the uncultured men of long beards.[16]

As my account of *The American Quarter* indicates, the novel unfolds as a collection of stories that serve to tell a street level history of Tripoli. This is partly a matter of social realism that serves to offset the ideological stories or myths that dismiss Tripoli as a mere hotbed of irrational violent fanaticism. Instead, we see how the novel's characters are products of their habitus or are accorded dispositions that can be seen to derive from their milieu. Beyond this, Douaihy's approach may be understood in terms of the Arab *maqāmāt* literary tradition, with respect to the structure of stories within a wider story and the way that the narrator offers us an intimate view of the worlds and struggles of forgotten or unimportant people, presented as neither heroes nor villains but as products of their environment. Regarding this, it is not just a mimetic picture of Tripoli that is offered to readers but a critique of Tripolitan society for the purpose of community guidance. That is, although *The American Quarter* has a retrospective structure, the novel examines the past to envision a way forward beyond wrong turnings and potential pitfalls.

It is in its ending especially that the novel looks ahead, imagining a new configuration for the rebellious residents of Tripoli. Ismail, proving his mother's fears correct, is recruited by Islamists into joining a jihadist mission in Iraq, reflecting the historical fact that scores of young men from Tripoli went to fight for Iraq.[17]

---

[15] Jabbour Douhaiy, *The American Quarter*, p. 99.
[16] Jabbour Douaihy, *The American Quarter*, p. 116.
[17] 'Lebanon: Tripoli's Poor Swell Ranks of Militant Islamic Groups', Integrated Regional Information Networks United Nations, 10 August 2007, https://www.worldpress.org/Mideast/2894.cfm.

However, on the brink of a suicide mission, Ismail encounters a young boy that reminds him of his younger brother, towards whom he is very protective. He is then unable to continue with his terrorist plan. Despite this change of plan, his presence in Iraq is nevertheless captured by television footage that is then broadcast in Lebanon. This takes us back to the start of the novel, when Intisar returns home to find locals gathered around the television at her house. They assume that Ismail has heroically become a martyr, and soon the neighbourhood is festooned with his martyr portrait to honour him. Ismail, meanwhile, clandestinely returns to Tripoli and seeks sanctuary at the house of Abdelkarim.

The reason Ismail turns to Abdelkarim is explained by an earlier episode in the novel. Having torn down the election posters of the corrupt politicians, Ismail goes into hiding at Abdelkarim's house to evade the police. While the two men are initially strangers, Abdelkarim, seemingly fascinated by Ismail's connection with the real life of the streets, bombards him with questions to learn all he can of him. In turn, Abdelkarim confides in Ismail, telling him the exotic story of his lost love, the ballerina. One night, Abdelkarim persuades Ismail to get drunk with him, and they collapse in bed together. The narration discretely hints that they have a sexual encounter, as their breathing becomes laboured and they wake up in a mutual embrace.[18]

When Ismail smuggles himself back into Tripoli and turns up at Abdelkarim's house, Abdelkarim is willing to be his comrade. He lets Intisar know her son is not dead and procures a gun for Ismail. The security police have intelligence that Ismail might be at Abdelkarim's house and post a surveillance team outside. Abdelkarim goes through the wardrobe of his ballerina lover, finding the long black trench coat that she wore when they first met. He persuades Ismail to use it as a disguise as he attempts to escape the house, while Abdelkarim continues with his usual ritual of blaring out operatic arias and getting drunk. Baffled by his strange behaviour, the security police accost Abdelkarim, who swears Ismail never returned and died a martyr. The novel ends with Intisar arriving at the house. She and Abdelkarim spontaneously embrace and he feels a strong surge of desire for her. Ismail's escape creates a special bond between Abdelkarim and Intisar and remains their secret as they anticipate his return one day.

The arc of the novel is striking, bringing together the characters of Abdelkarim, Ismail and Intisar as if their alignment constitutes hope for a revolutionary future. Abdelkarim has always felt alienated from the elite class that he belongs to, and we see him refusing to fulfil the vote-buying role of his class. His sensitive, sexually ambiguous masculinity goes against the masculine stereotypes of his society, while his passionate and hedonistic love of foreign cultures also positions him as a misfit cosmopolitan. Even so, he is more drawn to the authenticity of the disadvantaged of his society than he is to others of his class background. The implication is that

---

[18] Jabbour Douaihy, *The American Quarter*, p. 112.

men like Abdelkarim and men like Ismail have something to offer one another in their mutual quest for dignity, non-judgemental acceptance, and new ways of belonging. Indeed, these mutually held values may unite Tripolitans outside of the manipulations of identity politics. As for Intisar, she offers a feisty feminine resilience and supportiveness that both Abdelkarim and Ismail strongly admire. It is as if the combination of these three figures brings together the arts, culture, and civility, as represented by Abdelkarim; street-wise rebel integrity, as represented by Ismail; and womanly strength, as represented by Intisar. Intriguingly, this local alchemy can be seen to have manifested itself in the Tripoli uprisings of 2019, as I will indicate further after some reflection on the differing manifestations of riots and revolution, the latter viewed from the aspect of the Arab uprisings.

Riots and Revolutions

One reason that I have pieced together the stories of *The American Quarter* is that it is a challenging novel to summarize. Its mode of exposition is discontinuous and it does not rely on narratorial explanations in its presentation of events, leaving the reader to make connections. The implication of this is that it is a work written especially for local audiences with some prior knowledge of the novel's milieu, in contradistinction to certain postcolonial novels that are primarily angled towards a Western readership. The reason that I mention this is because, in my view, one means of differentiating riots and revolutions from each other is through their structures of interpellation and address. *The American Quarter* is not merely about Tripolitans but addressed to them in an acknowledgment of their struggles.

Typically, riots may be said to respond to hierarchical structures of interpellation where rioters address their rage and frustration to those in power. In contradistinction to this, one of the striking manifestations of the Arab uprisings, as I have examined in detail elsewhere,[19] is how they mobilized modes of interpellation that disregarded hierarchical structures in favour of lateral and reciprocal forms of recognition and welcoming receptivity. As will be seen, this disregard for hierarchy is reflected in Douaihy's narrative. In order to contextualize this observation before returning to the novel, I will briefly allude to the London riots of 2011 in relation to the start of the Arab uprisings in 2010 and 2011.

As I have considered elsewhere,[20] the London riots and the Arab uprisings were motivated by similar circumstances while they took different forms. For a start, the Tunisian and Egyptian revolutions and the London riots were each sparked

---

[19] Caroline Rooney, *Creative Radicalism in the Middle East: Culture and the Arab Left after the Uprisings*, London: I.B. Tauris), p. 78.

[20] Caroline Rooney, 'From Cairo to Tottenham: Big Societies, Neoliberal States and Colonial Utopias', *Journal for Cultural Research* 17, no. 2 (2013), pp. 144–163, doi: 10.1080/14797585.2012.756244.

by police clashes leading to deaths (Mohamed Bouazizi, Khaled Said, and Mark Duggan) that met with widespread popular outrage. The popular identification with victims of police brutality may be said to derive from a sense of how states, especially neoliberal ones, are organized to protect the lives of the privileged, while treating the lives of those abandoned by the system as having no value.

In the case of the London riots, politicians and the media widely characterized the rioters as an anti-social criminal class, as if they had no legitimate grievances. British Prime Minister David Cameron defined the riots as 'criminality, pure and simple', while Theresa May, then Home Secretary, spoke of the 'sheer criminality' of the rioters.[21] The point is that those in authority explained the riots by merely blaming them on a class of hooligans and losers when it was such contemptuous and dismissive attitudes that may be said to have *caused* the riots in that the rioters opposed themselves to the devaluation of those they saw as fellow citizens.

It is however the case that the London riots broke out in neighbourhoods known for their crime gang culture and that they engaged in criminal acts such as arson and looting. In an article on the London riots sardonically entitled 'Shoplifters of the World Unite', Slavoj Žižek comments on how members of local communities had to protect themselves from the riots. He observes:

> One of the forms this reaction took was the 'tribal' activity of the local (Turkish, Caribbean, Sikh) communities which quickly organised their own vigilante units to protect their property…. The truth is that the conflict was between two poles of the underprivileged: those who have succeeded in functioning within the system versus those who are too frustrated to go on trying. The rioters' violence was almost exclusively directed against their own.[22]

This observation relates to how neoliberal ideology relies on differentiating those deemed worthy of citizenship from those deemed unworthy and worthless, pitting these ideologically constructed groups against each other. This is loosely comparable to the 'slum warfare' in Tripoli where rival poles of the precariat also turned against each other. One difference, however, is that neighbourhood loyalties appear stronger in the Tripolitan context with battles between neighbourhoods rather than within them. The reason that neoliberal regimes mount their divide and rule strategies that create rivalries amongst the underprivileged is arguably to reroute the dissatisfactions that would otherwise entail anger against the privileged—dissatisfactions that are at the centre of *The American Quarter*. While neoliberal leaders may be seen to be criminally indifferent to powerless citizens, they deflect blame from themselves by the interpellation of certain deprived groups as a criminal class.

---

[21] Lemm Sissay, 'Who Are the Criminals?' 9 August 2011, https://blog.lemnsissay.com/2011/08/09/who-are-the-criminals-part-1-of-2/

[22] Slavoj Žižek, 'Shoplifters of the World Unite', *London Review of Books* 33, no. 16, 25 August 2011, https://www.lrb.co.uk/the-paper/v33/n16/slavoj-zizek/shoplifters-of-the-world-unite.

In his analysis of the anti-sociality of rioters that he sees as having given up on trying to be a part of society, Žižek broadens his critique to the protest movement of the Spanish *Indignados*. This movement began with 50,000 taking to the streets on 15 May 2011, to protest austerity measures following the 2008 financial crisis, and took place between the start of the Arab uprisings and the London riots. Žižek considers this movement to partake of a similar disappointing apathy in political terms. He writes of how the Indignados seek to unite across political constituencies to address inclusive social rights through a revolution that is non-violent and primarily ethical.[23]

The Indignados were clearly inspired by the Arab Spring, in terms of the emphasis on peaceful interventions, social unity, and the affirmation of civil society across the divisions of class and religion. That the Spanish protestors refer to themselves as the 'indignant' is telling, given that etymologically *dignus* refers to granting worth to someone, and is thus a question of dignity. One of the main rallying cries of the Arab Spring was a call for dignity or *karāmah*. While Žižek appears dismissive of the 'apolitical' appeal of these movements that place the emphasis on an inclusive society, it needs to be said this inclusiveness is the revolutionary alternative to the neoliberal abandonment of the social sphere where what is resisted is the treatment of the most powerless as superfluous. As I have maintained elsewhere, the Arab uprisings reversed the projection of superfluity onto precarious individuals or groups in positing ineffectual or useless leadership as superfluous.[24]

What is at stake in both riots and revolutions is confronting the ethical pretensions deployed to justify neoliberal hegemony. Some of those who took part in the London riots saw themselves as turning the tables. For instance, one rioter commented in an interview: 'They was the criminals today. We was enforcing the law.'[25] With this, the rioter proposes a carnivalesque or Bakhtinian inversion of roles. However, the London rioters were not truly able to extricate themselves from the structures of interpellation in play. This is indicated by a comment made by Labour MP John McDonnell, quoted in Slovo's verbatim play *The Riots*:

> Society has created a society of looters at every level: MPs fiddling expenses, bankers with their bonuses, corporations not paying their taxes, and all this was, was kids with the same moral values that have been inculcated in society motivated by the same level of consumerism, coming out and seizing their opportunity.'[26]

That is, while the state's political actors might be seen as the ultimate criminals more than those they demonize, the rioters were not sufficiently able to assert

---

[23] Slavoj Žižek, 'Shoplifters of the World Unite'.
[24] Caroline Rooney, *Creative Radicalism in the Middle East*, p. 89.
[25] Raekha Prasad, 'Reading the Riots', *Guardian*, 2 December 2011, http://www.guardian.co.uk/uk/2011/dec/05/riots-revenge-against-police.
[26] Gillian Slovo, *The Riots: From Spoken Evidence* (London: Oberon Books, 2011), pp. 53–54.

different values through a language of their own. As such, they remained caught within structures of mimetic or parodic interpellation, so that questions of status, identity, and pride took precedence over more revolutionary assertions of dignity and the ethical reconstitution of civil society. In order to clarify this, I will now turn to the Tripoli uprisings.

Tripoli, 'Bride of the Revolution'

In the years that preceded the 2019 uprising, it is striking to note that arts and culture were being used to confront social divisions and, especially, to dismantle the neighbourhood war between the gangs of Bab al-Tebanneh and Jabal Mohsen. A civil society movement called March was founded in 2011 to 'promote social cohesion and personal freedoms while advocating for equal rights through its work in peace-building and conflict resolution', making particular use of the arts to address divisions in Tripoli.[27] One of March's early projects (2015) was the staging of a play called *Love and War on the Rooftop—A Tripolitan Play*, written and directed by Lucien Bourjeily. It recruited sixteen young actors, eight from Bab al-Tebanneh and eight from Jabal Mohsen. While the actors initially came to rehearsals armed with weapons, the play was successful in rebuilding trust across these communities. Other March initiatives include the establishment of an inclusive cultural café *Kahwetna* ('our café') on Syria Street, the frontline between Bab al-Tebanneh and Jabal Mohsen, together with the rehabilitation of shops in the area that had been destroyed or run down by conflict. Part of the reconstruction project has been to train people in new skills. March founder Lea Baroudi states: 'We gave the men basic construction skills: electricity, paint, landscaping, everything. For the women, we taught them graphic design.'[28] Apart from the influential work of March, there had been other creative initiatives in the run-up to the uprisings. In 2017, for example, the duo Ashekman (two artist twins) staged a dramatic public installation in which they painted the word *salam*, meaning peace, across the rooftops of the conflicted neighbourhoods of Bab al-Tebanneh and Jabal Mohsen.[29]

When the Lebanese uprisings began in Tripoli, a city that was soon named 'bride of the revolution', surprise was registered that the city had taken the revolutionary lead in Lebanon, especially with such wedding-like exuberance, given its reputation as a place dominated by violent sectarianism and criminal gangs. Defying expectations, the protests of October 2019 were characterized by the good

---

[27] March website, 'Getting to Know Us', https://www.marchlebanon.org/about-us/.
[28] Maryam Haddar and Patricia Bitar Cherfan, 'Peace Takes Centre Stage with Lea Barodi', March website, 27 July 2020, https://www.marchlebanon.org/press/peace-takes-center-stage-with-lea-baroudi/.
[29] Ashekman, 'Operation Salam', Ashekman website, 1 February 2019, https://ashekman.com/portfolio-item/operation-salam/.

humour, creativity, inclusivity, and festiveness of the earlier Arab revolutions in Tunisia and Egypt. As Lina Khatib observes: 'The scenes in Tripoli have been deeply moving because many had written the city off as a hub of Sunni extremism.'[30] What was much in evidence was the peaceful street-level unification of the people. A protestor called Hammoud, quoted in *The New Yorker*, celebrated this fact: 'This is a revolution for the people. It's not political and it's not sectarian. There are no flags but Lebanese flags. The whole country is united.'[31]

The participants in the Tripoli uprisings conveyed their message through graffiti, slogans, and chants. Joey Ayoub, in addressing the revolution as one against divisive sectarianism, quotes the Tripolitan chant of: 'We are the popular revolution. You are the civil war.'[32] In addition, widespread accusations amongst protestors targeted political corruption with the denunciation *kellon yaani kellon* ('all of them means all of them'), along with the telling constant chant of 'thieves, thieves'. Novelist Elias Khoury, in broaching how the revolution began as a protest over a WhatsApp tax, states: 'The issue is not just taxes, taxes have revealed the reality of the compound of thieves that controls Lebanon.'[33] Khoury also calls Tripoli 'the light of the revolution'[34] for its role in exposing the fraudulence of the elites and in leading the protests. Commenting specifically on the acoustic nature of riotous Tripoli, Sabah Jalloul notes:

> In the streets of Tripoli ... the catchy chant that echoed in every corner was 'M'aalmeh, M'aalmeh' ('Hey, big boss, I know you're corrupt.... Hey, big boss, you're sucking my blood').... The famous 'M'aalmeh' chant was written by the activist Tamim Abdo, in a clear Tripolitan accent which utilizes witty satirical phrases to criticize politicians. With its catchy tune, the cheer spread with great momentum, reaching Beirut and other regions where protests were happening.[35]

Expanding further on the chants, she writes of the way the chants sound out against 'Tripoli's "bad name" of recent years as a city defined by the clashes between

---

[30] Richard Hall, 'A City Once Blighted by Extremism Has Become the Unlikely Focus of Nationwide Protests, *Independent*, 16 December 2019, https://www.independent.co.uk/news/world/middle-east/lebanon-protests-riots-tripoli-hezbollah-whatsapp-a9170611.html.

[31] Helen Sullivan, 'The Making of Lebanon's October Revolution', *The New Yorker*, 26 October 2019, https://www.newyorker.com/news/dispatch/the-making-of-lebanons-october-revolution.

[32] Joey Ayoub, 'Lebanon: A Revolution against Sectarianism', *CrimethInc*, 13 November 2019, https://crimethinc.com/2019/11/13/lebanon-a-revolution-against-sectarianism-chronicling-the-first-month-of-the-uprising.

[33] Elias Khoury, 'Letter to Samir Kassir', International Workers League—Fourth International, 28 October 2019, https://litci.org/en/elias-khoury-letter-to-samir-kassir/.

[34] Elias Khoury, 'Tripoli, Light of the Revolution', translated by Elias Abu Jaoudeh, Hummus for Thought blog, 27 October 2019, https://hummusforthought.com/2019/10/27/tripoli-light-of-the-revolution/.

[35] Sabah Jalloul, 'What it Takes to Protest: Adventures and Initiatives in the World of Lebanon's October 17 Uprising', *Assafir Al Arabi*, 18 December 2020, https://assafirarabi.com/en/36517/2021/03/08/what-it-takes-to-protest-adventures-and-initiatives-in-the-world-of-lebanons-october-17-uprising-2-2/.

the regions of Bab al-Tebanneh and Jabal Mohsen, and as an alleged "incubator for extremist Islamist groups"'. The chants mock these attempts to obliterate the city's identity and spirit, and condemn the politicians's repetitive and divisive exploitation of the Tripolitan youth for their own interests. Jalloul quotes the following example:

> 'They call me when there's a fight,
> and they say they are on my side....'
> 'Tebbaneh is the mother of all the poor,
> and you pigs will fall!
> Oh, beloved people of Mohsen,
> We won't let you down either!'[36]

As with the London riots, those accused of criminality and anti-social behaviour turn the accusation against the elites. However, this goes beyond a mere reversal, in that it is part of a wider battle to re-establish both solidarity and meaningful discourse. As Walid El Houri notes, 'Today it is a struggle over meanings.'[37]

The struggle over meanings is one that rejects the hypocritical rhetoric of politicians, whose claims manipulate voters, often employing divide and rule tactics. The first two lines of the chant above lines are an indication of the rejection of such rhetoric: a struggle over meaning that constitutes an ethical stance rooted in realities. For a start, this involves the state acknowledging the socio-economic realities that crush the powerless, but beyond this, it also demands a spirit of genuine solidarity. Accordingly, El Houri speaks of the Lebanese uprisings as constituting 'an ethical revolution', based on 'mutual help, solidarity and care'.[38]

In an article on the Tripoli uprising, Timour Azhari quotes a revolutionary as observing: 'The Tripoli they painted as a city of "terrorism", as Kandahar, a city of death and slaughter—here is the real Tripoli, a city of civilisation and culture where people want to live just like anywhere else.'[39] The interviewee, Ahmad, adds: 'The armed groups were created by politicians to make us hate each other, and we did, and we lost everything.... Now we are taking back our image. What you are seeing here is spontaneous; it comes straight from our hearts.' The desire expressed here is to reclaim Tripoli, a Tripoli grounded in the creative expression of its people.

---

[36] Sabah Jalloul, 'What it Takes to Protest'.
[37] Walid El Houri, 'Lebanon: A Revolution Defining a Country', *Open Democracy*, 8 November 2019, https://www.opendemocracy.net/en/north-africa-west-asia/lebanon-revolution-redefining-country/.
[38] El Houri, 'Lebanon: A Revolution Defining a Country'.
[39] Timour Azhari, 'Why Thousands Continue to Protest in Lebanon's Tripoli', *Al Jazeera*, 3 November 2019, https://www.aljazeera.com/news/2019/11/3/why-thousands-continue-to-protest-in-lebanons-tripoli.

In a blog post prior to the revolution, a review of the collective March's theatrical work states that 'Art prevails where the government fails.'[40]

In an article entitled 'All Love to Tripoli', journalist and writer Hazem El Amin comments:

> Tripoli is the capital of wreck and affinity, offering a complete and continuous story. What is going on today in Tripoli is an extension of that story. Youngsters are storming out of the city's alleys to reach Abdul Hamid Karami Square and scream their lungs out in the face of the state that is starving them. They are the children of the ladies whom Jabbour Douaihy described in *The American Quarter*.[41]

The character of Tripoli, with its continuous story of social struggles and rebellious defiance, is accurately captured by Douaihy's novel—where the revolutionaries of today are the sons and daughters of women such as Douaihy's spirited female character Intisar. One of the main slogans of the Lebanese movement was 'the revolution is a woman'. This is due to the very active and widespread involvement of women in the revolution together with their collective support of women's rights. Women also played a leading role in containing the violence between police and protestors by creating a women's front-line.[42]

The uprisings in Tripoli coincided with the start of the global pandemic, which disrupted the revolutionary momentum. On the one hand, public gatherings were discouraged on health grounds; on the other hand, the coronavirus crisis greatly worsened already desperate economic conditions. Formerly peaceful and convivial demonstrations gave way to angry, violent riots, such as those that occurred in Tripoli in January 2021. Grenades and Molotov cocktails were used in attacks on state institutions and in clashes with the police, while earlier riots in April 2020 had torched banks.

This resort to violence is symptomatic of increasing hopelessness. Ayoub, commenting on the 2019 uprisings, explains that the strategy of neoliberalism 'was sugarcoated in a language of hope: the narrative was that only through business ties could the menace of the civil war be kept at bay'.[43] The 2019 uprisings contested this false narrative of hope through a far more convincing experience of hope, as Ayoub goes on to address: 'As an organizer of the 2015 protests, who grew up in Lebanon and who has been writing about it since 2012, I could see right away that these protests were going to be different. I wasn't the only one taken over by that

---

[40] Najib, 'Art Prevails Where Our Government Failed', *BlogBaladi*, 8 June 2015, https://blogbaladi.com/art-prevails-where-our-government-failed-march-lebanon-uniting-bab-el-tebbeneh-jabal-mohsen-in-a-beautiful-play/.

[41] Hazem El Amin 'All Love to Tripoli', *Daraj*, 29 January 2021, https://daraj.com/en/66058/.

[42] See Alessandra Bajec, 'Lebanon's Revolution is a Reawakening for Tripoli Women', TRT World, 2 December 2019, https://www.trtworld.com/magazine/lebanon-s-revolution-is-a-reawakening-for-tripoli-women-31852.

[43] Joey Ayoub, 'Lebanon: A Revolution against Sectarianism'.

rarest of all feelings: hope.' It was the fact that this revolutionary hope was not sustained that led to the resumption of rioting. What this means is that protest movements in Tripoli have changing rhythms that reflect the varying affective structures of local circumstances, something that Douaihy's *The American Quarter* captures well.

As Douaihy's novel registers, and as Lefèvre's research confirms, the recent volatility of Tripoli is part of what El Amin calls its 'continuous history', where its earlier Marxist radicalism became re-routed into Islamist channels. This happened not so much for ideological reasons but as a consequence of the increasing conditions of hopelessness. *The American Quarter* holds out for the resumption of a revolutionary ethos, but not one configured in the old Marxist ways. Instead, this revolutionary ethos is predicated on a new ethical configuration of the arts and culture combined with popular rebellion, as well as on feminine and feminist orientations. This is what came to the fore in the Tripoli uprisings. In the final part of this discussion, I will further clarify the significance of this creative radicalism's demotic signifying practices.

Revolutionary Aesthetics

The aesthetics of the Tripoli protests have been described as carnivalesque, and the significance of this is addressed by Lebanese writer Rawi Hage:

> These are the seeds of a new form of religiosity that no longer treats the body as an object of submission and devotion, but as a way to challenge the austerity of our former god through joy and laughter....
> The carnivalesque celebrations and the abundance of creativity that were witnessed during the demonstrations are in themselves revolutionary. The 'rave parties' of Tripoli—a city historically stigmatized as an Islamic stronghold—are a manifestation of this. Men with beards, veiled women and people from different backgrounds swaying to the rhythms of a young DJ.[44]

Although Hage does not elaborate, it is clear that a popular sense of the sacred is at stake, where spiritual values are not aligned with religious or political authority. What matters more than those forms of authority is popular authorship, the repertoire of the people: a question of their collective cultural biography. What counts in this is not just a re-evaluation of the body, but an affirmation of the voice.

---

[44] Rana Andraos, Edgar Savidian, Danny Mallat, and Zena Zalzal, 'Five Lebanese Novelists Talk about the "Revolution"', *L'Orient Today*, 25 November 2019, https://today.lorientlejour.com/article/1196265/five-lebanese-novelists-talk-about-the-revolution.html.

The fact that Abdelkarim in *The American Quarter* is a lover of opera, and thus of the power of the voice and song, is not merely a personal quirk of his, but something that may be said to constitute a lifeline. We can explain this through Zeina Hashem Beck's poetry collection *3Arabi Song* (2016), which celebrates her hometown of Tripoli through her musical associations of growing up there. In 'Umm Kultum Speaks', Hashem Beck writes: 'I dressed my voice, first with boy's clothing, then with the Qur'an, and then with poems, then with Egypt.'[45] Yet we are told these provisional coverings have a more authentic source in a planetary spirituality. The poem ends with the ambiguous assertion that 'Everything about me orbits', as the singer both orbits and is orbited.[46] Across the poems, songs bind communities through time and space, song becoming a source of memories, of defiance, of emotional ties, of hope. While the voices and the music have strong local associations, the music can come from anywhere. '3Arabi Song', the title poem of the collection, references family preferences for Piaf, Aznavour, Dalida. The Italian song *Lasciate Mi Cantare*, which celebrates what it is to be 'a real Italian', is given a Tripolitan resonance with its cheerful greeting, *Buongiorno Dio* ('good morning God'). The poem also speaks of how the remake of 'the Guevara song' conquers the Arab world in the nineties (probably the remake of *Hasta Siempre, Comandante*), while Tripolitan youth are also dancing to Queen, wanting 'to break free, God knows'.[47] This is 'the god of joy and laughter' that Rawi Hage suggests the Tripoli revolution raves brought to the fore. That is, there was always a potentially creative Tripolitan popular culture despite Tripoli's reputation for destructive sectarianism.

In conclusion, the retrieval of meaning that the Tripoli uprisings effected, extending more widely to the uprisings of Lebanon and the Arab world, is not so much an ideological struggle as one against the manipulations of the ideological. Crucial to this is the rejection of hegemonic interpellations that self-righteously criminalize dissent, and thus constitute a hypocritical claiming of the moral high ground. Along with the refusal to accept hegemonic brainwashing, the insurrectionary contestation of political corruption draws on the retrieval of ethical values that are inspired and maintained by local popular cultures. These local cultures offer authenticity in conveying both the collective *bios* and collective ethos (affective and spiritual). They thereby come to reject identity politics in favour of local and hoped-for planetary solidarities, however deferred.

---

[45] Zeina Hashem Beck, *3Arabi Song* (Studio City, CA: The Rattle Foundation, 2016), p. 27.
[46] Hashem Beck, *3Arabi Song*, p. 27.
[47] Hashem Beck, *3Arabi Song*, pp. 31–32.

13
Taming 'the Square'

Documenting the Rioting Subject in Basma Abdel Aziz's *The Queue*

Rita Sakr

Introducing the Framework of the 'Riot' in *The Queue*

This chapter investigates the interconnections between violence and literary form in Basma Abdel Aziz's 2016 novel *The Queue* (originally published in 2013 in Arabic as *Al-Tābūr*), which reimagines the riot and the rioting subject. Abdel Aziz is an Egyptian creative writer, psychiatrist, human rights activist, and visual artist. Her work across these fields has focused on uncovering the impact of the oppressive police state's measures on the political body and body politic, including erasures of documentary evidence of harm and the misrepresentation of political agency during and in the aftermath of protests, particularly the 2011 Egyptian Revolution.

Throughout *The Queue*, readers encounter characters whose grasp on the violence of the riot is precarious. The novel stages a memorial disappearance, signifying a forced erasure of documentary evidence that records the repressive practices of state authorities against the rioting subject. More importantly, the novel is a powerful creative act that commemorates disappearances and their mechanisms. This commemoration is evident in the text's structure. The novel consists of six sections, each opening with a 'Document', and a final section that begins with an 'Annex', representing the police state's vanishing of evidence of harmed protestors. Each Document is followed by a series of chapters that imaginatively record, in narrative snippets, what was erased or misrepresented, particularly the manifestations of vulnerability, witness and resistance displayed by the rioting subject in gestures, sounds, symbols, and silence.

The character at the centre of *The Queue*, Yehya Gad el-Rab Saeed, is injured during an incident cryptically known as 'the Disgraceful Events'. He is subsequently denied surgery to extract a bullet lodged inside his body. The repressive measures against protestors condemned as troublemaking rioters during the Disgraceful Events occur some years after an uprising, known as the First Storm, failed to bring down the regime.[1] Instead, the First Storm led to the establishment of a centralised authority, the Gate, at which citizens must queue for weeks to gain permits, issued as documents, for basic rights including bread and healthcare.[2] After the Disgraceful Events, the reopening of the Gate for the processing of any requests becomes a matter of indefinite speculation and virtual immobility in a surveilled queue, dislocated from the space of violently repressed protest in 'the square'. By negating the basic infrastructural conditions of resistance in the public sphere, the Gate thus 'simply deal[s] out another form of punishment' that accentuates conditions of precarity among the queuing citizens.[3] *The Queue* examines this punishment and precarity by highlighting the ways in which the police state assaults the rebellious Egyptian body and body politic. These attacks comprise the combined practices of physical harm, the denial of resources and critical infrastructure to sustain resistance, and the distortion of facts pertaining to protestors, culminating in the breakdown of emergent solidarities in the square. In this chapter, I explore Abdel Aziz's engagement with the relations between enforced silence and vigorous expression across the urban geography of the riot, the body of the rioter in pain, and the literary text bearing witness to the harm inflicted on the city and its citizens.

The square that is continually referred to in relation to the riots remains unnamed in *The Queue*. Yet, given the repetition of the phrase 'the square' in literary and cultural representations of the 2011 Egyptian Revolution, this square is readily identifiable as Midan al-Tahrir in Cairo. Adopting a relational view of space, this chapter explores the implications of repressive measures implemented by the police state seeking to tame or erode the local, regional, and global significance of a riotous 'Tahrir'. I am approaching 'Tahrir' here not merely as a public space, but as a utopian national site where liberation struggles unfolded.[4] At the start of *The Queue*, we encounter the transformation of the national site into a dystopian space of failed liberation and suppressed riot, exemplified by the monitored queue.

In Abdel Aziz's novel, the narratological mapping of the life of the bullet lodged inside Yehya's pelvis after the Events in the square emerges as a differential articulation of slow necropolitical violence—which, in Achille Mbembe's theorization, 'proceeds by a sort of inversion between life and death, as if life was merely death's

---

[1] The 'First Storm' deliberately echoes the 2011 Egyptian Revolution, while the 'Disgraceful Events' fictionally anticipate the Egyptian military regime's return to power in 2013.
[2] Abdel Aziz states that she was inspired by a real queue in Cairo. 'Basma Abdel Aziz on Writing *The Queue*', *ArabLit* (31 August 2017), https://arablit.org/2017/08/31/basma-abdel-aziz-on-writing-the-queue/
[3] Basma Abdel Aziz, *The Queue*, trans. by Elizabeth Jaquette (Brooklyn, NY: Melville House, 2013), p. 33.
[4] On my earlier approach to 'Tahrir' in a broader Egyptian literary framework, see my chapter '"A Way of Making a Space for Ourselves Where We Can Make the Best of Ourselves": Writing Egypt's "Tahrir"', in Rita Sakr, *Anticipating' the 2011 Arab Uprisings: Revolutionary Literatures and Political Geographies*, Palgrave Pivot (Basingstoke: Palgrave, 2013), pp. 21–46.

medium'.[5] This necropolitical violence operates through the production of bodies in pain in the aftermath of the riot. In *Rebel Cities*, David Harvey argues that '[w]hat Tahrir Square showed to the world was ... that it is bodies on the street and in the squares, not the babble of sentiments on Twitter or Facebook, that really matter'.[6] As it focuses on the narrative of the bullet in Yehya's body, Abdel Aziz's novelistic engagement with the riot addresses the demise of the tortured body, rather than the space of the square that the riot has been widely associated with. The body, not the square, becomes the site where the relations of vulnerability, witness, and resistance are reconfigured.

The Queue opens with Tarek Fahmy, the doctor who performed an X-ray on Yehya. The narrative arc of the novel pivots around the disappearance of this X-ray and Yehya's agonistic quest to recover it while suffering from the impact of the bullet, which cannot be surgically removed due to the Gate's decree against extracting bullets from protestors's bodies. Like the other evidence of harm erased or misrepresented by the police state in the aforementioned Documents, the vanished X-ray carries legal and medical documentary weight. *The Queue* achieves an alternative literary archiving of this harm and its misrepresentation. Abdel Aziz offers an innovative narration of the 'riot' through *The Queue*'s engagement with the documentation of the rioting subject—through the novel's references to, on the one hand, the ephemeral existence of the X-ray and, on the other, the embodied documentation of harm evident in the trail of blood left by Yehya's body and the bodies of other protestors.

The tension between the transient nature of the riot and its lasting political significance is exemplified in Tarek's 'vague' and 'hazy' recollection of the Disgraceful Events. His opening summary of the protests and their repression blends dispersed documentary facts with quotes from the Gate's own account of the riot:

> The Events had begun when a small group of people held a protest on a street leading to the square. There weren't many of them, but they boldly condemned the Gate's injustice and tyranny. Their demands were lofty, the stuff of dreams, another doctor told Tarek during one of their night shifts together: the protestors called for the dissolution of the Gate and everything it stood for. Before long, others joined the demonstrations, too. They chanted with passion, their numbers grew, and the protest started to move, but they were quickly confronted by the

---

[5] Achille Mbembe, *Necropolitics*, trans. Steven Corcoran (Durham, NC: Duke University Press, 2019), p. 38. I am here combining conceptual frameworks based on both Rob Nixon, *Slow Violence and The Environmentalism of the Poor* (Cambridge, MA: Harvard University Press, 2013) and Mbembe's *Necropolitics* to engage the (in)visibility of corrosive mechanisms in neoliberal authoritarian systems. In such systems, sovereign politics is implemented through the production of death among the disempowered and political resistance is threatened by the spectacularized misrepresentation by the authorities of the vulnerability of the rioting body as paradoxically dangerous.

[6] David Harvey, *Rebel Cities: From the Right to the City to the Urban Revolution* (London: Verso, 2013), 179.

Gate's newly formed security units. These accused the protesters of overstepping their bounds, and said they wouldn't tolerate such insulting behavior. Then the forces attacked, to 'return people to their senses', beating them brutally. When the injured protestors scattered in retreat and ran into the streets, they were accused of 'spreading chaos', and attempting to undermine the blessed security that had finally—thankfully—returned under the Gate's rule.... The Quell Force had been created to suppress this kind of riot and was better armed than any government agency before it. On the final day, it cleared the square effortlessly, wiping out everyone at the rally in just a few hours.[7]

This passage is central to my argument and critical approach as it sets up the representational framework of the riot. The two secondary quotes—'return people to their senses' and 'spreading chaos', which are presumably linked to the Gate's widely propagated version of the Events—focus attention on the ways in which the seemingly chaotic and vividly sensory elements of the riot, including the chanting and the bodies massing in the square, threaten the police state. The implied propaganda—declaring that the Quell Force, which was 'created to suppress this kind of riot', easily 'cleared [the bodies of the rioters from] the square'—registers the protests as immediately destructive yet historically evanescent, eradicable from both the urban geography and the memory of the people. The success of the police state at abruptly clearing the square reveals the limitations of the participatory democracy that was momentarily enabled by what Jessica Winegar interprets as forms of 'aesthetic ordering'.[8] This aesthetic ordering was implemented by the 2011 revolutionaries through certain civic practices, like cleaning Tahrir Square after the toppling of Hosni Mubarak. Here, the political work of *The Queue* lies in exposing and countering official accounts and practices that distort the validity and undermine the potential continuity of revolutionary activity.

In *The Rebirth of History*, Alain Badiou extends this point of participation and prospective continuity, arguing that

> during a real change, we witness the production of a new site which is nevertheless internal to the general localization that is a world. Thus, in Egypt the people who had rallied in the square believed they were Egypt; Egypt was the people who were there to proclaim that if, under Mubarak, Egypt did not exist, now it existed, and them with it.... A political event occurring everywhere is something that does not exist. The site is the thing whereby the Idea, still fluid, encounters popular genericity. A non-localized Idea is impotent; a site without an Idea is merely an immediate riot, a nihilistic spurt.[9]

---

[7] Abdel Aziz, *The Queue*, pp. 7–8.

[8] Jessica Winegar, 'A Civilized Revolution: Aesthetics and Political Action in Egypt', *American Ethnologist*, 43, no. 4 (2016): pp. 614–617.

[9] Alain Badiou, *The Rebirth of History: Times of Riots and Uprisings* (London: Verso, 2012), p. 57, p. 92.

The Queue recovers the political agency of those who 'condemned the Gate's injustice and tyranny' and records both the 'passion' and pain that underpin their struggle for the Idea, which is their call 'for the dissolution of the Gate and everything it stood for'. In this context, the novel's articulation of the dynamics of vulnerable embodied agency and its precarious documentary traces—in public spaces, bodies, and paper—gestures towards the important socio-spatial, medical, legal, and discursive displacements and disappearances that result from the riot.

In both its formal techniques and semantic choices, Abdel Aziz's novel constructs a rebellious representational space where the terror of autocratic governance against the 'historical riot' might be recovered. In its close narrative engagement with harm in successive close-ups on resilient bodies in pain, *The Queue* materializes an alternative record—a counterpoint to the insidious precarity of official documentary evidence of the suppression of the 'riot'. I analyse this alternative record in relation to the vanishings staged in the dynamics of the 'Documents', and in the police state's repression of the significance of the sites and symbols deployed by the protestors. In the discussion that follows, I explore the novelistic record of the harm inflicted on Yehya and others, including a victim of the Quell Force killed for being a 'filthy rioter', the 'Lady with the Mask', and an injured protestor defending a bag of spent bullets while being wrestled by a policeman.

From 'the Square' to the 'Documents': Necropolitical Vanishings of the Rioting Political Body

The Queue is divided into seven sections. The first six sections follow the same structure. Each begins with a 'Document', followed by the doctor Tarek Fahmy's apprehensive reflection on it. They then contain a succession of chapters depicting, in interpolated narrative snippets, the lives and deaths connected with instances of rebellion and repression in the square and the queue. Each Document consists of amended, redacted records containing medical and personal information about Yehya. These records are reproduced in an italicized font that seems to textually embody a bending of factual information. Document No. 1 consists of primary 'Patient Information' related to Yehya. Document No. 2, entitled 'Time, Location and Circumstances of the Injury', reads:

> *Those accompanying him stated he was injured at approximately 1:30 p.m. while passing through District 9, where the Events occurred. They stated that he left company headquarters to meet some clients and employees on the other side of the square when clashes between unknown persons began. The unrest escalated and spread to the surrounding streets. Several of them witnessed his attempt to leave the area. He was injured, however, and they were unable to identify his assailant. They carried him to the hospital on their shoulders, and he was conscious upon arrival,*

despite a significant loss of blood. They stated that his documents were lost en route, and the bag of merchandise he had been carrying was stolen. As such, there is no evidence of the veracity of their account.[10]

This passage establishes the importance of documentary evidence in the battle for 'veracity' concerning the events and the injured. The official Document vanishes the power of the Idea that sustains the 'historical riot' into the chaos of what it represents as transient 'clashes between unknown persons' and 'unrest'. This vanishing accentuates the precarity of witness with respect to the rioting subject, whose documents are 'lost en route' to the hospital and whose belongings are stolen.

In Document No. 3, Abdel Aziz uses brackets to indicate redacted information, reproducing the authorities's manipulation of medical evidence of harm:

visible symptoms include: signs of choking and disruption of the nervous system, bleeding around entry and exit wounds caused by a [redacted], sign of recent abrasions and bruising on the back, pelvis, and forearm regions, [redacted; injury written above it] penetrating the pelvic region along with profuse bleeding, deviation of the wrist. Procedures conducted include [long sentence, redacted].[11]

In *Paper Knowledge*, Lisa Gitelman notes that nineteenth-century slave owners would place advertisements in Southern US newspapers, providing physical descriptions of escaped slaves's bodies to aid in their recapture. These same advertisements were then republished in the North as an indictment of slavery, as the descriptions unwittingly exhibited evidence of the harm done to the slaves. Gitelman argues that, 'Because it implies accountability, knowing and showing together constitute an epistemic practice to which ethics and politics become available, even necessary.'[12] This is the double know-show act that emerges in the use of the Documents across *The Queue*. The formal embedding of a Document at the start of each section highlights the workings of the police state that closely monitors, and hence contains and controls, the lives and deaths of its rebellious subjects by means of official paper knowledge. Yet the novel also reimagines the content of this distorted archive, allowing the reader to hold those who inflicted harm on the riotous political body, through injuries, and on the record, through redactions, to account.

Document No. 4 notes 'certain acts [committed by Yehya] that may be described as rebellious', such as being 'seen in the square on more than one occasion, when he had no reason to be there', 'an irrational belief that he can alter reality' and

---

[10] Abdel Aziz, *The Queue*, p. 24. Italics in original.
[11] Abdel Aziz, *The Queue*, p. 40. Italics in original.
[12] Lisa Gitelman, *Paper Knowledge: Toward a Media History of Documents* (Durham, NC: Duke University Press, 2014), p. 5.

'a clear tendency to act in a socially unacceptable and unhealthy manner.'[13] *The Queue* depicts many instances where those in wider society mirror the police state's misrepresentation, characterising the protestors's behaviour as chaotic. Prominent journalists quote eyewitnesses who insist 'that the people who caused the Disgraceful Events were just rioters who had suddenly "lost all moral inhibitions" and flown into a frenzy'.[14] The doctor at the state-run Zephyr Hospital asserts 'that the high mortality rate was due to the fact that these rioters were simply too sensitive'.[15] This pseudo-medical language echoes the now-defunct terminology of 'the excitable heart' that was used in the late 1900s to refer to sufferers of what is now recognized as PTSD.[16] It also recalls the recurrent diagnosis, fabricated by some Egyptian doctors working in prisons, of fatal 'shock' due to severe reduction of blood volume in prisoners's bodies.[17] In this context, Document No. 4, titled 'Patient History', compresses Yehya's life story into an amalgam of pseudo-medical knowledge. It thus amplifies the redactions in Document No. 3, with a citizen file typically held by the internal intelligence units of authoritarian regimes. Through this jibe at the warped construction of the 'History' of the rioting subject, Abdel Aziz highlights the tension between the enforced authority and order of the official record, and the imaginative narrative of the life and death of the political body that she explores in Yehya's story across the novel. The three striking lines from Document No. 4 quoted above also extend the significance of Document No. 2. They succinctly bring to mind the connections between the right to the city or 'the square', autocracy's distortions of the facts of revolutionary action into a spectacle of random riots disjointed from responsible citizenship, and the undermining of political agency or the future of the riotous Idea that underlies the potential to change historical realities.

Document No. 5, titled 'The Gate's Response', marks the shift from misrepresentation to complete erasure. The reaction of the anonymous absolute authority to the rioting subject disappears into a blank symbolic square on the page. This page is a visual equivalent of the socio-spatial vanishing of 'Tahrir': the correlation of the site and Idea is reduced to a mere geometric shape. The page is transformed into the representational equivalent of the secret torture sites where riotous energies are consumed and dissident lives vanish into a space of perpetual non-arrival. The repressive response of the police state to the 'historical riot' embodied in the mass of rioting subject(s) 'chant[ing] with passion' is symbolically represented in the technical play with (in)visibility on the page—the correlative of the Quell Force

---

[13] Abdel Aziz, *The Queue*, p. 102.
[14] Abdel Aziz, *The Queue*, p. 52.
[15] Abdel Aziz, *The Queue*, p. 52.
[16] Abdel Aziz, *Dhākirat al qahr: dirāsah ḥawla manẓoumat al-taʿdheeb (Memory of Repression: A Study of the System of Torture)* (Cairo: Dar al-Tanweer, 2014), p. 127.
[17] Abdel Aziz, *Memory of Repression*, p. 306.

'clear[ing] the square'.[18] Through this innovative formal technique, Abdel Aziz vividly demonstrates how documentary evidence of the authorities's persecution of the protestors is whitewashed and erased. Gitelman argues that 'documents help define and are mutually defined by the know-show function, since documenting is an epistemic practice: the kind of knowing that is all wrapped up with showing, and showing wrapped with knowing'.[19] As it engages the know-show function of the document, Abdel Aziz's formal mediation of the dynamics of the Documents, especially Document No. 5, exemplifies her intertwined roles as creative writer, visual artist, psychiatrist, human rights advocate and recorder of violations. In this respect, Abdel Aziz's insightful engagement with the psychological impact of the official Document's power is exemplified in Tarek's reaction as he looks at the empty square on the page. Terrorized by both his potential complicity with and nascent resistance to the Gate, Tarek imagines that the 'space on the page grew wider before his eyes, encompassing him, as if to swallow him whole and imprison him within it'.[20] Abdel Aziz thus renders the Documents as a surreal 'thirst for mysteries' in 'the service of visceral experiences'.[21] These mechanisms are manifested in the authority's dislocation of the embodied riotous square onto physical sites and psychological states of disorientation.

Document No. 6 exemplifies the bureaucratic workings of a police state. It becomes clear that the file, which was supposed to have been protected by the examining doctor, remains in the control of an invisible hand that continually adds information about Yehya, his friends, and Tarek. Ironically refracting the statement in Document No. 2 that there is *'no evidence of the veracity of their account'* (referring to those who carried Yehya to the hospital), the 'Follow Up' section of Document No. 6 warns that *'individuals responsible for observation and the collection of information are kindly asked to ensure its veracity before transmitting it to the record-keeper'.*[22] We are implicitly reminded that the record-keeper is the same Gate keeper who ensures the suppression of riotous political will in the square by establishing precarious access to conditions of life in the queue.

The six sections that each open with a Document are followed by a final section beginning with 'Annex 1' (with no further annexes) that 'contained the names of people who carried Yehya to the nearest hospital when he was shot'.[23] Yet, while the Documents enact the containment of riotous energies in cordoned sites, Annex 1 presents a significant formal break. This break marks the narrative movement towards the articulation of Tarek's shift to stand in solidarity with the political life

---

[18] Abdel Aziz, *The Queue*, p. 8.
[19] Gitelman, *Paper Knowledge*, p. 1.
[20] Abdel Aziz, *The Queue*, p. 141.
[21] Mbembe, *Necropolitics*, p. 51.
[22] Abdel Aziz, *The Queue*, p. 192. Italics in original.
[23] Abdel Aziz, *The Queue*, p. 201.

of his patient, the rioting subject. While Tarek cannot identify any name in the Annex except that of Yehya's girlfriend Amani,

> he was unable to ignore it all, either, or to pretend as if none of it has happened. The constant turmoil, and his own helplessness in controlling his thoughts and feelings, were choking him. He had been suspended in this gray area, doing nothing for months since he had first opened the file. Now, suddenly, in a moment of wild rage, he decided to go to the queue in search of Yehya.[24]

In the novel's final scene, Tarek reads a 'line he'd somehow missed [and previously unmentioned in the 'Documents']: *Yehya Gad el-Rab Saeed spent one hundred and forty nights of his life in the queue*.'[25] Against the suppressive state-controlled archival serialization of the Documents that (re)produces 'this grey area', *The Queue* offers an alternative representational space for the memorialization of Yehya's life as his condition deteriorates and he struggles to have the bullet removed from his body. (We should note here that the Arabic word Yeḥya means 'he will live' or 'long live'.) In its imaginative engagement with the aforementioned know-show function, *The Queue* presents the conflict between the competing claims of tyrannical politics and the rebellious political body. Simultaneously, the novel highlights the ways in which 'contemporary forms of subjugating life to the power of death (necropolitics) are deeply reconfiguring the relations between resistance, sacrifice, and terror'.[26] Tyrannical politics thrives through the interpolated dynamics of the riotous square's socio-spatial hypervisibility, and in the Documents' discursive vanishings of resistance and legal invisibility of state terror. While the riot is tackled by the police state as an eradicable threat to the wellbeing of the body politic, the political body is tortured, forcibly silenced, and murdered. What lives on is the Idea of dignified life, 'Yeḥya', that persists through Tarek's late change of heart at the conclusion of the novel. After reading the line that he missed establishing Yehya's death,

> Everything that had happened swirled in his [Tarek's] mind as if it were one long, uninterrupted scene.... There was no need to read the pages of the file another time.... He took a blue pen from his desk drawer instead, and as he hesitated for a moment on the paper it left a small dot of ink on the page. Then quickly, he added a sentence by hand to the bottom of the fifth document. He closed the file, left it on his desk, and rose.[27]

---

[24] Abdel Aziz, *The Queue*, p. 201.
[25] Abdel Aziz, *The Queue*, p. 217.
[26] Mbembe, *Necropolitics*, p. 92.
[27] Abdel Aziz, *The Queue*, p. 217.

Tarek's intervention in the empty square of Document No. 5 (the erased 'Gate's Response') illustrates how, working with documents, 'subjects know and show within and against the demands of an increasingly dense overlay of institutions and institutionalized realms'.[28] Accordingly, while the formal placement of the Documents at the start of each section highlights the repressive containment and interruption of the long duration of the 'historical riot' and the life of the rioting subject, the novel's conclusion opens out onto narrative futures.[29] These futures move beyond the apparent dichotomy of enforced silence and vigorous expression, optimistically suggesting 'possibilities that are unprecedented and previously unknown' in Egypt.[30]

The Protestor's Multiple Vulnerabilities: Bodily and Discursive Disfigurement in the Police State

The Queue offers an alternative, imaginative memorialization of the personal stories that escape an official archive maimed by erasure. Abdel Aziz achieves this in the series of chapters that follow each document, which depict the everyday violations of citizens's rights. Each chapter explores the simultaneous workings of discursive or semantic and bodily disfigurement, as well as the protestors's vulnerability, the precarity of eyewitness, and the tentative futures of resistance in the representational space of the riot. This complex process of memorialization is exemplified in the story of Mahfouz, whose life and death are narrated to others in the queue by his cousin, Shalaby.

Shalaby tells of how, as a member of the Quell Force (which 'had been created to suppress this kind of riot'), Mahfouz's 'truncheon crashed down on a filthy rioter's damn head, but the stubborn scum kept trying to get up so Mahfouz shot him. His blood gushed out and stained the square, and his soul left his body right there'.[31] Shalaby's objective in queuing before the Gate is to obtain recognition of and compensation for Mahfouz's presumably patriotic action; his cousin 'didn't endanger the country or its people like those rioters did'.[32] Shalaby believes that Mahfouz's actions prove he was 'a real man, while the man he's killed—probably without intending to—had just been a trouble-maker, a saboteur, out to frighten people and make their lives more difficult than they already were'.[33] In a later snippet, Shalaby concludes: 'It was those rabblerousers who'd crossed the line, and his

---

[28] Gitelman, *Paper Knowledge*, p. 20.
[29] By adapting the French historian Fernand Braudel's own adaptation of the concept of 'longue durée', I am also asserting the need for a long-historical perspective on necropolitical governance in Egypt especially as it is fictionalized through the demise of Yehya's body.
[30] Badiou, *The Rebirth of History*, p. 109.
[31] Abdel Aziz, *The Queue*, p. 8, p. 74.
[32] Abdel Aziz, *The Queue*, p. 77.
[33] Abdel Aziz, *The Queue*, p. 77.

cousin the martyr simply taught them a lesson—using his truncheon. He'd used it before, nearly every day, and according to the experts, truncheon blows never result in death.'[34] Shalaby's zealous defence of his cousin's actions demonstrates the way in which minds and bodies might be tamed through models of masculine power and gendered transgression, tied in with contradictory perceptions of vulnerability.[35] The paternalistic discourse that Shalaby channels illustrates how the authoritarian regime both aggravates the vulnerability of rioting subjects, while simultaneously instilling a sense of vulnerability in those same subjects.

Shalaby's statements also illustrate the police state's marshalling of expert reports, including those by medical professionals, to manipulate facts concerning torture, forced disappearances, and the killing of rioters. According to Shalaby, 'the doctors said they hadn't removed any bullets—not from the man, not from anyone.'[36] In a complex process of semantic misrepresentation, the political forces of protest and uprising are subsumed into the chaos of the immediate riot, then into the ensuing pattern of criminalization and systemic sabotage. This is a process that is repeated elsewhere: for example, Um Mabrouk refers to the protestors as 'meddlesome riffraff' when they begin to threaten the future of her makeshift coffee stand in the queue.[37] Um Mabrouk's compromised defence of her precarious and unregulated business typifies the forced collusion of the disenfranchised people that occurred with the crushing of dissent in Egypt. Living under a system that is both authoritarian and neoliberal, Um Mabrouk acts out of necessity, condemning the protest to save her business and provide for her family. Similar acts of discursive violence were common in the Egyptian state media's representation of protestors in Tahrir Square—typified by the use of the term *baltajiyya*, or thugs, to describe the protestors.[38] Like Um Mabrouk's castigation of the 'meddlesome riffraff', the other bystanders's collusion with the police state involves perpetuating the semantic distortion of the figure of the protestor or rebel into the anarchist or anti-patriotic rioter. These semantic distortions allow the bystanders to justify their failure to defend the protestors from violence—and, occasionally, their active participation in this same violence.[39]

---

[34] Abdel Aziz, *The Queue*, p. 165.

[35] As Judith Butler, Zeynep Gambetti and Leticia Sabsay note: 'Psychoanalytic feminists have remarked that the masculine positions are effectively built through a denial of their own vulnerability ... and project, displace, and localize it elsewhere ... it can work to exacerbate vulnerability (as a way of achieving power) or to disavow it (also as a way of achieving power)'. Judith Butler, Zeynep Gambetti, and Leticia Sabsay, 'Introduction', in *Vulnerability in Resistance*, ed. by Judith Butler, Zeynep Gambetti, and Leticia Sabsay (Durham, NC: Duke University Press, 2016), p. 4.

[36] Abdel Aziz, *The Queue*, p. 165.

[37] Abdel Aziz, *The Queue*, p. 89.

[38] Abdel Aziz quotes several protestors after their release on the subject of their representation as 'baltajiyya' that paradoxically sits alongside the protestors's own use of the same term to refer to state thugs. 'Memory of Repression', pp. 155–156.

[39] Abdel Aziz reports in her study that at the turn of 2014 bystander reactions changed dramatically. While they had previously attempted to ignore violations of rights, by 2014 they began to actively

This authoritarian integration and alienation of the body politic relies on the production of the ambiguous figure of the 'rioter' as an enemy of the state. In her study on torture, Abdel Aziz quotes an Egyptian director of criminal investigations accusing a group of 'troublemakers and brawlers' without identifying any specific person.[40] Interestingly, she notes, these derogatory terms morph into the more positive description 'real rebels' in the aftermath of the two post-January 2011 regime changes. This captures the equivocal complexity of the term rioter in Arabic, which may refer to either the 'mutaẓāhir' متظاهر—protestor—or the mushāghib مشاغب—troublemaker. In *The Queue*, the term rioter is used across multiple depictions of the protestors as irresponsible disruptors of civil peace. Shalaby is disconcerted when he learns 'that the young man Mahfouz had killed had been a believer, who'd prayed and fasted and went to mosque on Fridays, and that he probably wasn't a rioter, just a passerby'.[41] The opposition that Shalaby sets up between 'a rioter' and 'a passerby' presupposes that the passerby is the silent and therefore good citizen who would not protest loudly in public space. Shalaby's inability to adjust to the implications of his warped understanding of citizenship communicates a sense of imprisonment within an alternative, exhausted, and perpetually confused reality that seems to contain people who come from all walks of life and now stand in the queue. These masses are circumscribed by the parameters of the infernal urban space in which they remain ultimately immobile. They are both mentally and physically tamed.

Yehya's friend Nagy, a lecturer who has resigned from his job because of his dissident activities, is the only character who reflects on these patterns of socio-spatial and physiological taming. Such taming works to repress the energies that would otherwise fuel the 'historical riot'. Nagy 'wondered what made people so attached to their new lives of spinning in orbit around the queue' while suffering 'the same lethargy'.[42] Amidst 'the tear-gas canisters strewn in the stretches between the munitions', he sees a lady sitting on the ground begging, wearing 'a black gas mask hung around her neck'. He imagines presenting her to his students as 'the Lady with the Mask'—both a counter-monumental embodiment of precarity and resilience amidst socio-political violence, and an implicit commentary on the aestheticization of the figure of the protestor in the early aftermath of the Arab uprisings.[43] Abdel Aziz's introduction of this image-metaphor of 'the Lady with the Mask' functions as an imaginative corrective to the semantic disfigurement of the protestor as a mere troublemaker, intent on wreaking havoc. Nagy notes that 'during the times when the street had been filled with tear gas ... [s]he'd sat cross-legged in her

---

participate in the misrepresentation and repression of fellow citizens accused of being enemies of the state. Abdel Aziz, 'Memory of Repression', p. 300.

[40] Abdel Aziz, 'Memory of Repression', p. 208.
[41] Abdel Aziz, *The Queue*, p. 163.
[42] Abdel Aziz, *The Queue*, p. 90.
[43] Abdel Aziz, *The Queue*, p. 108.

usual place, not moving an inch, not trying to hide, a helmet on her head, a black mask hung around her neck, while everyone else was running all around her.'[44] If the protestor is often associated with the disruptive and ephemeral quality of the 'immediate riot', the Lady with the Mask instead speaks to the protracted, unending nature of socio-economic precarity in the authoritarian state. She represents the possibility of quiet revolutionary expression amidst the noise.

The Displaced 'Historical Riot': Disappeared Evidence and the (Re)production of Precarity

Through both its attention to bodily injury and resistance, and its formal experimentation with distorted or disappeared narrativity, *The Queue* registers several different phenomenological aspects of the violence experienced by protestors. The vanishing of the rebellious body politic in the narrative figures most clearly in the account of the Second Disgraceful Events, which occur 'at the edge of the main square':

> Eyewitnesses disagreed over how many were injured and killed, and though the wails of ambulances were heard, no one saw anyone being transported away. Here and there, people noticed deep, wide puddles of blood, but only rarely did they see someone bleeding. A grizzled, stubble-chinned driver swore to a group of people in the queue that with his own eyes he's seen a barefoot young man so wounded that his leg was about to fall off, his hand fiercely clasped around a clear plastic bag. Inside, the driver said he could make out small silver pellets, covered in a dark red liquid. The driver said that a plainclothes officer had offered to buy the bag and everything in it, but the young man had grimly refused. A violent struggle had ensued, which had ended with the officer stealing the bag.... The young man tried to chase after him, but his leg failed him, and he sat down on the ground and wept.[45]

In this passage, eyewitness testimony disintegrates. The surreal dissociation of blood from the bleeding subject lends a more-than-realist quality to the scene. This feeling is carried into the image of the man with the about-to-be-severed leg, who maintains a precarious hold on his bag of evidence and attempts, despite his considerable injury, to defend this evidence against the overwhelming power of the plainclothes officer. This episode can be read in dialogue with the questions raised in the introduction to *Vulnerability in Resistance*. Butler, Gambetti, and Sabsay ask: 'How are vulnerability and bodily exposure related, especially when we

---

[44] Abdel Aziz, *The Queue*, p. 108.
[45] Abdel Aziz, *The Queue*, p. 86.

think about the exposure of the body to power? Is that exposure both perilous and enabling? What is the relation between resistance and agency? In what ways is vulnerability bound up with the problem of precarity?'[46] The young man's attempted resistance is met with suppressive violence from the plainclothes officer, and the episode ends with his crushing recognition of his own vulnerability and defeat: he sits down and weeps. The disconnection of blood from bleeding subjects, and the violent dispossession of this (nearly) dismembered man, shed light on one of the police state's principal objectives in torturing the rioting subject: the victim's identity is destroyed, and their will to resist is broken, surrendered to the torturer. The tortured body, even if rarely seen, is then transformed into a public exhibition to terrorize society and crush potential resistance.[47] Yet this final objective is not necessarily fulfilled; in many police states, the exposure of the tortured body does not stop further acts of public protest.

In Abdel Aziz's novel, the authorities's (re)production of precarity through both physical attacks on protestors and the subsequent erasure of evidence culminates in the aftermath of the Second Disgraceful Events. The Gate begins by '[urging] citizens not be misled by what they had seen, no matter how confident they were in the accuracy of their vision'. It then follows this with an announcement that all radiology wards will now be closed 'in the interest of citizens's physical and psychological well-being', as it has 'determined that many of these devices gave false and inaccurate results and printed grainy or misleading images'.[48] Abdel Aziz here expands on her earlier exploration of the role of dissident documentation into the medical sphere. She draws this medical documentation into the realm of responsibility with respect to an ethics and politics of representation, the know-show function, in the struggle to bear witness to totalitarian repression of the 'historical riot'.

The Queue explores the relationship between violence, vulnerability, documentary evidence, and resistance in the aftermath of the riot by devoting considerable narrative attention to the physical details of Yehya's wounded body as he struggles to have the bullet removed. The first time we read of Yehya, he is 'dragging his feet and his stomach and his pelvis, all of it heavy, to stand in the queue without ever reaching the Gate'.[49] As he moves towards inevitable death, his (in)visible, tortured body paradoxically mutates into a spectacular site: 'The patches of blood on his clothes grew steadily larger; he was bleeding all the time now, no longer just when he urinated, and growing weaker from the loss of blood'.[50] Exposed to slow necropolitical violence, Yehya's bloodied body, like that of the man killed by Mahfouz whose blood 'stained the square', can be reimagined in connection to the

---

[46] Butler, Gambetti, and Sabsay, 'Introduction', pp. 1–2.
[47] Abdel Aziz, 'Memory of Repression', p. 144.
[48] Abdel Aziz, *The Queue*, p. 93.
[49] Abdel Aziz, *The Queue*, p. 10.
[50] Abdel Aziz, *The Queue*, p. 159.

aesthetic practice of the Egyptian graffiti artist Ammar Abo Bakr.[51] Bakr's representations of bloodied, tortured, and murdered protestors form a creative visual archive of the repressed 'historical riot' exhibited in the tortured city.[52]

We learn that Yehya's 'pain was so bad he couldn't bend his knees to lower his body that short distance to the ground'.[53] His everyday life is reduced to the inescapable fact that 'deep inside his body was a bullet that refused to leave him'.[54] In a surreal reordering of subject–object relations, the bullet gains a life of its own while Yehya fades away. He tells Tarek that '[i]t feels like the bullet is moving around in there', destroying his supposedly riotous energy and appropriating his right to free movement.[55] After his discussion with Tarek, Yehya is at first hopeful that

> the bullet might surrender and settle somewhere safe, surrounded by the protective tissue that the body naturally forms around any foreign object that disturbs its natural integrity. Then all these elements would be [sic] become one: the bullet, tissue, and various unknown secretions forming a tranquil, untroublesome mass that would stay with him for the rest of his life. But it seemed the bullet had chosen another path, launching an incursion into his intestines, puncturing them and perhaps soon poisoning his blood.[56]

This trajectory enacts a displacement of the now-tamed energy of 'the square' onto the tortured body in which the bullet runs riot. The imagined life of the bullet inside the body presents a physiological counterpart to the life of the tortured, riotous body politic as its course inevitably deviates from containment to slow, painful annihilation. The novel thus enables a critical corrective to historical timelines and political approaches that elide the complex dynamics of necropolitical violence—a violence that slowly erodes resistance by perpetuating bodies in pain.

Conclusion

After the Quell Force '[clear] the square' of the protestors, who '[chant] with passion' as their number increases and they take over the centre, 'the street looked like it had just emerged from an invisible war'.[57] When Yehya arrives at the hospital,

---

[51] Abdel Aziz, *The Queue*, p. 74.
[52] On Ammar Abo Bakr's exceptional contribution to rethinking graffiti in relation to urban violence and resistance in Egypt, see Mona Abaza, 'Mourning, Narratives and Interactions with the Martyrs through Cairo's Graffiti', *E-International Relations*, Oct. 2013, https://www.e-ir.info/2013/10/07/mourning-narratives-and-interactions-with-the-martyrs-through-cairos-graffiti/
[53] Abdel Aziz, *The Queue*, p. 14.
[54] Abdel Aziz, *The Queue*, p. 35.
[55] Abdel Aziz, *The Queue*, p. 56.
[56] Abdel Aziz, *The Queue*, p. 100.
[57] Abdel Aziz, *The Queue*, p. 8, pp. 29–30.

Tarek sees on 'his body a map of the battle', signifying intertwined topographies of the riot and the tortured body.[58] The harmed body and the bullet-strewn site of the riot are live evidence of the confrontation with the Quell Force, but their legal documentary power is also transient, as they are subject to erasure by the authorities. They are therefore connected to the paradox of the paper document as 'a figure both for all that is sturdy and stable' and 'insubstantial and ephemeral'.[59] This is a paradox that refracts the simultaneous durability and transience of the riot itself. By means of a figurative engagement with the ease with which the know-show function of the document can be manipulated, *The Queue* registers the impact of slow necropolitical violence that operates through both harming and vanishing of the riotous subject and assault on the significance of the 'historical riot'. Tarek realizes, as he reviews his files in the office, that he drew on Document No. 2:

> a figure resembling Yehya, nearly naked, and a small, solid circle, completely shaded in, occupying a space in the lower left part of his stomach.... He picked up an eraser and carefully erased what he'd drawn. He lifted the paper up to the light coming in through the window and looked at Yehya's outline and the shadow of the solid circle, no longer there.[60]

This surreal image-metaphor refracts the erasure in Document No. 5. Here, Abdel Aziz imaginatively indicates instances of medical complicity in eliminating evidence of persecution and abuse by the authorities against the rioting subjects. She also highlights the ways in which the 'battle' in 'the square' is interconnected with the struggle for 'veracity' through paper knowledge. Later, Yehya learns that the wounded who accepted under pressure:

> to undergo surgery at Zephyr Hospital emerged as they'd been before the Disgraceful Events. They didn't have a mark on their bodies, no signs of bullets or shrapnel, and the operations left almost no trace. But Yehya wasn't like them.... He possessed tangible evidence of what had really happened during the Disgraceful Events [...].[61]
>
> (115–116)

While Yehya is aware that the composition of his body-bullet is a valuable piece of evidence that has not yet been erased, Ehab, the journalist who was previously 'a rioter, an activist flush with enthusiasm', encourages him and his friends in their struggle to get the bullet removed.[62] After being tortured for seeking to obtain

---

[58] Abdel Aziz, *The Queue*, p. 25.
[59] Gitelman, *Paper Knowledge*, p. 3.
[60] Abdel Aziz, *The Queue*, pp. 25–26.
[61] Abdel Aziz, *The Queue*, pp. 115–116.
[62] Abdel Aziz, *The Queue*, p. 28.

the X-ray of Yehya's pelvis, his girlfriend Amani is convinced by the Gate's declaration that the riotous events in the square were 'a big-budget blockbuster'.[63] Deciding that the violence was 'all a simple fiction', she tries 'to convince Yehya that the bullet that had pierced his side and lodged itself in his pelvis was a fake bullet, that it wasn't important to remove it, and that he no longer needed to trouble himself with the matter of who had shot him'.[64] Despite the authorities's forceful attempt to forge a 'fiction of the events in the square', the reality of the harm remains as evidence deeply imbricated with the generative Idea of resisting tyranny despite repression: 'Yehya was not convinced, and he did not stop bleeding'.[65] From this perspective, *The Queue*'s imaginative attention to the expressive details of the harmed rioting body expands and complicates the view that 'the case of Tahrir Square highlights the revolutionary potential of the body'.[66] Abdel Aziz's novel recovers the vanishings and distortions that impact the life and death of the rioting subject. Displaced from the square to the queue, the subject inventively reimagines the know-show function of the documentary traces of harm. As such, the novel makes an important contribution to global literary representations of riotous events and authoritarian state responses to them, offering an alternative more-than-realist record of the riot's enduring political significance.

[63] Abdel Aziz, *The Queue*, p. 212.
[64] Abdel Aziz, *The Queue*, pp. 212–213.
[65] Abdel Aziz, *The Queue*, p. 205, p. 213.
[66] Nathan W. Swanson, 'Embodying Tahrir: Bodies and Geopolitics in the 2011 Egyptian Uprising', *Area* 48, no. 3 (2016): p. 301.

14
Mediating the Arab Spring's Riots

Reclaiming Egypt's Lost Archive

Jumana Bayeh

From the earliest crowd rumblings, assemblies and mass violence in 2011 Tahrir Square, Egypt's Arab Spring was a highly mediated series of events. Screened across the world on television sets, computer screens, and social media platforms, it is no wonder that Egypt's uprising was quickly referred to as 'the Facebook revolution'. While the use of this appellation has since declined, researchers continue to mine the vast collection of media platforms that recorded, disseminated, and archived the eighteen days that transformed Tahrir into a riotous battleground. Highly significant among the many digital media sites is *858.ma: The Archive of Resistance*, a treasure trove of raw footage, from major battles to sporadic street clashes, recorded by protestors engaged in street media activism. The hours of material on this site alone point to the sensory overload researchers face when sifting through the primary evidence on the Tahrir uprising. The team behind this website, the Mosireen Collective, were clearly aware of the daunting nature of this abundance of data, both in their own archive and beyond. In a statement on their site, the Mosireen team suggest that the way to give form to their digital collection is through narrative:

> 858 is, of course, just one archive of the revolution. It is not, and can never be, *the* archive. It is one collection of memories, one set of tools we can all use to fight the narratives of the counter-revolution, to pry loose the state's grip on history, to keep building new histories for the future.[1]

Taking inspiration from this observation on the significance of narrative for making sense of a plethora of media footage, this essay expands upon the Tahrir archives to include fiction, in particular the novel, to examine the role of authors in mediating the riots in Cairo.

Even before the publication of Mosireen's website, writers of fiction were instrumental in disseminating information about the various clashes that took place during the 2011 Egyptian Revolution that effectively ended the Mubarak regime,

---

[1] Mosireen Collective, 'About', *858.ma: An Archive of Resistance*, https://858.ma. Accessed 26 October 2021.

Jumana Bayeh, *Mediating the Arab Spring's Riots*. In: *Writing the Global Riot*. Edited by: Jumana Bayeh, Helen Groth, and Julian Murphet, Oxford University Press. © Oxford University Press (2023). DOI: 10.1093/oso/9780192862594.003.0015

as well as the battles that surrounded the counter-revolution of July 2013. Ahdaf Soueif, author of two critically acclaimed novels and several volumes of short stories, participated in the uprising and documented these events in articles for *The Guardian* and other media outlets. Likewise, Alaa al Aswany, most famous for *The Yacoubian Building* (2002), offered political commentary in the form of several newspaper articles and interviews, recording eye-witness accounts of the violence. Shifting from author of fiction to citizen journalist is hardly unheard of, and the same goes for moving in the opposite direction; yet what is of interest here is the fact that the revolution appears to have provoked some authors, like Omar Robert Hamilton and Yasmine El Rashidi, to move away from documentary forms like 858.ma and towards fiction. Following the uprising, Hamilton and El Rashidi published their debut novels, *The City Always Wins* (2017) and *Chronicle of a Last Summer* (2016)—prior to this, they had worked in documentary film production and journalism, respectively. Hamilton was a founding member of the Mosireen Collective, establishing 858.ma as well as contributing footage to it, while El Rashidi wrote several arresting articles for the *New York Review of Books* on the Tahrir uprising. Both authors expressed a particular need to turn to fiction, and to the novel specifically, in order to accommodate what they were hoping to convey about the aftermath of the uprising. Their novels demonstrate that while digital footage, street media and journalism are widely perceived as more accurate or closer to 'real life' than works of fiction, literary texts have also played an unexpected, if underappreciated, role in documenting Egypt's uprising.

There are also startling similarities between Hamilton and El Rashidi's justifications for their turn to fiction. As will be outlined below, they both express a fascination with sound, listening, and silence, and the desire to somehow narrate the intense sonic textures of the riots. Certainly, viewing any one of the many videos in 858's archive shows the degree to which the uprising was an extremely rowdy affair. Against the gunshots fired by the plain-clothed police—referred to as *baltajiyya* or thugs in local parlance—protestors pelted thousands of rocks that clattered onto the square like rain. Sound was also used strategically by both sides. Sonic booms from the military were deployed as a security measure to scare or disperse crowds, while protestors issued loud battle cries as a signal to attack or an attempt to confuse the opposition. As one rioter stated in an interview:

> At 9 a.m. came Thursday's first battle cry. It began with a rhythmic banging sound, as one man beat a pipe against the metal pole at the entrance to Cairo's underground train station. Then another joined in, banging a rock against a lamppost. And then dozens of men began whistling through their teeth, calling men to battle as they waved their hands, gesturing for hundreds to come forward.[2]

---

[2] Vivienne Walt, 'The Fighting Rages on in Tahrir Square', *Time Magazine*, 3 February 2011. Retrieved on 5 August 2021 from: http://content.time.com/time/world/article/0,8599,2045943,00.html

Lost in all that deafening sound, much like the abundance of data in the archives, are the stories that make sense of, comprehend, and give shape to the chaotic nature of the uprising. Encased in Hamilton and El Rashidi's novels are not only the sounds and voices of Egypt's Arab Spring, but also the stories that give these sounds their meaning; stories which are capable of building new histories of the past and new narratives of the future.

Why Fiction? Why Sound?

These lost sounds and stories are better explained with the aid of R. Murray Schafer's theorizations of lo- and hi-fi soundscapes. In 'The Music of the Environment' (1973), Schafer distinguishes between lo- and hi-fi frequencies, focusing on what each does and does not capture. A hi-fi system, he argued, 'is one possessing a favourable signal-to-noise ratio. The hi-fi soundscape is one in which discrete sounds can be heard clearly because of low ambient noise level. The country is generating more hi-fi than the city.'[3] By contrast, in a 'lo-fi soundscape individual acoustic signals are obscured in an overdense population of sounds. The pellucid sound—a footstep in the snow, a train whistle in the distance or a church bell across the valley—is masked by broad-band noise.'[4] In a context of sound studies, literature aligns with Schafer's hi-fi countryside while online data archives are more akin to noisy lo-fi cities where discrete sounds are obscured. Literature amplifies individual voices within the fictional spaces of a novel, voices that might otherwise be lost to the acoustic environment.

Both Hamilton and El Rashidi have explained turning to the novel when their original forms for mediating the events in Cairo—a documentary film and a non-fiction book—failed them. For Hamilton, the 2013 counter-revolution in which the military, with the support of protestors, ousted the democratically elected Muslim Brotherhood, was so violent and debilitating that it shut down not just public space but also discourse and dialogue, thereby silencing the riotous voices that participated in the 2011 uprising.[5] Unable to continue his activism in Cairo, Hamilton relocated to New York with multiple hard drives of the video footage the Mosireen Collective had amassed. His intention was to make a two-hour documentary using this footage, but when he sat down to write the script what spilled onto the page in an urgent and uncontrolled manner was prose fiction. Hamilton recounts altering his plan, thinking he might instead write a poetry collection or a journalistic book. 'It only became clear a little while later', he says, 'that a novel was

---

[3] R. Murray Schafer, 'The Music of the Environment', *No. 1 of an Occasional Journal devoted to Soundscape Studies*, 1973, Universal Edition No. 26912, p. 10.
[4] R. Murray Schafer, 'The Music of the Environment', p. 10.
[5] Omar Robert Hamilton, 'Omar Robert Hamilton on *The City Always Wins*'. Shakespeare and Company Bookshop, 27 Sept 2017, https://www.youtube.com/watch?v=jW7_lZD_9Ok. Accessed 9 August 2021.

the only form that could handle all the different things I wanted to ... say'.[6] These things included a commentary on the intense debates that the counter-revolution had suppressed, debates which *The City Always Wins* explores at length through dialogue, the inner-thoughts of characters, and in scenes where the protagonist, Khalil, creates audio files of mass protests and riotous activity.[7]

Likewise, El Rashidi found her way to fiction through a process of what she refers to as 'writing into failure'. While writing what she thought would be a work closer to journalism, El Rashidi became interested in explaining what she perceived as the silence of the Egyptian people prior to, and especially following, the Egyptian revolution. The silence she wanted to examine was not only the kind imposed by the state through censorship, but also the kind that permeates Egyptian society, shaping private lives and intimate relationships within households and between family members.[8] El Rashidi sought to explain the fact that the revolutionary 'eruption of this chorus of voices ... expressing a discontent about things ... we [Egyptians] had been living for decades' quickly and alarmingly receded back into silence. Writing into failure with her non-fiction work was the result of her realization that, as she states, 'the facts' did not provide 'the answers ... or I didn't know how to put them [the facts] together' to explain how the riot of voices reverted to silence. In order to not just write about the silence of the Egyptian people but actually give voice to this silence, El Rashidi needed to work in what she called 'a grey area where definite fact ends and possible fiction, or multiple truths, begin'.[9] For her, these grey areas could only be accessed in the form of the novel.

The multiple truths that El Rashidi associates with fiction are echoed in the statement from Mosireen, and by extension Hamilton. 858 distinguishes between the 'state's grip on history' (singular) and how their archive aids the creation of 'new *histories*' (plural). Recognizing the need to find ways to record or document multiple truths, histories, and voices has particular relevance for making sense of the overwhelmingly chaotic and untidy structures that define riots. In *Riotous Citizens*, Paul Bagguley and Yasmin Hussein caution against the way sociological and politically focused study of riots tend to impart a determined narrative sequence to what is instead an indeterminate series of events.[10] They argue that a significant

---

[6] Hamilton, 'Omar Robert Hamilton on *The City Always Wins*'.
[7] Hamilton, 'Omar Robert Hamilton on *The City Always Wins*'.
[8] In a book talk El Rashidi explains what she views as a culture of silence that pervades Egypt both in public and private. El Rashidi's point is that it is not just the state that encourages censorship but also the structure of domestic relations so that, for instance, children are encouraged by their parents to conform to certain behaviours. In light of this, El Rashidi concludes that Egyptian silence can only be understood in the 'everyday', within private relationships and intimate spaces, rather than just assumed to be a response to state-imposed repression. See Yasmine El Rashidi, 'Yasmine El Rashidi: *Chronicle of a Last Summer*', Politics and Prose Bookstore, 16 Aug 2016, https://www.youtube.com/watch?v=aCSz7Z9sk9g, 00:17:00-00:20:00. Accessed 9 August 2021.
[9] El Rashidi, 'Yasmine El Rashidi: *Chronicle of a Last Summer*'.
[10] Paul Bagguley and Yasmin Hussein, *Riotous Citizens: Ethnic Conflict in Multicultural Britain* (Abingdon: Routledge, 2016), p. 13.

pitfall in the research on riots is that it tends to 'reify' the crowd; that is, it treats the multifarious crowd as a stable object of inquiry. A consequence of this reification is that the crowd is depicted in an essentialist manner. Its members are assumed to embody the same characteristics that underpin the political grievances and shared motivations that propel their violent behaviour.[11]

This is no less the case when the research includes empirical data gathered from crowd participants. Despite being 'in a state of extreme narrative indeterminacy', both actors in the crowd and eye-witnesses tend to retrospectively 'naturalise events into logical and intelligible order', and 'analysts come along and generalize [those events] into patterns of disorder', lending them a sense of coherence, identifying patterns and stabilising, if only on paper, a highly volatile form. But this process fails to capture the changing nature of the crowd. While it is true that within the crowd there are degrees of coherence—rioting crowds usually form around common issues or grievances—these 'are multiple and mutate during [and after] the event'.[12] In other words, the crowd is not singular and does not possess a unified identity, nor are events reducible to a single narrative. Even though these may seem innocuous points to emphasise, they bear repeating because they help to explain why some of the same Egyptians who gathered in 2011 Tahrir Square demanding the end of the Mubarak leadership were also among those who mobilized in 2013 to undermine the elected Muslim Brotherhood, and who ultimately supported the rise of the military, which quickly transformed into a dictatorship not dissimilar to the Mubarak regime.

Unlike the social science research Bagguley and Hussein focus on, works of fiction are not compelled to make sense of events, to give riots a coherent shape, or to provide conclusions about a crowd's motivations by assuming it possesses a collective identity. Moreover, the imperative to make sense of public disorder and lend crowds coherence in this way might unwittingly, and ironically, reinforce the rhetoric and methods employed by those it seeks to critique: the agents of power, the state, or a dictator. The Libyan-British writer Hisham Matar, who reported on the Libyan uprising, identified the fault line between agents of power and writers of fiction as a battle over singular and multiple narratives: 'Dictatorship by its essence is interested in one narrative, an intolerant narrative, and writers are interested in a multiplicity of narratives and conflicting empathies and what the other is thinking and feeling. And that completely unsettles the dictatorial project.'[13] Authors like Hamilton and El Rashidi distort and unsettle both the reductive nature of riot analysis, as described by Bagguley and Hussein, and the mono-narratives of dictatorships by highlighting multiple voices within the crowd and employing fragmented episodic structures in their novels.

---

[11] Bagguley and Hussein, *Riotous Citizens*, p. 12.
[12] Bagguley and Hussein, *Riotous Citizens*, p. 13.
[13] Hisham Matar, 'Hisham Matar on the power of Libyan Fiction', *NPR*, 28 April 2011, https://www.npr.org/transcripts/135782783 Author interview. Accessed 10 August 2021.

Chronicle of a Last Summer

Chronicle of a Last Summer is the result of El Rashidi's recourse to the 'grey area' of fiction to explore Egypt's uprising and, more significantly, to probe the culture of silence that she perceives as a defining element of Egyptian society. For a novel that was, to adapt the author's words, written to explain how Egyptian silence was transformed into a riot of voices in Tahrir, it is remarkable that it is not set in that tumultuous period. The novel's episodic temporal structure side steps 2011 completely and instead focuses on three distinct periods of Cairo's history: the summers of 1984, 1998, and 2014. Although each section is introduced by specifying the urban space of Cairo, much of the story unfolds in the domestic sphere, within the nameless female narrator's once grand but now decaying family home. El Rashidi's novel, then, explores the significance of the 2011 uprising through both a wider temporal scope and in a narrower domestic context than is typically associated with an event like an uprising. In doing so it displaces the seminal significance that had been associated with both the city space of Cairo and the year 2011. This displacement is important because during the eighteen days of protests that forced Mubarak to resign, the uprising was considered by various political commentators and journalists as a watershed event, a moment heralding the possibility of democratic transformation for Egypt. However, the swift success of the counter-revolution a mere two years later and the rise of a military dictatorship suspended the fulfilment of the transformative promise of 2011. By decentring the uprising, El Rashidi's novel not only signals that the Egyptian revolution was not as formative as it once appeared, but also that 2011 needs to be historically and culturally contextualized to make sense of why Egyptians, boldly impassioned to raise their voices in 2011, apparently receded so quickly into silence.

There are two ways the novel contextualises the 2011 uprising. The first is that it makes ample reference to other riots and revolutions in twentieth-century Egypt, and the second is the attention to how political violence reverberates in an intimate setting. Regarding the former, references to political violence in Egypt's history appear early in the novel's 1984 instalment, when the narrator is still a child in primary school. In a conversation with her communist older cousin Dido, the narrator, having just been punished by her teacher for speaking Arabic, is informed by Dido that her English school will repress her Egyptian nationalism, and that the 1919 Wafd revolt was staged to liberate Egypt from British imperialism.[14] A subsequent conversation between Baba, the narrator's father, and Dido highlights that Egypt had 'two revolutions': the 1919 revolt, and the 1952 revolution when Nasser's Free Officers removed King Faruq and declared Egypt a republic. While Baba tells the narrator that these earlier revolutions 'came and went and all

---

[14] Yasmine El Rashidi, *Chronicle of a Last Summer: A Novel of Egypt* (New York, NY: Tim Duggan Books, 2016), pp. 24, 31.

their hopes were shattered', his words, from the vantage point of 1984, uncannily portend the outcome of 2011.[15]

These lost hopes are confirmed by Baba in 2014 when he states, while reflecting on 2011 with his adult daughter, that history operates in 'cycles' and that the Tahrir uprising repeats the violence of 1919 and 1952, so that 'we [Egyptians] were reliving the past, almost like déjà vu'.[16] The novel, however, does not rest on the cliched idea that history merely repeats itself, exploring instead how understandings of an uprising or riot are revised in social space. This is revealed during an extended discussion between the narrator and a shop owner, where they parse various meanings of the term revolution:

> 1919. The Wafd revolting against the British. It wasn't really a revolution, he says. It was a popular uprising. I raise my eyebrows. But it was a revolt, I say. But there wasn't a change of a system. The country didn't completely change. The British didn't leave until years later. So what is a revolution? I ask. *1952*. But it was also a coup? He shakes his head. It can *only* be called a revolution. Could it have been both? People didn't take to the streets, it was just one system of power ousting, usurping, another. That's a coup? Yes, he says, but it was against something that didn't represent the people, so it was a revolution for the people. Then 2011 was the same? I ask. That was a different kind of revolution, he says. But in the end all that happened is the army forced Mubarak to step down, as in '52? The people forced him out, he says. But the army wanted that?... He pauses. I offer: And 2013 was no different.... He tilts his head and thinks for a long time. He isn't sure. It's something he feels conflicted about.[17]

While there are other similar discussions in the text, this particular scene differs as it records in detail a debate about terms and the events they describe. In doing so, *Chronicle* challenges the idea of history being merely cyclical, exemplified in Baba's claim of 'déjà vu', and instead suggests that past and present overlap and reverberate within social settings and spaces, in the lived, quotidian discussions between, as in this instance, a store owner and his customer.

The significance of social space is further explored by El Rashidi when she reminds us that Egypt's past did not take place exclusively in city streets or public squares—the spaces that are widely associated with the 2011 uprising—but also unfolded inside ordinary Egyptian homes and shaped the lives of even those Egyptians who may never have stepped foot into Tahrir Square. This focus on the domestic space constitutes the second means by which El Rashidi challenges the central importance of 2011. The novel opens and largely remains within the

---

[15] El Rashidi, *Chronicle of a Last Summer*, p. 34.
[16] El Rashidi, *Chronicle of a Last Summer*, p. 146.
[17] El Rashidi, *Chronicle of a Last Summer*, pp. 157-158.

confines of a once grand Cairene family home. In the opening scene, the old two-storey house is described by the narrator as 'blistering', with damp towels placed on windowsills to block the entry of the summer heat.[18] The upper floor is inhabited by the narrator and her mother, while the lower floor—the domain of the narrator's grandmother until her death in 1983—has remained sealed and untouched for decades. According to the narrator, her Mama's reluctance to open up the space stems from a general Egyptian desire for stability: 'Ours wasn't a culture used to change. Permanency was valued. We lived in the same places we were born in. We married and moved around the corner.... The less change, the less movement, the better.'[19]

Mama's dislike of change is raised early in the text in relation to the impact of Nasser's 1952 revolution. In one of the rare moments when she verbally communicates her feelings, she tells the narrator about the friends she lost due to the changes ushered in by the new nationalist government:

> Mama pointed to the red villa and asked me if I saw it. *Yes.* The white villa on the corner. *Yes.* The villa across the street that's a school. *Yes.* Her friends used to live in those villas, then Nasser took them and they had to leave. Where did they go? They left the country. They packed their bags and left at dawn. They didn't even say goodbye. Was she sad? Very. Mama lost many friends because of Nasser.[20]

When the narrator asks, 'Why did Nasser make them leave?' her mother's response captures El Rashidi's attention to the domestic. Rather than responding by explaining the revolution's nationalist and socialist program to her daughter, Mama's brief response 'Because life is unfair' remains resolutely focused on the private impact of larger political events.[21] This stress on the way the revolution altered Mama's life privileges the intimate over the public, shifting the site of heightened political unrest away from its assumed topos of public space towards the domestic and private realms.

El Rashidi's interest in the impact of Egypt's history of civil unrest on the intimate lives of her characters is tied closely to her preoccupation with speech and silence. One of the key ways this is explored in the novel is through the narrator's film project, a university assessment. The film aims to investigate change, or a lack of change, in Egypt, and what that means for Egyptians. The narrator thinks she might begin the project by asking everyday Egyptians 'if they are angry.'[22] She knows, from experience, that this will be a challenge. While filming for a different assignment that involved asking 'passersby... what they would like to see improved

---

[18] El Rashidi, *Chronicle of a Last Summer*, p. 3.
[19] El Rashidi, *Chronicle of a Last Summer*, p. 129.
[20] El Rashidi, *Chronicle of a Last Summer*, p. 36.
[21] El Rashidi, *Chronicle of a Last Summer*, p. 36.
[22] El Rashidi, *Chronicle of a Last Summer*, p. 87.

in their city' she was met with subjects who not only 'walked away' but also looked at her 'skeptically ... asked who was really asking' and concluded that they 'couldn't answer such questions ... couldn't speak about the city ... couldn't speak about the country. Sorry. You know how it is. I don't want to get in trouble.'[23] When the narrator begins writing her film script, she reflects on the danger of not speaking in its opening lines, directing her communist and revolutionary cousin Dido to say: '*the only way our lives will change is if we demand it.... Leaving [Egypt] is the greatest evil. Then silence. Or maybe the other way around.*'[24] Two terms, '*languor*' and '*quotidian*', organize her ideas for the film.[25] For the narrator, these terms are linked by what she perceives as the sluggish everydayness that mirrors and accompanies the people's silence. It is this sluggishness that the narrator hopes to both capture and prise open in her film, and for this reason insists she must 'speak to people on the street about their desires and also capture this internal life, the intimate moments at home, the mundane. How did we land in our lives? The silence and the evenings in front of the TV are as comforting as they are fraught.'[26]

There are, however, explicit registrations of sound and voice in *Chronicle* that, read retrospectively, are illustrative of the persistent murmurs of unrest that foreshadowed the 2011 Egyptian Revolution. In the book's 1998 instalment, the narrator writes about Dido's activist work, focusing on his efforts to record 'oral histories of torture, abuse, arrests at the hands of state agents'.[27] Dido explains that he must create a language to document the 'emotions ... the trauma' of the victims, because they 'have no terms or designations' to describe their experiences. The victims not only have no 'voice' but also no 'real sense of who they are', approximating Judith Butler's argument that to be injured by speech, or a lack of it, 'is to suffer a loss ... [to] not know where [or who] you are'.[28] Dido's acts of recording and building a language of torture are prompted by a need to give order to the suffering of Egyptians, because while, as he insists, 'the streets are simmering, filled with people's outrage' their 'emotions are misplaced, making [them] silent'.[29]

Dido's resistance on an intimate or personal level is mirrored in the broader sound-based defiance that issues from religious quarters. The adhan, the Muslim call to prayer, interrupts the narrator and her mother's evening as it 'sounds from ... across the river and echoes into the house'.[30] This is not the first time that the adhan is mentioned in the text: in the 1984 instalment, the narrator notes how the call to evening prayer marks a shift in Saturday summer activities, where men leave

---

[23] El Rashidi, *Chronicle of a Last Summer*, p. 88.
[24] El Rashidi, *Chronicle of a Last Summer*, p. 111.
[25] El Rashidi, *Chronicle of a Last Summer*, p. 112.
[26] El Rashidi, *Chronicle of a Last Summer*, pp. 113-114.
[27] El Rashidi, *Chronicle of a Last Summer*, p. 80.
[28] El Rashidi, *Chronicle of a Last Summer*, p. 80; Judith Butler, *Excitable Speech: The Politics of the Performative* (New York, NY: Routledge, 1997), p. 4.
[29] El Rashidi, *Chronicle of a Last Summer*, p. 80.
[30] El Rashidi, *Chronicle of a Last Summer*, p. 105.

home first to attend mosque, with their families soon following.[31] By contrast, in the 1998 reference to the adhan, the narrator's focus on its intrusion into the house is infused with a sense of foreboding: 'The president had issued a decree banning mosque speakers above a certain decibel, but they had become louder again.... It's the most pertinent daily reminder of the increasing antagonism between the Brotherhood and the state.'[32] The trace of that antagonism between state and religion, which became the major battleline in post-Mubarak Egypt, is here reflected in the Muslim Brotherhood's weaponization of the adhan, a sound that is difficult to police given its sacred status.

This transformation of the adhan from a way to mark the changing rhythm of a summer's day to a deliberate act of political defiance, is not unlike the change in Mama's character that unfolds over the course of the novel. *Chronicle* opens by emphasizing Mama's inaudibility, as an 'old metal fan ... whirred, drowning out Mama's' voice.[33] The first two instalments of the novel also include instances of Mama gesturing with her eyes, using her mannerisms and hands as modes of communication. The narrator depicts her mother as a woman of few words, one who may have political views, but who does not show a willingness to participate in political activity. When readers meet Mama again in 2014, the 2011 uprising has intervened making her much more vocal and less reserved. As the narrator notes, 'Although I still see ... [Mama's] weariness, I know something has shifted. She laughs more.'[34] Laughter is not the only noise Mama makes; she has 'become involved with a community association, writes letters and petitions, joins marches, spends what little free time she has walking around the city talking pictures of things that need to change.'[35] During the marches against newly elected President Morsi and his controversial constitution, Mama joins the crowds on the streets while Baba, once the more likely of the two to participate in public action, remains at home.[36] By the end of the novel Mama has found her voice and speaks out about social and ecological justice in a way that provides a stark contrast to her silence and inertia prior to the revolution.

Mama's turn towards politics is evident not only in her activism but also in relation to her family home. One day in 2014 Mama tells her daughter that she views the house as 'the weight of a physical burden anchoring her down' and that through this realization she 'feel[s] reborn.'[37] Soon after, Mama decides to sell the only home she had ever inhabited. As she and her daughter pack the house, Mama plans a farewell party 'opening the house to all those who haven't been here in

---

[31] El Rashidi, *Chronicle of a Last Summer*, p. 48.
[32] El Rashidi, *Chronicle of a Last Summer*, p. 105.
[33] El Rashidi, *Chronicle of a Last Summer*, p. 3.
[34] El Rashidi, *Chronicle of a Last Summer*, p. 175.
[35] El Rashidi, *Chronicle of a Last Summer*, p. 174.
[36] El Rashidi, *Chronicle of a Last Summer*, p. 151.
[37] El Rashidi, *Chronicle of a Last Summer*, p. 179.

years' to recreate the social gatherings of the past. While these are seemingly contradictory acts—Mama plans to release herself from the past by selling her house but also wants to recreate that past with celebratory noise—they nevertheless highlight the impact of social change and unrest on the private lives of Egyptians. By ending here, inside Mama's home and her personal thoughts, *Chronicle of a Last Summer* orients the reader's attention towards the intimate and the private, affording insights into how riots and uprisings alter people's lives in ways that are better suited to being narrated in fiction—that 'grey area where definite fact ends and ... multiple truths begin' according to El Rashidi—as opposed to the more rigid forms that journalism demands.

The City Always Wins

Much like El Rashidi's novel, Robert Omar Hamilton's *The City Always Wins* utilizes sound to explore the aftermath of Egypt's Tahrir uprising. While not focused on the home space to the same degree as El Rashidi, Hamilton nevertheless examines the relationship between publicly staged riots and their impact on the private or personal lives of individuals and families. Opening in late 2011, Hamilton's narrative not only mirrors El Rashidi's avoidance of the eighteen days in January and February 2011, it also oscillates between public environments—the city streets and public squares where riots subsequent to 2011 took place—and private spaces, including the headquarters of a revolutionary movement; the homes of Khalil and Mariam, the novel's two central characters; and Khalil's recording studio. The role of noise and sound in the novel's more private settings is crucial to apprehending the broader impact of the riot's unwieldy form, and especially the way that it seeps into and shapes the lives of its two main characters.

One important way that sound is featured in *The City* is in its sustained engagement with multiple media forms. The narrative is centred around the activities of a newly founded collective, ChaosCairo, a team of revolutionaries who come together following the 2011 uprising to organize resistance and disseminate information. Information is packaged in podcasts, assembled video montage, text messages, and photographs, and disseminated via multiple social media platforms. This preoccupation with media in the novel, and in particular digital media, mirrors the early reception of Egypt's revolution, with the press dubbing it the 'Facebook revolution'. The use of new media technologies by Egyptian youth has also been interpreted as a pathway to modernity and a means by which Egyptians can become more politically engaged.[38] Such optimism is reflected in

---

[38] Xiaolin Zhuo, Barry Wellman, and Justine Yu, 'Egypt: The First Internet Revolt?', *Peace Magazine* 27 3.July–Sept. 2011, pp. 6–10. http://peacemagazine.org/archive/v27n3p06.htm. Accessed 26 October 2021.

the novel when Khalil, ChaosCairo's sound engineer, insists that the revolution is unstoppable: 'Chaos will carry the news.... They can't keep up with us. An army of Samsungs, Twitterers, HTCs, emails, Facebook events, private groups, iPhones, phone calls, text messages.... An army of infinite mobility—impossible to outmanoeuvre.'[39]

Amidst its attention to the role of media devices and platforms in facilitating the uprising, the novel also explores, through its characters, the dilemma of narrating the wider story of the events of 2011. Hafez, a filmmaker and member of Chaos, announces to the team that the story of the eighteen days in Tahrir can only be told through cinema:

> 'I got it!' he says. 'It's a *movie!*... It's the only way to do it. You can't write a thesis about it or a poem or a song or a book. It's too big. It's too cinematic ... it's gotta be a movie. The whole country pours out, takes the streets, beats the pigs, burns down their police stations. It's not about one hero ... it's just too big.... Think of all the stories. The guy's running into burning party headquarters ... people breaking out of prison ... burning down police station[s].... Shit, there's just so many scenes!'[40]

Although Hafez tragically dies before he can complete this cinematic work, his realization that no single voice or hero can tell the story of the uprising, and that many scenes are needed to capture the enormity of the narrative, is manifested in the very structure of *The City*.

While Khalil and Mariam, who voice increasingly conflicting views about what direction the revolutionaries should take, provide the two main perspectives that the omniscient narrator focuses on, the voices of a range of marginal characters are inserted as separate chapters or interludes throughout the novel. These characters operate outside of the ChaosCairo collective, and while not necessarily part of any organised revolutionary movement, they are all active in the resistance. The most significant of these alternative voices comes from Abu Bassem, the father of the martyr Bassem who was among those killed in Tahrir square. During the first of the three Abu Bassem interludes, readers learn that he is a supporter of the Muslim Brotherhood and is seeking justice for his son's death.[41] By our second encounter with Abu Bassem, his quest for justice has progressed. He has discovered the name of the police officer who killed his son and the station where the officer works.[42] Abu Bassem decides not to seek revenge immediately after he is advised by the Brotherhood leadership to be patient: 'We will avenge your son....

---

[39] Omar Robert Hamilton, *The City Always Wins: A Novel* (New York, NY: Faber and Faber, 2017), p. 20.
[40] Hamilton, *The City Always Wins*, pp. 81–2.
[41] Hamilton, *The City Always Wins*, pp. 28–9.
[42] Hamilton, *The City Always Wins*, p. 101.

But we must play the game, we must take power ... [through an] orderly path to the elections.... If a police station were to burn to the ground tonight, could there possibly be elections tomorrow? Of course not. So we must be patient.'[43] Upon receiving this message, Abu Bassem 'hears their logic' and waits.[44] In the end, however, Abu Bassem's patience is futile—the Brotherhood win the elections only to be removed from office during the counter-revolution. Having lost both his son and the Brotherhood, the final instalment of his story sees Abu Bassem sitting in a cybercafé, headphones over his ears, watching YouTube footage of his son, wondering what will happen if the footage he repeatedly watches 'breaks or is lost or deleted.... What if today is the day I find I have nothing left?'[45]

Abu Bassem's story is counterposed with that of another father, Abu Ramadan, whose son, Ramadan, was arrested on his way to work. Unlike Abu Bassem who is linked to the Brotherhood, neither Abu Ramadan nor his son are described as having a particular political affiliation, with Ramadan's arrest, according to his father, seemingly random.[46] During this tragic instalment, Abu Ramadan is at the morgue to identify his son's body, and speaks directly to him, asking him what it felt like to be gassed by the police.[47] There is also the story of Umm Ayman, the matriarch of a Coptic family, whose son 'went out like a man to stand up for his people and his church and his family, and he marched'.[48] Having left home that day without eating, Umm Ayman's son dies, she imagines, hungry. Her remedy for this and for her own grief is to continue to prepare his favourite meals and save him a portion.[49] There are several stories beyond these outlined but the cumulative effect of including these diverse perspectives ensures that *The City* is not just the story of one segment of Egypt's resistance as represented by ChaosCairo. The episodic structure of the novel and Hafez's words about the revolution's cinematic multiplicity of stories, align with Shaffer's observations about hi-fi frequencies and Bagguley and Hussein's views about the rioting crowd. Regarding the former, *The City* brings together multiple characters in the hi-fi dissonant chorus of Egypt's revolution, and illustrates that there is no one motivation or voice that can accurately capture the totality of the uprising.

This multiplicity of voices and perspectives is further emphasized through Khalil's activist work as ChaosCairo's sound and media engineer. In a pivotal scene, Khalil uses his skills to ensure that the news of Bassem's brutal murder is widely known. Sitting in his studio, he cuts a week's worth of footage into a montage that forms a sound-narrative of Bassem's death:

---

[43] Hamilton, *The City Always Wins*, p. 102.
[44] Hamilton, *The City Always Wins*, p. 102.
[45] Hamilton, *The City Always Wins*, p. 298.
[46] Hamilton, *The City Always Wins*, p. 240.
[47] Hamilton, *The City Always Wins*, p. 241.
[48] Hamilton, *The City Always Wins*, p. 38.
[49] Hamilton, *The City Always Wins*, p. 37.

Khalil hit pause, holding the moment, the intimacy of his sound studio with its low roll of acoustic cotton hanging down from the ceiling.... He takes a breath before placing the headphones over his ears. The conductor before his orchestra. A moment and he will begin flicking through the sound files one by one; scanning for highlights and grabbing them with loose, brutish cuts to drop them into his five categories: *essential, secondary, ambient, cutaway, effect.* Five colors for five pillars with which to build the week's aural architecture. Five colors with which to make the listener see the pain of Abu Bassem, to join his vigil. He presses play on the video once more. We know his name now. We know his name is Bassem.[50]

These attempts by Khalil to control sound, to shape a message through a curated method of 'aural architecture' in the intimacy of his studio, stands in stark contrast to the rowdy and violent riot scenes that pepper the narrative. During scenes of public violence, the narrator describes the crowds as an 'impenetrable herd' of wolves or buffalo that disperse when they hear a 'crackle of tasers snap [...] through the air'.[51] The crowd is dense and loosely organized, where a 'hundred people make up a front line ... of stone throwers and shit talkers hurling everything they have at the cops'.[52] Behind the front line are 'the fire starters and gas catchers hurling the smoking canisters back where they came from', and behind them 'are the spectators, the chanters, the drummers, the doctors, quarriers and hawkers'.[53] Khalil's incredible and vivid enumeration of the rioters highlights the degree to which the crowd is never simply a homogeneous, angry, undifferentiated mass; rather it is constituted by a range of actors, each armed to undertake different forms of resistance and violence. It is in these sites of chaos that Khalil records hours of ambient data to later give 'shape and rhythm [to] the battle', and to ensure that the deaths of the many martyrs like Bassem are neither unknown nor forgotten.[54]

Khalil's reliance on sound to narrate the street battles is counterbalanced by Miriam's investment in listening. One of the earliest scenes that details her internal thoughts takes place following several days of violent confrontation between rioters and state forces in November 2011. Standing in a morgue surrounded by an overwhelming number of dead bodies, Miriam reflects on the lost opportunity presented by the initial success of the uprising:

> We could have done more.... *We should have made the people listen sooner.* We were too slow and now they've made their deal with the Brotherhood and all we have are rocks.... The elections are upon us.... They think elections can end a revolution?.... Khalil is thinking about voting. How can he even think about

---

[50] Hamilton, *The City Always Wins*, p. 30
[51] Hamilton, *The City Always Wins*, p. 14.
[52] Hamilton, *The City Always Wins*, p. 41.
[53] Hamilton, *The City Always Wins*, p. 41.
[54] Hamilton, *The City Always Wins*, p. 41.

it? What is he thinking? What are we supposed to do—pack up the morgue and quietly file into the polling station?... That's what this death is for? To be forgotten with a ballot?[55]

For Mariam, curating sound files is ineffective unless people listen, and the ChaosCairo team has failed in her estimation because they were unable to make the masses listen to their messages. What is significant about this attention to listening is that it is raised in the shadow of the impending elections. In Arabic, the word for vote is *sawt*, literally 'voice'. To vote in Arabic is to give yourself a voice in political decisions. At first glance, it seems that Miriam's statement positions listening as the opposite of voice, and that she negates the power of *sawt* in favour of the potential power of listening, *sama3*. In Arabic these terms are not always constant in their meaning: there is an instance in the Arab world, in the Sufi tradition, where the person reciting a praise poem is referred to not as a moughani—a singer—but rather as a listener.[56]

In light of this, perhaps the novel, if not Mariam herself, is suggesting that it is not only 'the people' who needed to listen intently, but also those who had the opportunity to have their voices heard, that is those who emerged as leaders of the resistance and the uprising. Rather than focusing on broadcasting information, as did Khalil and the ChaosCairo crew, maybe what is needed is for members of movements like ChaosCairo to become listeners themselves, receivers of information to become more attuned with what was unfolding around them. This observation chimes with Khalil's realisation that, as his dead friend Hafez suggested, the uprising could only ever be conveyed in cinematic form: 'You're right, Hafez, it was a film, a cinematic dream where the good guys won ... with no room for ... doubt; *a narrative made by the bodies within it*'.[57] What Khalil conveys here is how hermetically sealed their film would have been, producing a one-sided visual and sonic spectacle that projects the 'bodies within it' onto the screen, yet fails to hear the voices and bodies operating beyond that inner circle. While the politics that Khalil and Miriam pursued involved delivering sound bites, bringing people to listen, making them aware of the names of the dead like Bassem, the novel hails the creators of sound, to hear and to listen to the varied of voices that constituted this riotous event in Egypt's history.

Both Hamilton's and El Rashidi's novels attempt to avoid the dangers of hermetically sealed narratives of Egypt's revolution. By turning to fiction, in particular the novel, both authors bypass the risk of reifying the crowd, which Bagguley and Hussein observe is a key flaw in social scientific methods used to study riots. The

---

[55] Hamilton, *The City Always Wins*, p. 60; emphasis added.
[56] Deborah Kapchan, *Theorizing Sound Writing* (Middletown, CT: Wesleyan University Press, 2017); and *Poetic Justice: An Anthology of Moroccan Contemporary Poetry* (Austin, TX: University of Texas Press, 2019).
[57] Hamilton, *The City Always Wins*, p. 276; emphasis added.

authors do this by skilfully lending nuance to the crowd, clearing narrative space to delve into the lives of individual rioters, showing their differing political affiliations, the hardships they face and the tragic impact of Egypt's history of uprisings on their families. While *The City* achieves this through the incorporation of multiple characters, *Chronicle*'s focus on the domestic sphere of the narrator highlights the transformative effects of the city's violence on the intimate lives of its citizens. The writers's shift to the novel, in an age of digital media density, to tell the story of the Egyptian uprising is central to their narration of the multiplicity and complexity of Egypt's riots and the crowds that massed in Cairo's streets. Adapting Schafer's work on sound, the novel approximates a hi-fi frequency, amplifying certain voices, sounds, and, in the space of a novel, stories, setting these sounds and stories against the noisy lo-fi soundscapes generated in digital media archives that drown out individual voices and narratives.

Selected Bibliography

Abaza, Mona. 'Mourning, Narratives and Interactions with the Martyrs through Cairo's Graffiti', *E-International Relations*, Oct 2013, https://www.e-ir.info/2013/10/07/mourning-narratives-and-interactions-with-the-martyrs-through-cairos-graffiti/

Achaari, Mohamed. 'Creativity as a Political Choice'. *Journal of North African Studies. Special Guest edited issue by Karima Laachir on 'The Aesthetics and Politics of Contemporary Cultural Production in Morocco'* 21.1 (2016): 12–21.

Ackbar, Abbas. *Hong Kong: Culture and the Politics of Disappearance* (Hong Kong: Hong Kong University Press, 1997), pp. 1–15.

Adorno, Theodor W. *Minima Moralia. Reflections on a Damaged Life* (London: Verso, 2005).

Ahmad, Aijaz. *Lineages of the Present: Ideology and Politics in Contemporary South Asia* (London: Verso, 2002).

Ahmed, A. Kayum. '#RhodesMustFall: How a Decolonial Student Movement in the Global South Inspired Epistemic Disobedience at the University of Oxford', *African Studies Review* 63, no. 2 (2020): 281–303.

Amin, Shahid. *Event, Metaphor, Memory: Chauri Chaura 1922–1992* (Delhi: Oxford University Press, 1996).

Anderson, Perry. *Lineages of the Absolutist State* (London: Verso, 1974).

Arendt, Hannah. *The Origins of Totalitarianism* (Milton Keynes: Penguin Classics, 2017).

Assmann, Aleida. *Cultural Memory and Western Civilization: Functions, Media, Archives* (New York, NY: Cambridge University Press, 2011).

Awadalla, Maggie, and Paul March-Russell (eds), *The Postcolonial Short Story: Contemporary Essays* (London: Palgrave, 2012).

Ayoub, Joey. 'Lebanon: A Revolution Against Sectarianism', *CrimethInc*, 13 November 2019, https://crimethinc.com/2019/11/13/lebanon-a-revolution-against-sectarianism-chronicling-the-first-month-of-the-uprising.

Azhari, Timour. 'Why Thousands Continue to Protest in Lebanon's Tripoli', *Al Jazeera*, 3 November 2019, https://www.aljazeera.com/news/2019/11/3/why-thousands-continue-to-protest-in-lebanons-tripoli.

Badiou, Alain. *The Rebirth of History: Times of Riots and Uprisings* (London: Verso, 2012).

Baer, Marc. *Theatre and Disorder in Georgian England* (Oxford: Clarendon Press, 1992).

Bagguley, Paul, and Yasmin Hussein, *Riotous Citizens: Ethnic Conflict in Multicultural Britain* (Abingdon: Routledge, 2016).

Bajec, Alessandra. 'Lebanon's Revolution is a Reawakening for Tripoli Women', TRT World, 2 December 2019, https://www.trtworld.com/magazine/lebanon-s-revolution-is-a-reawakening-for-tripoli-women-31852.

Baker, Keith Michael, and Dan Edelstein (eds), *Scripting Revolution: A Historical Approach to the Comparative Study of Revolutions* (Stanford, CA: Stanford University Press, 2015).

Baker, Phillip (ed.), *The Levellers: The Putney Debates* (London: Verso, 2007).

Bakhtin, Mikhail M. 'Discourse in the Novel', in Michael Holquist (ed.), *The Dialogic Imagination: Four Essays,* trans. Caryl Emerson and Michael Holquist (Austin, TX and London: University of Texas Press, 1981), pp. 259–422.

Baraka, Amiri. 'Black People', in William J. Harris (ed.), *The LeRoi James/Amiri Baraka Reader* (New York, NY: Thunder's Mouth Press, 1991).
Bauhinia Project (eds), *Hong Kong Without Us: A People's Poetry* (Athens, GA: University of Georgia Press, 2021).
Beaumont, Matthew. 'Cacotopianism, the Paris Commune, and England's Anti-Communist Imaginary, 1870–1900', *ELH* 73.2 (Summer, 2006): 465–487.
Beaumont, Matthew. '"A Little Political World of My Own": The New Woman, the New Life, and "New Amazonia"', *Victorian Literature and Culture*, 35.1 (2007): 215–232.
Benjamin, Walter. *Illuminations*, translated by Harry Zohn (New York, NY: Schocken Books, 2007).
Berman, Jessica. *Modernist Commitments* (New York, NY: Columbia University Press, 2011).
Berry, Michael. *A History of Pain: Trauma in Modern Chinese Literature and Film* (New York, NY: Columbia University Press, 2008).
Bevir, Mark. *Modernism and the Social Sciences* (Cambridge: Cambridge University Press, 2017).
Bohstedt, John. *The Politics of Provisions: Food Riots, Moral Economy, and Market Transition in England, c. 1550–1850* (London: Routledge, 2010).
Booker, M. Keith. *Ulysses, Capitalism, and Colonialism: Reading Joyce After the Cold War* (Westport, CT: Greenwood Press, 2000).
Bosman, Anston. 'Shakespeare and Globalization', in M. De Grazia and S. Wells (eds), *The New Cambridge Companion to Shakespeare* (Cambridge: Cambridge University Press, 2010), pp. 285–302.
Bourdieu, Pierre. *The Logic of Practice* (Stanford, CA: Stanford University Press, 1990).
Boyle, Michael Shayne. 'Theatrical Proletarians', in Mark Steven (ed.), *Understanding Marx, Understanding Modernism* (London: Bloomsbury, 2020).
Brenner, Robert. *Merchants and Revolution: Commercial Change, Political Conflict, and London's Overseas Traders, 1550–1653* (London: Verso, 2003).
Breton, Rob. 'The Sentimental Socialism of Margaret Harkness', *English Language Notes*, 48.1 (Spring/Summer, 2010), pp. 27–39.
Bronstein, Michaela. *Out of Context: The Uses of Modernist Fiction* (Oxford: Oxford University Press, 2018).
Brooks, Gwendolyn *Riot* (Detroit, MI: Broadside Press, 1969).
Bourke, Richard and Quentin Skinner (eds). *Popular Sovereignty in Historical Perspective* (Cambridge: Cambridge University Press, 2016).
Brown, Nicholas. *Utopian Generations: The Political Horizon of Twentieth-Century Literature* (Princeton, NJ: Princeton University Press, 2005).
Burke, Edmund. *Reflections on the Revolution in France* (London: Penguin, 2004).
Burke, Mary. 'The Riot of Spring: Synge's "Failed Realism" and the Peasant Drama', in Nicholas Grene (ed.), *The Oxford Handbook of Modern Irish Theatre* (Oxford: Oxford University Press, 2016), pp. 87–102.
Butler, Judith. *Excitable Speech: The Politics of the Performative* (New York, NY: Routledge, 1997).
Butler, Judith, Zeynep Gambetti, and Leticia Sabsay (eds). *Vulnerability in Resistance*, (Durham, NC: Duke University Press, 2016).
Cadzow, Allison, and Mary Anne Jebb. *Our Mob Served: Aboriginal and Torres Strait Islander Histories of War and Defending Australia* (Canberra: Aboriginal Studies Press, 2019).

Canetti, Elias. *Crowds and Power*, translated by Carol Stewart (London: Penguin, 1992)
Cenedese, Marta-Laura. '(Instrumental) Narratives of Postcolonial Rememory: Intersectionality and Multidirectional Memory', *Storyworlds* 10.1 (2018): 95–116.
Chalcraft, John. *Popular Politics in the Making of the Modern Middle East* (Cambridge: Cambridge University Press, 2016).
Chan, Cora, and Fiona de Londras (eds). *China's National Security: Endangering Hong Kong's Rule of Law?* (Oxford and New York, NY: Hart Publishing, 2020).
Chase, Malcolm. *1820: Disorder and Stability in the United Kingdom* (Manchester: Manchester University Press, 2013).
Chu, Yiu-Wai. *Lost in Transition: Hong Kong Culture in the Age of China* (Albany, NY: SUNY Press, 2013).
Clarke, Anna. *Scandal: The Sexual Politics of the British Constitution* (Princeton, NJ: Princeton University Press, 2004).
Cleary, Joe. *Outrageous Fortune: Capital and Culture in Modern Ireland* (Dublin: Field Day Publications, 2007).
Clover, Joshua. *Riot. Strike. Riot: The New Era of Uprisings* (London: Verso, 2016).
Clover, Joshua and Chris Nealon. 'The Other Minimal Demand', in Ruth Jennison and Julian Murphet (eds), *Communism and Poetry: Writing against Capital* (London: Palgrave Macmillan, 2019).
Clover, Joshua, Juliana Spahr, and Jasper Bernes, 'Elegy, or the poetics of surplus', *Jacket2*, February 2014, https://jacket2.org/commentary/elegy-or-poetics-surplus
Cole, Sarah. *At the Violet Hour: Modernism and Violence in England and Ireland* (Oxford: Oxford University Press, 2012).
Cooper, Wayne F. *Claude McKay, Rebel Sojourner in the Harlem Renaissance* (Baton Rouge, LA: Louisiana State University Press, 1987).
Cox, Glyn Salton. 'Uncivil Society', *Key Words: A Journal of Cultural Materialism* 16 (2018): 23-40, pp. 33–34.
Das, Veena. 'The Anthropology of Pain', in *Critical Events: An Anthropological Perspective on Contemporary India* (Oxford: Oxford University Press, 1995), pp. 175–196.
Davidoff, Leonora and Catherine Hall, *Family Fortunes: Men and Women of the English Middle Class, 1780–1850* (Chicago, IL and London: University of Chicago Press, 1987).
Dawson, Graham. 'Trauma, Place and the Politics of Memory: Bloody Sunday, Derry, 1972-2004', *History Workshop Journal* 59 (2005): 151–178.
Dean, Joan Fitzpatrick. *Riot and Great Anger: Stage Censorship in Twentieth Century Ireland* (Madison, WI: University of Wisconsin Press, 2004).
Debord, Guy. 'The Decline and Fall of the Spectacle-Commodity Economy', trans. Donald Nicholson Smith, *Internationale Situationniste 10* (March 1966), archived on *Situationist International Online*, https://www.cddc.vt.edu/sionline/si/decline.html
Defoe, Daniel. *A Hymn to the Mob* (London: S. Popping et al., 1715).
Deleuze, Gilles. 'Postscript on the Societies of Control.' *October* 59 (1992): 3–7.
Denney, Peter, Bruce Buchan, David Ellison, and Karen Crawley (eds). *Sound, Space, and Civility in the British World, 1700–1850* (Abingdon: Routledge, 2019).
Derrida, Jacques, and Derek Attridge. *Acts of Literature* (New York, NY: Routledge, 1992).
Dimock, Wai Chee. 'A Theory of Resonance', *PMLA* 112. 5 (October 1997): 1060–1071.
Duffy, Enda. *The Subaltern Ulysses* (Minneapolis: University of Minnesota Press, 1994).
Duffy, Enda. 'Disappearing Dublin: *Ulysses*, Postcoloniality, and the Politics of Space', in Derek Attridge and Marjorie Howes (eds), *Semicolonial Joyce* (Cambridge: Cambridge University Press, 2000), pp. 37–57.

Elam, J. Daniel. 'Commonplace Anticolonialism: Bhagat Singh's Jail Notebook and the Politics of Reading', *South Asia: The Journal of South Asian Studies* 39.3 (2016): 592–607.

Elam, J. Daniel. *World Literature for the Wretched of the Earth* (Fordham: Fordham University Press, 2020).

Elinson, Alexander. 'Opening the Circle: Storyteller and Audience in Moroccan Prison Literature'. *Middle Eastern Literatures* 12.3 (2009): 289–303.

Erll, Astrid, and Ann Rigney. 'Literature and the Production of Cultural Memory: Introduction'. *European Journal of English Studies* 10.2 (2006): 111–115.

Eshel, Amir. *Futurity: Contemporary Literature and the Quest for the Past* (Chicago, IL: Chicago University Press, 2013).

Ewick, Patricia, and Susan S. Silbey. 'Conformity, Contestation, and Resistance: An Account of Legal Consciousness', *New England Law Review* 26 (1992): 731–749.

Eyerman, Ron. 'The Past in the Present: Culture and the Transmission of Memory', *Acta Sociologica* 47.2 (2004): 159–169.

Fisher, Tony. *Theatre and Governance in Britain, 1500–1900: Democracy, Disorder and the State* (Cambridge: Cambridge University Press, 2017).

Flately, Jonathan. 'How a Revolutionary Counter-Mood is Made', *New Literary History* 43.3 (Summer 2012): 503–525.

Foley, Barbara. *Spectres of 1919: Class and Nation in the Making of the New Negro* (Chicago, IL: University of Illinois Press, 2003).

Gamedze, Thulile. 'Destruction Styles: Black Aesthetics of Rupture and Capture', *Radical Philosophy* 2.8 (2020): 55–65.

Gatrell, Vic. *The Hanging Tree: Execution and the English People* (Oxford: Oxford University Press, 1994).

Ginibi, Ruby Langford. *All My Mob* (St Lucia: University of Queensland Press, 2007).

Gordon, Avery. *Ghostly Matters: Haunting and the Sociological Imagination* (Minneapolis: University of Minnesota Press, 2008).

Hadley, Elaine. 'The Old Price Wars: Melodramatizing the Public Sphere in Early Nineteenth-Century England', *PMLA* 107 (1992): 524–537.

Hafez, Sabry. *The Quest for Identities: The Development of the Modern Arabic Short Story* (London: Safi, 2008)

Hammoudi, Abdallah. *Master and Disciple: The Cultural Foundations of Moroccan Authoritarianism* (Chicago, IL: Chicago University Press, 1997).

Harris, Cheryl I. 'Whiteness as Property', *Harvard Law Review* 106.8 (1993): 1701–1791.

Hartman, Saidiya. *Scenes of Subjection: Terror, Slavery, and Self-Making in Nineteenth-Century America* (Oxford: Oxford University Press, 1997).

Hartman, Saidiya. 'The Time of Slavery', *South Atlantic Quarterly* 101.4 (2002): 757–777.

Hartman, Saidiya. *Wayward Lives, Beautiful Experiments: Intimate Histories of Social Upheaval* (London: Serpent's Tail, 2019).

Harvey, David. *Rebel Cities: From the Right to the City to the Urban Revolution* (London: Verso, 2013).

Havel, Václav. *The Power of the Powerless* (Vintage Classics, 2018).

Hay, Douglas et al. (eds). *Albion's Fatal Tree: Crime and Society in Eighteenth-Century England* (London: Pantheon, 1976).

Haywood, Ian. 'Pandemonium: Radical Soundscapes and Satirical Prints in the Romantic Period', *Republic of Letters* 5.2 (2017): 1–26.

Holland, Oscar. 'From the Place Vendome to Trafalgar Square', *Key Words: A Journal of Cultural Materialism* 14 (2016): 98.

Holmes, Rachel. *Eleanor Marx* (London: Bloomsbury, 2014), p. 299.

Hourani, Albert. *Arabic Thought in the Liberal Age 1798–1939* (Cambridge: Cambridge University Press, 1983).
Hunt, Sarah Beth. *Hindi Dalit Literature and the Politics of Representation* (London: Taylor & Francis Group, 2014).
Hussain, Intizar. 'An Unwritten Epic', in Mushirul Hasan (ed.), *Inventing Boundaries: Gender, Politics and the Partition of India* (Oxford: Oxford University Press, 2000), 300–317.
Jameson, Fredric. 'Third-World Literature in the Era of Multinational Capitalism', *Social Text* 15 (1986): 65–88.
Janowitz, Anne. *Lyric and Labour in the Romantic Tradition* (Cambridge: Cambridge University Press, 1998), pp. 228–229.
Jones, Carol A. G. *Lost in China?: Law, Culture and Identity in Post-1997 Hong Kong* (Cambridge: Cambridge University Press, 2015).
Kapchan, Deborah. *Theorizing Sound Writing* (Middletown, CT: Wesleyan University Press, 2017)
Kornbluh, Anna. *The Order of Forms. Realism, Formalism, and Social Space* (Chicago, IL: The University of Chicago Press, 2019).
Koven, Seth. *Slumming. Sexual and Social Politics in Victorian London* (Princeton, NJ: Princeton University Press, 2004).
Krugler, David. *1919, The Year of Racial Violence: How African Americans Fought Back* (Cambridge: Cambridge University Press, 2015).
Laqueur, Thomas. 'The Queen Caroline Affair: Politics as Art in the Reign of George IV', *Journal of Modern History* (1982): 417–466.
Le Bon, Gustave. *The Crowd: A Study of the Popular Mind* (Dover: Dover Press, 1902).
Lefèvre, Raphaël. *Jihad in the City: Militant Islam and Contentious Politics in Tripoli* (Oxford: Oxford University Press, 2021).
Leung, Janny. 'Publicity Stunts, Power Play, and Information Warfare in Mediatised Public Confessions', *Law and Humanities* 11.1 (2017): 82–101.
Machilchrist, Felicitas, and Rosalie Metro (eds). *Trickbox of Memory: Essays on Power and Disorderly Pasts* (Brooklyn: Punctum Books, 2020).
Marx, Karl. *Capital: A Critique of Political Economy*, Vol. 1, trans. Ben Fowkes (London: Penguin, 1992).
Mbembe, Achille. *Necropolitics*, trans. Steven Corcoran (Durham, NC: Duke University Press, 2019).
Mbembe, Achille and Sarah Nuttall (eds). *Johannesburg: The Elusive Metropolis* (Durham, NC: Duke University Press, 2008)
Memon, Muhammad Umar. 'Partition Literature: A Study of Intiẓār Ḥusain', *Modern Asian Studies* 14.3 (1980): 377–410.
Menon, Ritu and Kamla Bhasin. *Borders and Boundaries: Women in India's Partition* (New Brunswick, NJ: Rutgers University Press, 1998).
Migdal, Joel S. 'Mental Maps and Virtual Checkpoints', in Joel S. Migdal (ed.), *Boundaries and Belonging: States and Societies in the Struggle to Shape Identities and Local Practices* (Cambridge: Cambridge University Press, 2004), pp. 3–26.
Mishra, Sudesh. 'Acts of Rememory in Oceania', *Symploke* 26.1–2 (2018): 19–32.
Moffat, Chris and J Daniel Elam. 'On the Form, Politics and Effects of Writing Revolution', *South Asia: The Journal of South Asian Studies* 39.3 (2016): 513–524.
Mohagheh, Jason Bahbak. *The Writing of Violence in the Middle East* (London: Bloomsbury, 2013).

Moody, Jane. *Illegitimate Theatre in London, 1770–1840* (Cambridge: Cambridge University Press, 2000).
Mosireen Collective, *858.ma: An Archive of Resistance*, https://858.ma. Accessed 26 October 2021.
Moten, Fred. *Stolen Life* (Durham, NC: Duke University Press, 2018), p. 131.
Moten, Fred, and Stefano Harney, *The Undercommons: Fugitive Planning & Black Study* (Colchester: Minor Compositions, 2013), pp. 132, 134.
Moten, Fred, and Stefano Harney, *All Incomplete* (Colchester: Minor Compositions, 2020).
Mufti, Aamir R. *Enlightenment in the Colony* (Princeton, NJ: Princeton University Press, 2007).
Neumann, Birgit. 'The Literary Representation of Memory', in Astrid Erll and Ansgar Nünning (eds), *Cultural Memory Studies: An International and Interdisciplinary Handbook* (Berlin: Walter de Gruyter, 2008), pp. 333–345.
Ng, Michael H.K. and John Wong (eds), *Civil Unrest and Governance in Hong Kong: Law and Order from Historical and Cultural Perspectives* (London: Routledge, 2017), https://doi.org/10.4324/9781315537252.
O'Neill, Morna. 'Cartoons for the Cause? Walter Crane's *The Anarchists of Chicago*', *Art History* (February 2015): 106–117.
Padamsee, Alex. 'Uncertain Partitions', *Wasafiri* 23.1 (2008): 1–5.
Parmaksız, Pınar Melis Yelsalı. 'Cultural Memory of Social Protest: Mnemonic Literature about Gezi Park Protests.' *Memory Studies* 14.2 (2021): 288–302.
Parsons, Cóilín. 'Planetary Parallax: *Ulysses*, the Stars, and South Africa', *Modernism/modernity* 24.1 (2017): 67–85.
Paulson, Ronald. *The Art of the Riot in England and America* (Baltimore, MD: Owlworks, 2010).
Perkins-Valdez, Dolen. '"Atlanta's Shame": W. E. B. Du Bois and Carrie Williams Clifford Respond to the Atlanta Race Riot of 1906', *Studies in the Literary Imagination* 4.2 (2007): 133–151.
Plotz, John. *The Crowd: British Literature and Public Politics* (Berkeley, CA: University of California Press, 2000).
Rai, Alok. 'The Trauma of Independence: Some Aspects of Progressive Hindi Literature 1945-7', in Mushirul Hasan (ed.), *Inventing Boundaries: Gender, Politics and the Partition of India* (New Delhi and Oxford: Oxford University Press, 2000), pp. 351–370.
Rancière, Jacques. *The Politics of Literature*, trans. Julie Rose (Cambridge: Polity, 2011).
Randall, Adrian. *Riotous Assemblies: Popular Protest in Hanoverian England* (Oxford: Oxford University Press, 2006).
Rigney, Ann. 'The Dynamics of Remembrance: Texts between Monumentality and Morphing', in Astrid Erll and Ansgar Nünning (eds), *Cultural Memory Studies: An International and Interdisciplinary Handbook* (Berlin: Walter de Gruyter, 2008), pp. 345–353.
Rigney, Ann. 'Mediations of Outrage: How Violence against Protestors Is Remembered', *Social Research: An International Quarterly* 87.3 (2020): 707–733.
Rinner, Susanne. *The German Student Movement and the Literary Imagination: Transnational Memories of Protest and Dissent* (New York, NY: Berghahn Books, 2012).
Robins, Jane. *Rebel Queen: How the Trial of Caroline Brought England to the Brink of Revolution* (London: Simon and Schuster, 2006).
Rogers, Nicholas. *Crowds, Culture and Politics in Georgian Britain* (Oxford: Clarendon Press, 1998).
Rogers, Nicholas. *Mayhem: Post-War Crime and Violence in Britain, 1748–53* (New Haven, CT and London: Yale University Press, 2012).

Rooney, Caroline. *Creative Radicalism in the Middle East: Culture and the Arab Left after the Uprisings* (London: I.B. Tauris, 2020).
Rooney, Caroline. 'From Cairo to Tottenham: Big Societies, Neoliberal States and Colonial Utopias', *Journal for Cultural Research* 17.2 (2013): 144–163, doi: 10.1080/14797585.2012.756244.
Ross, Kristin. *Communal Luxury. The Political Imaginary of the Paris Commune* (London: Verso, 2015).
Saint, Tarun K. ed. *Translating Partition* (New Delhi: Katha, 2001).
Saint, Tarun K. *Witnessing Partition: Memory, History Fiction*, 2nd edition (Abingdon: Routledge, 2017).
Sakr, Rita. '"A Way of Making a Space for Ourselves Where We Can Make the Best of Ourselves": Writing Egypt's "Tahrir"', in Rita Sakr, *Anticipating' the 2011 Arab Uprisings: Revolutionary Literatures and Political Geographies*, Palgrave Pivot (Basingstoke: Palgrave, 2013), pp. 21–46.
Sakr, Rita. *Monumental Space in the Post-Imperial Novel: An Interdisciplinary Study* (New York, NY: Continuum, 2021), pp. 41–81.
Sarkar, Bhaskar. *Mourning the Nation: Indian Cinema in the Wake of Partition* (Durham, NC: Duke University Press, 2009).
Schafer, R. Murray. *The Soundscape: Our Sonic Environment and the Tuning of the World* (London: Destiny Books, 1994).
Scott, James. *Domination and the Arts of Resistance* (New Haven, CT: Yale University Press, 1990).
Shaw, George Bernard. 'A Refutation of Anarchy', *Our Corner* 12 (July 1888): pp. 8–20.
Sherman, Louise and Christobel Mattingley (eds). *Our Mob, God's Story: Aboriginal & Torres Strait Islander, Artists Share Their Faith* (Sydney: Bible Society Australia, 2017).
Shingavi, Snehal and Charlotte Nunes. 'Bloomsbury Conversations that Didn't Happen: Indian Writing Between British Modernism and Anti-Colonialism', in Charles Ferrall and Dougal McNeill (eds), *Futility and Anarchy? British Literature in Transition, 1920–1940* (Cambridge: Cambridge University Press 2018), pp. 199–216.
Shoemaker, Robert. 'The London "Mob" in the Early Eighteenth Century' *Journal of British Studies* 26, vol 3 (1987), pp. 273–304.
Shoemaker, Robert. *The London Mob: Violence and Disorder in Eighteenth Century England* (London and New York, NY: 2004).
Silverman, Max. *Palimpsest Memory: The Holocaust and Colonialism in French and Francophone Fiction and Film* (New York, NY: Berghahn Book, 2013).
Skidan, Aleksandr. 'Political/Poetic', *Russian Studies in Literature* 54.1–3: 84–94.
Skinner, Quentin. 'Hobbes and the Humanist Frontispiece', in *From Humanism to Hobbes: Studies in Rhetoric and Politics* (Cambridge: Cambridge University Press, 2018), pp. 222–315.
Smith, Suzanne E. *Dancing in the Street: Motown and the Cultural Politics of Detroit* (Cambridge, MA: Harvard University Press, 1999).
Sorel, Georges *Reflections on Violence* (Cambridge: Cambridge University Press, 1999).
Spahr, Juliana. *Du Bois's Telegram: Literary Resistance and State Containment*, Kindle edition (Cambridge, MA: Harvard University Press, 2018)
Spence, Peter. *The Birth of Romantic Radicalism: War, Popular Politics and English Radical Reformism, 1810–1815* (Aldershot: Ashgate, 1996).
Stedman-Jones, Gareth. *Outcast London: A Study in the Relationship between Classes in Victorian Society* (London: Verso, 2013).

Steinhardt, H. Christoph, Li, Linda Chelan, and Jiang, Yihong, 'The Identity Shift in Hong Kong since 1997'. *Journal of Contemporary China* 27.110 (2018): 261–276.
Swanson, Nathan W. 'Embodying Tahrir: Bodies and Geopolitics in the 2011 Egyptian Uprising', *Area* 48.3 (2016): 300–307.
Swindells, Julia. *Glorious Causes: The Grand Theatre of Political Change* (Oxford: Oxford University Press, 2001).
Táíwò, Olúfẹ́mi O. *Elite Capture. How the Powerful Took Over Identity Politics (and Everything Else)* (London: Pluto Press, 2022).
Tarde, Gabriel. *On Communication and Social Influence* (Chicago, IL: University of Chicago Press, 2011).
Temple-Thurston, Barbara. 'The Reader as Absentminded Beggar: Recovering South Africa in *Ulysses*', *James Joyce Quarterly* 28.1 (1990): 247–256.
Terry, Jennifer. '"When the sea of living memory has receded": Cultural Memory and Literary Narratives of the Middle Passage.' *Memory Studies* 6.4 (2013): 474–488.
Thompson, Edward P. 'The Moral Economy of the English Crowd in the Eighteenth Century', *Past and Present* 50 (1971): 76–136.
Thompson, Edward P. *Customs in Common: Studies in Traditional Popular Culture* (London: Merlin, 1991).
Thompson, Edward P. *William Morris: Romantic to Revolutionary* (New York, NY: PM Press, 2011), p. 490.
Tilly, Charles. *Popular Contention in Great Britain, 1758—1834* (Cambridge, MA: Harvard University Press, 1995).
Touré, Asika (writing as Rolland Snellings). 'Keep on Pushin': Rhythm & Blues as a Weapon', republished under the name 'We Are on the Move and the Music Is Moving with Us', in John H. Bracey Jr, August Meier, and Elliot Rudwick (eds), *Black Nationalism in America* (Indianapolis, IN: The Bobbs-Merrill Company, 1970), pp. 449–450.
Trotsky, Leon. *Literature and Revolution*, trans. William Keach (Chicago, IL: Haymarket, 2005).
Viswanathan, Gauri. *Outside the Fold* (Princeton, NJ: Princeton University Press, 1998), pp. 220–222.
Wahrmann, Dror. 'Public Opinion, Violence, and the Limits of Constitutional Politics', in James Vernon (ed.), *Re-Reading the Constitution: New Narratives in the Political History of England's long Nineteenth Century* (Cambridge: Cambridge University Press, 1996), pp. 83–122.
Walkowitz, Rebecca. *Born Translated: The Contemporary Novel in an Age of World Literature* (New York, NY: Columbia University Press, 2015).
Walt, Vivienne. 'The Fighting Rages on in Tahrir Square', *Time Magazine*, 3 February 2011. Retrieved on 5 August 2021 from: http://content.time.com/time/world/article/0,8599,2045943,00.html
Webner, Pnina, Marin Webb, and Kathryn Spellman-Poots (eds), *The Political Aesthetics of Global Protest: The Arab Spring and Beyond* (Edinburgh: Edinburgh University Press, 2014).
Winegar, Jessica. 'A Civilized Revolution: Aesthetics and Political Action in Egypt', *American Ethnologist*, 43.4 (2016): 614–617.
Yarbakhsh, Elisabeth. *Iranian Hospitality, Afghan Marginality: Spaces of Refuge and Belonging in the City of Shiraz* (Lanham: Lexington Books, 2021).
Zhuo, Xiaolin, Barry Wellman, and Justine Yu, 'Egypt: The First Internet Revolt?', *Peace Magazine* 27.3 (July–Sept 2011): 6–10. http://peacemagazine.org/archive/v27n3p06.htm. Accessed 26 October 2021.

Publisher's Acknowledgements

Extract from 'Against the Police' by Miguel James (translated by Guillermo Parra), published in *Typo Magazine*, Issue 18, http://www.typomag.com/issue18/james.html. Used with permission.

Extracts from 'When You Hear People Say "Burn Down the American Plantation"' by Wendy Trevino, *Destituencies*, Issue Zero (November 2020), https://destituencies.com/2020/when-you-hear-people-say-burn-down-the-american-plantation/. Used with permission.

Extracts from 'Riot' and 'The Third Sermon of the Warpland' by Gwendolyn Brooks, published in *Riot* (Detroit, MI: Broadside Press, 1969). Reprinted by consent of Brooks Permissions.

Extracts from 'Keep on Pushing' by David Henderson, De mayor of Harlem: the poetry of David Henderson (New York, NY: E.P. Dutton, 1970). Permission sought.

Index

For the benefit of digital users, indexed terms that span two pages (e.g., 52–53) may, on occasion, appear on only one of those pages.

#metoo, 132, 167–168
#RhodesMustFall (Rhodes Must Fall), 78–79, 81–85, 87
858.ma: The Archive of Resistance, 238–239, 241–242

Abbas, Ackbar, 140, 151–152
Abbas, Khwaja Ahmad, 112
Abdel Aziz, Basma, 221–237
Aboriginal (indigenous, First Nations), 1 n.1, 2, 126, 129–131, 133–136
Achaari, Mohamed, 190–191, 197, 199–200
activism, 8–9, 61, 66–68, 77, 91, 99–100, 174187–189, 196, 213, 238, 240–241, 247–248
Adnan, Yacine, 200–202
Adorno, Theodor, 49–50
aesthetic, 2–3, 6–7, 11–12, 17, 58, 68, 69–70, 76, 80, 95, 102–103, 111–113, 147–148, 167, 171, 177–179, 184–185, 191, 192–193, 219–220
Akita, Koji, 16, 144
Ambedkar, B.R, 98–102 n.41, 102–103
Anand, Mulk Raj, 16. 88–103
Anderson, Perry, 45–47
anticolonial, 74–77, 85, 91–92
antisemitism, 126
Apter, Emily, 2–3 n. 4
Arab Spring, 6, 8–9, 11–12, 204–205, 214, 238, 240
Archer, Jayne Elisabeth, 48
archive, 2–3, 13, 17, 56–57, 138–139, 181–182, 226, 230, 234–235, 238
Arendt, Hannah, 126
assembly, 175–176, 180–181
Atlanta riot (1906), 13–14, 159

Badiou, Alain, 5–6, 8–9, 41–42, 224
Baer, Ben Consibee, 92–93 n.15
baltajiyya (thugs), 231, 239
Bakhtin, Mikhail, 142–143, 214
Baraka, Amiri, 14–15, 172, 178
barbarism, 15–16, 39–41, 48–50, 116–117, 131

Bauhinia Project, 145
Being HK, 147–148
Beaumont, Matthew, 66–67 n.34
Beck, Zeina Hashem, 220
Belkziz, Abdelellah, 193–194
Benabine, Mahi, 196–197
Benjamin, Walter, 49–50, 105–106, 113–115
Berghaus, Ruth, 53–54
Berman, Jessica, 92 n.15, 98
Bernes, Jasper, 184–185
Berry, Michael, 140
Besant, Annie, 58–64, 66–69
Bevir, Mark, 89–90
Bhalla, Alok, 59–60, 105, 112–113, 115–116
Black Lives Matter, 14–15, 165, 176–177 n.26, 182 n. 50
Bloody Sunday (*see also* Trafalgar Riots (1887), Chicago Haymarket Massacre (1886), Derry (1972)), 56–70
Bohstedt, John, 46
Du Bois, W. E. B., 13–14
Bonney, Sean, 171–172, 184–186
Bordiga, Amadeo, 39–41
Bosman, Anston, 40–41
Bourdieu, Pierre, 124–125
Boyle, Michael Shane, 51
bread riot, 80, 197
Breakazine, 146
Brecht, Bertolt, 15–16, 40–41, 49–55
Brenner, Robert, 52–53
Brooks, Gwendolyn, 14–15, 171, 175–178, 180–181
Brooks, Rayshard (Atlanta 2020), 174–175
Brown, Michael (Ferguson 2014), 174–176, 182
Burke, Edmund, 129–132, 135–136

Canetti, Elias, 4–5
Cantonese literature, 148
Cape Town, 74, 77–78
capitalism, 12–15, 40–41, 45–48, 77, 80, 156–158, 161–162, 169, 170, 175, 179, 192–193
Capitol Hill Riots (2021), 14–15, 132

264 INDEX

Chalcraft, John, 11–12
Chaucer, Geoffrey, 41–42, 47–48
Chughtai, Ismat, 110–111, 117
Clover, Joshua, 5–8, 54–55, 80, 155–158, 161–162, 164, 167–168, 170, 171, 175, 180–181, 184–185
Chander, Krishan, 110–113
Chicago Haymarket Massacre (1886), 57 n.4
Chugtai, Ismat, 110–111
Cole, Sarah, 2–3
colonialism, 73–74, 76, 77, 125–126, 151–152, 187 (*see also* anticolonial, decolonial, postcolonial)
Conrad, Joseph, 90–91, 163
Covent Garden theatre, 18, 26–27, 29
Crane, Walter, 58–59, 61–63, 68, 69–70
crowd, fickle 123–125, 127
  organised 5
  violent 124–126, 130

Dalits, 99–100, 188–189
Dar al Mulk, 196–198
Darwin, Charles, 89
Das, Veena, 113–116
Debord, Guy, 174–175
decolonial, 8–9, 16, 76, 87
Defoe, Daniel, 126–128
Deleuze, Gilles, 53–54
democracy, 84–85, 123–124, 130–131, 133, 135–136, 142, 161–162, 164, 190–191, 193–194 n.34, 194, 224
Derry (1972), 56–57
Detroit riot (1967), 14–15, 184
digital media, 3–4, 238, 248–249, 252–253
Dimock, Wai Chee, 6–7, 84–85, 87
Douaihy, Jabbour, 204–220
Doublespeak, 137–138, 141, 143–145
Dublin, 72–73, 75–77, 80, 82, 85–87
Duggal, Kartar Singh, 112–113
Durkheim, Emile, 16, 89, 94

Egypt, 9–11, 212–213, 215–216, 220, 221–236, 238–253
Egyptian Revolution, 221–222, 225, 229, 231, 238–239, 241
El Rashidi, Yasmine, 11, 238–242 n.8, 242–248, 252–253
empire, 15–17, 53–54, 58–59, 74–75, 77, 88, 90–91, 108, 199, 206
Endnotes (collective), 39–41, 54–55
Engels, Friedrich, 49–50, 68–69, 135–136
eyewitness, 61–62, 65, 66, 143, 226–227, 230, 233–234
extremism, 123, 215–216

Facebook Revolution, 238, 248–249
Fadel, Youssef, 196–197
February movement, 20 (Morocco), 26–27, 202
Federici, Sylvia, 40–41
Ferguson (2014), 8, 14–15, 174–175
Fiennes, Ralph, 54–55
Flately, Jonathan, 60–61
Floyd, George. 173–177
Forster, E.M, 83, 89–90, 98–102
Foucault, Michel, 149
French Revolution, The (1789-1799), 37, 126

Gangs, 204, 206–207, 215–216
Garm Hawa (film), 117–119
Garner, Eric (New York 2014), 182
Gause III, Gregory, 8–9
Gitelman, Lisa, 226–228
Georgian England, 18, 21
Gordon Riots, The (1780), 93

Hafez, Sabry, 109–110
Hage, Rawi, 219–220
Hamilton, Omar Robert, 11, 238–242, 248–253
Hammad, Isabella, 10–11
Haqqi, Mahmud Tahir, 9–11
Harkness, Margaret, 58–59, 61–63, 65, 66–70
Harlem riot (1964), 14–15, 175–176, 180–181, 183
Harlins, Latasha (Los Angeles, 1992), 174–175
Harris, Cheryl, 180–181
Hartman, Saidiya, 12, 175, 182
Havel, Václav, 145, 152
Harvey, David. 222–223
Hazlitt, William, 126
Hegel, G. W. F., 39–40
Helsinger, Elizabeth, 64
Henderson, David, 171, 175–184
Hindi (language), 110–111 n.27, 111–113
Hindus, 100–101, 110–111 n.27
Hobbes, Thomas, 43, 125–126, 131–132, 136
Basic Law (Hong Kong), 137–138, 151–152
National Security Law (NSL, Hong Kong), 137–138
Holland, Oscar, 57
Huxley, Aldous, 101–102, 145

Impressions, The (band), 175–178
India, 6–7, 11–12, 16, 59, 85, 91–92, 94, 97. 98–102, 104–105, 107–111, 115–120, 147, 188–189
Indigeneity, 129
Indigenous, 2, 125–126, 129–131, 133–136
Indignados, 214
Irish, 56–57, 59, 71, 74–77, 81, 84, 133

INDEX 265

James, Miguel, 171-172
James, William, 89
Janowitz, Anne, 57
Jouaiti, Abdelkarim, 190-191, 194, 196, 198-199
Joyce, James, 16, 71-78, 80, 83-87, 92

Kamleshwar, 110-113
Kelley, Robin D. G., 176
Kemble, John Philip, 26-32
Kermode, Frank, 46
Khatib, Lina, 215-216
Khoury, Elias, 216
King Hassan II (Morocco), 189, 191-192, 194-195, 197
King, Martin Luther, 2, 14-15
King Mohamed VI (Morocco), 195, 201
Kornbluh, Anna, 68
Ksikes, Driss, 193-194

Lai-Chu, Hon, 145-146
Lebanon, 11, 204, 206-207, 215-216, 218-220
  Beirut, 204, 206, 216
  Tripoli, 11, 204-220
Le Bon, Gustave, 4-5, 16, 88-90, 95-97
Lefèvre, Raphaël, 204-207, 209, 219
Lennon Walls, 142-143
Linnell, Alfred, 61-66
literary archive, 2-3, 13, 15
Lockman, Zachery, 9-10
Los Angeles riots (1992), 14-15, 174-175
Lucashenko, Melissa, 135-136
Lukacs, George, 108-109
Luxemburg, Rosa, 49-50

Machiavelli, Niccolò, 127
Mackey, Nathaniel, 176-177
Makhzen, 192-194 n.34, n.35, 194, 198, 199-201
Manto, Sa'adat Hasan, 110-117
maqāmāt literary tradition, 210
Martha and the Vandellas, 183-184
Marx, Eleanor, 61-63, 66-67
Marx, Karl (Marxism), 5-6, 51, 96-97, 135-136, 155, 156-157, 189, 206-207, 219
Matar, Hisham, 242
Matz, Robert, 44
Mayfield, Curtis, 175-176
Mbembe, Achille, 222-223
Memon, Muhammad Umar, 108, 112-113
Minneapolis riots (2020), 174-175
McKittrick, Katherine, 181-182
mob, 13-16, 19-20, 24-26, 30, 32, 35-38, 58-59, 61, 64, 67-68, 71-72, 90, 104-105, 116-117, 120, 122-136
Mohaghegh, Jason Bahbak, 8-9

mobile vulgus 123-125, 127
Morocco, 11, 187-203
Morris, William, 57-59, 61-70
Mosireen Collective, 238-241
Morrison, Toni, 11, 190-191
Moten, Fred, 13, 176, 177-180, 184-185
Mubarak regime, 238-239, 242
Muslim Brotherhood, 240-242, 246-247, 249-250
Muslims, 104, 106-107, 117-120

Native Title Act (1993), 1 n.1
Nebi Musa Riots (1920), 10
necropolitics, 222-223, 225, 229, 234-236
Nietzsche, Friedrich, 39-40
noise, 3-5, 15, 21, 24-25, 30-32, 61, 66, 178, 240, 247-248

Old Price Riots (1809), 17-18, 20-21, 26-35
Orwell, George, 145
Orwellian, 137, 142, 151

Padamsee, Alex, 110-111
Pakistan, 106-108, 115-116, 118-119
Paris Commune (1871), 57, 64
Partition, 16, 104-121
Peterloo massacre, 6, 34
Plotz, John, 7-8
Pogrom, 13-14, 105, 108-109, 120, 156
Polisario Front (Morocco), 196-197
Populism, 49-50, 123, 145
popular culture, 147-148, 204, 220
postcolonial, 75-78, 83-84, 98-99, 108-110, 117-118, 187, 188, 192-194, 212
Progressive Writers Movement, 110-111

qabaday (strongman), 207-209
Queen Caroline controversy (1820), 17-18, 34

race, 12, 44-46, 77, 80, 156-158, 166
Rai, Alok, 111-113
Ranciere, Jacques, 167
Reading the Riot Act, 18-19
Resonate, 148
Rhodes, Cecil, 77-78
Rif Revolt, The (1958-1959), 189
Riot Act, 6-7 n.19, 17, 19, 25-26. 27-30, 32, 34-35, 42-43, 56-59, 64, 66, 67
Rogers, Nicholas, 5, 24-26
Rowlett Act (1919), 17
Rudé, George, 5
rule of law, 132, 141, 146-147, 150, 152

Sailors' Revenge, The (Strand Riot, 1749), 22
Schafer, R. Murray, 240, 252–253
Schmitt, Carl, 43
Sectarianism, 215–216, 220
Shadwell, Thomas, 127–128
Shakespeare, William, 15–16, 39–55
Shaw, George Bernard, 57 n. 4
Shekhar, Hansda Sowvendra, 115, 121
Shelley, Percy Bysshe, 6–7, 20, 64
Sikhon, Sant Singh, 112–113
Six Acts, 18, 34, 38
Skinner, Quentin, 131–132
social media (Facbook, twitter, digital media), 3–4, 145, 222–223, 238, 248–249
Sorel, Georges, 90
Soueif, Ahdaf, 238–239
South Africa, 6–7, 16, 105–110, 112–113, 115
South African War (1899-1902), 71–72, 75–76
sound, 221, 239, 240, 246–253
sovereignty, 123–125 n.6, 124–134, 136
Spahr, Juliana, 14–15, 166–169, 184–185
Strand Riot, The (*see* The Sailors' Revenge)

Tahrir Square/ Midan al-Tahrir, 8, 11, 222–224, 227–228, 231, 236–239, 242, 243–245, 248, 249–250
Tam Wai-wan Vivian, 144
Tarde, Gabriel, 16, 89–90, 93, 95–96
Tazmamart prison, 192
Terrab, Sonia, 193–194
theatre, 18, 22, 26–30, 32, 40–41, 51, 71, 81–83, 169
Thomas, Howard, 48
Thompson, E.P., 5–6

Tilly, Charles, 4, 11–12, 80
Times, The, 26–27, 58–61, 63, 64
Tiananmen Square massacre, 6–7, 138–140, 150
totalitarianism, 123, 126
Touré, Asika, 183–184
Trafalgar Riots (1887), 17, 56–70
transhistory (transhistorical), 16, 50, 79–81, 84–85, 87
Turley, Richard Marggraf, 48

Umbrella Movement, 137–138, 142–143
Urdu, 106–108, 110–113

vawongsir, 149–150
Vendler, Helen, 41–42
Virk, Kulwant Singh, 112–113
Viswanathan, Gauri, 99–100
vox populi, 18, 21, 24–27, 34–35, 37, 38

Weber, Max, 89, 124, 125
Williams, Raymond, 122
Winegar, Jessica, 224
Winch, Tara June, 1–2
Women, 21–22, 26, 30, 32–35, 51, 76, 104, 114–115, 119, 120–122, 125, 127, 129–133, 136, 199–200, 215, 218–219
Woolf, Virginia, 16. 74, 88–103
World Literature, 75–76, 84–85, 99
world systems, 40–41, 46, 54–55

Years of Lead (1961-1999, Morocco), 189, 191–192, 195, 202–203

Yeung Tsz-chun, Raymond, 143